D1027710

SIX FACES OF GLOBALIZATION

Six Faces of Globalization

WHO WINS, WHO LOSES, AND WHY IT MATTERS

Anthea Roberts and Nicolas Lamp

Harvard University Press

Cambridge, Massachusetts & London, England

2021

Printed in the United States of America

First printing

Library of Congress Cataloging-in-Publication Data
Names: Roberts, Anthea (Writer on international law), author. |
Lamp, Nicolas, 1982– author.
Title: Six faces of globalization : who wins, who loses, and why it matters /
Anthea Roberts and Nicolas Lamp.
Description: Cambridge, Massachusetts : Harvard University Press, 2021. |
Includes bibliographical references and index.
Identifiers: LCCN 2021007194 | ISBN 9780674245952 (cloth)
Subjects: LCSH: Globalization. | Anti-globalization movement.
Classification: LCC JZ1318 .R6245 2021 | DDC 303.48/2–dc23
LC record available at https://lccn.loc.gov/2021007194

CONTENTS

ABBREVIATIONS vii

Part I: Globalization through Dragonfly Eyes

1 Unscrambling Globalization Narratives 3

2 Why Narratives Matter 20

Part II: Six Faces of Globalization

3 The Establishment Narrative 35

4 The Left-Wing Populist Narrative 55

5 The Right-Wing Populist Narrative 78

6 The Corporate Power Narrative 98

7 The Geoeconomic Narrative 122

8 The Global Threats Narratives 143

Part III: Working with Globalization Narratives

9 Switching Narratives 171

10 Overlaps among Narratives 184

11 Trade-offs among Narratives 203

12 Blind Spots and Biases 220

Part IV: From the Cube to the Kaleidoscope

13 Kaleidoscopic Complexity 245

14 Potential Alliances 262

15 Globalization for Foxes 280

NOTES 299

ACKNOWLEDGMENTS 365

INDEX 371

ABBREVIATIONS

AfD	Alternative für Deutschland (Alternative for Germany)
AFL-CIO	American Federation of Labor and Congress of Industrial Organizations
AI	Artificial intelligence
CCP	Chinese Communist Party
CEO	Chief executive officer
CETA	Comprehensive Economic and Trade Agreement
CPTPP	Comprehensive and Progressive Agreement on Trans-Pacific Partnership
ECB	European Central Bank
GATT	General Agreement on Tariffs and Trade
GDP	Gross domestic product
IMF	International Monetary Fund
IP	Intellectual property
ISDS	Investor-state dispute settlement
MBA	Master of Business Administration
NAFTA	North American Free Trade Agreement
SWIFT	Society for Worldwide Interbank Financial Telecommunication
TRIPS	Trade-Related Aspects of Intellectual Property Rights
TTIP	Transatlantic Trade and Investment Partnership
TTP	Trans-Pacific Partnership
UKIP	UK Independence Party
USMCA	United States–Mexico–Canada Agreement
USTR	United States trade representative
WHO	World Health Organization
WIPO	World Intellectual Property Organization
WTO	World Trade Organization

PART I

GLOBALIZATION THROUGH DRAGONFLY EYES

CHAPTER 1

Unscrambling Globalization Narratives

In recent years, it has seemed like the world is coming apart at the seams. Many of the apparent certainties of the post–Cold War era lie in tatters. In the West, what appeared to be a broad political consensus on the value of free markets and liberal trade has given way to increasingly acrimonious debates about who wins and who loses from economic globalization. Are Mexican workers stealing US and Canadian jobs? Has the global 1 percent rigged the game for its benefit? Is China engaged in a stealthy campaign for global supremacy? Are we all bound to lose in a world of untrammeled climate change and deadly pandemics?

From the collapse of the Soviet Union until the global financial crisis in 2008, the dominant narrative in the West highlighted the benefits of economic globalization. When the Cold War ended without shots being fired, the Western model of free market capitalism appeared to have vanquished all ideological rivals: the "end of history" was nigh.[1] Pro-market economic reforms swept country after country, trade and investment treaties were signed, new international institutions were created, and cross-border trade and investment soared.

Despite the dizzying pace of change, Western governments and the economic establishment heralded the developments as exciting and positive. Economic liberalization was portrayed as a "rising tide that lifts all boats," a way to "grow the pie" so that everyone—developed and developing countries, rich and poor—would be better off. Globalization was seen as an unstoppable but overwhelmingly beneficial force. Free trade was touted as a win-win outcome that would create peace and prosperity for all.

To be sure, globalization did not always run smoothly. As the economist Branko Milanovic pointed out in 2003, the prevailing view of globalization represented "only one, positive, face of globalization while entirely neglecting the malignant one."[2] Yet episodes such as the Asian financial crisis in 1998 and the Argentinian debt crisis in 2001 were largely treated as bumps in the road rather than signs that the world economy was on the wrong path. The voices of detractors in the West, such as the protesters who battled police in the streets of Seattle to derail a ministerial meeting of the World Trade Organization (WTO) in 1999, were drowned out as the political and intellectual elites enthusiastically embraced economic globalization.

But this dominant narrative has come unstuck. In the aftermath of the 2008 global financial crisis, rival stories about economic globalization began to make significant inroads in the West. Starting in 2011, the Occupy Wall Street protesters popularized the notion of a rift between the 1 percent and the rest of the population; they challenged the idea that the gains from globalization were either trickling down or being redistributed through government action, and they put concerns about inequality firmly on the political agenda. After the 2009 euro crisis and the arrival of refugees from the Syrian civil war, Europe was rocked by austerity politics and fears about Muslim immigration, which led to a hollowing out of centrist political parties in favor of more extreme parties on both the left and the right.

The virtues of economic interdependence came under sustained fire in many Western countries, but nowhere more prominently than in the United States and the United Kingdom, which had been bastions of both economic globalization and neoliberal ideology. In 2016, the United Kingdom voted to leave the European Union (EU) as Brexit voters vowed to "take back control" over borders and regulations. A few months later, Donald J. Trump was elected president of the United States, having risen to prominence by taking a firm stance against the establishment consensus in favor of free trade and globalization. Lambasting the "American carnage" of "rusted-out factories" in manufacturing communities and decrying the dangers posed by immigrants had been signature elements of Trump's campaign.[3]

By the end of 2020, the United Kingdom had left the EU, and the United States had charted a new approach to trade on everything from engagement with China to support of the WTO. The election of Joe Biden to the US presidency heralded a more moderate approach, but not a return to the old consensus. The sense that the West finds itself in an epochal struggle with China only intensified, while the rise of giant tech corporations with an unprecedented capacity to surveil and manipulate people's actions and beliefs created a lingering sense of dread. And the reality of greater—even potentially catastrophic—threats was crystallizing in many people's minds. The devastating impact of climate change, as well as our apparent political inability to do anything meaningful about it, began to hit home as fires swept across Australia, the Amazon, and California. These disasters overlapped with the coronavirus pandemic, which sparked unprecedented disruptions to public life, a severe economic downturn, and growing concerns about the risks posed by global connectivity and economic interdependence.

In sum, political life in Western countries has become more unsettled than at any other time since the end of the Cold War. The centrist consensus that sustained several decades of economic globalization has frayed. Views that were relegated to the political fringes even a few years ago have found their way into mainstream debates in many countries, and in some cases have come to shape government policy. In many Western democracies, the lines of political battle have not only moved but also multiplied: as the old division between left and right gives way to multiple vectors of political disagreement, old alliances are unraveling and new ones are being formed. Whether and when a new normal will be found, and what its contours might be, remains uncertain.

Unscrambling the Rubik's Cube

It is a confusing time, and our old mental models are increasingly unreliable guides to our complex and evolving reality. We are at a critical juncture: a relatively long period of stability in mainstream thinking about economic globalization has given way to a situation of dramatic flux. During such junctures, narratives assume particular relevance, because they offer new ways for us to understand what the problem is and what should be done about it. Narratives provide the tools to contest the old normal and establish the contours of the new.[4]

We are scholars of international trade and investment law who follow these debates intently, and the growing multiplicity of arguments about who wins and who loses from economic globalization reminded us of the confusion of a scrambled Rubik's cube (Figure I.1). The colors were all jumbled up, with each face representing an incoherent and confusing mix of arguments and concerns about trade, inequality, disintegrating

Fig. 1.1: A Scrambled Rubik's Cube
Credit: The image of the Rubik's Cube used by permission of Rubik's Brand Ltd. (www.rubiks.com).

communities, corporate power, public health, and environmental catastrophe. Could we unscramble this Rubik's cube? we wondered. Was there a way to arrange the different-colored pieces of the puzzle into coherent narratives, and to fashion a framework to show how these narratives relate to each other? Could this help us to better understand the political moment we found ourselves in and provide us with tools to analyze potential paths forward? As we disentangled the debates that had been playing out in the Western media, six prominent narratives about the winners and losers from economic globalization emerged, which we conceptualize as existing on the six faces of the Rubik's cube.

The Top Face of the Cube: Everybody Wins

According to some economists, if you think that globalization impoverishes countries and destroys communities, you have it all wrong. Sure, you may have lost your job because workers in other countries are paid less, but that is not at all different from losing your job because workers in the factory next door are more efficient or because technological progress has rendered your skills obsolete. The market is simply doing its work. You should improve your qualifications to get a better job; in the meantime, you still benefit from globalization since it gives you access to cheaper products. The process of adjustment may be hard at times, but it is a short-term cost that we have to accept in the interest of long-term prosperity. The end result will be a more efficient economy, lower prices, and more abundant consumer choice.

In this view, the pushback against economic globalization by people who feel that they have lost out is simply a natural reaction to the creative destruction that necessarily accompanies progress. The appropriate response is to help individuals adjust to the competition unleashed by globalization by offering them retraining and allowing them to share in the gains from trade. Adjustment assistance that eases workers into new jobs not only helps to realize the efficiency gains derived from the reorganization of the international division of labor but also is a political imperative, since it shores up public support for international integration. The bottom line is that the economic gains from trade more than suffice to compensate anyone who may have lost out, so that everyone can ultimately benefit from free markets and liberal trade.

We call this "everybody wins" view the *establishment narrative,* because it was the dominant paradigm for understanding economic globalization in the West in the three decades following the end of the Cold War. The view reflected a consensus of the main political parties in most Western democracies and beyond, and it has been espoused by many of the institutions that serve as the guardians of the international economic order, such as the World Bank, the International Monetary Fund (IMF), and the WTO. Many powerful actors still endorse this narrative, arguing that free trade not only increases prosperity but also supports other goals, such as promoting peace. Since the establishment narrative has been ruling the world and also represents the sunniest view of globalization, we visualize it as situated on the top of the cube.

The Four Sides of the Cube: Winners and Losers

The establishment narrative now finds itself besieged from all sides. Concerns about the impact of free trade on workers and the environment have bubbled up previously, but discontent with economic globalization tended to be suppressed in mainstream circles in the West. In the decade following the global financial crisis, however, narratives that highlight how economic globalization produces both winners and losers have returned to the center of political debate. These currents have pushed us off the sunny top of the cube, over the edges, and down to the four faces on the cube's sides (Figure 1.2). Instead of relatively limited squabbles between the center-left and center-right on whether, when, and how to redistribute the gains from trade, we now confront four narratives that

Fig. 1.2: The Solved Cube
Credit: The image of the Rubik's Cube used by permission of Rubik's Brand Ltd. (www.rubiks.com).

present a much more fundamental challenge to the assumptions underlying the establishment perspective.

The establishment narrative looks at the world economy as a whole and treats countries as the relevant actors; it is at these levels and units of analysis that the superior efficiency of a global division of labor in which every country focuses on its comparative advantage is most apparent. The narrative emphasizes absolute rather than relative gains, and the metric it employs is economic, typically gross domestic product (GDP). Proponents of the four challenger narratives do not necessarily contest that economic globalization has produced absolute economic gains at the aggregate level, whether measured nationally or globally. However, they focus on the distribution of those gains, both within and across countries, and derive much of their energy from channeling the disappointment, fears, and anger of the losers. Where these four narratives differ from each other is in which actors they identify as having won or lost, and in why they think it matters.

On the left of the political spectrum, we see two narratives that emphasize how gains from economic globalization have flowed upward to rich individuals and multinational corporations. The *left-wing populist narrative* focuses on the ways in which national economies are rigged to channel the gains from globalization to the privileged few.[5] Proponents of this narrative point out that even as countries have seen their GDPs rise, many have also experienced a sharp increase in inequality, with a growing divide between rich and poor and a hollowing out of the middle class. Left-wing populism expresses itself in vertical hostility; its proponents stand up for the ordinary people who have lost out to the corrupt elite.[6] Whereas some proponents point the finger at chief executive officers (CEOs), bankers, and billionaires (the top 1 percent), others take aim at the educated professional class and the upper middle class more broadly (the top 20 percent). Wherever the line is drawn, however, left-wing populists agree that the middle class, the working class, and the poor have lost out.

Instead of singling out domestic elites, proponents of the *corporate power narrative* argue that the real winners from economic globalization are multinational corporations, which can take advantage of a global marketplace to produce cheaply, sell everywhere, and pay as little in taxes as possible. These companies use their power to shape international rules in areas that advantage them, such as trade and investment, while lobbying against effective international cooperation on subjects that might disadvantage them, such as taxation. In this way, multinational corporations manipulate the network of domestic and international rules to maximize their profits and minimize their responsibilities. According to the corporate power narrative, economic globalization produces many losers—workers, communities, citizens, even governments—but only one winner: corporations.

Although both of these narratives focus on the upward redistribution of wealth, they differ in their emphasis. The left-wing populist narrative zeroes in on domestic problems, highlighting the explosion of inequality within countries. The corporate power narrative, by contrast, adopts a transnational approach and treats multinational corporations and the transnational working class as the key actors. The two narratives are often intertwined in places such as the United States and the United Kingdom, where many on the left are broadly critical of owners of substantial capital, whether individual or corporate. In many western European countries, by contrast, where levels of domestic inequality are lower, the corporate power narrative features more prominently, as was evident in the protests across Europe in 2015 and 2016 against the Transatlantic Trade and Investment Partnership (TTIP).

On the right of the political spectrum, we find two narratives about winners and losers that primarily see the gains from globalization flowing sideways to foreigners and foreign countries. In the *right-wing populist narrative,* workers, their families, and their communities lose from globalization, both economically and in a cultural sense.[7] This narrative's emphasis varies in different countries. In the United States, where the loss of blue-collar jobs to China and Mexico has devastated manufacturing communities, the narrative has a strong anti-trade element. In western Europe, anti-immigrant sentiment and concerns about a loss of sovereignty are central features of the narrative, whereas anxieties about the impact of international trade are less pronounced. In the United Kingdom, for instance, many of those who voted for Brexit did not oppose free trade; they rebelled against what they perceived as dictates from the EU institutions in Brussels and longed to regain control over immigration.

The right-wing populist narrative shares with the left-wing version a deep distrust of elites, but the two narratives part company on what they blame the elite for: whereas left-wing populists fault the elite for enriching themselves at the expense of the working and middle classes, right-wing populists denounce the elite for failing to protect the hardworking native population from threats posed by an external "other." The right-wing populist narrative thus has a strong horizontal us-versus-them quality, whether expressed through concern about protecting workers from the offshoring of jobs or guarding them against an inflow of immigrants who might compete for those jobs, live off the welfare system, or threaten the native community's sense of identity.[8] The right-wing populist narrative also highlights geographical divisions within countries, such as the diverging fortunes of thriving cities and declining rural areas. For proponents of the narrative, these geographical divides map onto different value systems: rural areas are bastions for conservative cultural values such as stability, tradition, patriotism, and loyalty, whereas urban centers represent an untethered and amoral "globalism."[9] For proponents of the narrative, these cultural cleavages are more significant than divisions based on class or income per se.

The *geoeconomic narrative* also focuses on an external threat, but of a different kind: it emphasizes economic and technological competition between the United States and China as great-power rivals. Although both countries have gained from economic globalization in absolute terms, in relative terms China has closed the gap on America. Concerns about the interplay of economic security and national security have waxed and waned over the years; the United States treated the Soviet Union as a security threat during the Cold War and Japan as an economic competitor during the 1970s and 1980s. But the United States increasingly perceives China as both an economic competitor and a security threat, lending the geoeconomic narrative an urgency that it did not have during the Cold War. Although the narrative features most prominently in America, it is gaining ground in other Western countries as well, where China is increasingly regarded as a strategic competitor and a potential security threat rather than merely as an economic partner. Instead of applauding trade and investment as enhancing economic welfare and increasing prospects for peace, the geoeconomic narrative emphasizes the security vulnerabilities created by economic interdependence and digital connectivity with a strategic rival.

Although both the right-wing populist and geoeconomic narratives emphasize external, horizontal threats, they differ in key ways. The former focuses on cultural as well as economic losses, while the latter is more mindful of relative economic power of countries and its capacity to undergird political and military power. The former primarily laments the loss of the manufacturing jobs of the past, while the latter focuses on winning the race in the technologies of the future, such as fifth-generation (5G) networks and artificial intelligence. And the former targets Polish plumbers who undercut local workers, whereas the latter casts a critical eye on Chinese scientists and engineers who might steal Western technology.

The Bottom Face of the Cube: Everybody Loses

The narratives we have discussed so far assume either that everyone wins from economic globalization (the top face) or that economic globalization produces both winners and losers (the four faces on the sides). By contrast, on the bottom face of the Rubik's cube, we locate narratives that see all of us as at risk of losing from economic globalization in its current form. These narratives portray economic globalization as a source and accelerator of global threats, such as pandemics and climate change. Some of these narratives focus on how global connectivity increases the risk of contagion, both of the viral and economic kind. Others warn that the skyrocketing carbon emissions associated with the global diffusion of Western patterns of production and consumption are endangering both people and the planet. These *global threats narratives* emphasize our common humanity; their proponents call for global solidarity and international cooperation in the face of common challenges.

Proponents of the global threats narratives start from the observation that everything is interdependent: our economic systems are located within our social and political systems, which in turn are embedded within our environmental ecosystems and planetary boundaries. According to these narratives, we need to redefine the goals of our economies to enable individuals and societies to survive and thrive within the limits of our planet. This can mean emphasizing resilience over efficiency in our supply chains and sustainability over profit-seeking in our economies. Unless we fashion a more sustainable and resilient global economy, they warn, we run the risk that everybody will lose. We will not lose equally, however: some people and some countries will suffer first or worst. Proponents of these narratives argue that we need to be attentive to these distributional questions, either for moral reasons (because we have an obligation to look out for those who are most vulnerable) or for instrumental reasons (because no one will be safe until everyone is safe).

Globalization through Dragonfly Eyes

Debates about economic globalization often revolve around the question of whether particular narratives about who wins and who loses are right or wrong. That is not the question that we seek to answer in this book. We will not tell you *what* to think about economic globalization. Instead, we try to show *how* we can think about the current controversies over economic globalization in productive ways.

We use the metaphor of the Rubik's cube as a meta-framework for understanding how the six main narratives in Western debates relate to one another. We show how the narratives stress different facts or interpret the same facts in divergent ways, as well as how they differ in their levels and units of analysis and their metrics of evaluation. We distill the narratives by grouping together story lines and arguments that share certain core elements, such as which actors they identify as winners and losers, and whether they view gains as having moved upward (to the elite) or outward (to a foreign "other"). In doing so, we provide a high-altitude map and analytical framework for understanding these confusing debates. A schema of the narratives is shown in Figure 1.3.

Narratives provide the story lines through which we perceive and communicate our understanding of reality and express our values.[10] Political scientists and policy analysts have long recognized that narratives not only reflect and affect our understanding of reality but also shape our actions.[11] Recent attention to narratives among prominent economists is particularly striking. Robert Shiller has called for the development of a "narrative economics" to analyze the narratives that people develop about

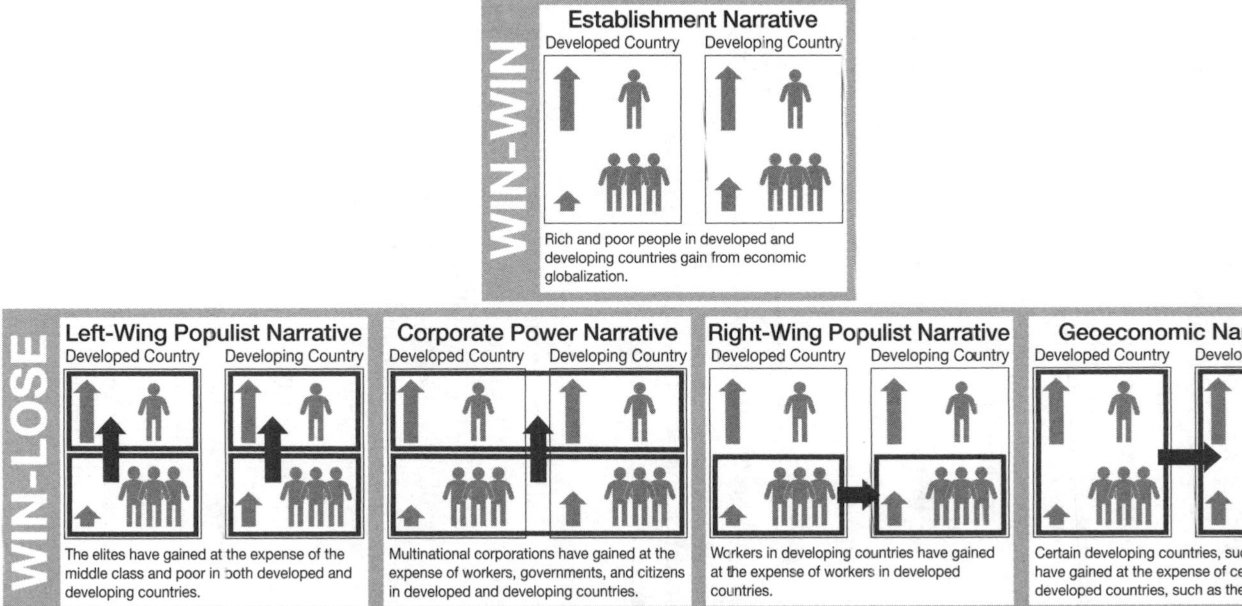

Fig. 1.3: Schematic Representation of the Rubik's Cube Narratives about Economic Globalization
Credit: © Anthea Roberts and Nicolas Lamp.

the economy and the pathways through which they spread, given that narratives represent "major vectors of rapid change in culture, in zeitgeist, and in economic behavior."[12] For John Kay and Mervyn King, narratives are the most powerful mechanism available for organizing our imperfect knowledge in conditions of radical uncertainty: in a complex world, narratives are necessary to help answer the question "What is going on here?"[13] Meanwhile, Dani Rodrik has argued that economic and cultural narratives are crucial to understanding the populist backlash against globalization, since they provide "direction and content" to the economic grievances caused by globalization.[14]

We construct the narratives that we present in this book from statements by politicians, journalists, academics, and citizens; they appear in various guises in our newspapers, magazines, books, and TV shows, on social media, and in personal conversations (Figure 1.4). Although some of the narratives have been strongly shaped by specific actors, they lie beyond the control of any particular actor, as anyone can employ the framing and analytical moves of a narrative. Right-wing populism lives on past Trump's presidency, for instance, just as left-wing populism continued to thrive after Elizabeth Warren and Bernie Sanders conceded the US Democratic primary. None of our narratives can be attributed to a single author, and even someone whom we identify as a proponent of a certain narrative may not subscribe to all of its elements. The same actor may embrace multiple narratives or different narratives in different settings.

Narratives are often resistant to change, even in the face of contradictory empirical evidence, because of their intuitive plausibility, the force of their metaphors, the emotions they provoke and channel, and the way they stabilize assumptions for decision-making. Accordingly, whether or not we think a narrative is factually correct, we need to understand its power in public discourse and in policy formation. We all gravitate toward certain narratives. But healthy public debate and deliberative decision-making require that, in addition to defending our preferred narratives, we understand the best versions of the arguments made by others. To further this objective, we try to present charitable and coherent versions of each narrative without sitting in judgment of them. Although assessing the accuracy of the narratives' empirical claims is essential for developing sound policy, the necessary first step is to understand one another's narratives and the values that animate them.

Our approach is informed by the conviction that when dealing with contested issues such as economic globalization, it is crucial to explore

Establishment

Left-Wing Populist

Right-Wing Populist

Corporate Power

Geoeconomics

Global Threats

Fig. 1.4: The Narratives Reflected in Covers of *The Economist*
Note: Covers of *The Economist* of March 18, 2017 ("On the up"), January 22, 2011 ("The rich and the rest"), March 26, 2016 ("Winners take all"), October 21, 2017 ("Left behind"), October 18, 2018 ("China v America"), and August 4, 2018 ("In the line of fire"), with labeling by the authors.
Credit: © The Economist Newspaper Limited, London.

multiple perspectives. No single narrative can capture the multifaceted nature of such issues, and no perspective is neutral. Each narrative distills a certain set of experiences and tells part of the story; none tells the whole. Each narrative embodies value judgments about what merits our attention and how we should evaluate what we see; none is value free. In Milanovic's words, globalization "presents different faces to different people. Depending on where we live, whether we are rich or poor, where we stand ideologically, we are bound to see the process differently." Considering multiple narratives in a structured way allows us to be conscious of how our approach fits within the broader discursive universe, and what others might be seeing and valuing that we might be missing. It forces us to take in the many faces of economic globalization.[15]

We live in highly polarized times. In many Western countries, the electorate is becoming more divided, and individuals are growing more distrustful of those holding different political views. People are increasingly sorting themselves geographically so that they are more likely to live and work with others who have similar backgrounds. Cable television and social media have encouraged the development of echo chambers that reinforce existing views even as they stigmatize and delegitimize alternative viewpoints. Our political discussions are rife with condescension and contempt—sometimes we treat others as though they were too stupid to understand the facts or their own interests, or too self-interested to care about the well-being of anyone other than themselves. At a critical juncture, when we need to have an open debate about the path forward, we have instead adopted some very bad habits in how we engage with one another.[16]

We believe that taking an empathetic approach is a first step to overcoming polarization and facilitating constructive disagreement. As social psychologist Jonathan Haidt explains: "If you really want to change someone's mind on a moral or political matter, you'll need to see things from that person's angle as well as your own. And if you truly see it the other person's way—deeply and intuitively—you might even find your own mind opening in response. Empathy is an antidote to righteousness."[17] Helping readers achieve that sort of cognitive empathy—where you understand another approach from within its own frame of reference, whether you agree with it or not—is a key purpose of this book.[18]

Our effort to differentiate various narratives and integrate them into a meta-framework is not just an attempt to get people with different perspectives to better understand *one another*. It is also informed by the science on how to best understand complex and contested issues such as economic globalization *themselves*.

Complex integrative thinking involves at least two steps. The first is the willingness to accept that there are different ways of looking at an issue and the ability to see problems from different perspectives (*differentiation*). The second step is the ability to draw insights from each so as to integrate them into a coherent understanding or approach (*integration*). As political scientist and psychologist Philip Tetlock has shown in his work on forecasting, our best chance of understanding complex issues lies in seeing them through "dragonfly eyes." Dragonflies have compound eyes made up of thousands of lenses that give them a range of vision of nearly 360 degrees. Dragonfly thinking involves synthesizing a multitude of points, counterpoints, and counter-counterpoints. Tetlock's studies show that people who integrate insights from multiple perspectives are likely to develop a more accurate understanding of complex problems than those who rely on a single perspective.[19]

Viewing complex problems through dragonfly eyes is also useful in identifying potential alliances and brokering compromises. In studies of peace and conflict, psychologist Peter Suedfeld and his colleagues found that leaders who demonstrate low levels of integrative complexity are less likely than their peers to produce negotiated outcomes and more likely to oversee violent eruptions. The inability to understand the perspectives of others or to see how different issues could be traded off detracts from our ability to find peaceful solutions. By contrast, leaders who score high on integrative complexity have a greater chance of finding peaceful ways to resolve conflicts. They can better understand the perspectives and priorities of different sides in a way that facilitates trade-offs and creative solutions that meet each side's core concerns.[20] These are precisely some of the qualities and approaches that we wish to foster in these debates.

From the Cube to the Kaleidoscope

The dragonfly approach to complex integrative thinking informs the plan of this book. After explaining in Part I what narratives are, why they are important, and why we need to consider multiple narratives, in Part II we lay out six competing narratives about the winners and losers from globalization. Each chapter takes the reader on a journey through a different narrative, presented on its own terms. We invoke the texture and feel of these narratives by recounting how prominent contemporary advocates have narrated these perspectives in public debates, particularly during the past few years, which have seen a marked unraveling of the mainstream consensus of the post–Cold War era. We focus primarily on the narratives that became salient in Western countries, particularly in the United States and the United Kingdom, where the pushback against economic globalization has been the most forceful.

But "solving" the Rubik's cube in this way not only clarifies the six main narratives that we believe are driving Western debates; it can also provide the starting point for further analysis. In Part III, we shift gears from a narrative approach to an analytical one. We move from presenting the narratives as freestanding intellectual constructs to showing how actors can (and often do) use them as tools to achieve strategic ends. Thus, we examine how different actors deliberately switch from one narrative to another to advance interpretations of policy challenges that suit their interests or accord with their values and how, in so doing, they highlight certain issues and possibilities while obscuring others. We explore how actors combine multiple narratives in formulating policies or reaching agreements, which creates both alliances and tensions. And we consider how the different values that the narratives embody require difficult trade-offs when actors seek to combine narratives.

The six faces of globalization that get most of the attention in Western debates also have blind spots and biases—a point we highlight by examining additional perspectives from outside the West.[21] Although the Rubik's cube narratives enjoy some currency around the world, other narratives that better reflect the distinctive historical experience and current positionality of countries outside the West are often more prominent. These tend to receive only passing attention in Western debates and sometimes run counter to dominant Western perceptions. To convey a sense of some of these alternative story lines, we sketch four additional narrative strands—the neocolonial narrative, various Asia-rising narratives, narratives against Western hegemony, and a "left behind" narrative. Understanding these narratives—an undertaking to which this book can make only a minor contribution—is indispensable for anyone trying to comprehend truly global issues.

In Part IV, we move from analysis to method. We explore how we can use multiple narratives to understand other multifaceted and evolving phenomena, including climate change and the coronavirus pandemic. Viewing these phenomena through multiple lenses allows us to blend the insights of different narratives and to appreciate these phenomena in their kaleidoscopic complexity. In some ways, different narratives complement each other by reinforcing similar concerns from different angles or by shedding light on different aspects of a phenomenon. In other ways, the narratives offer contradictory accounts of what has happened and how to evaluate it. These moments of conflict can help guide our analysis and search for more facts, and sometimes indicate the contours of trade-offs that will need to be made. This method bears a closer resemblance to turning a kaleidoscope than to solving a Rubik's cube: with each turn, the colored pieces shift, new reflections are created, and new patterns appear. But there is no end to the process and no single solution to the problem.

Trump's defeat has revived optimism among some commentators about a reset on economic globalization, but few expect a wholesale return to the free market liberalism that led to the explosion of trade and investment flows during the 1990s and 2000s. Any attempt to define a new normal will need to be sensitive to the critiques we describe and to the ways in which the world has changed since the high point of economic globalization following the Cold War. Biden's trade agenda reflects this insight: it embraces the establishment narrative's enthusiasm for trade's potential to generate prosperity while tempering it with a commitment to prioritizing the welfare of US workers (a concern of both right-wing and left-wing populists), an awareness of the need for greater regulation of corporate power (including in the areas of taxation and antitrust), and a determination to compete aggressively with China economically and technologically while cooperating on global threats such as climate change and pandemics. In the penultimate chapter of the book, we explore the potential for similar combinations of narratives in relation to the role of work and workers in society, international economic interdependence, and policy responses to climate change.

Ultimately, this book offers a meta-framework for understanding Western debates about economic globalization and a kaleidoscopic method for identifying factual and normative disagreements, as well as common themes and potential alliances, across various narratives. The book also showcases a method—looking at complex issues through dragonfly eyes—that can serve us well in examining other contentious debates and policy challenges, from pandemics to the climate crisis. We hope that this approach will enable us to understand not only where we have come apart but also how we might come back together.

CHAPTER 2

Why Narratives Matter

Facts do not speak for themselves. Instead, we use narratives to understand and communicate what they mean. And we can often tell multiple stories about the same facts. Take the Elephant Graph, which was created by the former World Bank economist Branko Milanovic, as an example. Named for its distinctively shaped curve, this graph shows the relative rise in real incomes for people in different income brackets throughout the world over a twenty-year period of intense globalization, from 1988 to 2008 (Figure 2.1). The graph shows, for example, that people in the 30th percentile of the global income distribution have seen their incomes rise by over 50 percent during that period.[1]

But the graph only represents facts; it does not provide a narrative. There are no characters—we do not know who the people in the 30th percentile are and whether we should focus on them or, say, those in the 80th percentile. There is no plot—we do not know why the line goes up and down. And there is no "moral of the story"—the graph does not tell us whether what is happening is good or bad. The narratives that we analyze in this book supply these elements, helping us make sense of factual representations such as the Elephant Graph. And they supply them in ways that embody widely divergent interpretations of the same set of facts.

The Elephant Graph is commonly interpreted as a challenge to the establishment narrative's claim that economic globalization is a win-win scenario that leaves everyone better off. Although the incomes of individuals in most income brackets rose, those who started in the 75th and 85th percentiles globally saw their real incomes stagnate or, on some versions of the graph, decline (marked as point 2 on the graph). These individuals are overwhelmingly the poor, working class, and middle class in

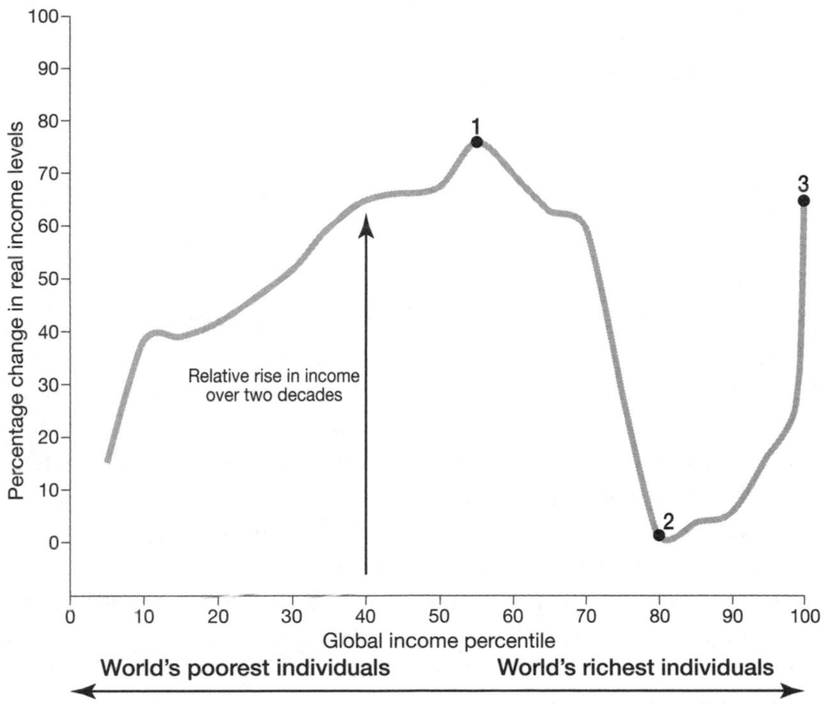

Fig. 2.1: Branko Milanovic's "Elephant Graph"

Note: This graph shows the relative rise in income of individuals at different points of the global income distribution between 1988 and 2008.

Credit: Data source: Branko Milanovic, Global Inequality: A New Approach for the Age of Globalization *(Cambridge, MA: The Belknap Press of Harvard University Press, 2016), 11.*

developed countries. By global standards, their absolute income levels remain high. In relative terms, however, their fortunes have stalled or regressed while others have surged ahead.[2]

That has not kept proponents of the establishment narrative from marshaling evidence and arguments that we are basically on the right path. Proponents of this narrative often point to the beneficiaries of globalization, including the hundreds of millions of workers in developing countries who have been lifted out of poverty (at point 1) and the rich and professional classes who have been able to take advantage of the globalized economy to reap ample rewards for their skills (at point 3). To the extent that the narrative acknowledges that the people at point 2 have been "left behind," it argues that the reasons are largely homegrown, such as inflexible labor markets, obsolete education systems, and an unwillingness to "adjust."

Yet the experiences of those stuck in the sharp dip of the Elephant Graph provided an opening for proponents of other narratives to challenge the establishment narrative's win-win claims. In the 2016 US presidential election, different politicians appealed to these disaffected voters by providing rival explanations of who had won at their expense and by offering competing prescriptions for what should be done about it.

In Donald Trump's narrative, the main protagonists were developing countries and their workers: he accused China and Mexico of "raping" and "killing" the United States by taking advantage of the "terrible" trade deals negotiated by previous US presidents. By likening the results of economic globalization to a crime scene, Trump not only furnished his narrative with a gripping plot but also left little doubt as to the moral of the story: America had been wronged. The United States needed to fight back by protecting itself, its workers, and its manufacturing communities against unfair foreign competition. In Trump's telling, the working class in America had lost out to the individuals at point 1 on the Elephant Graph, who overwhelmingly represent the working and middle classes in developing countries (Figure 2.2).[3]

Bernie Sanders appealed to the same victims but identified a different villain. "The global economy is not working for the majority of people in our country and the world," he explained. "This is an economic model developed by the economic elite to benefit the economic elite." Rather than blame workers in developing countries, Sanders pointed the finger at the richest 1 percent, at point 3 on the graph. In his narrative, America's economic elite was in the driver's seat and was making off with ill-gotten gains at the expense of the country's less fortunate citizens (Figure 2.3). The moral of the story was different as well. Instead of proposing tariffs to keep jobs at home and walls to keep foreigners out, Sanders argued for creating "national and global economies that work for all, not just a handful of billionaires."[4]

The battle between these right-wing and left-wing populist narratives in the 2016 US presidential election shows how narratives can be used to make sense of the same facts in divergent ways. By combining different causal accounts and normative evaluations, narratives provide alternative story lines about what has happened and why, what we should make of it, and what might be done in response.

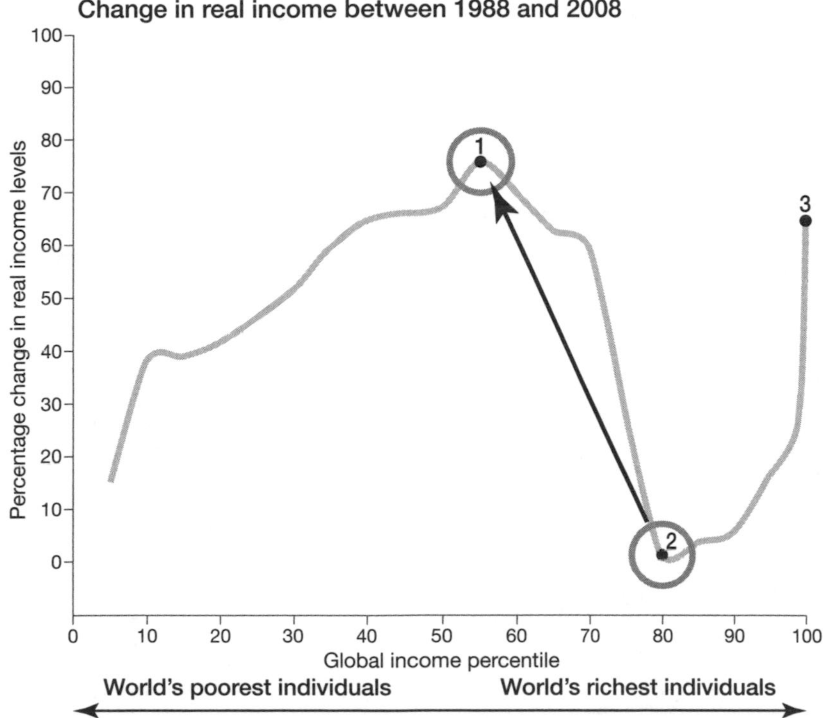

Fig. 2.2: Winners and Losers as Portrayed by the Right-Wing Populist Narrative
Note: The right-wing populist narrative argues that globalization has transferred income from the middle class in developed countries (origin of the arrow at point 2) to the middle class in developing countries (endpoint of the arrow at point 1).
Credit: Data source: Branko Milanovic, Global Inequality: A New Approach for the Age of Globalization *(Cambridge, MA: The Belknap Press of Harvard University Press, 2016), 11.*

Building Blocks of Narratives

Narratives consist of four main building blocks: they set the scene for analyzing issues in a particular way; they identify specific protagonists as winners and losers, or villains and victims; they provide a plot (an account of the sequence of events and the causal mechanisms that have led to a particular outcome); and they suggest a moral of the story (a normative assessment of what has happened, and prescriptions for what should be done about it). In doing so, narratives furnish a window into their proponents' experiences, concerns, values, and policy preferences.[5]

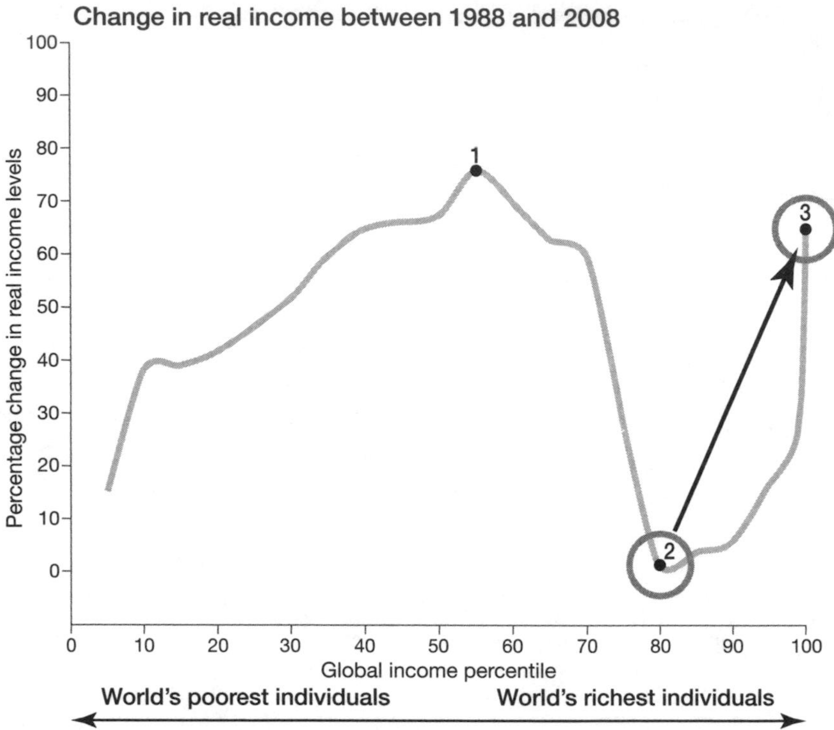

Fig. 2.3: Winners and Losers as Portrayed by the Left-Wing Populist Narrative
Note: The left-wing populist narrative argues that globalization has transferred income from the middle class in developed countries (origin of the arrow at point 2) to the top 1 percent of the global income distribution (endpoint of the arrow at point 3).
Credit: Data source: Branko Milanovic, Global Inequality: A New Approach for the Age of Globalization *(Cambridge, MA: The Belknap Press of Harvard University Press, 2016), 11.*

Setting the Scene and Identifying the Characters

Before you can tell a story, you need to frame the scene. Do you direct the focus to manufacturing communities in northern England that are socially disintegrating after factories close? Do you chronicle the explosive growth of Chinese technology companies and their potential digital reach into Western countries through 5G networks? Or do you contrast the situation of a fast-food worker in New York City who is working three jobs to make ends meet with that of the owner of a $45 million apartment overlooking Central Park? Simply by setting the scene, the narrator frames the problems created by economic globalization in a specific way.[6] In his book *Frame Analysis,* sociologist Erving Goffman explains that frames are like windows through which we see the world: they organize the central ideas on a complex issue, shaping what we see and do not see.[7] Framing plays an essential scene-setting role by identifying the appropriate units of analysis, level of analysis, and metrics of evaluation.

One of the differences between Trump's and Sanders's narratives is their choice of characters, or, put in more abstract terms, their units of analysis. Sanders is famous for railing against the billionaire class and the top 1 percent of the income distribution; he often contrasts their power and influence with the declining fortunes of the middle and working classes. This framing puts representatives of certain classes into focus. By contrast, Trump's narrative directs attention to the fate of manufacturing workers and their communities, on the one hand, and competition between developed and developing countries, on the other hand. His units of analysis are a specific group of US workers and the communities they sustain, as well as China and Mexico, whose workers compete with US nationals.

Besides their choice of characters, Sanders's and Trump's narratives differ in their level of analysis. For Sanders, the increasing divide between the haves and have-nots stems largely from the corruption of the US political and economic system. Like many other left-wing populists, he focuses primarily on the domestic policy arena and thus largely adopts a national level of analysis. For Trump, by contrast, the devastation of US industrial communities cannot be understood without examining the trade practices of other countries that have been taking advantage of America's openness. Like other right-wing populists, Trump adopts an international level of analysis where blame is directed externally to other countries and the actors that represent them. Of course, these are not the only options. The corporate power narrative, for instance, adopts a transnational level of analysis and treats multinational corporations and the transnational working class as key units of analysis. By adopting different levels and units of analysis, different narratives direct attention to different phenomena.

The framing used by a narrator often also lays the groundwork for the moral of the story by suggesting a specific metric of assessment. The metric can be primarily economic, such as GDP growth or the share of income that accrues to different classes. Or the metric can be noneconomic, such as the integrity of the social fabric, a country's security,

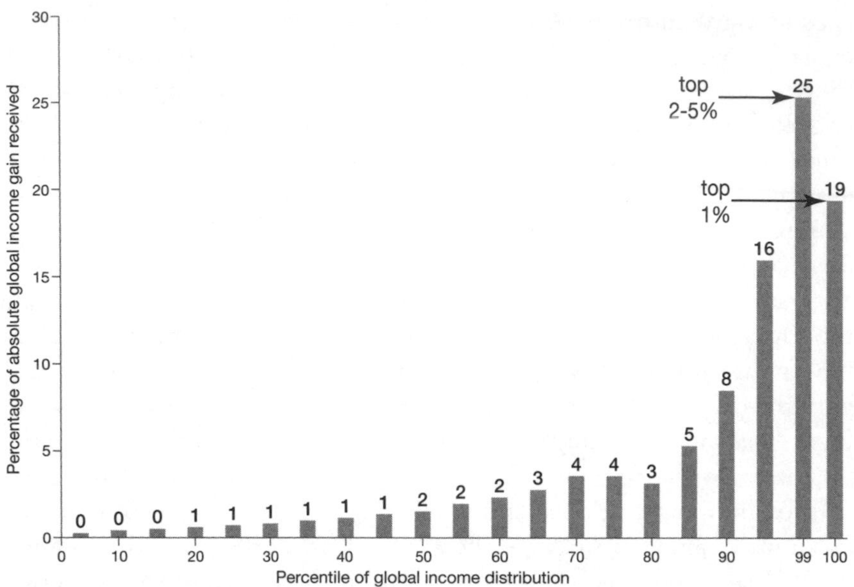

Fig. 2.4: Who Has Gained the Most in Absolute Terms?
Note: This graph shows the percentage of absolute real income gains received by individuals at different points in the global income distribution from 1988 to 2008 (the same period that is covered by the Elephant Graph).
Credit: Branko Milanovic, Global Inequality: A New Approach for the Age of Globalization *(Cambridge, MA: The Belknap Press of Harvard University Press, 2016), figure 1.2.*

or environmental sustainability. Different metrics of assessment not only embody different values but also produce divergent perceptions about the underlying realities. For example, if we look at income gains using the metric of absolute rather than relative gains, the clear winners appear to be the global rich, who began rich and became much richer (Figure 2.4). Although Asia's middle classes gained the most in relative terms, their incomes were low in the first place, so their absolute gains were not that high. These sorts of framing choices do not necessarily precede the development of empirical and normative accounts, since these choices often depend on prior empirical assumptions and normative commitments.

Developing the Plot and Distilling the Moral

Having adopted a framing, narrators relate a "plot," an account of a sequence of events and causal relationships that explains who has won at the expense of whom and why. The plot transforms the photographic stills of the frame into a motion picture. It connects actors and events over time. These plots go hand in hand with normative assessments about whether the developments they describe are good or bad and what should be done about them. Was the loss fair or the result of exploitation? Is it a cost that society has to accept or an intolerable imposition that should be rolled back?

Narratives often build normative judgments into the language they use. They might characterize jobs as "stolen" or the system as "rigged." They often employ distinctive metaphors, such as describing economic gains as "growing the size of the pie," export subsidies as "weapons of job destruction," and corporations as "leeches" or "vampires." These choices also give each narrative a distinctive feel: one need only compare the upbeat mood of the establishment story with the ominous sensation created by the global threats narrative.

By framing the problem in a specific way, narratives set the stage for policy prescriptions. Trump saw the problem as the shipping of good manufacturing jobs offshore. His solution? Impose tariffs and bring the jobs back home. By contrast, Sanders saw the problem as the elite rigging the rules of the game. His answer? Impose a wealth tax, strengthen worker rights, and provide universal healthcare. Even when there is agreement on a problem's diagnosis, there can be disagreement about which remedies will fix it. It is possible to agree that manufacturing communities have been hard hit by economic globalization and yet disagree that tariffs will bring those jobs back. Particular framings, however, tend to narrow the range of solutions that are considered.

When evaluating various narratives, it is useful to assess their empirical claims, some of which may be stronger than others. But narratives cannot be assessed through appeals to "the facts" alone. Narratives invariably embody normative judgments that cannot be reduced to empirical disagreements, from the question of how to identify the relevant facts in the first place to the values embedded in the different "morals of the story."

Why Study Multiple Narratives?

The art of advocacy lies in convincing others to view the world through the lens of your chosen narrative so that your viewpoint becomes accepted as the correct way of understanding reality. The aim is to render the narrative as natural and taken-for-granted, and to present the world through a single story, as though no other stories were relevant or true. The goal of the sort of meta-framing that we engage in, by contrast, lies in highlighting a multiplicity of narratives and showing how they set forth complementary and sometimes contradictory understandings of reality. The aim is to expose the danger of a single story by showcasing diverse angles and perspectives.

The reason a single narrative can be dangerous is that it may ring true but represent only a one-dimensional understanding of a three-dimensional reality. Sociologist Gareth Morgan makes a similar point about metaphors: "Metaphor is inherently paradoxical. It can create powerful insights that also become distortions, as the way of seeing created through the metaphor becomes a way of *not* seeing."[8] The same is true of economic models: "Models are never true; but there is truth in models."[9] Narratives, metaphors, and models are useful because they permit us to gain traction on complex issues, but none will ever give us the full picture.

Our work on narratives stands within a general lineage of writings that foreground the importance of ideas in the construction of economic regimes. We view ideas and interests as interrelated and mutually constitutive. In order to know what your interests are in a given situation, you first need to have some sense of what the problem is and how it impacts you; different ways of framing the problem can affect the way you understand your interests. But actors with particular interests can also propagate different ideas in order to achieve their goals.[10] Narratives are stories we tell ourselves to make sense of the world, but they are also stories we tell *others* to influence *their* understanding of the world.

Ideas can be powerful in different ways at different times, but they are particularly significant during periods of political flux. The political scientist Mark Blyth has argued that new ideas achieve their greatest impact when they explain aspects of people's experiences that do not cohere with the dominant paradigm. Actors who want to challenge the status quo can then use these ideas to destabilize the existing consensus and to lay out a blueprint for a new consensus.[11] How does one set of ideas come to challenge or dislodge another? The answer often lies in crisis, either intellectual or social. At such junctures, battles are fought over which idea or combination of ideas should provide the basis for the new normal.[12] We trace multiple narratives at this time because the dominant establishment narrative has been dethroned, though it is not yet clear what narrative or combination of narratives will take its place.

Although we focus on the narratives in their current incarnation, we recognize that our narratives have a long lineage. For example, in the

1970s Robert Gilpin identified three contrasting perspectives on the political economy of multinational corporations. The liberal perspective, which reflects what we identify as the establishment narrative, views international economic relations as cooperative and corporations as drivers of global economic welfare. The mercantilist perspective, which is embodied in the right-wing populist and geoeconomic narratives, views international economic relations as conflictual and worries that corporations might act contrary to the interests of their countries. And the Marxist perspective, which accords with the corporate power narrative, also views international economic relations as conflictual but views the conflict as occurring between the transnational capitalist class (including multinational corporations) and everyone else.[13] Although tracing the intellectual lineages of the narratives could yield fascinating insights, it is beyond the scope of this book.

How Should We Analyze Narratives?

We tend to remember political candidacies for sound bites of two kinds. The first are slogans that encapsulate a worldview or purport to express a deep insight into how the world works. Bill Clinton's "It's the economy, stupid," Barack Obama's "Yes, we can," and Trump's "Make America great again" fall into this category. So do former UK prime minister Margaret Thatcher's stark pronouncements championing individualism ("There is no such thing as society") and neoliberal economic reforms ("There is no alternative").

The second kind are offhand remarks, often made in private, that appear to reveal a candidate's disparaging view of certain parts of the population and can have a devastating impact on the candidate's electoral prospects. In Mitt Romney's case, his candidacy was undone in part when he was recorded as saying that "there are 47 percent who are with [Obama], who are dependent upon government, who believe that they are victims, who believe the government has a responsibility to care for them, who believe that they are entitled to health care, to food, to housing, to you-name-it. . . . I'll never convince them they should take personal responsibility and care for their lives."[14] For Hillary Clinton, it was her statement that "you could put half of Trump's supporters into what I call the basket of deplorables. Right? The racist, sexist, homophobic, xenophobic, Islamophobic—you name it."[15]

What made these comments so devastating was that they seemed to show a presidential candidate express contempt for a substantial part of the American population. Contempt is a feeling that obliterates any basis for dialogue, any sense of a shared purpose or project, any semblance of empathy and caring, any chance of a genuine engagement.[16] Current political debates are often shot through with contempt. Such contempt is frequently an expression of righteous anger; proponents of one narrative may genuinely despise the political convictions and normative attitudes of proponents of other narratives. But contempt generally serves only to rally the troops—it will never win anyone over.

In exploring different narratives on economic globalization, we try to remove contempt from the discussion. Each of the narratives that we reconstruct in this book could easily be caricatured; one would need only to cite its most extreme proponents and most exaggerated arguments. That, however, is not our purpose. We seek to reconstruct the narratives in sympathetic ways, putting them in their best light rather than seeking to discredit and denigrate them. In this way, we hope to provide a workable framework for people with diverse views to engage in productive debates.

Another pitfall of political discourse that we try to avoid in this book is exemplified by then-candidate Obama's infamous comments about Americans living in cities ravaged by deindustrialization. Speaking about residents of small towns in the Midwest, where jobs had disappeared and not been replaced, Obama concluded: "It's not surprising then that they get bitter, they cling to guns or religion or antipathy to people who aren't like them or anti-immigrant sentiment or anti-trade sentiment as a way to explain their frustrations."[17] Obama did not express contempt for these voters; instead, he belittled them by suggesting that they were deluded about the real causes of their situation.

The inclination not to take people's expressed views at face value can also be found among journalists and academics. In his book *What's the Matter with Kansas,* historian and journalist Thomas Frank explored why people vote Republican when doing so would seem to go against their economic self-interest. The answer to this paradox, he concluded, lay in "bait-and-switch" political campaigns. Conservative politicians had hoodwinked voters into casting their ballots against their economic self-interest by pairing a rich person's "economic agenda" with the "bait" of social issues such as abortion and gun control: "Vote to stop abortion; receive a rollback on capital gains taxes. . . . Vote to get government off our backs; receive conglomeration and monopoly everywhere from media to meat packing. Vote to strike a blow against elitism; receive a social order in which wealth is more concentrated than ever before in our lifetimes."[18] In a similar vein, Dani Rodrik's distinction between the demand side of populism (which he views as being based on economic anxiety) and its supply side (where populist politicians propound "cultural" narratives to channel economic concerns into anti-immigrant sentiment) appears to be based on an assumption of the primacy of economic concerns over other values as the real cause of the problem.[19]

We take a different approach. A considerable body of literature exists on whether the underlying drivers of different populist narratives are economic or cultural.[20] In our view, both factors are likely at play, it is often not easy to separate the two, and each affects the other. Economic divisions between the working and professional classes are not just about money; they also reflect and reinforce cultural differences, including with respect to values.[21] Disparities in educational attainment not only lead to different economic outcomes but also reflect and reinforce cultural differences in openness to experience and comfort with diversity.[22] And economic and cultural factors may exacerbate each other; for instance, in conditions of perceived economic scarcity, instincts to protect one's community may become more salient.[23] However, our aim is not to adjudicate these debates; instead, we believe that we can best encourage dialogue across diverse camps if we take the narratives at face value and presume that their proponents are genuine.

We leave to others the very important job of assessing the underlying empirical claims of the narratives, weighing the value of their normative commitments, and debating the merits of their proposed solutions. These tasks are more vital than ever: we are living in times in which misinformation abounds and in which more actors than ever before have the means to manipulate people and their sense of reality.[24] Powerful actors sponsor research and narratives that suit their interests, as can be seen in the case of fossil fuel corporations sowing doubt about climate change.[25] Politicians may also stoke fear about internal and external threats in order to suit their agendas and solidify their power.[26] Anyone who wishes to assess narratives for their truth or persuasiveness needs to be attentive as to whether these story lines represent the facts accurately, what monied interests might be behind different narratives, and whose interests these narratives serve and undermine.

But that is not our goal here. In many ways, our project precedes such political, economic, and philosophical analyses.[27] We eschew extreme narratives such as conspiracy theories and climate change denial, instead constructing six mainstream narratives that form the basic architecture of the Western debates. Rather than picking a battle and choosing a side, we step back to create a meta-framework that enables the reader to understand different perspectives and encourages actors to be conscious of how their approaches fit within this broader schema.[28] Our hope is to facilitate good-faith debates about the merits of different narratives, including as to which facts are relevant, what causal mechanisms explain them, how they should be evaluated normatively, and what policies should be enacted in response.[29] By rendering competing narratives explicit and providing a structure for guiding good-faith debates, this book contributes the kind of meta-framework that current debates about economic globalization are lacking.

PART II

SIX FACES OF GLOBALIZATION

IN THIS PART, WE TAKE READERS ON A JOURNEY to experience how economic globalization looks from the vantage point of each narrative. We draw primarily on the themes, arguments, metaphors, and images invoked by proponents of the narratives, though we also rely on commentators who describe the narratives without necessarily endorsing them. We aim to be illustrative rather than exhaustive. Our approach is curated, not comprehensive, and qualitative, not quantitative.

These narratives are our own intellectual constructs based on a broad range of sources. They are quite capacious; each narrative accommodates multiple subplots. We group certain story lines together under a single narrative when they share core building blocks—for instance, when they use the same units and level of analysis, see the gains from economic globalization flowing in the same direction, and affirm the same values. Some actors we identify as proponents of a given narrative may endorse some subplots but not others. Others may blend elements from different narratives.

Some readers will take issue with some of the narrative's causal claims; for example, many economists argue that the effects that advocates of the right-wing populist narrative attribute to trade are caused by technological change. Others may disagree with the narratives' normative commitments; for instance, some commentators criticize the corporate power narrative for focusing only on how multinational companies hurt people rather than on the ways in which they help them. Still others may argue that the policies advocated by a particular narrative are ineffective at best and counterproductive at worst; many doubt, for example, that a policy of degrowth is either feasible or desirable.

These are important issues that are worthy of serious debate. However, we leave these empirical, normative, and policy questions to the side so that we can fully immerse readers in these different discursive landscapes. We want to evoke the concerns and complaints of each narrative in an interpretive and sociological way rather than assess and critique them with the methods of political science or economics. Whether one likes a particular narrative or not, and whether one agrees with its empirical claims and normative evaluations or not, it is important to understand these narratives on their own terms, as they are all present and powerful in current Western debates.

CHAPTER 3

The Establishment Narrative

The international economic order that has been built over the past 70 years has many defenders. Economists point to the variety and cheapness of the products that we enjoy, and to the hundreds of millions of people who have been lifted out of poverty in China and India in recent decades. Officials of international organizations highlight the contribution that international rules make to the peaceful settlement of disputes. And, at least until recently, the majority of politicians in mainstream political parties across the developed and developing world saw trade agreements as an integral part of their strategies to boost economic growth. Because of the widespread support that the narrative about the benefits of economic globalization has enjoyed in many established institutions, we call it the establishment narrative.

The events of the past decade have given the establishment narrative a bad name. Few economists predicted the 2008 global financial crisis that led to what was then the deepest recession since the Great Depression. Economic growth in Western countries has been accompanied by rising inequality since the 1970s. The effects of deindustrialization have left formerly thriving regions in desolation, as the knowledge economy clusters in a few booming global cities that provide focal points for communications, financial, and transport networks. To its critics, the establishment narrative's response to these developments has been lackluster: data-heavy reports issued by international organizations that tell people who have lost their jobs to be "mobile" and "adjust" in response to the changing world fail to convince those who have heard politicians promise too many times that trade agreements will lead to better, higher-paying jobs. And high-flying 1 percenters who casually suggest that displaced workers should be mollified with welfare handouts inspire deep resentment.[1] Not surprisingly, political outsiders in many Western countries have gained traction by broadcasting their anti-establishment credentials, sometimes riding the wave of discontent all the way to public office.

In this chapter, we first restate the establishment narrative's basic case that economic liberalization, coupled with good governance and the rule of law, will lead to prosperity and peace. From this perspective, what matters first and foremost is to grow the size of the economic pie; questions of distribution are of secondary importance. We then discuss the biggest split among proponents of the narrative that has resurfaced in the current crisis: the debate on whether and, if so, how to help the losers from economic globalization so as to counter the rise of left-wing and right-wing populist sentiment across many developed countries. Finally, we survey the establishment narrative's response to the biggest intellectual challenge that it has encountered in decades: the effects of the "China shock" on manufacturing jobs in developed countries such as the United States and the United Kingdom.

The Benefits of Free Trade

Imagine you found yourself, Robinson Crusoe style, on a small island somewhere in the ocean. You are scrambling to survive. You spend your days collecting fruit and firewood, constructing makeshift shelters, and watching out for danger. You are just scraping by.

Then one day a wooden box is washed ashore. You open it and discover a big black machine. Fortunately, the instructions came in a sealed plastic bag and are still readable. They consist of two short sentences: *1. Insert any product into the machine. 2. Say what you need, and the machine will convert the product you inserted into the product you want.*

Intrigued, you try out the machine. You put a bunch of bananas into it and ask for a tent. Lo and behold, the machine spits out a tent. You put another bunch of bananas into it and ask for firewood. Again your wish is fulfilled.

The machine profoundly changes your life. No longer do you have to try to produce everything yourself; instead, you can focus on one product and use the machine to get everything else. Your island abounds in bananas, so you decide to harvest bananas. Whereas previously it took you two hours each day to collect one box of firewood, now you need only five minutes to harvest some bananas, put them into the machine, and get your box of firewood.

But it gets better than that. As you focus on harvesting bananas, you get more proficient at it. You develop a special cutting technique to harvest bananas more quickly, and you build a transportation system to carry the bananas to the machine. Even more amazingly, you discover that, over time, the machine continually gives you more for any given quantity of bananas that you put into it: you used to get only one box of firewood for a bunch of bananas, but now you get two boxes. You can hardly believe your good luck.

What does this seemingly far-fetched Robinson Crusoe story have to do with economic globalization? For most mainstream economists, the answer is simple: economic globalization is the big black machine. It is an almost miracle-like force for good—a form of "magic." Economist Alan Binder declares, "Like 99% of economists since the days of Adam Smith, I am a free trader down to my toes." That free trade is beneficial, Gregory Mankiw (another economist) concludes, "is something that is universally believed by economists."[2]

These economists point out that most human beings were in the position of the hardscrabble Robinson Crusoe as recently as 200 years ago. What allowed them to escape from that position were three processes facilitated by the big black machine of economic globalization. First, they were able to *specialize*. Just as the machine allowed you, a lonely islander, to focus on the one activity (harvesting bananas) that you were relatively good at, so the advent of the global market allowed millions of people to focus on their relative advantages and exchange the products of their labor for the products of other people's labor.

Second, economic globalization spurred investment in *technology*. As a lonely islander, you had neither the time nor the incentive to invest in improving your banana-harvesting technology: your own demand for bananas was limited by how much you could eat, and you had to spend time gathering other resources. Just as the advent of the big black machine with its insatiable demand for bananas and the ability to provide you with all other necessities gave you the incentive and opportunity to improve your banana-harvesting technology, so economic globalization created massive rewards for those who invested in technologies—new machines, new ways of organizing production—that allowed them to produce more with less.

Finally, just as the machine gives you ever more for the same input, so economic globalization allows everyone to benefit from the productivity increases that *others* realize through specialization and improved technology. When others do well from free trade, it does not come at your expense; you benefit from their increased productivity, as they benefit from yours. Free trade is truly a win-win outcome.

Indeed, if you substitute countries for individuals, the happy story above captures the essence of David Ricardo's theory of comparative advantage. In the classic example used by Ricardo, England was more efficient at producing cloth than wine, and Portugal was more efficient at producing wine than cloth. Ricardo showed that both countries would end up better off if each concentrated on producing what it did best (i.e., its *comparative* advantage) and traded for the rest, rather than if both countries tried to make both products. This outcome holds true even if Portugal was more efficient than England at producing both cloth and wine (i.e., it had an *absolute* advantage). Portugal would still be better off if it focused on making wine and used the excess money it received from trading wine to buy more cloth from England.[3]

We have become utterly dependent on specialization and trade. As an illustration, consider two experiments. Thomas Thwaites, a British designer, tried to declare his independence from the division of labor by building a toaster from scratch. He spent several months and £1,187.54 trying to replicate a product that he had bought for £3.94, with pitiful results. And the French documentary filmmaker Benjamin Carle, also known as Monsieur Made-in-France, tried to say "no thank you" to trade by living only off French products for a year; he had to make do without a washing machine, a bike, or a kettle (he cheated by continuing to use his computer). "Just as it is nearly impossible for individuals to produce all the things they wish to consume," economist Kimberly Clausing concludes, "it would be foolish for one country to make everything its people desire."[4]

Free Market Capitalism and Economic Growth

Perhaps the best illustration of the phenomenal growth in income experienced by the world's population over the past 200 years is the "hockey stick of human prosperity" (Figure 3.1). It shows per capita incomes hovering just around subsistence levels for millennia before shooting up around the early 1800s, when the invention of steam power gave rise to the first Industrial Revolution (which allowed workers to become much more productive) and radically reduced transport costs (which facilitated trade by making it possible to produce goods in one place but sell them in another).[5]

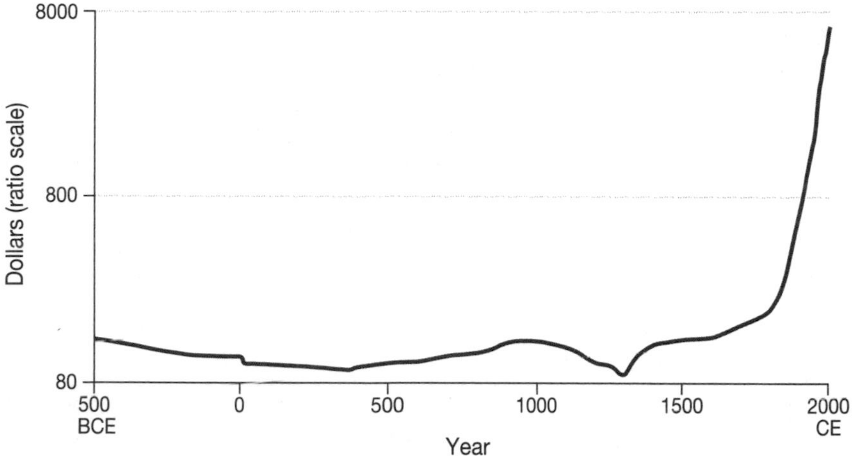

Fig. 3.1: The Hockey Stick of Human Prosperity
Note: This graph shows annual world GDP from 500 BCE to 2000 CE (in 1990 international dollars).
Credit: Reformatted from Victor V. Claar, "The Urgency of Poverty and the Hope of Genuinely Fair Trade," Journal of Markets and Morality *16, no. 1 (Spring 2013): 273–279, figure 1.*

This first Industrial Revolution ushered in 200 years of unprecedented changes in human living conditions. Over this period, the majority of people in Western countries moved from rural areas to cities, and from agriculture into manufacturing and then into service sector occupations. For instance, 220 years ago, 75 percent of Americans worked in agriculture, driving plows pulled by horses and harvesting crops by hand, whereas now less than 3 percent of America's population is needed to grow its food.[6] Although these changes caused enormous dislocations, the establishment narrative points out that specialization, technological innovation, and trade have made us vastly more productive. And since our productivity determines our standard of living, that is all that matters. Compared with where we were 200 years ago—and in most cases even fifty years ago—individuals in developed countries today are unfathomably rich.

But economic globalization does not merely benefit rich developed countries; it has also played a key role in lifting hundreds of millions of people out of poverty in developing countries, as successive waves of development have swept the globe, moving from Europe and North America in the nineteenth and early twentieth centuries to the newly industrializing

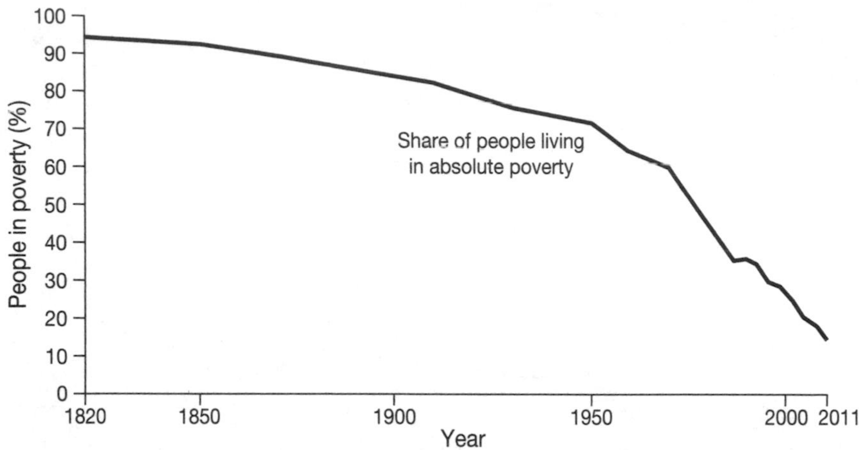

Fig. 3.2: The Declining Share of People Living in Absolute Poverty
Note: This graph shows the declining share of people living in absolute poverty from 1820 to 2011.
Credit: Reformatted from Max Roser and Esteban Ortiz-Ospina, "Global Extreme Poverty," Share of the World Population Living in Absolute Poverty, 1820–2015, https://ourworldindata.org/extreme-poverty, based on data from François Bourguignon and Christian Morrisson, "Inequality among World Citizens: 1820–1992," American Economic Review *92, no. 4 (2002): 727–744 and from the World Bank.*

economies in East Asia in the second half of the twentieth century and the big emerging economies over the past twenty-five years (Figure 3.2). The last two waves have led to sharp reductions in poverty, particularly in China and India, which saw their GDP and per capita incomes soar after opening up to foreign trade and investment.

Proponents of the establishment narrative describe the feat of raising more than a billion people above the global poverty line as "truly the most astounding economic progress in the history of the world," and they give free trade much of the credit.[7] As economist Paul Krugman notes: "The raw fact is that every successful example of economic development this past century—every case of a poor nation that worked its way up to a more or less decent, or at least dramatically better, standard of living—has taken place via globalization; that is, by producing for the world market rather than trying for self-sufficiency."[8]

For proponents of the establishment narrative, the lesson from this experience is that free market capitalism is the key to unlocking economic growth. In the words of *Financial Times* columnist Martin Wolf, the basic takeaway is that a "world integrated through the market should be highly beneficial to the vast majority of the world's inhabitants" because the market is "the most powerful institution for raising living standards ever invented: indeed there are no rivals."[9]

International Trade Agreements as Guarantors of Peace

For proponents of the establishment narrative, the evidence of the benefits of free trade is so overwhelming that countries should be prepared to liberalize their economies unilaterally, regardless of what other countries are doing. If governments heeded this advice, there would be no need for international trade agreements to set tariff rates—any agreements would only be about harmonizing standards and setting the "rules of the road" to ensure that trade across borders is as frictionless as trade within borders.[10] But historical experience has shown that governments are often reluctant to dismantle barriers and expose certain domestic producers to competition, and that they are prone to reacting to trade restrictions imposed by their trading partners by retaliating with restrictions of their own. The most famous example of this dynamic is the escalation of trade restrictions that followed the imposition of the highly protectionist Smoot-Hawley Tariff by the United States in 1930, which raised import duties to protect US businesses and farmers. In the establishment narrative's telling, the collapse in world trade that arose from the subsequent tit-for-tat escalation of tariffs aggravated the effects of the Great Depression and provided fertile ground for the rise of extremist parties in Europe, which ultimately paved the way for World War II.

When trade officials set out to rebuild the international trade regime after World War II, the link between unchecked protectionism and military conflict was foremost in their minds. President Franklin D. Roosevelt's secretary of state, Cordell Hull, had long believed that "unhampered trade dovetailed with peace; high tariffs, trade barriers, and unfair economic competition, with war."[11] In the 1930s, Hull had attempted to redress the damage done by the Smoot-Hawley Tariff and to avert a new war by launching an ambitious program of bilateral trade agreements.[12] After World War II, when US trade officials kick-started the negotiations that led to the conclusion of the General Agreement on Tariffs and Trade (GATT), they frequently referenced the "restrictionism of the Thirties" as the evil to avoid.[13] Similar statements became a constant refrain in trade negotiations, as negotiators regularly reaffirmed their "resolve that the tragedy of the 1930s, arising from protectionism embodied in economic blocs, should never be repeated."[14] In a speech to the United Nations in the 1970s, the GATT's director-general stated: "I imagine that few people would argue that the world would be better off without any generally-accepted rules for trade. The law of the jungle applied to international trade in the 1930s, and the world paid dearly for the fact. For the past generation the GATT has provided the rule of law that was lacking in world trade during the Great Depression years."[15]

The notion of a strong link between open trade and peaceful international relations has carried over into the era of the WTO, which succeeded the GATT in 1995. In describing the benefits of the multilateral trading system, the WTO leads with the argument that "the system helps promote peace" because it ensures that "disputes are handled constructively."[16] According to the WTO, trade reduces the prospects of war: since salespeople usually hesitate to fight their customers, healthy commercial relations should usually mean that there is little political support for conflict between two countries. "Protectionism can easily plunge us into a situation where no one wins and everyone loses," another WTO publication warns, since destructive trade tensions can easily escalate into armed conflict.[17] During the Great Recession of 2008, the WTO's director-general compared the trajectory of the crisis favorably with the events of the 1930s. "The existence of an institutional setup of international trade rules," he argued, was a "vital factor" in preventing the "contagion of inward-looking trade policy and protectionism" that had characterized the Great Depression.[18]

The conviction that international economic integration is the most reliable safeguard against war also motivated the most far-reaching regional integration project of the past century, the European Union. The foundation for European integration was laid in 1952 with the establishment of the European Coal and Steel Community, a supranational organization that, not coincidentally, regulated the production of materials essential to any military campaign. According to the foreign minister of France at the time, Robert Schuman, joint oversight of coal and steel production would "make it plain that any war between France and Germany becomes not merely unthinkable, but materially impossible."[19] Sixty years later, the European Union was awarded the Nobel Peace Prize in recognition of its role in transforming Europe from a "continent of war" into a "continent of peace," not just by preventing another war between Germany and France but also by integrating eastern European countries after the collapse of communism and facilitating reconciliation

Fig. 3.3: World Peace through World Trade
Note: This stamp was issued on the occasion of the Seventeenth Congress of the International Chamber of Commerce, which took place in Washington, DC, April 19–25, 1959.
Credit: National Postal Museum, Smithsonian Institution.

among the Balkan states.[20] In the context of the Brexit debates in the United Kingdom, the European Union's role as a guarantor of peace in Europe was frequently invoked by those on the "Remain" side, perhaps most powerfully by veterans of World War II.[21]

The idea that trade promotes peace—also known as the "capitalist peace"—has also been championed by philosophers, journalists, and businesspeople.[22] In the eighteenth century, German philosopher Immanuel Kant argued that "the spirit of commerce . . . is incompatible with war,"[23] and French philosopher Montesquieu concluded: "Peace is the natural effect of trade. Two nations who traffic with each other become reciprocally dependent."[24] In 1909, British writer and politician Norman Angell reasoned that the interdependence of modern economies through trade reduced the prospects of war because it made war much more unprofitable.[25] And in the twenty-first century, *New York Times* columnist Thomas Friedman formulated the Golden Arches Theory of Conflict Prevention, according to which no two countries with McDonald's franchises will ever go to war against each other.[26] He later developed this proposition into the Dell Theory: no two countries that form part of the same major global supply chain, such as Dell Computer's, will ever fight a war against each other.[27] The private sector has also enthusiastically embraced the thesis that trade leads to peace. In the 1950s, the International Chamber of Commerce commissioned a book about its own history called *Merchants of Peace*,[28] and the United States issued a stamp featuring the phrase "World peace through world trade" to commemorate the seventeenth congress of the chamber (Figure 3.3).

The lesson of the twentieth and twenty-first centuries is that trade certainly does not suffice to prevent war: Europe descended into the horrors of World War I a few years after Angell's book was published, and Friedman's Golden Arches Theory was falsified when the NATO countries bombed Yugoslavia in 1999 and Russia invaded Georgia in 2008 and Ukraine in 2014. Nonetheless, the idea that trade integration plays a central role in safeguarding international security maintains a strong hold on the imagination of proponents of the establishment narrative.

No Pain, No Gain

The massive changes wrought by economic globalization that have made most of us fabulously rich (by historical standards) do not come without downsides. Imagine you are back on your small island (before the machine arrived), but instead of you being there alone, someone else is shipwrecked along with you. Over time, you develop an elementary division of labor: you focus on harvesting bananas and your companion concentrates on collecting firewood, and at regular intervals you meet to exchange bananas for firewood. She builds her hut on the part of the island where most of the firewood is found, and as the years go by, her identity starts to revolve around her work as a firewood collector.

One day, the machine is washed ashore. All of a sudden, you do not need her firewood anymore: you can get firewood much more easily by exchanging bananas for firewood through the machine. When she tries to use the machine to get bananas in exchange for firewood, she discovers, to her dismay, that the number of bananas she receives for a box of firewood is only a small fraction of the number she could harvest herself in the time it takes her to collect the box of firewood. In fact, you soon discover that you can eliminate your need for firewood entirely by using the machine to get a propane stove and a battery-powered lamp!

What should she do? Her first impulse is to push the machine back into the sea. You are appalled, because you realize how much worse off you would be without the machine. You try to convince her to move to your side of the island and start harvesting bananas. In that way, she too would be better off, though she would have to abandon her old way of life. Eventually she reluctantly agrees.

You managed to convince your companion on the island to do exactly what the proponents of the establishment narrative say to those who see themselves as losers from economic globalization: *Adjust! Don't try to protect yourself by preventing technological progress or shutting the door on trade. You can't stop the inevitable, and you're just going to make everyone worse off if you try.* Economist Richard Baldwin calls it the pain-gain package: "The iron law of globalization and automation is that progress means change, and change means pain." According to Baldwin, the disruptions caused by economic globalization should be embraced because they ultimately make the world a "much nicer place."[29]

This confidence that things will get better underpins the establishment narrative. "The story of economic progress is a story of economic change," the director-general of the WTO tells us. Some workers might suffer from short-term pain, but in the end free trade will make everyone better off because the "ability of workers to move from lower- to higher-productivity jobs, and from declining sectors to rising ones, is the essential mechanism by which trade and technological progress increase overall economic efficiency, promote development and improve living standards."[30] The need to adapt to progress through trade and technological development is part and parcel of what economists call "churn" and what the political economist Joseph Schumpeter termed "creative destruction." "It has been part of economic life for centuries and it can bring pain," the WTO explains. "But history tells us that countries seeking to block incoming goods, services or ideas often find their economies stagnating."[31]

In the 1990s and 2000s, there was a strong sense that globalization was an unstoppable force; resistance would be futile and wrongheaded. "I hear people say we have to stop and debate globalization," said UK prime minister Tony Blair, but "you might as well debate whether autumn should follow summer. . . . The character of this changing world is indifferent to tradition—unforgiving of frailty. No respecter of past reputations. It has no custom and practice. It is replete with opportunities, but they only go to those swift to adapt, slow to complain, open, willing and able to change."[32] "Global economic forces are unstoppable, just like technology itself," explains the fictitious president in the television series *West Wing*. "Should we have banned ATMs to protect bank tellers or digital watches to prop up the folks who fix grandfather clocks?" The question was rhetorical because the answer was assumed to be obvious. "Free trade creates better, higher-paying jobs," the White House employees chant in unison.[33]

The Need to Adjust

Adjustment is not always easy, and proponents of the establishment narrative have come to disagree profoundly on whether and to what extent governments should help the (short-term) losers from economic globalization to adjust.

When the issue first took center stage in developed countries in the 1950s with the decline of the textile industry, one school of thought that quickly emerged was what we call the No Differentiation School.[34] This school refuses to differentiate between the causes of dislocation; it does not look into the big black machine to see whether workers have lost their jobs due to domestic competition, international competition, changes in consumer tastes and needs, or technological progress. For this school, there is simply no intellectually defensible reason to treat international trade differently than other sources of economic change. As economist Donald Boudreaux has put it, "Competition that domestic producers endure from foreign rivals differs in precisely zero economically relevant ways from competition that domestic producers endure from each other."[35]

In the view of the No Differentiation School, any policies designed to help workers adjust—investments in education, a social safety net, active labor market policies—should be available to all workers irrespective of what caused their job loss. Providing special assistance to those harmed by trade not only is unfair to those who lose their jobs for other reasons, but also "perpetuates the myth that freeing trade creates special 'victims' who deserve special programs simply because of the reason for their unemployment" and "has the effect of demonizing trade as some nefarious thing that merits skepticism and concern." The No Differentiation School argues that nobody "loses" from trade per se. International trade is simply one form of market competition, and there is no reason (other than unfounded anti-foreigner bias) to single out trade as a unique ill.[36]

Other proponents of the establishment narrative adhere to what one could call the Trade Is Special School. In contrast to the No Differentiation School, the Trade Is Special School is willing to look into the big black machine and offer special support to those who lost their jobs because of international trade. Proponents of this view justify it on two grounds, one political and one moral.

The political reason is straightforward. Representatives of the Trade Is Special School recognize that open trade is much more vulnerable politically than technological progress and domestic competition. Producer interests have a long history of successfully lobbying governments to increase tariffs or at least to leave them in place to protect those producers. The Trade Is Special School holds that to ensure continuing political support for international trade, losers from trade should be given special attention. To make the inevitable job losses acceptable, political leaders need to find ways of "sharing the gains and the pains," Baldwin argues, "or at least offering a perception that everyone has a fighting chance of being a winner." On this view, helping the losers from free trade is necessary to "save the political consensus in favor of free trade."[37]

The moral rationale for giving special attention to people who lose their jobs from trade is more complex. One argument is that "unemployment caused by Government action, as in the lowering of tariffs, should be of particular concern to the Government." In other words, the government bears special responsibility for those displaced by trade liberalization because it more directly causes their misery (or at least allows it to happen) than it does with technological progress and domestic competition. Another moral justification for the Trade Is Special School is that displaced workers are taking one for the team. As Edward Alden, fellow at the Council of Foreign Relations, reports, one of the original proponents of adjustment assistance claimed that it was "unreasonable to say that a liberal trade policy is in the interest of the entire country and then allow particular industries, workers, and communities to pay the whole price."[38]

However much they disagree on whether and how to help people adjust, the bottom line of both schools is that we have to keep our eye on the ball: international trade is a source of wealth. Pushing the big black machine back into the sea is not an option. Instead, one way or another, and with help or without, people will have to move to the other side of the island, learn new skills, and adjust.

Responding to the China Shock

The establishment narrative about the benefits of trade has never faced a bigger challenge, both politically and intellectually, than in the period since 2016. The surprise election of Trump to the US presidency propelled working-class discontent to the top of the political agenda, while the Brexit vote in the United Kingdom sent shock waves through Europe. What happened? wondered many proponents of the establishment narrative.

Further questions were prompted by the work of economists who focused on the differential effects of trade on particular communities and groups. Pathbreaking research by labor economist David Autor and his colleagues—presented in an article evocatively titled "The China Shock"—showed that trade had caused deep and prolonged misery in the

US manufacturing communities that were most exposed to imports from China, as job losses in manufacturing were not offset by equivalent employment gains in other sectors. The effect on non-college-educated men of working age was particularly pronounced and led to detrimental impacts on their health and marital prospects. Research by economists Anne Case and Angus Deaton on the rise in the white working class's opioid abuse and suicide rates compounded the atmosphere of doom. Some began to wonder whether making an economic actor as large as China part of the big black machine—by admitting it to the WTO in 2001—had been a step too far. After taking some time to regroup, the proponents of the establishment narrative hit back with five arguments.[39]

Technology Is to Blame

The first line of defense by proponents of the establishment narrative is that much of the misery caused by the decline in manufacturing employment is due to forces operating in the big black machine *other* than trade, in particular the automation of production. Although US manufacturing employment has declined precipitously over the past decades, the value of manufacturing output has actually risen, and reached a new record high in 2018.[40] US manufacturers have been producing more than ever; they are just able to do it with far fewer workers (Figure 3.4). Proponents of this narrative cite various estimates to the effect that trade accounts for only between 13 and 20 percent of the decline in US manufacturing employment.[41] As the WTO's *World Trade Report* argues, "The disappearance of factory jobs today, like the disappearance of agricultural jobs in the past, has more to do with automation and digitization than with offshoring and outsourcing."[42]

The Benefits of Trade Continue to Exist

Even with China inside the big black machine, the benefits of free trade continue to flow. One of these benefits is *specialization*. Just as your companion on the island did not have to sit idly by after her firewood-collecting skills were no longer needed, so most US workers have moved on to other jobs, many of which were made possible by trade with China. The arrival of the big black machine on the island freed up resources (such as your companion's time, since she no longer had to collect firewood) and created additional demand (without the big black machine, there would not be enough demand for bananas for your companion to focus on harvesting bananas as well). China's integration into the world

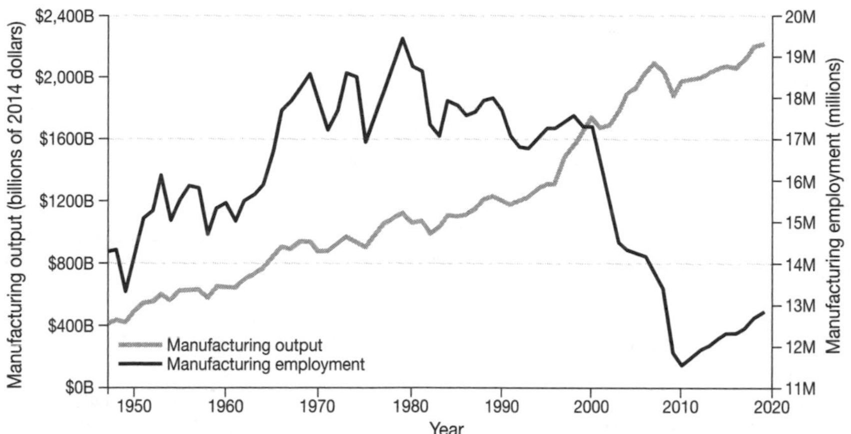

Fig. 3.4: Fewer Workers Are Producing More Goods

Note: This graph shows manufacturing employment and manufacturing output in the United States from 1947 to 2014.

Credit: Reformatted from Mark J. Perry, "Today Is Manufacturing Day, So Let's Recognize America's World-Class Manufacturing Sector and Factory Workers," Carpe Diem (American Enterprise Institute Ideas), *October 1, 2015, figure 1 with additional data supplied by Mark J. Perry.*

economy has had the same effect, creating new opportunities for US workers. Whereas jobs have been lost in manufacturing, the United States has been gaining jobs in services, construction, and retail. Before the onset of the coronavirus pandemic, overall US employment stood at an all-time high. As a result of the reallocation of resources resulting from the China shock, more Americans work with their minds than with their hands (Figure 3.5). And—at least according to the proponents of the establishment narrative—they tend to like it that way: as Trump's first director of the National Economic Council, Gary Cohn, put it, most Americans prefer sitting in an air-conditioned office to working in front of a blast furnace.[43]

Moreover, just as you became *more productive* at harvesting bananas once you were able to specialize in it, the US workforce as a whole became more productive as a result of the China shock. Productivity increased partly because companies innovated and invested in response to increased competition. China's emergence as a manufacturing powerhouse induced many US manufacturing companies to shift the focus of their US workforce to higher-value-added activities, such as research and

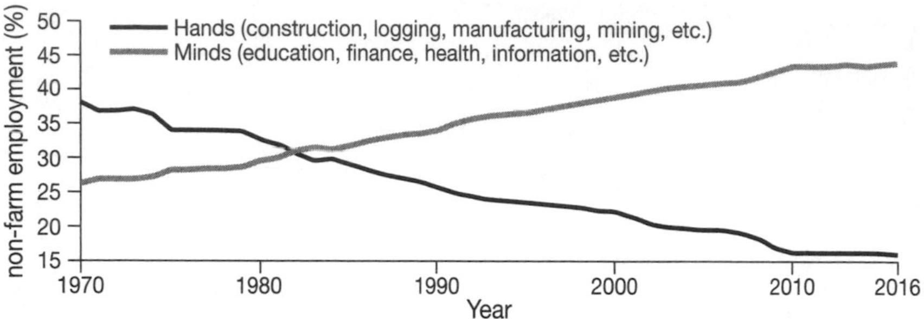

Fig. 3.5: More People Are Working with Their Minds Rather than with Their Hands

Note: This graph shows the share of private non-farm employment by type of work in the United States from 1970 to 2016.

Credit: Reformatted from Caroline Freund and Christine McDaniel, "The U.S. Needs to Invest in Minds, Not Miners," Bloomberg, June 6, 2017, figure "From Hands to Minds." Used by permission of Bloomberg LLP.

development, design, and marketing. The difference between these positions is illustrated by the "smile curve," which graphically depicts where in the production process the greatest amount of value is added.[44] The US workforce moved from the low-value-adding activities at the center of the curve toward the high-value-adding tasks at the curve's ends (Figure 3.6). In fact, some commentators have suggested that companies that still conduct most of their manufacturing in the United States, such as Tesla, should follow the example of companies like Apple and "leave 'production hell' to other people" by outsourcing the manufacturing to low-wage countries, since "the real money isn't in building beautiful things. It's in creating them." Proponents of the establishment narrative note that even those workers who left the employ of manufacturing companies often moved into higher-paid occupations. Colin Grabow, of the Cato Institute, has pointed out that the average pay in construction (one of the sectors that saw an increase in employment) substantially exceeds the pay in the textile industry, which has lost employees.[45]

And finally, just like your bunch of bananas went further in purchasing goods as time went by, consumers can buy much more by working for the same amount of time, proponents of the establishment narrative stress. For example, the average amount of time US workers have to put in to afford a range of home appliances declined by 70 percent between 1973 and 2009 (Table 3.1). TVs, for instance, cost 84 percent less in 2009

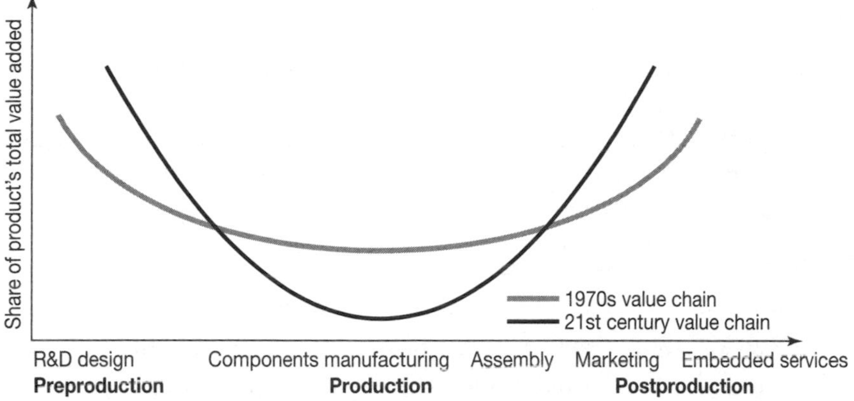

Fig. 3.6: The "Smile Curve" of Value Added in Manufacturing
Note: This graph provides a stylized representation of the share of a product's value that is added at different stages of the manufacturing process in the typical twenty-first-century value chain, compared to the typical value chain in the 1970s.
Credit: Reformatted from Mary Hallward-Driemeier and Gaurav Nayyar, Trouble in the Making? The Future of Manufacturing-Led Development *(Washington, DC: World Bank, 2018), figure 1.2. © World Bank. CC BY 3.0 IGO.*

Table 3.1 People Need to Work Less to Afford Basic Household Appliances

Household Appliances	Retail Price 1973	Hours of Work at $4.12	Retail Price 2009	Hours of Work at $18.72	% Change 1973 to 2009
Washing machine	$285	69.2	$400	21.4	–69.1
Clothes dryer	$185	44.9	$400	21.4	–52.4
Dishwasher	$310	75.2	$570	30.4	–59.5
Refrigerator	$370	89.8	$425	22.7	–74.7
Freezer	$240	58.3	$265	14.2	–75.7
Stove	$290	70.4	$650	34.7	–50.7
Color TV	$400	97.1	$300	16.0	–83.5
Coffeepot	$37	9.0	$30	1.6	–82.2
Blender	$40	9.7	$32	1.7	–82.4
Toaster	$25	6.1	$30	1.6	–73.6
Vacuum cleaner	$90	21.8	$100	5.3	–75.5
				Average	–70.8

Note: The table shows that the typical worker in the United States needed to put in 70 percent fewer hours on average in 2009 than in 1973 to afford basic household appliances. The wage per hour is the average hourly wage across all industries.
Source: Mark J. Perry, "The Rich Are Getting Richer and the Poor Are Getting Richer; The Good Old Days Are Now," Carpe Diem *(blog), November 28, 2009.*

than in 1973. One study cited by defenders of the establishment narrative found that the benefits consumers derived from lower prices of Chinese imports amounted to over $202 billion, which works out to $101,250 for each manufacturing job that was lost because of such competition. As Clausing notes, we are all consumers, and "in our role as consumers, international trade is nearly unambiguously good."[46]

Better Communication Is Required

The problem is not with free trade, the establishment narrative suggests; it is that the benefits of free trade are not communicated clearly enough to allow people to understand that it makes them better off. The idea that everybody ultimately wins from trade can seem counterintuitive, and job losses are often easier to see than consumer savings. As Clausing observes, "Economists peddling international integration have not always explained clearly and persuasively what is at stake."[47] Faced with rising pushback against free trade, the Group of 20 (G20) concluded in 2016 that "the benefits of trade and open markets must be communicated to the wider public more effectively." Responding to the G20's call, the IMF, World Bank, and WTO issued a report highlighting examples of governments working to communicate the benefits of trade to the public, including the European Commission's series Exporters' Stories, which showcases how individual EU companies profit from trade agreements, and the US Council of Economic Advisers' report *The Economic Benefits of U.S. Trade*, which finds that the typical US worker has received about $1,300 in annual earnings as a result of US export growth over the last twenty years.[48]

The Alternatives Are Terrible

Another argument that proponents of the establishment narrative deploy is that the alternatives to free trade are invariably worse. Blaming foreigners (whether trading partners or immigrants) is "quick and easy," but acting on that blame by imposing tariffs and building walls is "dangerous," "wrongheaded," and "shortsighted." "Tariffs are regressive taxes," the Organisation for Economic Co-operation and Development (OECD) affirms, because they have a disproportionate impact on those who are less well-off and spend a higher proportion of their income on goods. Tariffs also involve large costs to the economy overall. US tariffs on Chinese tires from 2009 to 2012 were estimated to have cost at least $900,000 per year for each job they saved—about twenty-two times the average wage of workers in the industries that benefited from the protection. Tariffs are not just expensive; they often also merely delay the inevitable. For instance, the Australian government spent over AUD 2 billion per year to support the automotive sector from 1997 to 2012, but this tactic simply put off the structural adjustment for the industry, with General Motors closing its local factories in 2020 despite decades of subsidies. According to the establishment narrative, the better response is to protect workers, not specific jobs.[49]

Redouble Efforts to Help Workers Adjust

Some proponents of the establishment narrative—especially those who belong to the Trade Is Special School—concede that we need to share the gains from trade more fairly and also offer more support to workers in adjusting to the inevitable shifts in job opportunities. They argue, however, that this is strictly a task for domestic policies. "Trade makes the pie bigger; domestic policies divide the pie up. Never the twain shall meet" is how trade law professor Timothy Meyer has summarized the establishment narrative's mantra.[50] At their 2016 Hangzhou Summit the leaders of the G20 declared that free trade "must be . . . accompanied by appropriate domestic policies to ensure that benefits are widely distributed."[51] The IMF, World Bank, and WTO concur: "Domestic policies to address trade-related adjustments are critical." Countries have a role to play in "easing worker mobility across firms, industries, and regions" with a view to minimizing adjustment costs and promoting employment. This agenda can include policies such as job search assistance, training programs, and wage insurance. Social safety nets can confer protection such as unemployment insurance and guarantee access to necessities including healthcare and education. Some countries have also offered trade adjustment assistance programs that are targeted specifically at workers who lose their jobs as a result of trade. "Mitigating adjustment costs can help to alleviate resulting negative attitudes toward trade," the IMF, World Bank, and WTO conclude, which makes "trade openness more socially sustainable."[52]

Conclusion

The establishment narrative provides an upbeat account of economic globalization. It argues that there is no question that globalization has promoted international specialization and technological progress—processes that have made most people in the West unfathomably rich by historical standards. The wisdom of the establishment narrative has been widely accepted by many governments in past decades. It had a sense of inevitability: "There are many speeds that a country can go at down this globalization path. . . . But there is only one right direction" is how Friedman, one of the best-known champions of the narrative, captured the sentiment.[53] Yet the establishment position has increasingly come under pressure by those who question both the speed and the direction of travel.

CHAPTER 4

The Left-Wing Populist Narrative

Gains from specialization. Increased productivity. Cheaper products. If the benefits advertised by the establishment narrative are real, why do so many people feel as if economic globalization has pulled the rug out from under their feet? The answer, argue the proponents of the left-wing populist narrative, is plain to see. The specialization promoted by globalization results in bifurcation—between takers and makers, billionaire CEOs and minimum-wage workers, highly paid professionals and precariously employed service providers. The rewards from the productivity gains have been appropriated largely by the top 1 percent and the professional class. And cheaper goods are little consolation when the cost of the real staples of a middle-class life—education, healthcare, and housing—has skyrocketed.

The proponents of the left-wing populist narrative have been ascendant since the 2008 global financial crisis. That crisis exposed a stark contrast: The bankers, who had run the system into the ground, emerged largely unscathed, having been saved by government bailouts and massive liquidity infusions from central banks. The masses, who were either unwitting participants in the bankers' schemes or innocent bystanders, suffered the consequences of the collapse. Many lost their homes and jobs, or were punished by austerity measures that governments implemented to address swelling budget deficits. All over the Western world, populist politicians on both the left and right rode the resulting groundswell of discontent to political prominence and, in some cases, to public office.[1]

The left-wing populist narrative challenges the establishment narrative's cheerful account of globalization in three respects. First, the establishment narrative is premised on the idea that international integration will grow the economic pie, which can then be divided at the national level so that everyone ends up better off. But if that redistribution never occurs or is inadequate, the fundamental premise on which many people accepted the establishment narrative's designs is called into question. People do not care whether the economy grows in the aggregate; they want most of all to be secure and prosperous in their own lives. For that to happen, it does not suffice that the winners *could* fully compensate the losers in theory; the winners must *actually* compensate the losers in practice. This redistribution has often not taken place, especially in countries with relatively weak welfare states, such as the United States—a point that some proponents of the establishment narrative have been willing to concede.

But the left-wing populist challengers go further. They do not believe that the great divide between the haves and have-nots is due simply to the insufficient redistribution of market outcomes. Rather, they see the problem in the legal rules and political dynamics, both global and national, that generate those market outcomes in the first place. Left-wing populists charge the political and economic elite not simply with a sin of omission (failing to redistribute) but also with a sin of commission (actively rigging the game—and thereby "pre-distributing" economic gains—in its favor).[2] They point to rules that permit corporate CEOs to pay themselves hundreds of times what their average employee earns; to dynamics that drive families into the red to pay for essentials such as housing, childcare, and education; to laws that allow private equity firms to buy up Main Street businesses, load them with debt, and pay themselves exorbitant fees while workers' pensions evaporate; and to arrangements that force governments to subject their populations to painful austerity measures while ensuring that international creditors are reimbursed.[3] Far from cushioning the losses caused by economic globalization, the domestic political and economic system is rigged to channel the gains generated by it to the privileged few.[4]

Proponents of the left-wing populist narrative further point out that the elite's embrace of international integration is highly selective, which compounds the asymmetric impact of globalization. Even as trade deals force manufacturing workers to compete with foreigners, the members of the professional elite use restrictive licensing and qualification requirements to shield themselves from foreign competition and to protect their high salaries. As a result, members of the working class lose twice over: they have to accept lower wages and inferior working conditions to compete internationally, while paying exorbitant fees for the services of lawyers, accountants, dentists, and doctors who can shelter themselves in their domestic markets.[5] At the same time, the elite can use globalization to increase the size of the market for their services while also hiding their fortunes abroad and structuring their assets so as to minimize their tax obligations at home. In this way, the left-wing populist critique interweaves concerns about economic globalization and domestic inequality.

Wage Stagnation and Income Inequality

Something remarkable happened in the US economy in the late 1970s and early 1980s: working-class people stopped getting rewarded for becoming better at what they did. During the previous twenty-five years, their wages had risen in line with the growth in productivity. By and large, if workers could produce twice as much as before, their wages doubled. This is more or less what happened between 1948 and 1973: the fortunes of most workers roughly tracked the fortunes of the overall economy. The rising tide actually lifted all boats. Around the mid-1970s, however, wage and productivity growth began to decouple: though productivity continued its steady upward climb, the typical worker's wages almost flatlined (Figure 4.1).[6]

This decoupling of wage growth for typical workers and productivity growth in the economy in the 1970s is central to the left-wing populist narrative: it marks the point at which the economic fortunes of the vast majority of the population started to diverge from the health of the economy as a whole and an exceedingly small share of the population began to appropriate an ever-larger share of the economic pie. In the thirty years following World War II, the US economy grew while income inequality fell. From around the mid-1970s, that pattern was reversed: the economy grew, but so did income inequality (Figure 4.2). From this point onward, economic growth no longer lifted all boats; instead, it lifted only the yachts.[7]

This change resulted in a fundamental restructuring of American society. In 1956, the sociologist C. Wright Mills described American society as "less a pyramid with a flat base than a fat diamond with a bulging middle."[8] But this diamond has disappeared. "The social shape of America now looks more like a contorted 'hourglass,'" writes economist and financial journalist Stewart Lansley, "with a pronounced bulge at the top, a long thin stem in the middle, and a fat bulge at the bottom."[9] Not all

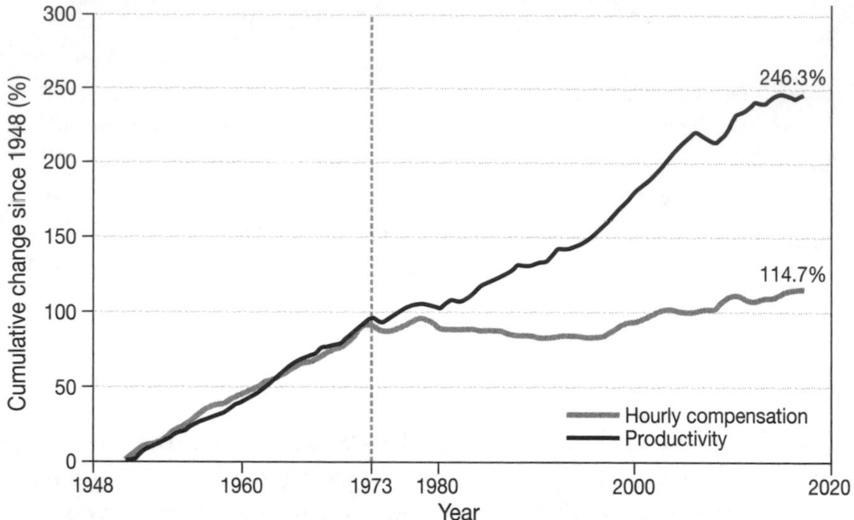

Fig. 4.1: The Productivity-Wage Gap

Note: This graph shows the growth of productivity and the typical worker's hourly compensation in the United States from 1948 to 2017. The "productivity" graph shows the growth in the output of goods and services minus depreciation per hour worked. The "hourly compensation" graph shows the growth in wages and benefits of production or non-supervisory workers in the private sector.

Credit: Reformatted from "The Productivity-Pay Gap," Economic Policy Institute, July 2019, figure "The gap between productivity and a typical worker's compensation has increased dramatically since 1973." By permission of Economic Policy Institute.

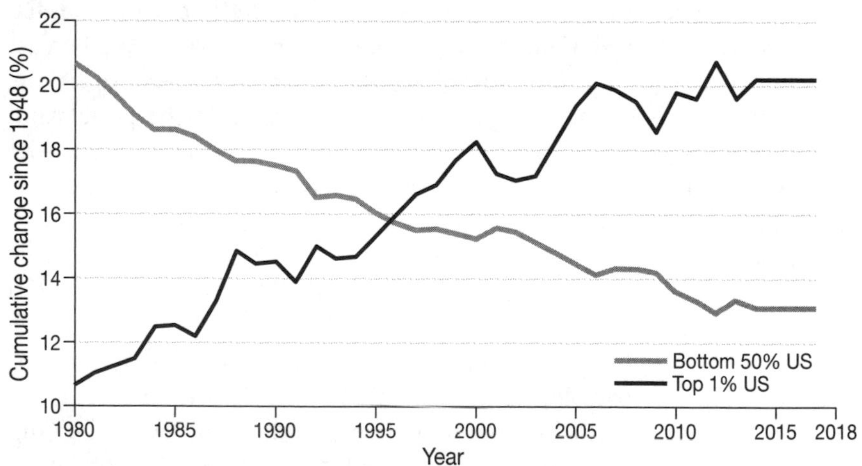

Fig. 4.2: The 1 Percent Gets an Ever-Bigger Share of the Pie

Note: This graph shows that in the United States, the share of national income received by the top 1 percent of the income distribution increased from just over 10 percent in 1980 to more than 20 percent in 2018, whereas the share of the bottom 50 percent of the income distribution fell from over 20 percent to 13 percent over the same period.

Credit: Reformatted from Facundo Alvaredo et al., World Inequality Report 2018, *figure 2.3.2a. CC BY-NC-SA 4.0.*

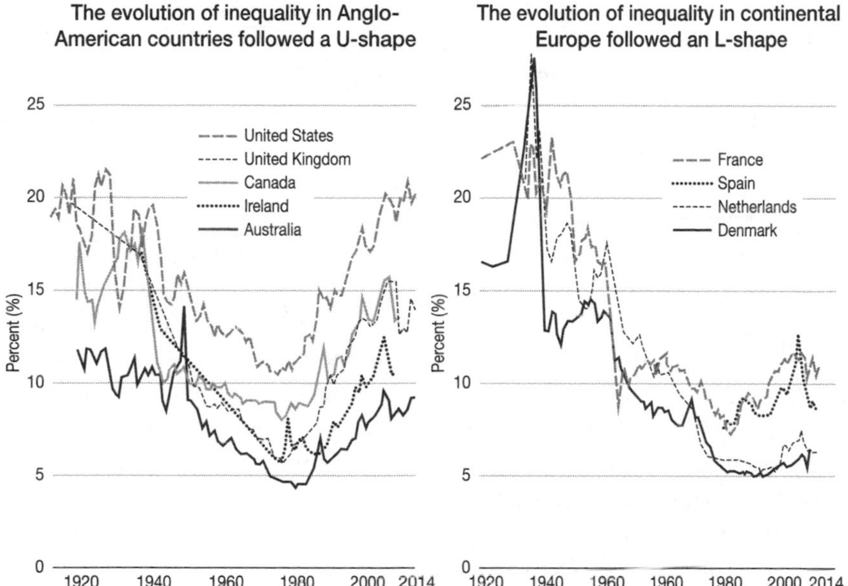

Fig. 4.3: The Evolution of Inequality Is Not Uniform across the West

Note: These graphs show the share of total income going to the top 1 percent of the income distribution since 1900 in Anglo-American Western countries and in continental Europe. Although income inequality fell in both groups until the 1980s, it has been rising quickly in the Anglo-American Western countries since then.

Credit: Reformatted from Max Roser and Esteban Ortiz-Ospina, "Income Inequality," Our World in Data *(2013), "Share of Total Income Going to the Top 1% since 1990," https://ourworldindata.org/income-inequality, based on data from the World Wealth and Income Database (2018).*

Western countries have experienced the same evolution as America. As Figure 4.3 shows, the trajectory of the income share of the top 1 percent since the 1920s follows a U shape in the United States and other Anglo-American countries: the share fell until the 1970s but has been rising consistently ever since. In continental Europe, by contrast, the income share going to the top 1 percent roughly tracks an L shape: its decline until the 1970s mirrors the decline in the United States, but it has largely flatlined since.

Proponents of the establishment narrative offer a benign explanation for the decoupling of productivity growth and wages since the 1970s. In their account, it reflects the shift to an increasingly technologically sophisticated economy in which innovators, superstar firms, and highly skilled workers can achieve massive economies of scale and can earn outsize returns as a result. In this view, the reason many people feel left behind is that they lack the skills it takes to succeed in an economy that increasingly rewards "human capital." The solutions offered by proponents of the establishment narrative include greater investments in education and training to "upskill" the workforce.[10]

Proponents of the left-wing populist narrative do not buy this explanation. They see the increasing gulf between what the economy produces and what the vast majority of the population takes home in pay as the result of a deliberate "war on the middle class." The middle class "has been chipped, squeezed and hammered," not because the skills demanded by the economy are shifting but because the elite have been allowed to manipulate the rules of the game to appropriate an ever-larger share of the economic pie. "We're not broke, we're being robbed" is the diagnosis of former UK Labour Party leader Jeremy Corbyn. The result is what economic historian Peter Temin calls a "dual economy," composed of high-wage finance, technology, and electronics sectors and low-wage service sectors employing semiskilled and unskilled workers, with a vanishing middle.[11]

Who Are the Winners?

But who is the ruthless elite? Proponents of the left-wing populist narrative differ on where exactly to draw the line between the winners and the losers. The narrative divides into two main branches. One focuses on the extraordinary gains that have been made by the superrich (e.g., CEOs and billionaires) and contrasts the ballooning wealth of the top 1 percent with the flagging fortunes of the bottom 99 percent. The other branch highlights the division between the college-educated professional classes and the rest of the population; this branch draws the line (roughly) between the top 20 percent and the bottom 80 percent.

The first view was popularized by the Occupy Wall Street protests. "We are the 99 percent" was the famous slogan of the movement that sprang up in New York in 2011 in response to rising inequality and the bailouts of the financial sector. Occupy Wall Street aimed at "fighting back against the corrosive power of major banks and multinational corporations over the democratic process, and the role of Wall Street in creating an economic collapse that has caused the greatest recession in generations."[12] Although the movement embraced people from diverse backgrounds, "the one thing we all have in common," it declared, is that

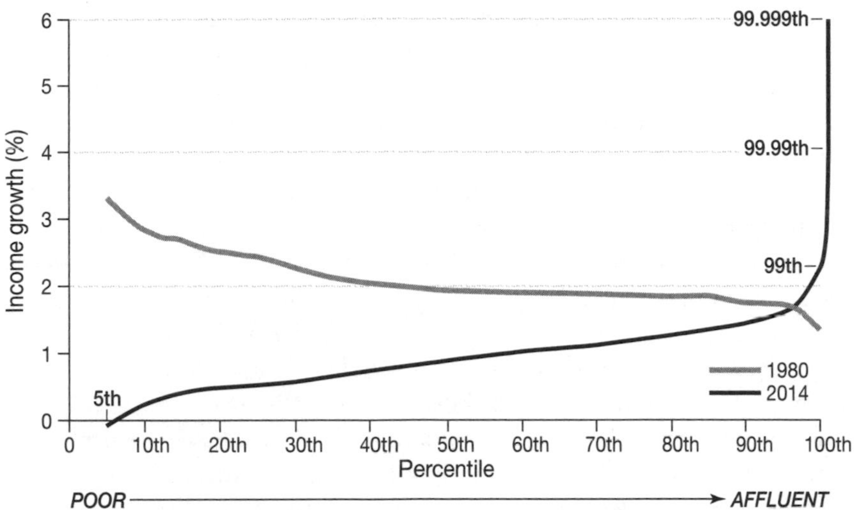

Fig. 4.4: The Hockey Stick of Inequality

Note: This graph shows growth for different parts of the income distribution in 1980 and in 2014. In 1980, those at the bottom of the income distribution experienced the highest relative income growth. In 2014, the incomes of the top 1, 0.1, and 0.01 percent grew much faster than those of anyone else.

Credit: Reformatted from Thomas Piketty, Emmanuel Saez, and Gabriel Zucman, "Distributional National Accounts: Methods and Estimates for the United States, Data Appendix," National Bureau of Economic Research, November 9, 2017, figure S.40b.

we "will no longer tolerate the greed and corruption of the 1%."[13] The skyrocketing fortunes of the 1, 0.1, and 0.01 percent, which are captured in images such as the hockey stick of inequality in Figure 4.4, explain why many left-wing populists see the main fault line in American society as between the top 1 percent and everybody else.[14]

Others disagree: "The big divide in America is not between the top 1 percent and the bottom 99. It's between the top 20 percent and the rest," argues *New York Times* columnist David Brooks. "These are the highly educated Americans who are pulling away from everybody else and who have built zoning restrictions and meritocratic barriers to make sure outsiders can't catch up." Proponents of this view point out that the upper middle class has prospered in recent decades and that many of the obstacles that have shut those lacking a university degree out of the middle class have been erected and perpetuated not by billionaires but by the "dream hoarders" of the upper middle class.[15]

One way the professional elite has been able to protect and legitimize its position at the top of the hourglass is through the idea of meritocracy. As law professor Daniel Markovits explains, meritocracy promises equality of opportunity by opening a previously hereditary elite to outsiders who are able to climb the ladder on the basis of their talent and hard work. Yet, in practice, children from more modest backgrounds lose out in school to children of rich parents, just as most adults lose out to elite graduates in the workplace. When everyone is judged according to the same meritocratic criteria, rich families, which can invest enormous amounts of time and resources into developing the human capital of their children, come out ahead. Intergenerational mobility is low in the United States and much of Europe, yet those who lose the meritocratic competition for income and status are told that they only have themselves to blame since they lack the talent or work ethic to succeed. One group graduates from college to become "superordinate" workers as lawyers, bankers, and doctors, whereas the other struggles to find secure and satisfying employment as "subordinate" workers: Uber drivers, Amazon stock fillers, and fast-food workers.[16] In the words of Michael Lind, author and cofounder of the New America Foundation, the old hereditary caste system has been replaced by a meritocratic one consisting of "managers and proles" in which "degrees are the new titles of nobility and diplomas the new coats of arms."[17]

The Banks versus the People

The global financial crisis was brought on by excessive risk-taking by US financial institutions, which made housing loans to people who would not be in a position to repay their loans unless housing prices continued to rise. US banks repackaged these loans into novel, lucrative, and supposedly safe debt instruments such as mortgage-backed securities and collateralized debt obligations, which they sold to banks in Europe and across the world that were trying to get in on the debt-fueled bonanza. When the housing bubble burst and borrowers began to default en masse, the crisis thus infected economies across the globe.

The fallout from the crisis served as a catalyst for the left-wing populist narrative. After the financial services firm Lehman Brothers collapsed in 2008, the US government pumped trillions of dollars of liquidity into the US financial system. The government acted to save the banks and insurance companies, in the hope of shoring up the financial system and the broader economy. The only way to save Main Street, the government claimed, was to save Wall Street. Main Street, however, did not see it that way. In the years following the global financial crisis, many in the working and middle classes who had tried to use debt to maintain their standard of living despite stagnant wages and the rapidly rising cost of living lost their homes to foreclosure and their jobs to the contracting economy. Even though Wall Street bankers had brought financial ruin to so many, not one was charged. When Wall Street firms announced the next year that they were returning to business as usual by paying large bonuses, the indignation was palpable. The bailouts created the perception that Wall Street was being allowed to privatize its profits and socialize its losses, playing a "heads I win, tails you lose" game.

Owing to the connectivity produced by economic globalization, the effects of Wall Street's financial recklessness were felt far beyond America's shores. The ripple effects helped to trigger the Greek debt crisis, which soon engulfed other eurozone countries, such as Italy and Spain. Here, the conflict between the banks and the populations of the affected countries played out on the international level. Most of Greece's debt was held by European banks. When it became clear that the debt burden was unsustainable, the international institutions that took charge of the crisis—represented by the so-called troika, composed of the European Commission, the European Central Bank, and the International Monetary Fund—faced a choice. They could acknowledge that Greece would never be able to repay its debt and force Greece's creditors to write down a part of the debt and restructure the rest—a course of action that probably would have required the governments of Germany and France to bail out their own banks, which would have suffered heavy losses. Alternatively, they could insist that Greece repay its private creditors, which was possible only if Greece received massive bailouts from its eurozone peers.

The international lenders chose the latter course. In return for the bailouts, the troika demanded that Greece adopt strict austerity measures and prioritize servicing its debt above all else. The resulting wage and budget cuts shifted the "burden of adjustment entirely onto the shoulders of Greek workers and taxpayers," giving the European banks the opportunity to divest their holdings of Greek debt—largely by offloading it onto the balance sheet of the European Central Bank (ECB)—and to minimize their losses when a partial restructuring of the debt was ultimately negotiated.[18] Although the European banks had been able to profit from lending to Greece, the troika allowed them to socialize their losses when those loans turned sour. By providing funds to the Greek government to repay its private creditors or by taking the debt off their hands directly (through ECB bond buying), the troika transformed Greece's obligations from debt owed to the private sector (the banks) into debt owed to the public sector (the ECB, the IMF, and ultimately eurozone governments). The troika then employed its superior leverage to ensure that Greek workers, taxpayers, and pensioners would have to make enormous sacrifices to repay that debt.[19]

The Greek population ultimately rebelled, electing the left-wing populist Syriza party in 2015 and overwhelmingly rejecting the terms of the bailout in a referendum. Syriza came to power with the goal of achieving debt relief, which, it argued, was "not an exercise in creating moral hazard" but—in light of the humanitarian crisis that was playing out in Greece—a "moral duty." On the day of his election, Prime Minister Alexis Tsipras declared that "Greece leaves behind catastrophic austerity, it leaves behind fear and authoritarianism, it leaves behind five years of humiliation and anguish."[20] What the Greeks discovered, however, was that in the context of an international debt crisis, the policy preferences of the citizens of a peripheral debtor country hardly mattered. Syriza ultimately had to cave because the cards were stacked against it at a level that escaped the reach of national politics. Greece's creditors were able to bring to bear what political scientist Jerome Roos has called the "structural power" of finance to impose bailout terms on Greece's new populist government virtually at will.[21] As the Syriza government's finance minister Yanis Varoufakis described it, the troika simply used its control of Greece's access to financing to "asphyxiate" the Syriza government until it capitulated to the troika's demands.[22]

Greece was not the only country in southern Europe whose politics were upended by the financial crisis. In Spain, the economic crisis of 2008 led to soaring inequality, which gave rise to the anti-austerity social movement 15-M (Los Indignados, "the indignant ones") and the emergence of Podemos in the European elections of 2014.[23] Podemos divides society into two opposing camps: "the people," on one hand, and "the caste," composed of politicians, bankers, big corporations, speculators, and any other privileged group, on the other hand.[24] Podemos claims to represent a large majority ("those below") seeking to wrest control back from a corrupt and self-interested elite ("those on top"). "We're going to throw out the political and economic mafia," "reclaim Madrid for its people," and "put an end to this austericide," its crowds chant.[25]

Making and Taking

"For decades, Washington has lived by a simple rule: If it's good for Wall Street, it's good for the economy," explains US senator Elizabeth Warren. According to Warren, rich Wall Street donors have pumped millions of dollars into the political system to enforce this rule, and Washington has showered big banks with favors, including no-strings-attached bailouts during the global financial crisis, sweeping deregulation, and special tax breaks. "Here's the problem with the belief that helping Wall Street always helps the economy: it isn't true," Warren argues. Financial sector profits have gone from 10 to 25 percent of total corporate profits, while most individuals have lived through a generation of stagnant wages. Not only do the fortunes of Main Street not seem to follow those of Wall Street, but the opposite is often the case, left-wing populists contend: "Wall Street is looting the economy and Washington is helping them do it."[26]

"Finance has become a headwind to economic growth, not a catalyst for it," explains *Financial Times* columnist Rana Foroohar. The financial sector is supposed to support Main Street by connecting savers with borrowers as efficiently as possible and spreading risk. The problem is that much of what the financial sector does and encourages represents "taking" rather than "making," according to Foroohar, or "value extraction" rather than "value creation," as economist Mariana Mazzucato puts it. Instead of working to support the real economy, finance is leeching off the real economy, leaving it sick and anemic.[27]

Nowhere is the problem of value extraction clearer than in the role of private equity companies, which have been accused of engaging in "legalized looting" in country after country.[28] The private equity playbook is simple. The firm will purchase a company using a little bit of its own capital and a large amount of debt. Once it has acquired the company, it transfers the debt to the company, which now has to service the debt. All the while, the private equity company pays itself "managing fees" and "consulting fees." This fate has been suffered by many well-known companies, including Remington, the oldest US gun manufacturer, which had to file for bankruptcy in 2018 and 2020, and Toys "R" Us, which closed all its stores in the United States and terminated its 33,000 employees in 2018. The two private equity firms that bought the shoe retail chain Payless paid themselves $700 million in dividends in 2012 and 2013 before the chain entered into bankruptcy in 2017.[29]

The descriptions of private equity firms in the left-wing populist narrative are particularly emotive. They are said to "loot" and "pillage" companies and are characterized as "vampires—bleeding the company dry and walking away enriched even as the company succumbs."[30] A German minister of the economy compared private equity firms to rapacious insects: "Some financial investors do not spare a thought for the people whose jobs they are destroying—they remain anonymous, do not show their face, and attack enterprises like swarms of locusts, devour them, and move on. This is the form of capitalism that we are fighting."[31]

But the problem extends well beyond private equity firms. In the 1980s and 1990s, the prevailing wisdom in many Western countries advised that corporate executives be paid in stock-based compensation to give them incentives to maximize shareholder value, which was intended to improve the performance of the economy as a whole.[32] This approach, however, has led to a broader "financialization" of the economy: more and more companies are focusing on making money for their shareholders through financial engineering rather than on making products and providing services.[33] A key mechanism to "make money out of money" is through share buybacks and dividends. Firms in the Standard and Poor's 500 stock-market index now spend $1 trillion a year on share buybacks and dividends, the equivalent of 95 percent of their net earnings.[34] These buybacks boost the value of shares and thus yield bumper remuneration for shareholders and CEOs paid in share options. But these short-term measures leave less and less money for investment in research, product development, and other activities that contribute to the companies' long-term health.[35]

CEOs and Billionaires

Left-wing populists are not simply concerned about wrongdoing by Wall Street and major corporations; they also worry about the increasing prevalence of superrich individuals—CEOs and billionaires—and their growing share of the pie. As many people have struggled to keep afloat and not slide backward, soaring executive salaries have increased inequality. Indeed, in 2015, the average CEO in the United States earned more than 275 times as much as the average worker, compared with just 33 times as much in 1980 (Figure 4.5). The world is seeing a rising number of billionaires and, as a 2017 Oxfam report noted, just eight billionaires have as much net worth as "half of humanity."[36] A system that permits this level of wealth and inequality is not just rigged, the left-wing populists say, but immoral.

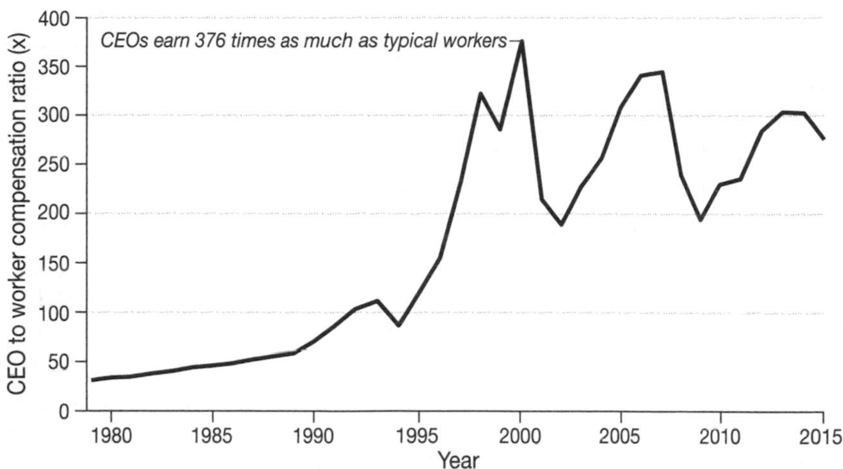

Fig. 4.5: CEOs in the United States Make Hundreds of Times More than Most of Their Employees

Note: This graph shows the ratio of the compensation of CEOs to the compensation of the typical worker in their industries in the United States. In 2015, CEOs earned on average 276 times as much as their typical employee.

Credit: Data source: Lawrence Mishel and Alyssa Davis, "Top CEOs Make 300 Times More than Typical Workers," Economic Policy Institute, Issue Brief #399, June 21, 2015.

Whereas ordinary workers face fierce competition for their jobs, the pay of top executives is not determined in anything resembling a normal market. As economist Dean Baker has argued, most shareholders do not have enough at stake to exert the considerable effort required to rein in the pay of CEOs. Boards of directors, the members of which are often selected with input from the CEO and who receive significant payments themselves, have little incentive not to sign off on excessive pay packages, if they are even aware of how much their CEOs are paid. As a result, corporate CEOs in America get away with "ripping off" their companies to the tune of hundreds of billions of dollars.[37] Although CEO pay has risen in other developed countries, the ratio of CEO pay to that of the median worker in the United States is significantly higher than elsewhere.[38]

Left-wing populists are increasingly taking on the entire "billionaire class." Some are categorical: "A system that allows billionaires to exist" is immoral, declares Alexandria Ocasio-Cortez, a congressional representative from New York. It is "wrong" that billionaires should be able to coexist in a country alongside "parts of Alabama where people are still getting ringworm because they don't have access to public health."[39] Sanders concurs: "When you have a half a million Americans sleeping out on the street today, when you have 87 million people uninsured or underinsured . . . and then you also have three people owning more wealth than the bottom half of American society, that is a moral and economic outrage."[40] Corbyn agrees: "There are 150 billionaires in the UK while 14 million people live in poverty. In a fair society there would be no billionaires and no one would live in poverty."[41]

Beyond the exorbitant wealth of CEOs and billionaires, a broader professional class has also profited handsomely from the globalized economy. Many of these superordinate workers are based in what sociologist Saskia Sassen calls "global cities" such as New York and London and provide professional services—accounting, legal, public relations—to multinational corporations and the superrich.[42] These professionals specialize in skills such as legally "coding capital" so that it can be recognized and enforced across borders and constructing complex corporate structures to minimize tax payments.[43] They, in turn, are serviced by a plethora of precariously employed and underpaid workers, often recent immigrants, who offer everything from childcare and yoga classes to pedicures and dry cleaning. It is the hourglass, pure and simple.

Regressive Taxation

It is not just the amount of money made by the superrich that the left-wing populists view as problematic; they are also outraged by the low rates of taxes paid by the very rich. The superrich have enjoyed lower and lower effective tax rates over time by dint of a combination of cuts, avoidance, and evasion. In 1950, the wealthiest Americans paid around 70 percent of their income in taxes. By 2018, that figure had declined to only 23 percent. Billionaire investor Warren Buffett famously stated that billionaires pay lower tax rates than their secretaries. Although some argued that this observation was not necessarily the norm when he originally made it in the late 2000s, it is now clearly the case.[44]

One reason for this anomaly is that tax codes in many countries have become less progressive and, in some cases, regressive. According to economists Emmanuel Saez and Gabriel Zucman, "The tax code, like everything else, [has been] rigged. . . . In 1970, the richest Americans paid, all taxes included, more than 50% of their income in taxes, twice as much as working-class individuals. In 2018, following the Trump tax reform, and for the first time in the last hundred years, billionaires have paid less than steel workers, school teachers, and retirees."[45] Another reason for this inversion is that an army of lawyers and accountants has sprung up since the 1980s and 1990s to help the rich exploit loopholes and structure their affairs to minimize their tax obligations, sometimes by crossing the line from lawful avoidance to unlawful evasion.[46]

Outrage about tax evasion and avoidance is shared widely across the West. In France, the leader of the Left Party and founder of the movement La France Insoumise (Insubordinate France), Jean-Luc Mélenchon, regularly points out that "the tax system burdens the middle class while the richest go abroad." Pablo Iglesias, the leader of Podemos, argues that in Spain it is only "workers and small businesses" that pay taxes. Irene Montero, another prominent Podemos politician, notes that thirty-three of the thirty-five companies included in Spain's leading stock market index "do not pay taxes in Spain." And the promise to "stand up to the tax-evading economic oligarchy" was a central plank of Syriza's plan to tackle the Greek debt crisis without further dismantling public services.[47]

Some proponents of the left-wing populist narrative draw a sharp contrast between the morals of ordinary citizens and those at the top. In one of her first speeches on the national stage—at the Democratic National Convention of 2012—Warren told the crowd: "I talk to small business owners all across Massachusetts. And not one of them—not one—made big bucks from the risky Wall Street bets that brought down our economy. I talk to nurses and programmers, salespeople and firefighters—people who bust their tails every day. And not one of them—not one—stashes their money in the Cayman Islands to avoid paying their fair share of taxes." The concern of ordinary Americans, in Warren's telling, is not wealth per se but how that wealth is generated and protected: "These folks don't resent that someone else made more money. We're Americans. We celebrate success. We just don't want the game to be rigged."[48]

Whereas some proponents of the establishment narrative concede that there has been insufficient redistribution to help those left behind by globalization, the left-wing populist diagnosis is much starker: redistribution has been occurring, but in the wrong direction. "We have witnessed an enormous transfer of wealth from the middle class and the poor to multimillionaires and billionaires," says Sanders.[49] How have the elite accomplished this? The left-wing populists argue that even as those at the top of the income distribution have been allowed to keep an ever-greater share of the pie, they have put downward pressures on the middle and working classes. The elite has taken aim at the middle of the income distribution, most prominently through a multipronged attack on unions, which has resulted in decreasing wages and benefits for many who formerly fell squarely within the middle class. They have also worked hard to keep the bottom of the income distribution down, including by resisting attempts to raise the minimum wage.

Attacking the Middle

When workers wanted to stand up for themselves, they used to be able to form or join a union. But various anti-union laws and practices have led to declining union numbers and membership across many Western countries over the past few decades. These effects are part and parcel of the neoliberal market reforms implemented during the era of Reagan and Thatcher. In Britain, for example, the percentage of unionized workers decreased from 38 percent to 23 percent between 1990 and 2016; the figure was as low as 8 percent for those between sixteen and twenty-four years old. In the United States, the percentage of unionized workers in the public and private sectors combined almost halved between 1983 and 2015, dropping from 20 percent to 11 percent.[50] These numbers show that the power of organized labor has been eviscerated, allowing capital owners not only to drive down wages and conditions for workers but also to exert disproportionate influence on politicians.

Whereas the right-wing populist narrative rails against the movement of manufacturing jobs to China and Mexico, US proponents of the left-wing populist narrative highlight a different trend: the increasing concentration of manufacturing activity in states in the American South. In these states, so-called "right-to-work" laws, which some advocates argue would more accurately be described as "anti-union-fee" laws, permit workers to refuse to pay any fees to the union that represents them. The laws thereby undermine the financial viability of unions and diminish their ability to bargain and lobby on behalf of workers. US employers are not alone in taking advantage of this legislative environment: much of the manufacturing boom in the southern US states is driven by foreign corporations attracted by low wages and generous government incentives.[51]

The right-to-work legislation and anti-union climate in the southern US states is only the starkest manifestation of the embattled situation of unions in the United States. Some employers require new hires to watch propaganda videos depicting unions as greedy and self-interested, and others illegally fire workers who attempt to organize. Under the circumstances, perhaps it is little wonder that by 2010 fewer than 7 percent of US private sector workers belonged to a union, and support for organized labor unions reached an all-time low. In the 1970s, nearly 300 large strikes (those involving at least 1,000 workers) occurred every year. After the market reforms championed by Reagan, that number shrank to fewer than sixty. Today, such strikes are rarely held. Between 2008 and 2018, the average number of large strikes per year was a mere thirteen.[52]

"No other industrial country treats its working class so badly," the former *New York Times* journalist and labor expert Steven Greenhouse observes, and there's one big reason for that: "Labor unions are weaker in the United States than in other industrial nations." Studies suggest that one of the potent factors behind America's soaring income inequality is the decline of labor unions, which has hampered the ability of workers to get a better deal from their employers. The diminished power of labor is also skewing politics and policymaking. One study found that in the 2016 US election cycle, for instance, business outspent labor by a ratio of sixteen to one. Money talks, as Tamara Draut, of the think tank Demos, explains: "Without the countervailing force of a vibrant working class, historically powered by organized labor, the door was propped wide open for the rise of corporate power and politics dominated by big money. It became easier for Congress to deregulate and loosen worker protections. It became easier for leaders to champion free-trade agreements that sold out labor and enriched capital. And it became easier to load up the tax code with benefits for big business and the wealthy."[53]

Keeping the Bottom Down

A major difference between the middle and professional classes, on the one hand, and the working class, on the other, is in how they earn their wages, Draut explains. Nearly six out of ten workers in America are paid hourly wages, as opposed to annual salaries. Eight out of ten of these hourly workers do not hold a bachelor's degree. Many of them punch the clock when they arrive and leave, have uncertain hours, and need to request permission for a bathroom break. A large number—retail salespeople, cashiers, food service and prep workers, and janitors—are adults trying to support themselves and their families rather than teenagers seeking to earn some extra cash. They often lack not only job security but also benefits, and must cobble together multiple jobs to get by. Even when they are able to find full-time work, they frequently do not earn a living wage because the minimum wage is so low.[54]

Battles over the minimum wage represent another capital-versus-labor fight that motivates left-wing populist outrage. For Sanders, the matter is clear: "If somebody is going to work, that person has got to receive at least a wage that they can go out and live with dignity on."[55] To proponents of the left-wing populist narrative, the reality that someone can work full-time and yet not make enough to earn a living is unconscionable; it reflects a failure to respect the dignity of work. At 34 percent of the median wage, the $7.25 minimum wage in the United States ranks as the lowest among Western developed nations in comparison with the general wage level.[56] In inflation-adjusted terms, the US minimum wage has *fallen* 37 percent since 1968.[57] At the same time as the number of unionized manufacturing jobs continues its steady decline, ever more people are forced to take up jobs in the service sector, where the low union density and high share of low-wage jobs mean that the level of the legislated minimum wage can make the difference between a decent livelihood and a destitute existence in the ranks of the working poor.

The precarious situation of low-wage workers is compounded by underemployment—they often cannot get enough hours. Nearly 40 percent of those who are working part-time would prefer to have a full-time job.[58] At a Senate hearing, Sanders recounted a conversation with African American youths in Detroit, Michigan: "There are kids there who are desperately trying to do the right thing. . . . The best job that they can get if they're high school graduates, even with some college . . . is working in a fast-food restaurant at $7.25 an hour. They can't even get 40 hours a week; they're getting 20 hours a week, 30 hours a week. They are desperately trying to bring themselves out of poverty, and they're going nowhere in a hurry."[59] Sanders has assailed corporations such as Walmart for paying "starvation wages," which are "so low that many of these employees are forced to rely on government programs like food stamps, Medicaid and public housing in order to survive."[60] According to Sanders, taxpayers would save $150 billion annually on assistance to the working poor if corporations paid their employees a living wage.[61]

These "poverty jobs" are marked by more than low pay, unpredictable schedules, and too few hours. They are often attended by a lack of respect as well. According to Draut, low-wage workers feel "invisible," "unappreciated," and "disrespected." The center of gravity of the working class has shifted from white males who make things to a much more diverse group—including women, blacks, and Latinos—who serve people. The diversity of this group and its incorporation of many historically disadvantaged populations have made the group harder to mobilize and easier to "ignore, dismiss, and marginalize." And the work these people do, from cooking and serving meals to cleaning houses and hotels, is imbued with "historical baggage" that contributes to their being and feeling overlooked and undervalued.[62] Dignity comes from making a living wage and being respected as a person, not just being treated like an expendable widget or servant.

Middle-Class Dreams Slip Away

When Warren started studying bankruptcy proceedings in the early 1980s, she expected to find that the people who ended up in bankruptcy would be of a certain kind: profligate spenders who had taken on unreasonable risks and adopted irresponsible lifestyles. What she found instead was that the vast majority of people filing for bankruptcy were from ordinary middle-class families who had been tripped up by an unforeseen setback—the loss of a job, a divorce, or a health emergency. Such setbacks were nothing new, of course, so Warren started to wonder why bankruptcies in the United States had nevertheless risen precipitously over the years. What she discovered was a complex mix of factors. The entry of women into the workforce had led to higher household incomes, but also higher expenses, such as the need to pay for the care of children and elderly parents. Moreover, the higher incomes had enabled families to bid up the price of housing in good school districts, leading to debt levels that left no room for error. Financial services firms, which preyed on financially imperiled families by offering easily accessible but expensive credit, compounded the debt spiral that families fell into once things started going wrong.[63] The picture that emerged from Warren's research was far from the one painted by the establishment narrative, which emphasizes how automation and trade have led to lower prices. Although families may have been able to afford cheaper televisions and washing machines, they were brought to the edge of financial ruin by the rising cost of housing, childcare, college tuition, and healthcare. Many needed only a little bit of bad luck to be pushed over the edge.

As Figure 4.6 shows, the developments that Warren describes reflect the experience of the United States and most other major Western countries,

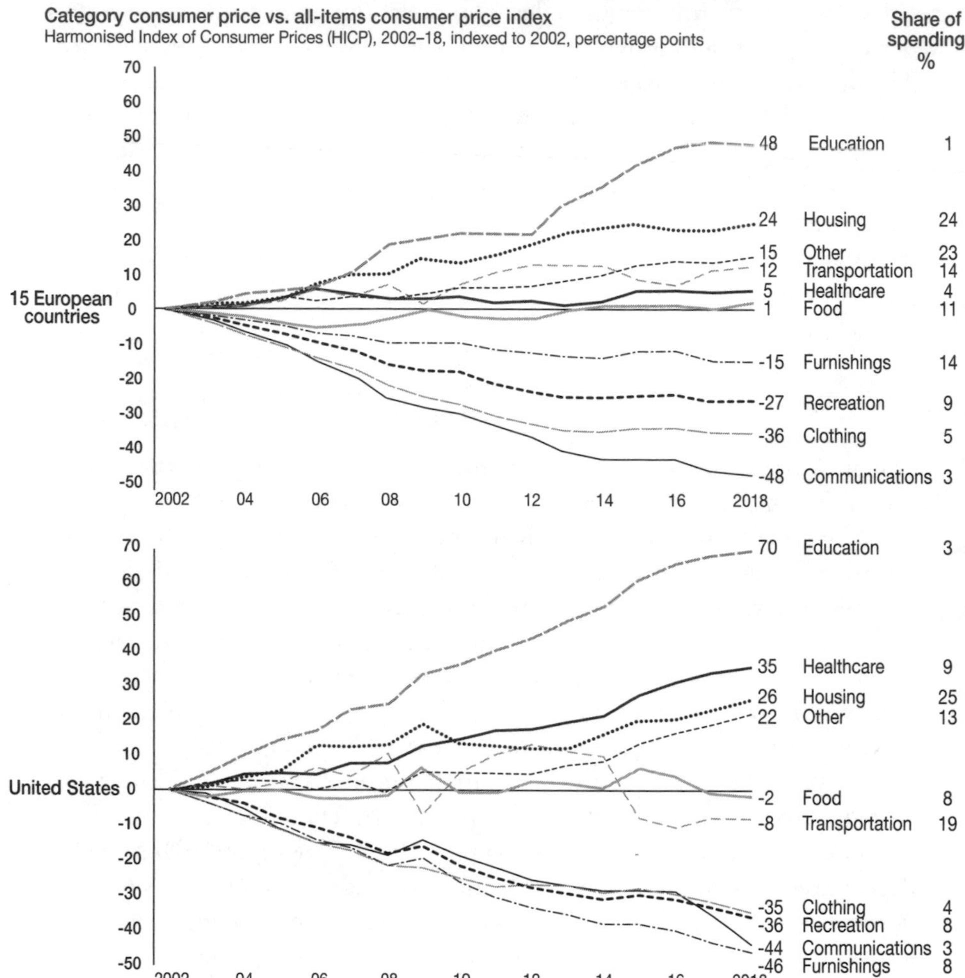

Fig. 4.6: The Rising Cost of the Staples of a Middle-Class Life

Note: These graph shows that while consumer prices of discretionary goods and services decreased, the cost of necessities such as housing, healthcare (especially in the United States), and education grew faster than general consumer prices.

Credit: Extracted and reformatted from James Manyika et al., "The Social Contract in the 21st Century," McKinsey Global Institute Report, February 2020, exhibit E4.

but the increase in the cost of education and especially of healthcare in the United States stands out. Technological innovation and economic globalization have brought about falling prices for discretionary goods and services. From 2002 to 2018, the cost of communication fell by 43 percentage points, furnishings by 33 percentage points, clothing by 31 percentage points, and recreation by 30 percentage points on average in twenty countries studied. Overall, however, consumer prices have increased significantly—by 33 percent—driven by rising housing, healthcare, and education costs. The cost of housing alone has increased by an average of 37 percent across these countries. In many cases, this increase has translated into a fall in the real income of the average worker. Even in countries where workers have seen nominal income gains, such as Australia, France, and the United Kingdom, the increasing cost of these essential items eroded between 54 and 107 percent of those gains for average households in the period 2000 to 2017. If all else remained constant, consumers in ten Western countries would have had to work an additional four weeks a year to be able to afford the same amount of housing, healthcare, and education that they had two decades ago.[64]

Warren's discoveries proved to be a political awakening for her. Having been a Republican and strong supporter of capitalism, she began to believe that the cards were stacked against middle-class families in both direct and more indirect ways. Take the cost of housing. On the surface, the families themselves were at fault because they overextended themselves by buying houses they could not afford. But Warren drew attention to the underlying rules that motivated them to do so—namely, the rules that make access to schools dependent on your zip code. In taking these decisions, families were trying to safeguard the professional future of their children. Others have pointed to another factor that drives up the cost of housing: the role of zoning. In his book on "dream hoarding," Richard Reeves, a senior fellow at the Brookings Institution, notes how local zoning boards restrict the supply of housing in desirable areas, which makes real estate more expensive, excludes less well-off families, and forces middle-class families to take on mortgages they cannot afford to obtain the best education for their children.[65]

Lack of affordable housing is one of the key reasons that the middle class is being squeezed out of London. In 1980, 65 percent of its residents were categorized as being in the middle—neither rich nor poor. In 2015, that number had declined to 37 percent, whereas the ranks of the rich and poor swelled.[66] As a global city, London attracts a wealthy professional class of lawyers, bankers, and accountants, as well as superrich individuals from countries such as Russia and China who buy up property as an [illegible] ment. As Corbyn has argued, homelessness "becomes inev[illegible] government sells off council homes, refuses to build [illegible] and encourages the development of luxury flats whi[illegible] they're acquired purely as investment opportunities by [illegible] The situation looks little different in other global cities, suc[illegible] Toronto, or Paris. "It's becoming impossible to afford to liv[illegible] laments Jagmeet Singh, the leader of Canada's New Dem[illegible] while Mélenchon blames "the financialization of housing" [illegible] that house prices in Paris have increased by 350 percent in [illegible]

Healthcare is another area in which left-wing populists in [illegible] States see the rules as obviously rigged. Many bankruptcies in th[illegible] States are the direct consequence of a medical emergency, eve[illegible] people have insurance, because the rules have allowed insurance c[illegible] nies to deny or limit coverage. Although the problems of the US he[illegible] care system are unique in the developed world, the systems in o[illegible] Western countries disadvantage the working and middle classes in oth[illegible] ways. In Germany, the doctor and politician Karl Lauterbach has long campaigned against a healthcare system that reproduces and entrenches the class divisions of German society: state employees and the rich have access to private insurance, whereas most of the population pays into the public system. Lauterbach argues that the privately insured are in a parasitic relationship with the public system: private insurance is affordable only because of the economies of scale generated by the public system, but at the same time the privately insured siphon off the time and attention of the best doctors for themselves.[69]

Not only do the high costs of middle-class life make it easier to fall off the ladder, but broken and missing rungs are making it harder to climb up. A growing number of people in Western countries no longer believe that their children will benefit from a better life than they did. In 2016, only 24 percent of Americans thought that life for their children's generation would be an improvement over their own, and only 11 percent of Trump supporters felt that way.[70] In place of optimism for the future, many feel that society is broken and it is harder and harder to achieve the middle-class dream. And this feeling has a basis in fact: levels of social mobility have fallen across an array of Western countries, and particularly in the United States. Philip Alston, the UN special rapporteur on extreme poverty and human rights, concluded in a 2017 report that "the American

dire consequences of job losses in the manufacturing sector in the United States to nativist concerns about the *Überfremdung* (over-foreignization) of societies from excessive rates of immigration in Germany. Although the decline in manufacturing employment is common to all developed countries, the anti-trade sentiment that Trump rode to the presidency figures most prominently in the United States. In Europe, the economic and cultural anxiety produced by economic globalization and social change primarily manifests itself in a backlash against immigration and a desire to regain control of the countries' destiny from faceless international bureaucrats, as reflected most famously in the Brexit vote.[3]

Not all proponents of this narrative embrace all elements of it, and we sometimes refer to the strands separately, such as the protectionist narrative or the anti-immigration narrative. What is common to these strands is the sense of threat from an external other and the perceived need to protect one's group—one's family, community, country, or ethnic group—from this external threat. Like the left-wing populist narrative, the right-wing populist narrative is marked by a deep distrust of elites. But while the former faults the elite for enriching themselves at the expense of the working and middle classes, the latter denounce the elite for failing to protect the lower classes from the predations of an external other. Right-wing populists express ire upward and outward.[4] As Trump put it in his inaugural address: "Washington flourished—but the people did not share in its wealth. Politicians prospered—but the jobs left, and the factories closed. The establishment protected itself, but not the citizens of our country."[5]

Rejecting the Establishment's Trade-off on Trade

More than eighty years before Trump was elected president, the impact of trade on communities preyed on the mind of Joseph Martin. The representative from Massachusetts was listening to the debate in the US House of Representatives on the Reciprocal Trade Agreements Act, draft legislation that would authorize President Franklin D. Roosevelt to negotiate tariff reductions with foreign countries. Proponents of the legislation admitted that it might lead to the demise of "inefficient" industries in the United States, such as those producing fine textiles, lace, and toys, but gave assurances that the gains would be worth the pain. Yet Martin was disturbed by the legislation's potential effects and scornful of the attitude of those advocating it:

> Theorists with a passion for experiments sitting in their comfortable offices might easily . . . classify any industry as economically unsound, and consequently be the basis for increasing our . . . export trade. The fact that these industries have been the means of providing the livelihood of countless thousands for generations would be of no avail. The fact that entire communities were dependent for their existence upon the industry might easily be passed over. The planners, dreaming of a new order, might casually decide these people must be sacrificed for the general good, and they would be given transportation and sent to some other part of the country to start life anew.[6]

Martin's speech bears the hallmarks of protectionist concerns that have accompanied US trade policy ever since the passage of the Reciprocal Trade Agreements Act in 1934.[7] The protectionist narrative takes issue with what it sees as the callousness of proponents of trade liberalization, who are prepared to bargain away the livelihoods of workers for the gains of export industries; it deplores their high-handedness in passing over the human cost of "adjustment"; and it underlines their lack of respect for communities that have grown over generations. Martin warned: "Trade off these many thousands of workers and you may as a result sell a trifle more cotton abroad. But you will swell the ranks of the unemployed and swell the relief bill of the Nation. Trade off these workers and you destroy purchasing power at home—purchasing power which contributes to the prosperity of the cotton grower, the automobile manufacturer, and the western farmer."[8]

Martin rejected the trade-off at the heart of the establishment narrative's case for free trade, in particular the narrative's willingness to prioritize aggregate gains for the many over individual losses for the few. Proponents of the protectionist narrative cast doubt on the value of what is gained and emphasize the value of what is lost. Yes, we might export more raw cotton, Martin says, but we will deprive our workers of their livelihoods. Yes, we might get access to cheaper products, but we will sacrifice communities that are the pillars of our nation. For protectionists, the larger pie is simply not worth it, since cheaper products do not make up for the harm of lost livelihoods and destroyed communities.

Fast-forward to the twenty-first century. The loss of community-sustaining jobs that had been a trickle in the 1930s has become a flood. Although the textile manufacturers that prompted Martin's foremost con-

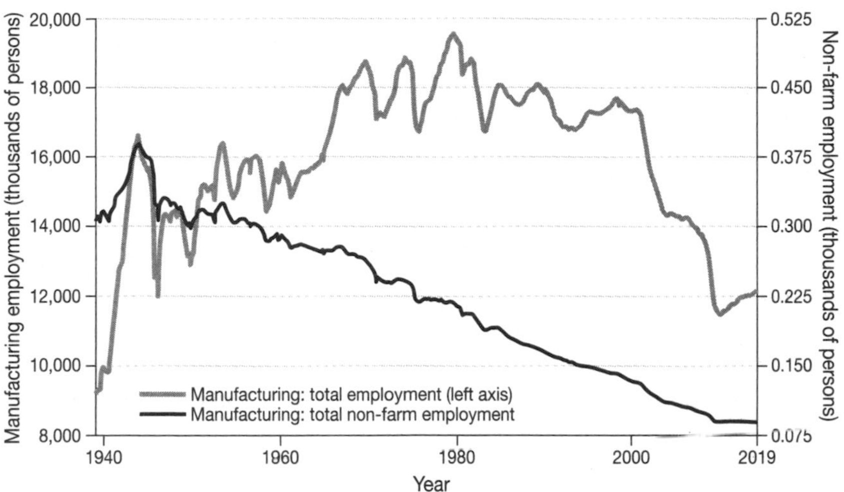

Fig. 5.1: The Inexorable Decline of Manufacturing as a Source of Employment in the United States

Note: This graph shows that US manufacturing employment reached its peak in the late 1970s, declined unevenly afterward, and dropped off sharply after 2000. The share of manufacturing employment in total non-farm employment has declined steadily since World War II.

Credit: Reformatted from The FRED Blog, *April 21, 2014, figure "The Decline of Manufacturing."*

cern were exposed to tough competition from low-cost producers from the 1930s onward, overall manufacturing employment in the United States kept on growing for decades; at its peak in 1979 the sector employed almost 20 million people before entering a persistent decline. Today, approximately 12 million workers are engaged in manufacturing in the United States. The decline of the sector's share of total employment has been even more marked: whereas manufacturing accounted for almost 40 percent of US jobs at the height of World War II, today a mere 8 percent of the US workforce has a manufacturing job (Figure 5.1). By far the most workers are now employed in the service sector.

For the establishment narrative, this development resulted naturally from the productivity growth in the manufacturing sector that was facilitated by the arrival of the big black machine. Proponents of that narrative point out that despite the decline in manufacturing employment, manufacturing *output* has reached record highs; the diminished number of manufacturing jobs simply mirrors the steep decline in farm jobs on account of soaring productivity in the early twentieth century. Proponents of the establishment narrative do not deny that these developments pose challenges: just as displacement forced farmhands to give up their rural life and move to towns to take up manufacturing jobs, so those seeking the new service-sector jobs will find them mostly concentrated in large metropolitan areas. Not all of these occupations will replicate the perks of the typical manufacturing job, which offered secure lifelong employment with benefits for those with limited education.[9] Yet for the establishment narrative, these are just the perennial challenges of adjustment, which can be overcome with investments in retraining and incentives to relocate. In short, the establishment narrative has a simple message for the millions of workers affected by factory closures: *Educate yourself. Move. Change!*

Trump arrived with an equally simple message to those factory workers: *You have been wronged. Those jobs are rightfully yours. Your feckless leaders have allowed Mexico and China to steal them, but I will bring them back.* To laid-off workers, these words were music to their ears. Trump promised to restore their communities to their former glory. He tapped into a deep psychological need not just for work to pay the bills but also for the dignity that stems from feeling valued in society.

Manufacturing Jobs, Communities, and the Multiplier Effect

What is at stake with the loss of manufacturing jobs? Many proponents of the protectionist strand of the right-wing populist narrative see manufacturing jobs as key engines of US prosperity. They emphasize the high wages of manufacturing workers compared with those in the service sector and the resulting multiplier effect—that is, their potential to support jobs in other industries.[10] As Trump's director of trade and manufacturing policy, Peter Navarro, has put it: "A manufacturing job has inherently more power to create wealth, because they on average pay more and also . . . create more jobs. . . . If you have the manufacturing job as the seed corn, then you have jobs in the supply chain. Then towns spring up around that where you have the retail, the lawyers, the accountants, the restaurants, the movie theaters."[11]

Most mainstream economists accept the multiplier effect of manufacturing jobs but argue that production adds the least value in the value chain and that the future of developed countries' workforce lies in the creative and professional jobs that can also form part of the manufacturing value chain but are not necessarily classified as manufacturing jobs.[12] Protectionists do not buy this view. They maintain that there are simply not enough jobs in the creative industries and that most former manufacturing workers, if they do not wind up on the unemployment or disability rolls, can only find service sector jobs that pay less and provide fewer benefits than their previous occupations. Moreover, these jobs are often not located in the communities where manufacturing workers live, and thus cannot sustain those communities.[13]

The flipside of the multiplier effect of manufacturing jobs is that communities unravel when these jobs disappear. Economist Enrico Moretti finds that for every manufacturing job lost in America, another 1.6 service jobs are also lost. In Navarro's words, "When you lose a factory or a plant in a small- or medium-sized town in the Midwest, it's like a black hole. And all of that community gets sucked into the black hole and it becomes a community of despair and crime and blight rather than something that's prosperous." For many proponents of the protectionist narrative, this "black hole" effect of factory closures means that much more is at stake in the loss of manufacturing jobs than lost income—the ripples travel much further. One of the most striking illustrations of this effect is the rise in "deaths of despair" among middle-aged, non-university-educated, non-Hispanic white workers, particularly men, in the United States (Figure 5.2). According to photographer Chris Arnade, who has spent years documenting the lives of people in "back row America," drugs become a way to "dull the pain of not being able to live good lives in the economy" the elite have created for them.[14]

As rural areas and industrial towns have stagnated or declined, the fortunes of the large metropolitan centers, including London, New York, and Silicon Valley, have risen. Even as globalization and technological progress have meant that much manufacturing has moved offshore, workers in the innovation sector, such as high-tech research and development in Silicon Valley, have benefited from technological advancement and increased global demand for their products and services. Far from the "death of distance" promised by early proponents of the internet—whereby the internet was predicted to make distance irrelevant, thereby enabling almost anyone to work at almost any job from anywhere—these high-tech firms often cluster around one another, profiting from the positive spillover effects of proximity. The multiplier effect works here too, as each high-tech job supports another five jobs in these cities.[15] Such agglomeration means that a rift has opened up in countries such as the

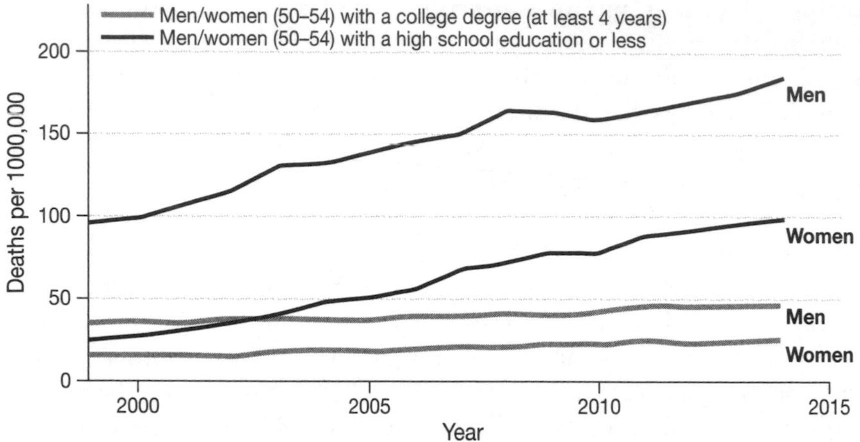

Fig. 5.2: Deaths of Despair among the White Working Class in the United States
Note: This graph compares the death rates from drugs, alcohol, or suicide of non-Hispanic whites ages 50–54 with a high school education or less (in black) with the death rates of non-Hispanic whites with a tertiary education in the same age group (in gray).
Credit: Reformatted from Anne Case and Angus Deaton, "Mortality and Morbidity in the 21st Century," Brookings Papers on Economic Activity, *Spring 2017, 397–476, figure 11.*

United States. Today, there are three Americas: brain hubs—metropolitan areas with a well-educated labor force and a strong innovation sector that are growing in size and wealth; cities and towns that were once dominated by traditional manufacturing, but are now declining rapidly and losing jobs and residents; and places in between that could go either way. These disparate experiences reflect a more general economic and social division between "hubs and heartlands." The United States might be growing economically at the aggregate level, but the distribution of this growth is highly uneven, both across classes (as highlighted by the left-wing populist narrative) and across geographical areas (as highlighted by the right-wing populist narrative).[16]

What is true for America also holds true for many other Western countries. A fundamental cleavage exists between London and Great Britain's post-industrial towns, between Paris and *la France périphérique* (peripheral France), between Rome and Italy's *mezzogiorno* (southern Italy). According to French social geographer Christophe Guilluy, economic globalization comes with a new social geography: employment and wealth have become more and more concentrated in the big cities. Indeed, between 2000 and 2010, 75 percent of all growth in France occurred in the fifteen largest metropolitan areas. The deindustrialized regions, rural areas, and small and medium-sized towns, where many working-class people live, become less and less dynamic. It is from these peripheral locations that the right-wing populist revolt springs, with the losers of economic globalization determined to make themselves seen and their voices heard after decades of marginalization and neglect. The economic divide between the metropolises and the periphery also reflects a physical separation of the elite and the rest, resulting in the perception that the elite have gradually forgotten a group of people they no longer see.[17]

The Importance of Place

Whereas adherents of the establishment narrative dismiss lack of mobility as a source of labor market "friction" and suggest the provision of relocation allowances in response to factory closures, the importance of place echoes in the reflections of many blue-collar workers. When Arnade asked residents in dwindling American towns why they stayed, they looked at him like it was a crazy question, because the answer was so obvious. "This is where I am from," says Randy. "[Cairo, Illinois] is my home. It is a small community, and it is my family," explains Marva. "There is a lot to improve. But it is my home. When you don't have anything else all you got is your home." "I didn't want to leave," explains Jim. "I wanted this. . . . Being able to see people I was born with every day and staying close to my family. I live on land where my two grown boys and their families live just nine hundred feet away. I can see them every day, and do. What more could you ask for?"[18]

Jonathan Achey Jr. had worked for twenty-eight years at General Motors in Lordstown, Ohio, when in 2018 the factory was "unallocated"—left without a car to produce. He told the *New York Times:* "Thank God my dad was lucky enough to spend 35 years at Lordstown. He bought a house a couple of miles away from where he grew up, where my grandparents lived. And I loved the fact that, when I was a kid, it took us not even 10 minutes to go to the place where my dad grew up. I thought that was the coolest thing ever. And right now, [my son] Michael has that option: He can go to my mom's house and say his dad was born and raised in that house."[19]

Moving away from one's community also poses practical difficulties. Many blue-collar workers rely on their extended families for support. As Sherria Duncan, another worker at the Lordstown plant, says: "Family is important to us, and the possibility of having to leave the area is hard, because our family would probably be separated. Both of our mothers help a lot, and we really rely on our parents because we work separate shifts." "They say 'Family first' at G.M., but it isn't true, because they don't understand that a lot of people have children in school," Duncan reflects. "So that's very scary if we have to transfer plants, because we won't have that safety net."[20] When faced with the choice of losing their jobs or ripping their family apart, many people choose to stay in their community.

Professional classes often derive much of their identity and respect from their professions, so moving for work seems like an obvious thing to do. Working-class people, by contrast, are more likely to draw identity and respect from their place in and commitment to their family and community. For those who take pride in the notion that "family comes first," law professor Joan Williams explains, moving for work might suggest that they value their job more than their communities. Their lower earning power also means they rely more on close networks of family and friends for many kinds of assistance that professionals pay for, from childcare and elder care to home improvements. Moving would uproot them from their communities and this extended network of support: "You can't provide childcare for your grandchildren via Skype."[21]

Loyalty and Betrayal

A sense of loyalty to the community often goes hand in hand with a sense of patriotism and a rejection of cosmopolitan values. At a Conservative Party conference in 2016 following the Brexit vote, the new British prime minister, Theresa May, famously declared: "If you believe you're a citizen of the world, you're a citizen of nowhere. You don't understand what the very word 'citizenship' means." The "spirit of citizenship," May argued, is what helps to make societies work. It means "a commitment to the men and women who live around you, who work for you, who buy the goods and services you sell." It is the social contract that motivates you to train local people before hiring cheap labor from overseas. It is what connects you to your country and your compatriots, rather than to other international elites in other global cities.[22] It lies at the heart of French politician Marine Le Pen's distinction between the "patriots" and the "globalists."[23]

The loss that the workers at the shuttered General Motors plant in Lordstown felt was compounded by a sense of betrayal at the breach of this social contract. As Achey put it: "My whole life has been General Motors. I have 28 years invested in the company that is doing this to me. I understand it's a business, and they have to make decisions when it comes to business. If this is what they feel they have to do, then I'll have to accept it. But it's hard when you see money going to other places, when you see CEOs making the money they're making. Do I feel like I got slapped in the face? Absolutely."[24] When Trump talks about other countries "stealing US jobs," he suggests that US workers have an entitlement to these jobs that is akin to a property right. This conception of jobs as property echoes the sense of workers such as Achey that they have "invested" in their companies and are losing much more than a job—they are losing a part of their identity, a part of their family history, and a part of their community. The jobs-as-property metaphor also captures the feeling of being wronged—"slapped in the face"—when the job is taken away and given to a foreigner just for profit. "Workers who believe their country cares more for cheap goods and cheap labor than for the job prospects of its own people feel betrayed," suspects philosopher Michael Sandel.[25]

Autoworkers in the United States and Canada are put off by a suggestive symbol of this betrayal: cars manufactured in Mexico. In a small act of rebellion, many autoworkers refuse to buy models of their (former) companies' cars manufactured in Mexico. When General Motors closed its plant in Oshawa, Ontario, the Canadian union Unifor organized a public educational campaign about the models imported from Mexico (Figure 5.3), even taking out a Super Bowl ad that evoked the fraying social contract between companies and their workers by telling GM: "If you want to sell here, build here." The sense of betrayal and disrespect is compounded when the companies ask the soon-to-be-laid-off workers to train their Mexican or Chinese replacements. The establishment narrative's emphasis on automation as the primary cause of the decline in manufacturing employment rings hollow to workers whose "last act at the factory was to unbolt the machine and load it up to be shipped off to China."[26]

Traditional Values

Theresa May's comments about "citizens of nowhere" reflect a division that British journalist David Goodhart argues helps explain the Brexit vote: the split between Somewheres and Anywheres. The establishment narrative reflects the views and values of the Anywheres. Most of them

Fig. 5.3: A Canadian Union's Campaign against Cars Made in Mexico
Note: This image was part of a campaign by Unifor, the largest private sector union in Canada, against the closure of the General Motors plant in Oshawa, Ontario.
Credit: Reprinted with permission by Unifor.

left their hometowns to get a post-secondary education and become professionals. They tend to be highly schooled and mobile, value autonomy and openness, and handle social change comfortably. The larger though typically less influential group, the Somewheres, are more rooted and less well educated, value security and familiarity, and are more connected to group identities. In this view, votes such as the Brexit referendum reflect pushback by the Somewheres against the Anywheres.[27]

Will Wilkinson calls the geographic sorting of Anywheres and Somewheres the "density divide." People who move to cities in search of work are typically more educated, ethnically diverse, and open to change than those who stay behind. This sorting process is exacerbated by the departure of the best-educated from rural areas for college, which encourages them to become more liberal and to relocate to cities to work. As J. D. Vance, the author of *Hillbilly Elegy,* recalls one of his professors telling him about higher education: "The sociological role we play is to suck talent out of small towns and redistribute it to big cities."[28] Low-density populations are much more likely than high-density ones to vote for right-wing populist positions or parties, from Brexit in the United Kingdom to the National Front in France and the Alternative für Deutschland (AfD) in Germany.[29] Whereas Anywheres celebrate change, Somewheres are more likely to appeal to traditional values, including character, stability, community rootedness, and established gender hierarchies. "The professional elite values change and self-development; working-class families value stability and community," Williams observes, "for families a few paychecks away from losing their homes and stable middle-class lives, respect for stability reigns supreme."[30]

The loss of traditional blue-collar jobs strikes a particularly hard blow for some men, as their loss of breadwinner status leads them to question their very worth as men. Rick Marsh, an autoworker who lost his job at the General Motors plant in Lordstown, wondered: "Without the ability to feed my family and pay for my children and feed my children, what am I as a man?"[31] Participation by men of prime working age in the workforce has been declining for decades, but the effect is most concentrated among men with a high school degree or less.[32] Suggesting that working-class men should respond by moving into "pink-collar" jobs, such as hospitality and nursing, is perceived as adding insult to injury. For those who feel humiliated and frustrated by a changing economy and social values, this suggestion simply fans the flames of resentment.[33]

But the problem is not just one of wounded male pride. Economists have linked declining work prospects and rising idleness among men of prime working age to rising drug and alcohol abuse and falling marriage rates.[34] "Work is meaningful," explains the executive director of the think tank American Compass, Oren Cass, who has become one of the most prominent proponents of this narrative in the United States, "because of what it means to the person performing it, what it allows him to provide for his family, and what role it establishes for him in his community. . . . Where fewer men work, fewer marriages form. Unemployment doubles the risk of divorce, and male joblessness appears to be the primary culprit."[35]

The right-wing US commentator Tucker Carlson concurs. He argues that the pathologies of today's America, including "stunning out of wedlock birthrates," "high male unemployment," and a "terrifying drug epidemic," are in no small part due to the fact that "manufacturing, a male-dominated industry, all but disappeared over the course of a generation." Often what jobs remained were mainly in schools and hospitals, both traditional employers of women, and so women frequently ended up earning more than men. "Now, before you applaud this as a victory for feminism, consider the effects," he says. "Study after study has shown that when men make less than women, women generally don't want to marry them. Maybe they should want to marry them, but they don't. Over big populations, this causes a drop in marriage, a spike in out-of-wedlock births, and all the familiar disasters that inevitably follow—more drug and alcohol abuse, higher incarceration rates, fewer families formed in the next generation. . . . But increasingly, marriage is a luxury only the affluent in America can afford."[36]

As a presidential candidate and later as president, Trump took male anxiety about the loss of breadwinner status and transformed it into an aggressive assertion of manly entitlement to traditional blue-collar jobs. For Trump, work in a steel mill, a car plant, or a coal mine not only allows men to provide for their families but also validates their manhood. Trump often ridiculed the idea that blue-collar workers should be expected to adjust to changes in the economy. At his rallies, he juxtaposed "big, strong" steelworkers and coal miners with huge hands with those working on "little," effeminate computer parts: "I said to these beautiful guys, these—the West Virginia, big, strong guys, their fathers were in the mines, their grandfathers, their great—that's what they do. I said, fellas, supposing we take you to Silicon Valley . . . [laughter] And we'll teach you, like, how to make these beautiful little keyboards, these beautiful computers. They looked at me like, hey—you know the expression. We want to dig coal." Trump communicated to blue-collar men that they do not have to change—a message he reinforced in the case of the General Motors plant in Lordstown by exhorting workers to stay put: "Don't move, don't sell your house."[37]

For Trump, the traditional manly blue-collar jobs also have a central place in the national psyche. By describing the "hundreds" of steelworkers that are "back on the job" thanks to his steel tariffs as "pouring 2.7 million tons of raw American steel into the spine of our country," he suggested that a country without a thriving steel industry is spineless.[38] By contrast, Trump rarely ever mentioned the textile industry, even though textile workers have been exposed to cutthroat international competition for much longer than workers in the steel and auto industries. The reason may be that the textile industry predominantly employs women, and its shrinkage therefore does not threaten the position of men to the same extent as the loss of jobs in the steel, coal, and auto industries.[39] From the perspective of some proponents of the right-wing populist narrative, this makes such job losses less damaging to the social fabric.

Protecting against Outside Threats

One of the hallmarks of the right-wing populist narrative is the desire to protect the security of one's group—one's family, community, nation, or ethnic group—against external threats. In-group identification often translates into out-group hostility. Such hostility does not just manifest itself in attempts to prevent jobs from being shipped abroad. It also finds expression in resistance against immigration. In the United States, Trump gave expression to this nativist sentiment through his repeated references to Mexican immigrants as rapists and criminals, his promises to build a wall, and his "Muslim ban." In Europe, the anti-immigration sentiment has been the most visible manifestation of the economic and cultural anxieties brought on by slowing growth, austerity measures, and the large influx of refugees from poor and war-ravaged countries of the Middle East and Africa.

Those who are concerned about immigration explain their resistance in multiple ways. First, some bemoan the "stealing" of their jobs and the downward pressure immigrants can place on wages. According to author Michael Lind: "Instead of bringing jobs to low-wage workers abroad, employers can encourage the importation of low-wage workers to their home countries to suppress wages, deter unionization, and weaken the bargaining power of native and immigrant workers alike."[40] In October 2015, for example, the Walt Disney Company fired 250 IT workers—not because their skills had become redundant or their work had been automated, but because the company had found it could more cheaply bring in workers from India under the H-1B visa category. Adding insult to injury, Disney required the fired workers to train their replacements as a condition for receiving severance pay, which the US workers found "humiliating."[41] The suspicion that even well-qualified immigrants are brought in to undercut the wages of local workers rather than to fill real needs also animates right-wing populist concerns in other countries, such as France, Germany, and the United Kingdom. "If the international division of labor makes it possible to reduce wage costs by replacing European workers with Chinese and Indian workers," explains Guilluy, "immigration allows industries and services that cannot be moved offshore to practice social dumping" by bringing cheap labor onshore.[42]

A second concern is that immigrants are "parasites" feeding off national welfare systems.[43] In the Brexit vote, the UK Independence Party (UKIP) campaigned to limit free access to the National Health Service to legal residents. In Germany and other western European countries, it is widely suspected that the waves of migrants from the Middle East and Africa are not fleeing conflict or persecution but are flocking to Europe in search of a better life. Some right-wing populists regard "immigration into the welfare state" ("Einwanderung in die Sozialsysteme") as especially corrosive, as it undermines the principle of reciprocity that undergirds the system. "The wealth that is produced in this country must benefit in the first place those who produced it," says Björn Höcke, the AfD's leader in the east German state of Thuringia. "A welfare state can only have a future . . . in a country that has closed borders."[44] The elite congratulate themselves on being cosmopolitan and open, yet they often cloister themselves in expensive neighborhoods and self-select out of the public schools and hospitals, so immigrants live near, but not among, the upper class. This segregation means that the elite do not experience the same competition for public services with immigrants as do members of the native working class.

Third, those concerned about immigration invoke the need to protect society from violence and crime perpetrated by outsiders. On New Year's Eve 2015, for instance, raucous celebrations in the plaza facing Cologne's main train station featured intoxicated young men shooting fireworks into the crowds. The following day, dozens of women reported to police that they had been surrounded by groups of men who appeared to be of North African and Middle Eastern origin. The women were groped, sexually assaulted, and in some cases raped, and their cell phones were stolen. Overall, around 650 women were attacked that night in Cologne alone, and hundreds more were subjected to similar assaults in other German cities.[45] Although the German police and the mainstream media were initially reluctant to identify the perpetrators as foreign out of fear of stoking anti-immigrant sentiment, the attacks became a symbol of the danger that large numbers of young immigrant men posed to the safety of the native population, and particularly of women.

For many Germans, what made the attacks such a powerful symbol of otherness was the collective nature of the crime: the assailants were seen not as individual deviants but as groups of foreign men living according to their own norms, which were fundamentally at odds with German values. Another frightening aspect was the ability of these groups to take over a public place and turn it into a lawless space. The attacks made it seem as though refusal to go along with mass immigration was necessary to protect "a liberal and open society"; closing the border came to appear to be a matter of "defending the safety of public spaces for everyone (including women)" and "resisting imported antisemitism and homophobic and misogynistic attitudes." For the AfD, the lesson was that we can protect our community by not letting "these people" in; we do not need to allow the "importation of criminality," the AfD politician Alexander Gauland avowed.[46]

Yet perhaps the most vital threat that the right-wing populist narrative identifies is the one that immigration poses not to economic vitality and physical safety but to the cultural identity of the native population.

Strangers in Their Own Land

In September 2015, as tens of thousands of refugees made their way across the Balkans toward northern Europe, the German chancellor Angela Merkel decided to let them enter Germany. Remarking on the challenges of accommodating such a large group of newcomers, Merkel commended Germany's "welcome culture" in responding to refugees. But it proved to be a galvanizing moment for the young AfD. Apart from the size of the influx, the loss of control—the perception that suddenly anyone could enter the country, to be processed months or years later, if ever—was highly unsettling to the increasing numbers of AfD members and sympathizers. What was at stake for them was not just public safety and economic well-being but the very identity of the German people. For many AfD members, the admission of hundreds of thousands of immigrants from predominantly Muslim countries called into question the continued existence of the "German people" as an "ethno-cultural unity."[47]

An important source of these fears was the perception that immigrants from Muslim countries do not integrate into German society but rather establish "parallel societies" that have minimal interaction with the German mainstream: they attend mosques where the imam preaches in Turkish or Arabic, frequent their own restaurants and shops, and mostly keep to themselves. Because they bring their own culture with them, the places where immigrants live soon start to look and sound different: German-owned stores are replaced by Muslim barber shops, halal grocers, kebab shops, and shisha bars. Many immigrants speak languages other than German in the street, and some women wear veils. Moreover, there is a perception that Muslim immigrants regard German society and its values with disdain. They are viewed as signaling their rejection of German values, such as equality of men and women, by the clothes they wear, by their disrespect for German figures of authority such as teachers and police (especially female officers), and by their disregard for German laws.[48]

Many Germans are unwilling to accept these changes, which make them feel like "strangers in [their] own country." The fear of over-foreignization has also penetrated areas with very few immigrants: Germans who live in the east German countryside vote for the AfD because they do not want their towns and villages to change in the way major cities such as Berlin and Hamburg have changed. A similar phenomenon can be observed in other European countries, as resistance to immigration is often high in areas with few migrants whose inhabitants reject the changes they perceive in the major cities. For several years, more than half the British people have agreed with some version of the statement "Britain has changed in recent times beyond recognition, it sometimes feels like a foreign country and this makes me feel uncomfortable." Older, less well educated, and less wealthy people are the most likely to subscribe to this view. Similar sentiments have fueled the rise of right-wing populists in France. "This election is a choice of civilisation," warned Le Pen in the run-up to the 2017 presidential election: "After decades of cowardice and laissez-faire . . . will our children live in a country that is still French and democratic? Will they even speak our French language?" For proponents of the right-wing populist narrative, immigration at the level and speed with which it has taken place in many European countries over the past decades, specifically when it comes without integration, threatens the sense of "ontological security" (*Weltvertrauen*) that allows people to feel comfortable in their societies.[49]

The disconnect between elite and working-class views on issues such as the benefits of free trade and the value of immigration fuels resentment against and distrust of elites, whom many working-class people consider not just arrogant but "morally wrong in their core values."[50] In signing trade deals and permitting immigration, the elite enabled economic and cultural attacks against the nation. The resulting feeling of betrayal is compounded by the sense that the elite have effectively silenced the views of anti-immigration proponents of the right-wing populist narrative by dismissing them as racist, sexist, or nativist and enforcing political correctness. One American southerner explained that she loved Rush Limbaugh, the late US radio commentator, because when she listened to him it felt as though he was defending her against insults liberals were lobbing at her community: "Oh, liberals think that Bible-believing Southerners are ignorant, backward, rednecks, losers. They think we're racist, sexist, homophobic, and maybe fat." Politicians like

Trump have allowed people to feel released from the censure of the political correctness police and finally permitted them to say in public what they have been thinking in private. Trump was an "emotions candidate" whose speeches evoked "dominance, bravado, clarity, national pride, and perhaps personal uplift." "We have passion," he told a Louisiana crowd. "We're not silent anymore; we're the loud, noisy majority." Trump gave his adoring fans "a giddy release from the feeling of being a stranger in one's own land."[51]

Taking Back Control

"Let's take back control" was the slogan of the Vote Leave campaign for Brexit. "We want our country back" was UKIP's refrain. The desire to take back sovereignty formed a core part of the motivation for the Brexit vote. The Leave campaign had won a victory for "real people," UKIP leader Nigel Farage declared, and the date of the Brexit vote should go down as the country's "independence day." "Leaving the EU would be a win-win for all," Boris Johnson asserted, because the European Union "subverts our democracy" and the United Kingdom is "big enough and strong enough to stand on its own."[52] On arriving in the United Kingdom shortly after the vote in June 2016, Trump tweeted: "Place is going wild over the vote. They took their country back, just like we will take America back."[53]

One of the hallmarks of economic globalization has been the transfer of control over many economic and regulatory issues to supranational bodies. This loss of control in the West is exemplified by the formation and development of the European Union, to which European nations have delegated many fields of economic policymaking, especially since the mid-1980s. This loss of control was not accidental but, rather, by design; it was deemed necessary to create a more integrated and efficient market so as to realize on the European continent the economic gains promised by the establishment narrative.[54]

But this ceding of control has raised nationalist ire and helped feed right-wing populist narratives. The spark that triggers this fury varies from country to country, but a desire to reclaim sovereignty, particularly over immigration, is a common theme. In Spain, for instance, the right-wing party Vox tweeted its approval of Trump's election in 2016: "The Americans also say yes to their national sovereignty, yes to the control of their borders and no to the globalism of the corrupt establishment." Its leader Santiago Abascal declared that "VOX defends national sovereignty against the globalist and multicultural model that is dictated from the offices of international progress." The Italian politician Matteo Salvini has similarly argued that Italy should reject "orders" from Berlin, Brussels, and Paris: "For me, Italy is Italy: a proudly free and sovereign country!" Far-right Australian politician Pauline Hanson sings a similar tune: the "push for globalization, economic rationalism, free trade and ethnic diversity has seen our country's decline. This is due to the foreign takeover of our land and assets."[55]

Concerns about the loss of control over immigration have been particularly pronounced in the United Kingdom. In the run-up to the Brexit vote, Farage claimed that Britain was "impotent on matters of security and migration. We have given up our sovereignty to Europe."[56] Although immigration from outside the European Union is highly controversial in all EU member states, the United Kingdom also harbored particularly strong opposition to immigration from other EU members, especially eastern European countries. This opposition is partly explained by the unique position of the United Kingdom, which, under the influence of the internationalist Blair government, was the only large EU member to immediately open its labor market to workers from the ten new EU member nations that acceded in 2004, while the other large EU member countries made use of the right to impose temporary restrictions on the freedom of movement of workers from eastern Europe.[57] Faced with much higher inflows of eastern European immigrants than other countries were, subsequent UK governments sought to stem the flow. But their ability to do so was hampered by the circumstance that freedom of movement, as one of the four fundamental freedoms of the European single market, is largely removed from national control.

The powerlessness of the UK government to respond to public sentiment against high levels of immigration exposed the country's loss of control in the process of European integration and led to the Brexit movement's rallying cry, "Take back control." "There's not much point in having a United Kingdom if we're governed from somewhere else," Farage argued. "We may as well become a satellite state of the European Union because that's virtually what we are. Our courts aren't supreme. Our parliaments aren't supreme."[58] A fundamental element of the right-wing populist narrative is a desire to reassert control—over national policies, identity, and the future.

Conclusion

Proponents of the establishment narrative describe those who subscribe to the right-wing populist narrative as having been "left behind." This metaphor suggests that the world has moved on, and that those who have lost out need to catch up through "adjustment" or be mollified through welfare handouts. Arguably, this view profoundly misreads what animates the right-wing populist narrative. Although some proponents of the narrative do feel forgotten by the establishment, they have no interest in catching up. As they see it, the problem is not that the world has been moving too fast but that it has been moving in the wrong direction. They do not want to follow that path. What motivates the right-wing populist narrative is not anger at having been left behind but, rather, mourning for what has been left behind—a world that provided plenty of stable, respectable, and community-sustaining jobs for men and women with limited education, and that imparted the security of relative ethnic and cultural homogeneity and of stable social and gender hierarchies.[59]

As Steve Bannon, one of the most recognizable proponents of this perspective, has stated, the narrative is not primarily concerned with economics; rather, "it's about human dignity and self-worth." "Here's the bottom line," Bannon declared: "The party of Davos"—his term for proponents of the establishment narrative—"has been arrogant. The party of Davos hasn't worried about what people's patriotism is, what their love of country is, what their love of their cultures are [*sic*] . . . they look at the little guy, it's just another unit of production, unit of consumption."[60] What emerges from the different strands of the right-wing populist narrative is that much more is at stake than money: family, community, nation, history, dignity, a sense of self-worth, a sense of place. All these facets of life are under threat not just from free trade agreements and immigration but also from changes in culture and attitudes that have become enmeshed with the process of economic globalization.

CHAPTER 6

The Corporate Power Narrative

Neither the benefits nor the ravages of globalization come about by themselves; someone has to decide to source products from overseas rather than the supplier next door, to shift production offshore rather than keep the local factory open, or to move capital into tax havens rather than invest it at home. Individuals who choose imports over domestic products, consume services abroad, or hold their assets offshore play a role in this process. But it is largely the production, sourcing, and investment decisions of multinational corporations that drive the process of economic globalization. For proponents of what we call the corporate power narrative, the rise of multinational corporations has fundamentally changed the distribution of gains from economic globalization in a way that the establishment narrative has failed to recognize. As Jerry Brown, former governor of California, has argued:

> Listening to free trade cheerleaders, one would never guess that the doctrine for free trade was invented back in the late 18th and early 19th centuries when conditions were totally different from our own. Then, companies were grounded in a specific country and not footloose to open and close factories whenever they found lower wages and taxes or weaker health and safety laws. In those days, business capital was not mobile in the way it is today and was normally guided by national interests and loyalty to the country of its origin. Today, the transnational corporation has virtually no allegiance except to its own global expansion and profit. What brings financial value to the shareholder is the only criterion even if jobs are destroyed and whole communities are devastated.[1]

The corporate power narrative argues that, in their role as drivers of globalization, corporations benefit from three sources of power. First, their ability to move capital across the globe freely and to export their products almost anywhere at negligible cost has given corporations enormous *bargaining power* vis-à-vis workers and governments: they can use the threat of decamping to another country as leverage in negotiations with workers over wages and with governments over regulations and taxation. As a result, corporations can set off a "race to the bottom" on labor and environmental standards, wages, and tax rates.[2]

Governments are not just passive bystanders, however. In their eagerness to help corporations take advantage of the opportunities of globalization, governments have concluded trade and investment agreements that give those corporations a second source of power: *legal entitlements* to influence regulatory processes, extend their markets, protect their investments and intellectual property, and in certain circumstances sue governments for measures that diminish the value of the corporations' assets.[3]

For some multinational corporations, these advantages combine with other factors, such as technological change and domestic policy choices, to produce a third source of leverage: *market power.* Globalization and technology (which give rise to worldwide markets and massive economies of scale) interact with network effects (which provide increasing returns to existing market leaders) and lax antitrust enforcement (particularly in the United States) to concentrate market share in many industries in a handful of superstar firms, skewing the distribution of gains from globalization toward corporations and away from workers and governments.[4]

The corporate power narrative has a long lineage. "Citizens beware" was the opening sentence and theme of US political activist Ralph Nader's 1993 pamphlet against the North American Free Trade Agreement (NAFTA) and the imminent conclusion of the Uruguay Round of trade negotiations, which would result in the establishment of the WTO in 1995. Nader had spent the preceding twenty years fighting for product safety standards and consumer protections in the United States. In the early 1990s, he saw those gains as being threatened at the international level: an "unprecedented corporate power grab," warned Nader, was "underway in global negotiations over international trade." The leading global corporations, he argued, were circumventing democratic processes at the national level to impose their "autocratic" agenda at the international level. "Global commerce without commensurate democratic global law may be the dream of corporate chief executive officers," he warned, "but it would be a disaster for the rest of the world."[5]

Nader was one of the first proponents of the corporate power narrative to identify the first two sources of power that corporations derive from international trade and investment agreements. First, by exposing countries to the competitive pressures of a global market, economic liberalization creates incentives to lower standards so as to attract investment. Freedom for capital allows corporations "to pit country against country in a race to see who can set the lowest wage levels, the lowest environmental standards, the lowest consumer safety standards." As a result, "workers, consumers, and communities in all countries lose; short-term profits soar and big business 'wins.'"[6]

Second, Nader pointed to opportunities for corporations to have more direct influence on standard-setting. Instead of working indirectly through market pressure, this mechanism creates legal constraints on countries' regulatory freedom that are imposed at the international level and circumvent domestic regulatory processes. In particular, Nader and his colleagues had their eye on agreements negotiated in the context of the Uruguay Round that aimed at "harmonizing" technical and sanitary standards across the global economy—leaving little room for national democratic influence and considerable room for corporate capture.[7]

However, recent concern about corporate power has arisen most palpably at the intersection of globalization, technology, and antitrust policy, particularly in the area of Big Tech. Advocates ranging from law professors Lina Khan and Tim Wu to public officials such as Elizabeth Warren and EU commissioner Margrethe Vestager to journalists such as *Financial Times* columnist and author Rana Foroohar are clamoring to curb the power of Big Tech companies. "The challenge for us today," Foroohar argues, "is figuring out how to put boundaries around a technology industry that has become more powerful than many individual countries."[8]

Who loses as corporations exploit their bargaining leverage, legal entitlements, and market power to protect their assets and maximize their profits in the course of economic globalization? Proponents of the corporate power narrative argue that, except for the shareholders and managers of the corporations themselves, virtually everyone does. Most apparent is the impact on workers across the globe, as corporations dictate wages and working conditions by threatening to decamp to low-wage countries or by exploiting their status as the dominant employer in a particular area. Consumers, however, lose out as well, since corporations can whittle down safety standards, delay or prevent the introduction of consumer protection legislation, overcharge for goods and services, and harvest their data. Finally, people also suffer in their role as citizens, because the ability of corporations to evade taxation, chill regulation, exert political influence, and manipulate societal debates leaves them with a diminished welfare and regulatory state and a compromised democracy.[9]

Drawing on historical and contemporary examples, this chapter illustrates the corporate power narrative's concerns about (1) bargaining power over taxes and wages, (2) legal entitlements with respect to standard-setting, intellectual property rights, and international dispute settlement, and (3) corporate concentration.

Bargaining Power: Corporate Taxes

The corporate power narrative's first concern relates to the opportunities for global arbitrage that globalization creates. Corporations can take advantage of differences in wages, regulations, or taxes among different countries by moving—or they can bolster their bargaining position where they are by threatening to move. The fear that these dynamics would lead governments to lower their standards has been borne out most clearly in the area of corporate taxation.[10] "For years, multinational corporations have encouraged a race to the bottom," economist Joseph Stiglitz explains, "telling each country that it must lower its taxes below that of its competitors."[11] Between 1985 and 2018, the global average statutory corporate tax rate fell by more than half, from 49 percent to 24 percent. In recent years, the United States cut its rate from 35 percent to 21 percent, and the United Kingdom cut its from 19 percent to 17 percent (Figure 6.1). As corporations pay less in taxes, countries' revenue base for providing public services dwindles.

Proponents of the corporate power narrative assert that Western governments' aggressive attempts to lure corporations with ever lower tax rates are largely futile, as corporations increasingly shift their profits to tax havens, such as Bermuda, Ireland, and Luxembourg, which offer rock-bottom rates that major countries cannot hope to match. These small nations create large holes in international tax collection. One study found that close to 40 percent of foreign profits by multinational companies was shifted to tax havens.[12] US multinationals are estimated to book about half of their foreign profits in tax havens where they face effective rates of just 7 percent.[13] Economist Gabriel Zucman reckons that 55 percent of all foreign profits of US firms are kept in tax havens at a cost of $130 billion per year in lost tax revenue. The establishment

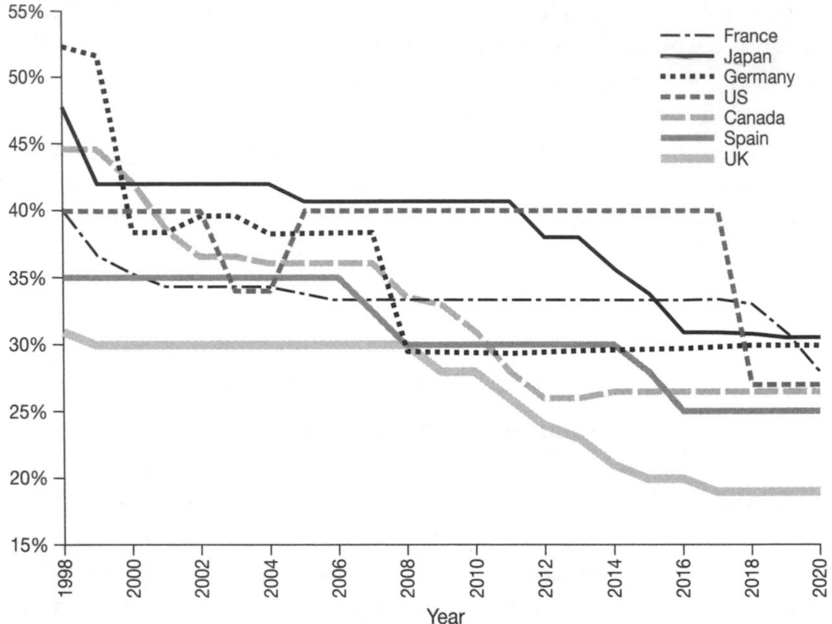

Fig. 6.1: The Race to the Bottom on Corporate Taxes

Note: This graph shows the annual corporate tax rates of major Western countries between 1998 and 2018.

Credit: Reformatted from Jeffrey Kleintop, "Tax War: Will Global Competition to Lower Taxes Lift Growth?," Charles Schwab Market Commentary, *October 12, 2020, figure "Effective Corporate Tax Rates."*

narrative heralds the free market, but, as Zucman notes, "nothing in the logic of free exchange justifies this theft."[14] Proponents of the corporate power narrative received unexpected backing for these claims in 2019 when economists working for the IMF concluded that "almost 40 percent" of global foreign direct investment constituted "phantom investment into corporate shells with no substance and no real links to the local economy."[15]

The increasing economic importance of intangible property, such as patents, trade secrets, and trademarks, in the global economy plays a significant role in enabling tax avoidance because intangibles are not physically present in any country. This lack of physicality has made it easier for intellectual-property-rich corporations to book profits associated with such intangibles with subsidiaries that they conveniently locate in low-tax jurisdictions, thereby avoiding taxation in the countries where most of their economic activity occurs (for instance, where the product is made or sold) or where the parent company is headquartered.[16] Apple, for example, created two Irish subsidiaries that own most of the company's intellectual property. It then claimed that these companies were the source of much of its global profits, as they licensed this intellectual property to other global Apple subsidiaries that are selling or licensing Apple products throughout the world. Apple used this to avoid paying high taxes in its home country and many of the countries in which it was operating. Furthermore, instead of paying Ireland's already low corporate tax rate, Apple then struck an agreement with Ireland that lets it pay as little as 0.005 percent of its profit to the government.[17]

Apple's example shows how corporations engage in contortions to minimize their obligations, often through behavior that is lawful but awful in the view of proponents of the corporate power narrative. They support international rules that permit them to manufacture and sell in any country around the world, but they resist international rules that might ensure that corporations pay their fair share in taxes in the countries in which they are headquartered, the places where their goods are manufactured, or the markets in which they sell. When multinationals avoid taxes, either the public coffers are depleted or others—often law-abiding, middle-class households—end up paying instead. The Tax Justice Network highlights the losses that the public suffers: "Tax is the return due to society on its investments—the roads, educated workforces, courts and so on—from which companies benefit. If they avoid or evade tax, they are free-riding off benefits provided by others." Apple, Google, Starbucks, and companies like them all claim to be socially responsible, but as Stiglitz reminds them, the "first element of social responsibility should be paying your fair share of tax."[18]

Bargaining Power: Workers' Wages

An automobile factory in the United States or Canada closes. Production of the vehicle model in question is moved to a new plant in Mexico or China. This scenario has played out countless times over the past three decades. How should we make sense of what is happening?

For protectionists, the answer is clear. The factory closures are an unmitigated loss for the United States and Canada and a gain for Mexico and China, because the manufacturing jobs at issue are "good" jobs that yield a decent standard of living and are essential to sustain manufacturing communities. Proponents of the establishment narrative offer a different reading: the "really good" jobs—those in research and development, design, and marketing—are likely to stay in the developed country, and their number might even increase, as the company can broaden its product offering by dint of the more cost-effective production. In other words, workers in developed countries get to move up the two ends of the smile curve where their work creates more value added, resulting in higher profits for companies and higher wages for workers in these countries.[19] Proponents of the establishment narrative acknowledge that short-term pain will ensue but claim that everyone will gain in the end: the Mexicans or Chinese will be able to get factory jobs, and the average productivity of workers in the United States and Canada will increase.

The corporate power narrative argues that both of these readings miss a crucial part of the story, since they ignore what happens to the jobs as they are moved from the developed countries to the developing countries. In the words of Canadian union leader Jerry Dias, international agreements such as NAFTA have allowed corporations to take "good Canadian jobs and [make] them bad ones in Mexico."[20] What was a well-paying union job with health insurance and a pension in Canada becomes a Mexican minimum-wage job without benefits. At the same time, corporations can use the threat of moving ever more jobs to Mexico to pressure Canadian and US workers to accept lower wages and inferior working conditions. As the American Federation of Labor and Congress of Industrial Organizations (AFL-CIO) has argued, NAFTA makes "it easier for global companies to suppress wages, disrupt union organizing, and skirt clean air and water obligations by relocating or threatening to relocate production elsewhere . . . [B]y providing incentives that make offshoring decisions more attractive (including [investor-state dispute settlement], guaranteed market access, excessive intellectual property protections and a low-standards regulatory framework), these deals provide added leverage for employers to actively hold down wages and standards by 'predicting' workplace closures and offshoring of jobs if workers form a union or refuse to give back hard-won wages and protections during negotiations."[21]

The corporate power narrative thus differs from both the establishment and the right-wing populist narratives in how it identifies the winners and losers from the offshoring of production: it holds that corporations and their owners win, and workers in both developed and developing countries lose. Along these lines, the AFL-CIO pointed out that, as a conse-

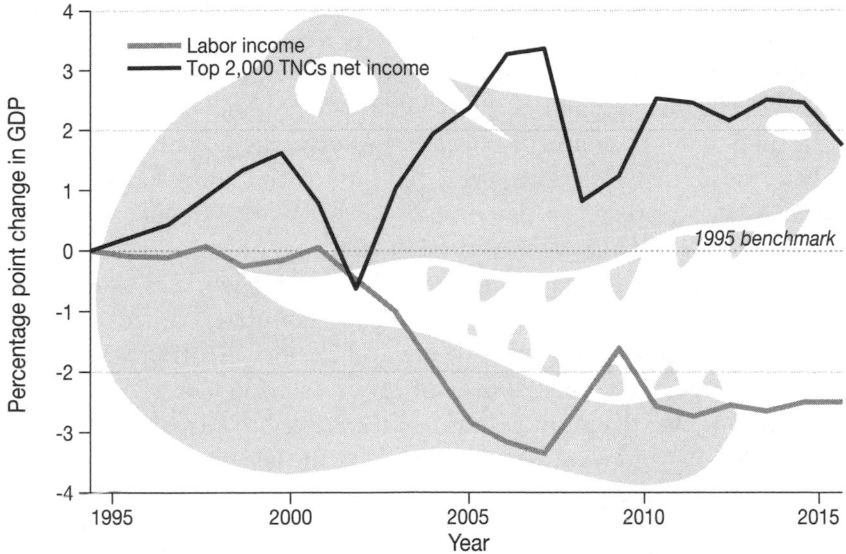

Fig. 6.2: The "Crocodile Curve"

Note: This graph shows the profits of the top 2,000 transnational corporations (in black) compared with the global labor income share (in gray), as percentage point changes in GDP.
Credit: Reformatted from Kevin P. Gallagher and Richard Kozul-Wright, "A New Multilateralism for Shared Prosperity: Geneva Principles for a Global Green New Deal," Boston University Global Development Policy Center and United Nations Conference on Trade and Development, May 2019, figure 6.

quence of NAFTA "dragging down taxes, wages and standards towards their lowest level within the trade bloc," the income distribution in all three NAFTA countries has "become more unequal as capital captures an ever-larger share and workers an ever-smaller share."[22] As a result, corporate profits have steadily increased and the labor share of income has concomitantly declined, which is reflected in the "crocodile curve" (Figure 6.2).

In contrast to the protectionist viewpoint, which pits workers in developing and developed countries against each other and attributes all outsourcing of jobs to "cheating" by developing countries, proponents of the corporate power narrative such as labor advocate Jeffrey Vogt concede that "developing countries should be able to attract investment based on a comparative wage advantage." Yet the corporate power narrative also contradicts the establishment narrative's contention that workers invariably win; rather, the narrative maintains that workers lose—both individually and collectively—whenever wages "are artificially low due to labor repression."[23] Dani Rodrik emphasizes the need to "distinguish cases where low wages in poor countries reflect low productivity from cases of genuine rights violations."[24] Violations of worker rights in developing countries concern the corporate power narrative not only because such violations affect the fate of the individuals involved but also because they can determine whether workers collectively gain from economic globalization. As the AFL-CIO has pointed out, "Rais[ing] the wages and protect[ing] fundamental rights for workers in Mexico" would help workers in all three NAFTA countries, since it would "limit . . . the ability of corporations and Mexico's ruling elite to use Mexican wages as an instrument of labor arbitrage."[25] If workers in Mexico and other developing countries were able "to bargain collectively for better wages and working conditions, . . . the benefits of trade [would] accrue not only to capital but also to labor."[26]

It follows that for proponents of the corporate power narrative such as journalist William Greider, thinking about the winners and losers from economic globalization "does not begin by examining Americans' own complaints about the global system. It begins by grasping what happens to people at the other end—the foreigners who inherit the American jobs," since the misery of workers in developing countries is "the other end of the transmission belt eroding the structure of work and incomes in the United States." That is why proponents of the corporate power narrative do not see the solution as closing the border. "The only plausible way that citizens can defend themselves and their nation against the forces of globalization is to link their own interests cooperatively with the interests of other peoples in other nations—that is, with the foreigners who are competitors for the jobs and production but who are also victimized by the system."[27]

To North American proponents of the corporate power narrative, Exhibit A for what happens when tariff reductions put workers in different countries in competition with each other without the same labor protections is the conditions in the maquiladoras that sprang up on the Mexican side of the border in the 1980s. Writing in the early 1990s, Greider described the slums of Ciudad Juárez as a "demented caricature" of suburban life in America: the employees of US flagship companies, including General Electric, Ford, and General Motors, lived in "squatter villages," subsisting on wages that did not pay for basic necessities. "With the noblesse oblige of the feudal padrone, some U.S. companies dole[d] out occasional *despensa* for their struggling employees—rations of flour, beans, rice, oil, sugar, salt—in lieu of a living wage."[28]

Instead of creating broad-based prosperity, on this account, the presence of US corporations in Mexico perpetuated misery. The working conditions were so deplorable that turnover among the employees was high and the often very young employees did not have an opportunity to acquire useful skills that would spill over into the economy at large. The corporations created an "enclave" economy that left no lasting prosperity before they decamped to places with even cheaper labor.[29] As Nader sums it up, "The corporate-induced race to the bottom is a game that no country or community can win. There is always some place in the world that is a little worse off, where the living conditions are a little bit more wretched. . . . The game of countries bidding against each other causes a downward spiral."[30]

Proponents of the corporate power narrative argue that little has changed in the twenty-five years since NAFTA originally entered into force. The AFL-CIO points out that since the conclusion of NAFTA, "wages in Mexico have lost purchasing power, and the U.S.-Mexico wage gap actually has increased."[31] Mexican workers are far from being able to afford the standard of living that US workers whose jobs the Mexican workers inherited used to have. Dias frequently notes that Mexican workers cannot afford the cars they produce even though Mexican manufacturing productivity has been rising rapidly: between 1994 and 2011, productivity increased by almost 80 percent, whereas real hourly compensation *fell* by 17 percent (Figure 6.3).[32] These statistics mean that despite "producing more, millions of Mexican workers are earning less than they did three decades ago."[33] The increasing gap between productivity and wages is the basis for the corporate power narrative's claim that workers in developing countries are not really "winning": these workers are not fairly rewarded for their work. Instead, the corporations that employ them are the ones that come out ahead, as they are able to appropriate a greater share of the gains from trade at the expense of *both* the Canadian and US workers who have lost their jobs *and* the Mexican workers whose wages do not reflect their rapidly rising productivity and barely allow them to subsist.

As NAFTA was being renegotiated in 2017 and 2018, Dias traveled to Mexico to put into action this insight into the interlinked fate of workers in developed and developing countries. Speaking into a bullhorn at a large protest in Mexico City, he conveyed a message of worker solidarity: "We

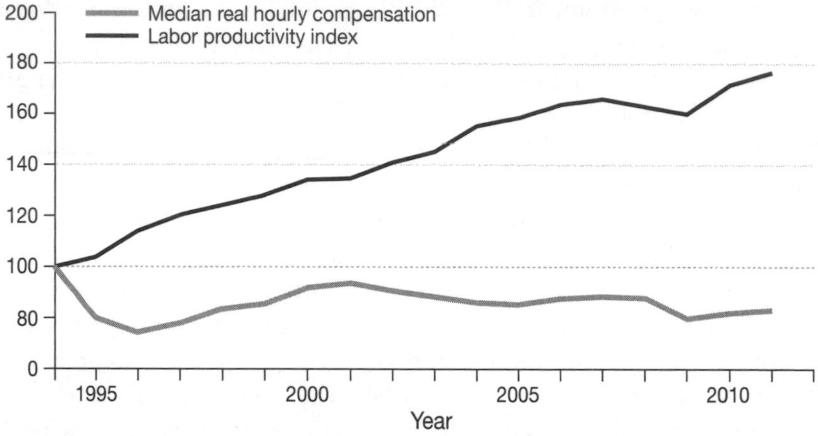

Fig. 6.3: Mexicans' Productivity Is Catching Up; Their Wages Not So Much
Note: This graph shows the growth in Mexican labor productivity (in black) compared with the growth in real compensation (in gray) between 1994 and 2011.
Credit: Reformatted from Harley Shaiken, "The Nafta Paradox," Berkeley Review of Latin American Studies, *Spring 2014, p. 40.*

all stand together, because the corporations only care about their profits, they don't care about us. They take more and more and more, and we have less and less and less. They're driving down the standards of workers in Canada, the United States and Mexico. So our strength has to be our unity. . . . They try to exploit workers. They pit workers against workers in each of our three countries. . . . Canadian and American workers know that our fight is not with Mexican workers. Our collective fight is with the governments, the international corporations."[34]

Legal Entitlements: Standard-Setting

The corporate power narrative's second concern stems from corporations' ability to use the legal tools of the trade regime to attack standards set by democratic governments. The most frequently cited example is the repeated attempts by the US government—acting at the behest of US agribusiness—to dismantle regulations adopted by the European Union on the basis of the "precautionary principle." The approach to regulation expressed by this principle insists that the safety of a food additive or a new genetically altered variety of a plant must be proven before it will be approved for public consumption, in contrast to the US approach, which allows the use of such additives or organisms by default unless they have been shown to be harmful. The precautionary principle served as the basis for the European Union's ban on beef from cattle that had been administered growth hormones, as well as its moratorium on the approval of genetically modified organisms. Though the United States challenged only the European Union's regulations in the WTO, proponents of the corporate power narrative argue that the WTO cases were "also meant as a warning to other countries" not to adopt similar restrictions.[35]

For proponents of the corporate power narrative, it was not just consumers who lost when these regulations were found to be inconsistent with WTO law (though the European Union refused to comply with the ruling on hormone-treated beef and has been dragging its feet on approving genetically modified organisms). Rather, something bigger was at stake. Rodrik highlights the European Union's argument that "regulatory decisions . . . cannot be made purely on the basis of science" but must also take into account "a society's risk preferences," which may result in entirely legitimate regulatory differences between countries.[36] The activist Thilo Bode, who is arguably the most prominent proponent of the narrative in Germany, has gone even further, claiming that the precautionary principle is integral to the "European understanding of the state and democracy" and as such is part of the European identity. Bode asserts that we need to recognize that the world is not only a "global marketplace" and that "the interest of international corporations in harmonized standards" should therefore not prevail over all other considerations.[37]

The experience of US attacks on the precautionary principle, which demonstrated the potential for corporations to use trade law in an attempt to preempt regulatory choices by democratic bodies, was one of the driving forces behind European protests against the proposed TTIP agreement with the United States in 2015. Advocacy groups used the prospect of the forced opening of the EU market to US-origin hormone-treated beef, genetically modified corn, and "chlorinated chickens"—poultry washed in chlorine to kill pathogens—to rally the public against the agreement. The advocates feared that the agreement's mechanisms for "regulatory cooperation" would give US corporate lobbyists the chance to water down European regulations before they would even see the light of day: under TTIP, Bode warned, "the influence of corporate interests would rise immensely," since US and European corporations could band together "at the tables of the transatlantic regulatory cooperation council."[38] It would have been the "ultimate corporate power grab" that Nader had foreseen more than twenty years earlier, an example of "legislation by treaty" involving a "massive transfer of power from democratic legislatures to corporate managers and bankers."[39]

In this way, the corporate power narrative highlights the power of multinationals to exploit differences among countries in some areas (by taking advantage of differential tax rates and wage levels) while using their power to eliminate differences in other areas (such as different regulatory standards for products). The result is a system that puts workers in different countries in competition with each other but does not ensure that they enjoy the same labor protections, and that curtails food and environmental regulations while not putting a floor under tax and regulatory competition. "Even as [corporations] have exploited opportunities for international tax arbitrage, firms and lobbies in the post–Cold War era of globalization have also promoted . . . the selective harmonization of laws and rules, when it has been in their interest to do so," notes Michael Lind. "The economic sectors chosen by Western governments for arbitrage and harmonization reflect the interests not of national working-class majorities but of national managerial elites. Harmonizing labor standards or wages would undercut the corporate search for the cheapest labor, while transnational crackdowns on tax avoidance would thwart the strategy of tax arbitrage by transnational firms."[40]

For proponents of the corporate power narrative, this model of globalization represents exactly the opposite of what is normatively desirable: the lack of international regulation in some areas creates *illegitimate* sources of comparative advantage—such as artificially cheap labor due to the violation of worker rights—whereas regulatory competition and harmonization in other areas push countries to eliminate *legitimate* regulatory differences that reflect diverging democratic choices about questions such as acceptable levels of risk and the size of the welfare state.

Legal Entitlements: Intellectual Property Rights

"This is not mainly about trade," said Lori Wallach, director of Public Citizen's Global Trade Watch, about the Trans-Pacific Partnership (TPP). "It is a corporate Trojan horse. The agreement has 29 chapters, and only five of them have to do with trade. The other 24 chapters either handcuff our domestic governments, limiting food safety, environmental standards, financial regulation, energy and climate policy, or establishing new powers for corporations." Economist Paul Krugman agreed: "This is not a trade agreement. It's about intellectual property and dispute settlement; the big beneficiaries are likely to be pharma companies and firms that want to sue governments." For Krugman, this meant that it was "off-point and insulting to offer an off-the-shelf lecture on how trade is good because of comparative advantage" in defense of the agreement. The aim of the TPP, according to this view, was to minimize regulatory differences between the parties and afford broad-based protection to economic assets, thereby creating a "generalized freedom to operate" for corporations across the participating countries.[41]

Rodrik has long argued that "the label 'free trade agreements' does not do a very good job of describing" what recent international economic agreements "actually do." Rather than pursuing "efficiency-enhancing policies," as the establishment narrative claims, trade and investment agreements often reflect "rent-seeking, self-interested behavior" by corporations that may well "produce welfare-reducing, or purely redistributive outcomes under the guise of free trade."[42] On this view, it is possible to be in favor of free trade yet against free trade agreements, because the two are fundamentally different. The establishment narrative presents free trade as good for countries in general because it gives them a way to protect the gains for the many (lower prices, greater choice) against the narrow interests of protectionists, who would seek to shut out cheap imports to maintain their domestic market share. According to this view, governments know that enacting free trade policies is in their long-term interest, so tying their hands to the mast by signing on to trade agreements helps them avoid the temptation to backslide by giving in to strong protectionist interests for political gain.[43]

According to Rodrik, this account might have been accurate when trade agreements dealt only with limited issues such as reducing tariffs. But modern trade agreements have a much wider purview. Far from reining in protectionists, Rodrik suggests, modern trade agreements "empower another set of special interests and politically well-connected firms, such as international banks, pharmaceutical companies and multinational corporations."[44] As a consequence, these agreements might produce welfare-enhancing outcomes by opening markets and allowing them to be served more efficiently, but they can also produce welfare-reducing or redistributive outcomes under the mantle of free trade.

A classic example of this concern is the protection of intellectual property rights in trade agreements. Intellectual property rights used to be the exclusive remit of the World Intellectual Property Organization

(WIPO), but US companies became frustrated with WIPO for being, in their view, an ineffective UN agency with no leverage over developing countries. In the 1980s, a concerted push by Western corporations led to the incorporation of intellectual property protections in the multilateral trade regime, in the form of the Trade-Related Aspects of Intellectual Property Rights (TRIPS) agreement.[45] The United States and other Western countries also began including intellectual property rights in their bilateral and regional free trade agreements and investment treaties from the 1990s onward.

Intellectual property protection was a feature of international trade agreements that flew under the radar of publics in most Western countries for many years because it primarily targeted developing countries. As the world's economy moved from the industrial era to the knowledge-based era, intellectual property protection became a vital way of protecting the advantages and market position of companies and countries that owned a lot of intellectual property. Initially, the intellectual property elements of these agreements had little effect in most Western countries since they often reflected standards that were already embodied in domestic legislation. It was primarily NGOs such as Doctors Without Borders that drew attention to how these agreements impeded access to essential medicines in developing countries by forcing them to use their public health budgets to purchase brand-name products instead of cheap generic versions.[46]

Only when the governments of countries with the most valuable intellectual property stock, including the United States and the European Union, started to use every new trade agreement to further ratchet up intellectual property protections did Western publics start paying attention. For example, one aspect of the Comprehensive Economic and Trade Agreement (CETA) between the European Union and Canada that caught the public's eye was that the Canadian government had agreed to extend patent protection for medicines by two years, which delayed the market entry of cheaper generic versions of those medicines. Estimates placed the cost of these changes to Canada's public health budget at between CAD 795 million and CAD 1.95 billion annually—an amount that was likely to exceed the projected gains to Canada's GDP (CAD 850 million) from the elimination of tariffs by CETA. As one member of the Canadian Parliament put it during hearings on the agreement, "all Canadians will lose" owing to the increased costs of drugs.[47]

This example lends credence to the argument of Dan Ciuriak, a Canadian economist, that modern trade and investment treaties have become primarily "asset value protection agreements," in that the economic value of the protection that they afford to various types of assets dwarfs the economic effect of any efficiency gains they may generate.[48] It is not surprising, then, that studies find that Big Pharma and other firms with intangible assets, ranging from Hollywood to Silicon Valley, play an influential role in lobbying for free trade agreements.[49] These agreements do not discipline corporate power; rather, they enable it.

In the digital economy, this asset value protection also takes the form of guaranteeing the free flow of data across borders. Take, for example, the Comprehensive and Progressive Agreement on Trans-Pacific Partnership (CPTPP)—the version of the TPP that the remaining participants agreed to after President Trump withdrew the United States' signature. The CPTPP enacts what legal scholar Thomas Streinz calls the "Silicon Valley Consensus," pursuant to which countries must not restrict cross-border data flows and must refrain from requiring the use of local computing facilities, unless there are public policy justifications for such measures. These provisions work to the advantage of multinational companies, particularly Silicon Valley ones, which can move data across borders without restrictions and store the data wherever they like. The ability to pool data from many countries in one place is a tremendous advantage when it comes to machine learning and AI. At the same time, these provisions make it harder for other countries to develop domestic digital economies and to share in the gains from the digital economy.[50]

Protecting intellectual property rights and ensuring the free flow of data are two ways in which modern trade agreements advantage major multinational corporations; another is by allowing investors to sue countries through a process called investor-state dispute settlement (ISDS).

Legal Entitlements: ISDS Claims

In 2015, hundreds of thousands of people took to the streets of Berlin, Hamburg, Munich, and Frankfurt. For the first time since the founding of the Federal Republic of Germany in 1949, its citizens were protesting trade agreements, specifically the proposed TTIP agreement, between the European Union and the United States, and the CETA, between the European Union and Canada. The German public's opposition to these agreements presented a puzzle. Germany had been running record trade surpluses with the rest of the world for years, and the dependence of

Germany's economy on open trade was a widely accepted truism. So why were Germans taking to the streets?[51]

The German public's opposition to TTIP and CETA was not motivated by concerns about trade; what drove the protests was the fear that these agreements would give large North American corporations the right to sue European governments for taking measures in the public interest and to obtain large damage awards under an obscure investment arbitration system known as ISDS. To understand how ISDS became "the most toxic acronym in Europe," one needs to go back to the late 1950s, when Germany concluded its first bilateral investment treaty with Pakistan. The treaty protected investors of one party to the agreement against expropriation without compensation or discriminatory treatment in the territory of the other party. In practice, that protection largely benefited German investments in Pakistan as there were few Pakistani investments in Germany.[52]

It is safe to say that the German public took no note of this treaty. Under the treaty, in the event of a dispute the foreign investor's home country could sue the host country in which the investment was made. But it did not take long before this clause was supplemented in many investment treaties by ISDS, which permitted foreign investors themselves to sue governments directly before arbitral tribunals. Still, the public in Germany and other European countries paid little attention while their governments went on to conclude hundreds of similar treaties with developing countries over the following decades. This lack of attention was not surprising: the chance that a developed-country government would be sued by an investor from a developing country was slim, because the flows of investments protected by these treaties were largely a one-way street from developed to developing countries.

This state of affairs changed in the 1990s. In NAFTA, a deal between Canada, Mexico, and the United States, the procedure under which investors could sue governments was included for the first time in a treaty involving two developed countries. And investors did not hold back: US investors sued Canada, and Canadian investors sued the United States. Indeed, Canada quickly became the "most sued developed country in the world." By 2016, as the protests against TTIP and CETA were roiling Europe, the advocacy group Council of Canadians warned that Canada had paid out CAD 200 million to American corporations and had spent more than CAD 65 million in legal fees fending off a total of thirty-seven investor-state claims under NAFTA. The council noted that "almost two-thirds of claims against Canada involved challenges to environmental protection or resources management that allegedly interfered with the profit of American corporations."[53]

But the European public had already received its own wake-up call. In 2011, following the Fukushima nuclear disaster in Japan, the German government decided to accelerate Germany's "exit" from nuclear power, a decision that enjoyed broad public support. Although the major energy companies challenged the decision in German courts, one company—the Swedish energy giant Vattenfall—went further and sued the German government for $4.9 billion in compensation under the ISDS procedures of the Energy Charter Treaty, which had been concluded by European governments in the 1990s with a view to safeguarding western European investments in energy infrastructure in eastern Europe. At the time it was ratified, few if any would have foreseen that it might one day be used to challenge a popular decision of a democratically elected government to phase out nuclear power. But it was. The Vattenfall dispute galvanized the German public and helped propel the TTIP protests.

The prospect that TTIP would expose European governments to multibillion-dollar suits by US investors sent shudders down many Europeans' spines. Bode, who wrote a best-selling anti-TTIP book in German, describes ISDS as a system of "parallel justice" for investors and captures the sense of shock felt by the German public when it learned about the system. He finds it "unfathomable" that "sovereign states with a democratic constitution voluntarily agree to become liable for compensation vis-à-vis private persons and private enterprises simply because they are fulfilling their task, namely, to adopt laws for and on behalf of their citizens." Pia Eberhardt, a member of the nonprofit watchdog Corporate Europe Observatory, describes ISDS as "a global legal straightjacket that makes it very, very difficult and expensive for governments to regulate corporations." "It is dangerous for democracy," Eberhardt concludes.[54]

To proponents of the corporate power narrative, ISDS epitomizes the attempt to use international agreements to privilege the interests of corporations over the rights of citizens and to undermine democratic institutions in the process. Germany ultimately settled claims by four nuclear operators, including Vattenfall, for nearly 2.6 billion euros ($3.1 billion) in compensation.[55] If the Vattenfall matter was one example, a case involving tobacco products company Philip Morris was another. When Australia passed a public health measure requiring plain packaging of tobacco products, Philip Morris brought an ISDS case claiming that by preventing it from using its trademarks, Australia was indirectly expropriating its intellectual property and should be liable for billions of dollars in compensation. Would this not lead to regulatory chill, critics asked, by putting pressure on Australia to repeal its law and scaring off other countries from adopting similar public health measures? The concern about regulatory chill was only heightened when New Zealand announced that it was holding off on passing similar legislation until the Philip Morris case was resolved.[56]

ISDS has become a leitmotif of the corporate power narrative, and some prominent Western politicians are now denouncing it as an illegitimate and dangerous constraint on sovereignty. In seeking to defeat the TPP, for instance, Bernie Sanders asked with respect to the Vattenfall case: "Should the people of Germany have the right to make energy choices on their own or should these decisions be left in the hands of an unelected international tribunal?" Elizabeth Warren similarly condemned ISDS as "rigged, pseudo-courts" that are "tilt[ing] the playing field" in favor of big multinational corporations and undermining US sovereignty, and cautioned that if the TPP agreement included such a clause, "the only winners will be multinational corporations." As more countries experiment with legislation to speed up the transition to renewable energy, there are also intensifying concerns about the use of ISDS claims by coal, oil, and gas companies to target government measures that affect their bottom line.[57]

Market Power: Corporate Concentration

For proponents of the corporate power narrative, corporations are the winners from globalization not only because international economic agreements protect their investments and intellectual property, constrain national regulation, and allow them to play workers and governments off against each other to keep wages and taxes low. The narrative also draws attention to how globalization, technological change, and domestic policy choices—specifically, lax antitrust enforcement—have led to changing market structures and an ever-higher concentration of revenues and profits among a few dominant firms. This corporate concentration is problematic because dominant firms tend to have a lower-than-average labor share of income, use their market power to inflate prices and squeeze suppliers, and wield disproportionate political and social influence.

The increasing dominance of ever more markets by a small number of firms is a widely observed fact. Americans went from being able to choose between twelve major airlines in 1990 to only four large carriers in 2019, and even fewer on most routes. Many have a choice between only one or two internet providers. This is not an isolated, industry-specific phenomenon. Between 1997 and 2012, 75 percent of US industries became more concentrated.[58] Globally, the dominance of a few superstars is particularly evident within digital markets: Google, Apple, Microsoft, Facebook, and Amazon dominate the markets for search, hardware, PC software, social networking, and online shopping, respectively, not just in the US, but in many other countries too. For instance, Google's and Apple's operating systems run on 99 percent of all cell phones globally, while Apple and Microsoft supply 95 percent of the world's desktop operating systems.[59]

Big Tech firms are now the richest and most powerful companies on the face of the planet, and Silicon Valley has been the single greatest creator of corporate wealth in history. The combined market capitalization of Facebook, Apple, Amazon, Netflix, and Google exceeds the size of the economy of France. But that extraordinary growth and concentration has come with downsides for business dynamism, consumer privacy, and democracy, claim proponents of the corporate power narrative. "Today's big tech companies have too much power—too much power over our economy, our society, and our democracy," declared Elizabeth Warren during her primary campaign. "They've bulldozed competition, used our private information for profit, and tilted the playing field against everyone else. And in the process, they have hurt small businesses and stifled innovation."[60]

What explains the increased concentration that has allowed a handful of firms to attain dominance in each industry and to accrue ever-rising profits? Three different factors are at play, and their roles vary depending on the industry. International economic agreements have played a part: the lowering of barriers to trade in goods and services, the hitherto relatively unrestricted flow of data, and the virtually worldwide protection of intellectual property have created global markets in many sectors and have enabled firms to reach unprecedented economies of scale. These economies of scale allow market leaders to drive down their production costs and to harvest copious amounts of data, which they can monetize or use for research and development, both of which put pressure on less competitive firms and create barriers to new entrants seeking to match the incumbents' offerings.

Especially in the digital sphere, these economies of scale have been compounded by market characteristics such as network effects, information asymmetries, economies of scope, and lock-in effects that create winner-take-all dynamics and make it almost impossible for upstarts to displace established firms. Network effects exist where the more users a given product or service has, the more attractive it is to new users. With products like phones and services like social media, the more users a network has, the more attractive it is to potential new users, so the more new users it gets, the more attractive it becomes to the next set of potential users, and so on. The result is sometimes described as the "Matthew effect" based on the biblical phrase: "For to every one who has will more be given, and he will have abundance; but from him who has not, even what he has will be taken away."[61]

As Ciuriak explains, these dynamics were already strong in the knowledge-based economy when globalization and technology worked to give increasing returns to market leaders and trade agreements extended the reach and strength of intellectual property protections. The divide at that time was between the intellectual property haves and have-nots. However, in the data-driven economy, these disparities are becoming even more marked. The data-advantage of established market leaders, coupled with technological innovations in machine learning and artificial intelligence, mean that gains accrue to companies relative to consumers, and to market leaders relative to market laggards, at a much faster rate. The fact that some modern trade agreements also ensure the free flow of data across borders only further entrenches the global dominance of data-rich companies.

Proponents of the corporate power narrative also emphasize a third factor that has exacerbated the trend in favor of market concentration: lax antitrust policy. Corporate concentration is particularly pronounced in the United States, where regulators have been much less aggressive in scrutinizing mergers and enforcing antitrust laws than in Europe. In the United States, judge and legal scholar Robert Bork popularized a narrow approach to antitrust, the "consumer welfare" principle, which focuses only on whether a given practice, such as a merger or acquisition, would result in higher prices for consumers.[62] On this view, the dominant position of the tech companies is often not a concern. After all, companies such as Facebook and Google offer free services to consumers. One of the upshots of this narrow approach to antitrust is that the largest US tech companies have been allowed to achieve extraordinary levels of market power. Facebook has reached a 69 percent share of the world market in the social networking sector, and Google has consistently dominated the search engine market with a 90 percent world market share.[63] This concentration follows both companies' extensive efforts to buy up potential competitors: Facebook has concluded at least 67 unchallenged acquisitions, while Google has swallowed at least 214 companies.[64]

For proponents of the corporate power narrative, the increase in market concentration is worrying for four principal reasons. The first is the traditional concern that firms with market power will exploit their position to prey on consumers—and there is plenty of evidence that they do: "big business is overcharging you $5,000 a year," a *New York Times* headline declared in November 2019. From cell phone and broadband service to airline tickets, consolidation has predictably led to higher prices, as Philippon has shown.[65] The second concern is that, without the pressure of competition, dominant firms become less innovative and dynamic, putting less money into research and development. As Wu argues, "Both history and basic economics suggest we do much better trusting that fierce competition at home yields stronger industries overall."[66]

Third, rising corporate concentration has also further skewed the gains from globalization toward the top of the income distribution in several ways. One is the fact that superstar firms tend to have a lower-than-average labor share of income, even though their workers tend to be more productive and earn higher wages than the average worker. To the extent that superstar firms come to dominate markets, the labor share of income will fall.[67] Another reason is that firms that are dominant within particular markets can use their market power to depress wages. In an increasing number of labor markets in the United States, firms have "monopsony" power: they are the only ones offering jobs in a particular line of work, and hence can keep wages low.[68]

But it is not only workers who are getting squeezed as a result of monopsony power: "platform" firms, such as Amazon, have famously escaped the scrutiny of competition authorities because they were, if anything, pricing below cost—and thus benefiting consumers—in an aggressive effort to gain market share. Once these platform companies gain a dominant position, however, they have virtually complete control over the suppliers who sell or advertise on their platform and can force them to bear ever-greater costs.[69]

These dynamics are compounded by the increasing importance of data, machine learning, and artificial intelligence in the economy. Machine learning will put new pressure on white-collar jobs as much cognitive work will be capable of being outsourced to machines, just as the automation of manufacturing work previously put pressure on blue-collar jobs. As a result, increasing gains will accrue to major data-rich companies and their owners and shareholders, leaving many white-collar workers to fall behind in the manner that blue-collar workers did a generation before them, further accentuating the divide between the top 1 percent and the bottom 99 percent.[70]

Proponents of the corporate power narrative have a final, broader concern with the increasing concentration of corporate power, namely, its impact on politics and the social sphere. They fear the return of a new "gilded age" in which "extreme economic concentration yields gross inequality and material suffering" and warn of the power that companies like Google, Amazon, and Facebook wield over "not just commerce, but over politics, the news, and our private information."[71] Whether it is Facebook refusing to clamp down on misinformation and disinformation that is disseminated via its platform, or Twitter using its power to provide or deny a vital channel of communication to political figures, digital companies are affecting people's lives and the functioning of democracies in profound ways. Moreover, "social media's toxicity is not a bug—it's a feature," explains Jim Balsillie, the retired co-CEO of Research In Motion and chair of the Centre for International Governance Innovation. "Behavioral scientists involved with today's platforms helped design user experiences that capitalize on negative reactions because they produce far more engagement than positive reactions."[72]

This ominous sense of Big Tech's power is just the latest instantiation of the corporate power narrative. The internet "runs through our lives the way our blood vessels run through our bodies," explains EU commissioner Vestager, who is at the forefront of the global battle to curb the power of (American) Big Tech. "The giants of the Internet have worked out how to turn those huge flows of data in their favour," and, as the power of the internet has increased, "their power to control the flow of information . . . has become power over the way our economies and societies work." Vestager concludes that we need new rules in place to "make sure our democracies, and not just a handful of big platforms, make the decisions that determine our future."[73] And whether it is new attempts to fix international tax policies at the OECD, newly launched antitrust actions against Big Tech in many countries, or battles to get Big Tech to pay for local news services when they operate in foreign markets, many governments around the world seem to agree.

Conclusion

The corporate power narrative argues that multinational corporations are the real winners from economic globalization. They have used their market power and international mobility to avoid paying their fair share of tax, weaken the power of labor, and pit countries against each other in regulatory competition. They have worked to internationalize protections they favor, such as intellectual property rights, the free flow of data, and ISDS, but have resisted the internationalization of standards they disfavor, such as those on labor and the environment. There are many losers from economic globalization, according to this narrative, but powerful multinational corporations are the clear winners.

CHAPTER 7

The Geoeconomic Narrative

For the past forty years, the Chinese Communist Party (CCP) has been playing a beautiful game. It is sophisticated yet simple. It is a competition to gain control and influence across the planet—and to achieve that outcome . . . without resorting to military engagement," explains retired US brigadier general Robert Spalding. Flying quietly below the radar like a stealth bomber, the CCP has been acquiring technology without paying for it, infiltrating Western corporations and science laboratories, and encouraging Western firms to relocate to China. This twenty-first-century "stealth war" is different in kind from the military conflicts of the twentieth century. "Instead of bombs and bullets, it's about ones and zeros and dollars and cents: economics, finance, data information, manufacturing, infrastructure, and communications."[1]

Leaders in the West have been slow to grasp this strategy, Spalding warns: "Blinded by our own greed and the dream of globalization, we've been convinced that free trade automatically unlocks the shackles of authoritarianism and paves the way for democracy. The promise of cheap labor, inexpensive goods, and soaring stock prices has been spellbinding, but by giving up our manufacturing expertise and dominance, we have given up our independence and sold out our own citizens by stripping them of work." China is not a market economy or a democratic state, and it does not play by the rules of free and fair trade. By promising short-term financial rewards, China has succeeded in co-opting Western corporations to serve its own interests. Now Western countries face their biggest challenge since World War II—how to "stop the authoritarian juggernaut, the stealth war, that is being waged against [them]."[2]

If the period of high globalization saw the ascent of "doves" and "panda huggers," recent years have seen the rise of "hawks" and "dragon slayers." According to the latter, international trade and investment is a zero-sum game in which China's gain has been America's and the West's loss. China's authoritarian regime has used its state-led model to engage in "economic aggression" against other countries. Its weapons of choice include massive subsidies to Chinese companies, forced technology transfer, intellectual property theft, and industrial espionage. After decades in which Western governments held fast to the naive belief that the integration of China into the world economy would lead to fundamental changes in its political and economic system, a major reckoning is in order. China has become a fierce strategic rival, and the economic and security stakes in the West's relationship with China are existential.

Taking Sino-American great-power rivalry as its premise, the geoeconomic narrative involves a shift in focus from absolute economic gains, which both China and the United States have unquestionably derived from their economic relationship, to relative economic gains, which help to determine the strategic position of these two great powers vis-à-vis each other. Far from celebrating economic interdependence as maximizing economic efficiency and increasing the prospect for peace, this narrative warns about security and strategic vulnerabilities caused by interdependence and calls for increased self-sufficiency, resilience, and some level of economic and technological decoupling. The battle for technological supremacy in emerging technologies, such as 5G, artificial intelligence, and quantum computing, plays a key role in this narrative because innovation promises economic gains and bolsters both defensive and offensive strategic capabilities. The narrative thus reflects a "securitization" of economic policy and an "economization" of security policy.[3]

The interplay of economics and security is not limited to the Sino-American relationship, nor is it a novel concern.[4] But the salience of the narrative with respect to trade, investment, and technology has risen dramatically in recent years, particularly in the United States where strategic competition with China represents a point of continuity between the Obama, Trump, and Biden administrations. Antony Blinken, US secretary of state, has described the relationship with China as America's "biggest geopolitical test of the 21st century." From the US perspective, "China is the only country with the economic, diplomatic, military, and technological power to seriously challenge the stable and open international system—all the rules, values, and relationships that make the world work the way we want it to."[5] For this reason, even though interstate rivalries and concerns about the economic-security nexus have broader relevance and a longer lineage, this chapter focuses primarily on current debates about China in the United States and its Western allies.

Rising Dragon, Falling Eagle

For almost a century, the United States had been the eagle soaring over the world economy. With the largest and most innovative economy in the world, America took the lead in developing international trade and investment rules, opening up markets, and supporting the global operation of its multinational companies. But as the Chinese dragon has risen, the new geoeconomic narrative started to gain prominence in the United States. Following the Cold War and the economic rise of Japan, strategist Edward Luttwak argued that competition and rivalry among countries would principally play out in the economic arena rather than the military realm—a phenomenon he described as "geoeconomics."[6] More recently, foreign policy experts Robert Blackwill and Jennifer Harris invoked the term to describe the "use of economic instruments to promote and defend national interests, and to produce beneficial geopolitical results."[7] We use the term to describe the narrative that moves great-power competition, strategic rivalry, security concerns, and ideological conflict to the center of debates about the winners and losers from economic globalization.[8]

Security interests have never been absent from the international economic order, but they were not central to its day-to-day operations during the period of high globalization in which neoliberal ideas reigned supreme. The establishment narrative took it for granted that security and globalization were mutually reinforcing. New trade and investment agreements were understood to increase economic interdependence, which in turn would promote peace and cooperation by raising the costs of conflict between countries. And while most trade and investment agreements included broadly phrased security exceptions, countries largely refrained from invoking these clauses; every country realized that normalizing the use of the exception would give carte blanche to its trading partners to cite national security as a pretext for trade restrictions.

Consequently, the ordinary rules that underpinned the day-to-day working of trade and investment treaties during the 1990s and 2000s reflected an economic mindset: rather than focusing on security, they prioritized the dismantling of trade barriers and the protection and promotion of foreign investment. Corporations restructured their supply chains in hopes of minimizing costs and maximizing profits, which created deep interdependencies across national borders. Economic efficiency was the primary goal; peace was seen as a bonus. According to Robert Lighthizer, US trade representative between 2017 and 2021, a "lemming-like desire for 'efficiency'" caused many US companies to move their manufacturing offshore, even though "offshoring creates risks that often outweigh the incremental efficiencies."[9]

Concerns about security did not take center stage in the international trade and investment regime during this period partly because the United States did not view itself as having an economic rival that was simultaneously a strategic competitor. During the Cold War, the United States and the Soviet Union were strategic competitors, but over time it became clear that the Soviet Union was no match for the United States economically. Japan emerged as an economic competitor to the United States in the 1970s and 1980s, but it was a US security ally rather than a strategic competitor. US concerns about Japan's technological rise led to protectionist responses, but America did not cast Japan as a great-power rival nor as a combined economic and military threat. After the Cold War, the United States achieved both economic and strategic predominance; lacking peer competitors in both areas, its security focus turned to the Middle East and terrorism.

By the late 2000s, however, America's perception of China's economic rise started to change. In absolute economic terms, the United States and China both gained tremendously from economic globalization, but in relative terms, China had begun to close the gap between them. This convergence is apparent in the relative share of the world's GDP contributed by each state (Figure 7.1). This changing balance of economic power was brought into sharp relief when the US economy precipitated the global financial crisis and China's economy emerged as the world's second-largest. Instead of accepting the establishment's win-win narrative, many in the United States began to wonder whether China was winning at America's expense. At the same time, China was becoming more authoritarian at home and more assertive in the South China Sea, pricking American concerns across multiple domains—economic, military, and political.

Responding to shifts in the economic and strategic landscape, President Obama announced the US "Pivot to Asia" in 2011. As US secretary of state Hillary Clinton explained: "The future of politics will be decided in Asia, not Afghanistan or Iraq, and the United States will be right at

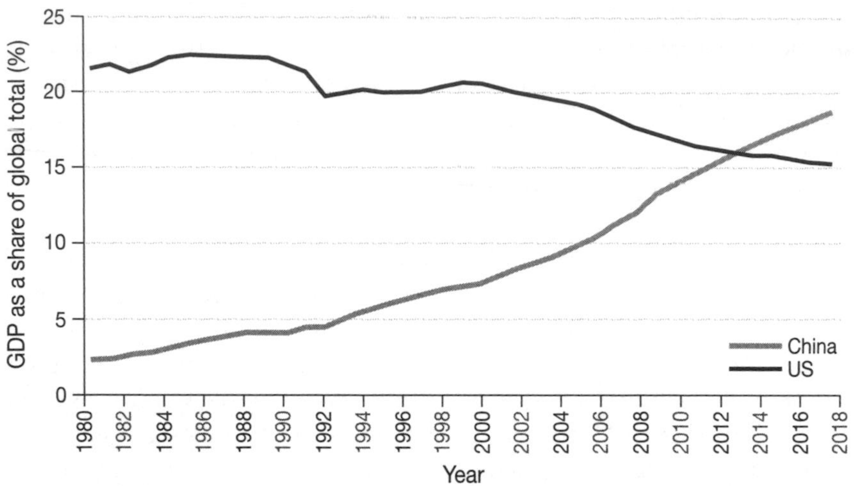

Fig. 7.1: China Has Overtaken the United States in the World Economy
Note: This graph shows the GDP of China and the United States as a share of global GDP in purchasing power parity terms.
Credit: Manas Chakravarty, "The Trade War Is a Symptom of the Waning Clout of the US," Livemint, *March 27, 2018, figure "Rising dragon, falling eagle."*

the center of the action." Clinton also announced the need for the United States to develop better "economic statecraft" policies. In this vein, Obama urged the Senate to ratify the TPP by warning that "if we don't write the rules . . . China will." US secretary of defense Ashton Carter declared, "In terms of our rebalance in the broadest sense, passing TPP is as important to me as another aircraft carrier." US commentators such as Blackwill began citing national security and geopolitical considerations as justifications for negotiating and passing the TPP, calling on the United States to play the "geoeconomics game."[10]

Trump withdrew the United States from the TPP on his first day in office, but his administration doubled down on treating China as an economic and strategic threat. In 2017, the US National Security Strategy described China as a "revisionist power" and "strategic competitor" that uses "predatory economics" to intimidate its neighbors and "steal" American intellectual property. China wants to "shape a world antithetical to U.S. values and interests," the document warned, and "seeks to displace the United States in the Indo-Pacific region, expand the reaches of its state-driven economic model, and reorder the region in its favor."[11] "Interstate strategic competition, not terrorism," had again become "the primary concern in U.S. national security," concluded the 2018 National Defense Strategy.[12] "America had hoped that economic liberalization would bring China into a greater partnership with us and with the world," explained then vice president Mike Pence, but instead "China ha[d] chosen economic aggression, which ha[d] in turn emboldened its growing military."[13]

The Biden administration accepts the geoeconomic diagnosis, though some of the remedies it prescribes differ from those of Trump's administration. Biden has described China as a "special challenge," noting that "China is playing the long game by extending its global reach, promoting its own political model, and investing in the technologies of the future." According to Jake Sullivan, Biden's national security advisor, "the signs that China is gearing up to contest America's global leadership" are "unmistakable" and "ubiquitous," and include attempts by China to shape "the world's economic rules, technology standards, and political institutions to its advantage and in its image." Some geoeconomic policies are continuous between the two administrations, such as movements toward technological decoupling. Others, such as Biden's emphasis on forging alliances with other democracies to counter China, differ: "When we join together with fellow democracies, our strength more than doubles. China can't afford to ignore more than half the global economy."[14] As Blinken sums it up: "Our relationship with China will be competitive when it should, be collaborative when it can be, and adversarial when it must be."[15]

Clash of the Economic Titans

A key element of the geoeconomic narrative is the shift in focus from absolute gains (based on the assumption of a positive-sum game) to relative gains (based on the concern that one party has gained disproportionately compared with the other or that one party's gain amounts to the other party's loss—that is, a zero-sum game). This shift from a fairly cooperative mindset to a more competitive and conflictual one comes in two varieties: one focused primarily on economic competition, and the other focused on security threats.

The focus on economic competition is supported by the increasingly widespread perception in the United States that China is winning only or partly because it is cheating. "The Chinese government is fighting a generational fight to surpass our country in economic and technological leadership. But not through legitimate innovation, not through fair and lawful competition," explains Christopher Wray, director of the US Federal Bureau of Investigation. "Instead, they've shown that they're willing to steal their way up the economic ladder at our expense. . . . We see Chinese companies stealing American intellectual property to avoid the hard slog of innovation, and then using it to compete against the very American companies they victimized—in effect, cheating twice over."[16] The US government accuses China of engaging in wholesale intellectual property "theft" through cyberespionage, piracy, and counterfeiting, "stealing" the West's innovation advantage. In addition, China uses "forced technology transfers"—requiring Western companies to hand over trade secrets and intellectual property—as a condition of access to the Chinese market. The CCP backs "national champions" through low-interest loans, subsidized utility rates, and lax environmental, health, and safety standards so that its companies can outcompete companies from other countries.[17]

Part of the problem is the lack of a level playing field, but part of it is that China and America are playing fundamentally different games. It is as though the world's two top football teams are meeting up for a match but playing different sports. The US team is like the World Cup champions; the game of football that it plays is soccer. Fast and nimble, the US players move fluidly and feature a range of individual styles and tactics. The players are not centrally coordinated. They wear shin guards but are not heavily protected. The team is quick and innovative; individual members can move the ball in many directions at great speed and with daunting skill. Counterintuitively, the Chinese team is like the Super Bowl champions; they play American football or what we call gridiron. Their plays are more centrally coordinated. The players wear full body protection, including helmets, shoulder and rib pads, and other types of protective gear. The game is not as quick or flexible. But the team has had great success in cooperating internally to move the ball down the field and overcome competitors along the way.[18]

China claims that it is deploying a legitimate variety of capitalism, just like gridiron is a legitimate variety of football.[19] Not so, say US proponents of the geoeconomic narrative. For them, the only legitimate game is soccer, and China's use of central coordination, generous support for its players, and aggressive tackling of the other side's players is cheating. US commentators claim that America permitted China to join the game of international trade on the understanding that China would conform, over time, to the free market rules and spirit of that game, and that China would become more liberal and democratic in the process.[20] That expectation has been disappointed. America and its allies now feel that they need to protect themselves by putting on helmets and additional padding; if soccer players had to play gridiron players on the same field, of course they would adapt their game and equipment.

Sports-based analogies underscore the competitive element of both the protectionist and geoeconomic narratives, but the latter often goes one step further toward adversarial conflict. Many proponents of the geoeconomic narrative do not share the establishment narrative's confidence that trade will lead to peace; instead, they highlight the importance of peace as a precondition for economic interdependence. As they see it, long periods of peace allow countries to develop strong trade and investment ties, but when the conditions for peace no longer obtain, economic interdependence becomes unsustainable as well. As countries enter into strategic competition, proponents of the geoeconomic narrative sometimes invoke metaphors from the battlefield, not just the sporting arena. China's illegal export subsidies are "weapons of job destruction" with "considerable firepower," Navarro argues, while defensive efforts to protect America's technological crown jewels "contribute to our arsenal of democracy alongside the Abrams tank, the Arleigh Burke class destroyer, and the Tomahawk missile." China's Made in China 2025 policy is a "declaration of war directed at the Western industrialized nations," argues German journalist Theo Sommer.[21]

Economic Security Is National Security

"Globalisation is not necessarily in itself a threat to national security," a report titled *Breaking the China Supply Chain* states. "However, during times of geopolitical tension, or in the face of a global pandemic or a similar challenge, dependency on foreign suppliers can become a threat to national security, particularly if a major supplier emerges as a geopolitical and/or an ideological rival." The report finds that the five countries that make up the intelligence grouping known as the Five Eyes—the United Kingdom, United States, Australia, Canada, and New Zealand—are strategically dependent on China in 831 categories of goods, and it warns of the need to break this reliance by decoupling in key sectors. "Without the capacity to produce vital goods that our militaries need, like medicine or rare-earth minerals, our nations are critically vulnerable," explains US senator Marco Rubio, a signatory to the report.[22]

According to a US Department of Defense report, competitors' trade and industrial policies, particularly China's "economic aggression," are playing a role in degrading the viability, capabilities, and capacity of the US national security innovation base. China's "domination" of the rare earth market illustrates the "dangerous interaction between Chinese economic aggression guided by its strategic industrial policies and vulnerabilities and gaps in America's manufacturing and defense industrial base." China strategically flooded the global market with rare earths at subsidized prices, which allowed it to drive out competitors and deter new market entrants, the report claimed. "When China needs to flex its soft power muscles by embargoing rare earths, it does not hesitate, as Japan learned in a 2010 maritime dispute."[23] Dependence on a foreign country—particularly a strategic rival—is dangerous.

"We cannot have national security without economic security," Trump declared in 2017.[24] The Biden administration's *Interim National Security Strategic Guidance* echoes this view: "In today's world, economic security is national security."[25] A country will not be able to defend itself abroad if it lacks economic prosperity at home, since economic heft undergirds military might. Even if a country is prosperous, reliance on foreign countries, including potential adversaries, for key defense supplies will jeopardize its ability to defend itself. Global supply chains may be efficient, but they create vulnerabilities. As Navarro explains: "We face numerous so-called 'single points of failure' where we have only one source of production—shafts for our ships, gun turrets for our tanks, space-based infrared detectors for missile defense, fabric for the lowly but increasingly high-tech tent. Our defense industrial base is also far too dependent on foreign suppliers for printed circuit boards, machine tools, and many other items critical to national security."[26]

This approach allows national security to become the exception that swallows the rule, object China and US allies alike. The international economic regime was premised on the prohibition of economic nationalism (protectionism) with exceptions for national security (protection). But if economic security is national security, how can one draw the line between protection, which is allowed, and protectionism, which is prohibited? If national security is defined to mean that a country must be economically prosperous and self-sufficient, including at surge capacity during wartime, the concept can be used to justify protective/protectionist measures across an enormous range of industries, from steel manufacturing to tent making. The Trump administration embraced this approach, protecting strategic industries even where that meant placing tariffs on aluminum imports from Canada. Others call for a more targeted approach on the basis that broadly restricting the flow of goods and people could undermine America's innovation advantage and, with it, the country's prosperity and security.[27]

Weaponized Interdependence

Concerns about the vulnerabilities associated with interdependence have been heightened by the increased connectivity resulting from globalization. Networks of interdependence, such as supply chains or telecommunications infrastructure, can be used by countries that control important nodes to engage in both the authorized and unauthorized collection of data to disrupt flows for strategic reasons, or even to cut off adversaries completely from access to the network. The upshot is a new or renewed focus on "weaponized interdependence," in the language of political scientists Henry Farrell and Abraham Newman, or "connectivity wars," in political scientist Mark Leonard's terminology.[28] The growing geostrategic rivalry between the United States and China is unfolding in a world of deep economic integration and growing digital connectivity. During the Cold War, little economic interaction took place between the strategic rivals, the United States and the Soviet Union.[29] By contrast, the economies of China and the United States have become deeply integrated with each other (Figure 7.2), as well as with those of other countries. The rising geopolitical tensions are bringing the strategic opportunities and risks associated with economic and digital interdependence into sharp relief. "It is widely believed that interdependence promotes cooperation," notes Thomas Wright of the Brookings Institution, referring to the assumptions underlying the establishment narrative, "but in the coming decade it is more likely to be perceived as a source of vulnerability and strategic competition."[30]

The risk of the weaponization of connectivity is greatest when interdependence is asymmetric, which enables the party in the stronger position to exert pressure on the party in the weaker position. According to Leonard: "Interdependence, once heralded as a barrier to conflict, has turned into a currency of power, as countries try to exploit the asymmetries in their relations. Many have understood that the trick is to make

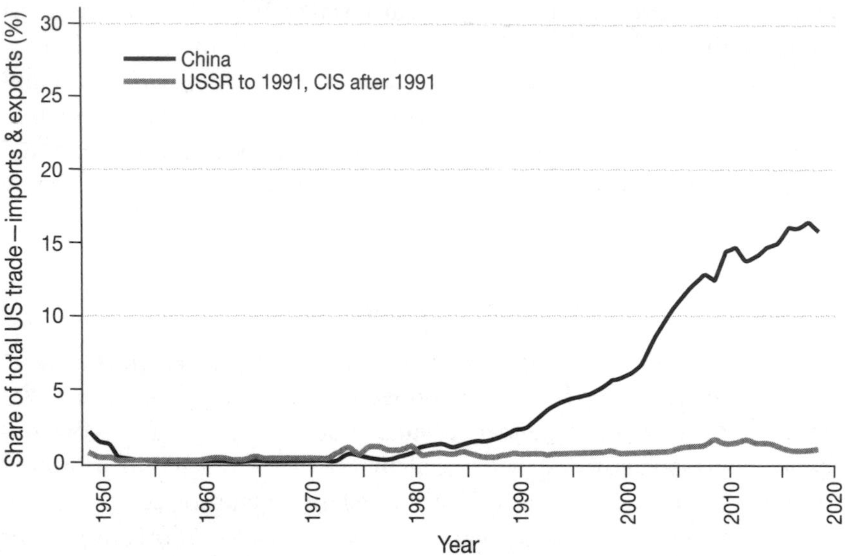

Fig. 7.2: The United States and China Are Economically Interdependent; the United States and the Soviet Union Never Were

Note: This graph shows the shares of US trade with China (in black) and the Soviet Union (until 1991) and the Commonwealth of Independent States (after 1991) (in gray), as a percentage of total US imports and exports, since 1950.

Credit: Reformatted from Andrew Batson, "The Difference between the New and Old Cold Wars," Andrew Batson's Blog, *May 12, 2019, figure "US trade with China is much larger than it ever was with the USSR."*

your competitors more dependent on you than you are on them—and then use that dependency to manipulate their behaviour."[31] Countries with power over central nodes in international networks through which money, information, and goods flow can exercise control over those nodes to impose costs on others. So far, the United States is the country that has most successfully exploited its position of dominance in international networks, such as the Society for Worldwide Interbank Financial Telecommunication (SWIFT) payment system, to sanction other governments and to ensure that foreign companies comply with its laws far beyond its borders; however, the focus of the geoeconomic narrative in the United States is on China's actual or potential weaponization of connectivity.

For example, the United States is concerned that by funding and building infrastructure projects through the Belt and Road Initiative, China is developing networks of interdependence that it may be able to exploit for political, economic, and military goals in the future. For European observers, China's investments in eastern and southern European countries have been a particular cause of concern. The European Union has allowed "Beijing to use its billions to drive a wedge" between its members, warns Sommer.[32] For example, after European lenders urged Greece to privatize state assets in order to pay down its crushing debt, the Chinese shipping conglomerate Cosco leased half of the port of Piraeus—the first European port after ships exit the Suez Canal. The company is now building a railway line from the port to the Hungarian capital, Budapest, that will allow it to outcompete northern European ports on shipments from Asia to Europe. These investments have bought China not only economic clout but also political influence, proponents of this narrative say. For instance, in 2016, Greece and Hungary vetoed an EU resolution that would have condemned Beijing's policy of expansion in the South China Sea.[33]

Western geoeconomic concerns about connectivity reach their peak regarding China's Digital Silk Road. China's regulatory approach to the internet differs starkly from the Western model in that it features much greater government surveillance, control, and censorship. Proponents of the geoeconomic narrative claim that China is using its internet companies and its investment in digital infrastructure along the Belt and Road to export "digital authoritarianism."[34] As Sommer warns, the "establishment of the Chinese techno-police state with the help of digital image recognition, improved data analytics, and artificial intelligence is not just an inner-Chinese development, it also opens up a new front line of geopolitical rivalry."[35] This stratagem will not only enable other authoritarian regimes to crack down on dissent domestically but also fashion the digital highways through which data can be siphoned back to Beijing for use in espionage and the development of artificial intelligence. These concerns underlie one of the most important current geoeconomic battlegrounds: the rollout of 5G technology.

My Way or the Huawei

In 2018, agents of the Australian Signals Directorate, the country's foreign signals intelligence agency, engaged in a digital war game. "We asked ourselves, if we had the powers akin to the 2017 Chinese Intelligence Law to direct a company which supplies 5G equipment to telco networks, what could we do with that and could anyone stop us?" explains Simeon

Gilding, one of Australia's former top cybersecurity officials. "We concluded that we could be awesome, no one would know and, if they did, we could plausibly deny our activities, safe in the knowledge that it would be too late to reverse billions of dollars' worth of investment. And, ironically, our targets would be paying to build a platform for our own signals intelligence and offensive cyber operations." This assessment became a turning point. A few months later, the Australian government invoked national security in effectively blocking Huawei, a leading Chinese telecommunications company, from taking part in the country's 5G rollout. As Gilding stated, "The fundamental issue is one of trust between nations in cyberspace," and the CCP had "destroyed that trust through its scaled and indiscriminate hacking of foreign networks and its determination to direct and control Chinese tech companies." Allowing Huawei to build the country's 5G network would have been like "paying a fox to babysit your chickens."[36]

Numerous countries now view 5G technology as the backbone of their country's critical infrastructure, providing the arteries through which everything in society will be connected, from the power grid to the water supply. According to the economic mindset that underlies the establishment narrative, if a foreign company can produce high-quality 5G networks for a low price, using that product constitutes a great way to maximize economic gains. Few doubt that Huawei fits that description, even in the United States. As the *New York Times* reported in 2018, "Huawei is essential for many wireless carriers that serve sprawling, sparsely populated regions because its gear for transmitting cell signals often costs far less than other options."[37] Prohibiting the use of Huawei equipment would make the expansion of wireless networks into many parts of rural America prohibitively expensive and deprive farmers and rural communities of access to vital technology, a move that looks deeply problematic from the establishment perspective. The security mindset underlying the geoeconomic narrative, however, sees giving control over critical infrastructure to a foreign company, particularly one that might be subject to the power of an authoritarian regime such as the CCP, as an unacceptable security risk.

Allowing Huawei to build 5G networks in your country today is "like allowing the KGB to build its telephone network during the cold war," remarked Tom Cotton, a US senator.[38] America knows the quality and quantity of information it gained from its control over US information technology companies, a point made clear to the world after Edward

Snowden, a former US National Security Agency contractor, leaked a trove of documents in 2013. Under the PRISM program, the US government enjoyed broad legal authority to compel technology companies to release records and information regarding non-US individuals. And the United States utilized this to its advantage. As former US National Security Agency director Michael Hayden declared: "This is a home game for us. . . . Why would we not turn the most powerful telecommunications and computing management structure on the planet to our use?"[39] But, of course, America is a democracy with checks and balances that can be trusted to rein in abuses, proponents of this narrative reason. Not so with China.

Worried that China might exercise similar or more intrusive controls over its information technology companies, the US government has launched an all-out assault on Huawei. In addition to banning Huawei from supplying equipment for its own 5G rollout, the United States has engaged in a campaign to convince its allies that they should also exclude Huawei from their 5G networks and has placed Huawei on the export ban list, depriving it of access to US-made semiconductors. When these restrictions proved ineffective, as Huawei shifted its demand to Taiwanese and South Korean producers, the US government weaponized its control over the semiconductor supply chain by banning any company using US software, intellectual property, or capital equipment (including the large Taiwanese and South Korean producers) from selling semiconductors to Huawei. But not everyone shared America's risk assessment. During one closed-door session, senior representatives from European telecom operators reportedly pressed a US official for hard evidence that Huawei presented a security risk. "Where is the smoking gun?" one executive demanded. "If the gun is smoking, you've already been shot," the US official replied, adding, "I don't know why you're lining up in front of a loaded weapon." The implication was that company-specific evidence of past wrongdoing was not required; the strategic risk associated with 5G and the company's country of origin was so great that the potential risk sufficed.[40]

"Chinese technology giants are not purely private actors, but instead function as at least de facto tools of the Chinese Communist Party when it matters most," is how Christopher Ashley Ford, US assistant secretary of state for international security and non-proliferation, describes the situation. These companies are "instruments of China's geopolitical strategy" and "when push comes to shove with the nominally private Chinese technology firms—that is, when Chinese Communist Party authorities really

The effect of stricter foreign investment revi
States and Europe, coupled with the more gen
war and stricter capital controls in China, has
nese investment in the United States and a de
Europe.[53] But clamping down on transacting i
effect of increasing China's attempts at making (
on indigenous innovation and self-reliance) and
nage), some warn. For instance, German intellig
that an uptick in Chinese acquisitions of German
a sharp decline in Chinese cyberespionage; as sc
plain: "As if with the flip of a switch, China mov
nology to buying it. But as legitimate avenues to
close, Beijing will flip the switch back."[54] In turn,
provoke further US actions to stifle rising Chinese
pions and spur its own industrial policy and investı
development.

Geoeconomic Competition and Third Co

To many countries, watching the downward spiral of
lationship is like watching their parents fight. These
their parents to get divorced, but if a divorce become
want an amicable shared-custody arrangement to be ag
vent their having to pick sides. "The fundamental prob
US and China is a mutual lack of strategic trust," note
Lee Hsien Loong of Singapore, but there is "no strate
about a US-China face-off." Instead, the two countries n
gether to update the global system rather than upend it and
must understand the other's point of view, and reconci
interests."[55]

If most countries feel like the kids, the European Union
only other adult in the room, meaning the only other great
resisted the rising geoeconomic narrative in the United
because it is so committed to the win-win establishment na
global trade and the benefits of multilateralism. It is also
ally and institutionally poorly set up to deal with the fusion
and economics since it was premised on the "commercial
underlying the establishment narrative. While European go
have centralized most trade and investment policy at the Euro

Endorsing the establishment narrative, Cha
Germany warns against seeing China as an
because it is economically successful"; she cauti
be "like closing your eyes to what others are able
hawkish. As Reinhard Bütikofer, a member of
and China hawk (by European standards) has
to partner with China where possible, but it wo
you can be systemic rivals on Monday and th
for the rest of the week as if you were not. .
naive 'win-win' rhetoric that oftentimes allow
Still others call for Europe to develop "strategi
logical sovereignty" to protect against both
In its New EU-US Agenda for Global Cha
tion, the European Commission declared, "As
and market economies, the EU and the US a
lenge presented by China's growing internat
we do not always agree on the best way to add
approaches broke into the open when the Eu
Comprehensive Agreement on Investment ju
inaugurated. European officials defended the
cremental strategy to open up China's marke
human rights record, but some observers saw
the economic rewards of pursuing a less co
China than the United States. Few doubted
vided West that was created by the deal was

Conclusion

The geoeconomic narrative draws attention
which China has closed the gap with the Uni
strategic and security concerns about interde
stead of assessing gains through an econom
assumption that all countries can benefit fr
this narrative focuses on great-power rivalry
threats, and technological competition.

CHAPTER 8

The Global Threats Narratives

On December 31, 2019, "the morning sky above Mallacoota turned black as coal."[1] Instead of celebrating New Year's Eve, 4,000 tourists and locals huddled on the beach and jetty as fire encircled the Australian coastal hamlet, cutting off all roads to the outside world. "It's mayhem out there, it's Armageddon," one person exclaimed.[2] "It was like we were in hell," said another. "We were all covered in ash."[3] To shelter from the flames, emergency officers instructed people to walk into the waves. It was just one among hundreds of out-of-control fires in Australia's worst fire season ever.

On the same day, China sent a notice to the World Health Organization (WHO) about a previously unknown form of pneumonia that had infected patients in Wuhan. Local doctors who had seen the lung scans of affected patients sent worried messages to their families and colleagues, warning them to protect themselves, as it looked like another highly contagious respiratory virus had emerged.[4] Although local authorities initially sought to silence those who expressed concerns, within weeks the government had locked down tens of millions of people in an unprecedented move to prevent the epidemic's spread.

What the world witnessed in Mallacoota and Wuhan were local manifestations of global threats. At first, the world watched the outbreak of the novel coronavirus as though it were a local Chinese health crisis. Within months, however, the coronavirus had turned into a global pandemic, leading governments across the world to shut their borders and lock down their populations, causing a Depression-level collapse in economic activity. Meanwhile, the effects of climate change were encroaching on humanity from all sides in the form of melting permafrost in Siberia and Alaska, scorching summers from India to France, devastating flooding in China and Bangladesh, and torrential downpours from the United Kingdom to the Philippines.

The increasing alarm about climate change and the heightened sense of vulnerability created by the coronavirus pandemic have fueled narratives that cast economic globalization as a source and accelerator of global threats. Some focus on how global connectivity increases the risk of viral and economic contagion. Others warn that the global diffusion of Western patterns of production and consumption is endangering both people and the planet. As supply chains failed and carbon emissions soared, many have called for greater resilience and sustainability. In stark contrast to the win-win picture of globalization painted by the establishment narrative, proponents of these narratives argue that we are all bound to lose if we do not change our economic system in fundamental ways.

Narratives about global threats urge us to refocus our attention from "national security" to what Anne-Marie Slaughter, CEO of the think tank New America, calls "global security."[5] Climate change knows no borders. Viruses do not discriminate based on nationality. In the face of "catastrophic global risks that menace our future," the Commission for the Human Future—an Australian group dedicated to developing solutions to large scale, interconnected global threats—calls on "the nations and peoples of the Earth to come together, as a matter of urgency, to prepare a plan for humanity to survive and thrive."[6] We must "redouble our efforts to build more inclusive and sustainable economies and societies that are more resilient in the face of pandemics, climate change and other global challenges," urges the UN secretary general, António Guterres.[7]

Resilience Narratives

The speed with which the coronavirus spread across the globe caught almost everyone by surprise. The highly infectious virus hitched a ride with the millions of air travelers who weave the webs of global commerce and tourism. The lockdowns that followed in its wake produced economic shocks that cascaded through global supply chains, spreading pain far and wide through the arteries of the global economy. "If ever we needed reminding that we live in an interconnected world, the novel coronavirus has brought that home," observed the UN high commissioners for human rights and refugees.[8]

The health crises and supply chain shocks caused by the coronavirus propelled narratives about resilience to the center of discussions about economic globalization. The problem, explains business professor Roger Martin, is that we have been trained to think of the economy as a well-oiled machine that we should fine-tune and optimize for efficiency. But our economies are more like vast gardens with many interconnected elements that give rise to unpredictable outcomes. We need to carefully tend and cultivate such complex ecologies—monitoring, recalibrating, and adapting to changes where necessary—if we want our gardens to remain healthy and productive over time. This also means overcoming our fixation with economic efficiency. "Rather than striving singularly for ever more efficiency" based on the mental model of a perfectible machine, explains Martin, we need to adopt ecological metaphors and "strive for balance between efficiency and a second feature: resilience."[9]

Resilience is generally understood to describe the capacity of a system to absorb a shock or stressor while persisting or adapting without being incapacitated. According to the United Nations International Strategy for Disaster Reduction, it is the "ability of a system, community or society exposed to hazards to resist, absorb, accommodate to and recover from the effects of a hazard in a timely and efficient manner."[10] For many governments and observers, the coronavirus pandemic showed that our systems were not resilient in the face of a large shock. As countries found that their foreign suppliers of personal protective equipment were either cut off or unable to keep up with skyrocketing demand, they began to rethink the relative merits of self-reliance and economic interdependence. As the centrality of China's manufacturing juggernaut to the world economy became clear, governments began to emphasize the value of diversification over concentration. And as "just-in-time" approaches to inventory management became "absolutely-too-late" for production, firms were forced to reappraise the virtues of slack and redundancy.

Connectivity and Contagion

The establishment narrative celebrates the greater connectivity across countries that is a defining feature of globalization. Global supply chains allow a wide range of products to be produced cost-effectively, with different countries playing to their comparative advantage. Connectivity promotes specialization and exchange, economies of scale, and efficiency. It allows for sharing and coordination across borders to the benefit of most countries and people, creating broad networks of interdependence. The global flow of people has heightened cross-cultural communication, fostering innovation and exchange.

But connectivity also comes with risks. Globalization is a "double-edged sword that can be a force for progress as well as a source of great harm," explain globalization scholars Ian Goldin and Mike Mariathasan.[11] According to an OECD report on emerging risks in the twenty-first century, "connectedness multiplies the channels through which accidents, diseases, or malevolent actions can propagate."[12] As professor of engineering systems Yossi Sheffi argues in *The Power of Resilience:* "The growing interconnectedness of the global economy makes it increasingly prone to contagion. Contagious events, including medical and financial problems, can spread via human networks that often strongly correlate with supply chain networks" producing global crises that deliver near-simultaneous blows to multiple countries and multiple industries.[13]

The global flow of people represents a key vector through which infections spread across borders. "Pandemics are among our gravest security challenges in the twenty-first century precisely because the world has become an interlocking set of networks connected by a perilously small number of major hubs," warns Slaughter. "The great strength of the system for spreading knowledge, economic growth, and positive innovation becomes, in the face of communicable diseases, its greatest weakness."[14] The coronavirus pandemic has brought this double-edged character of global connectivity into sharp relief: while it allowed the disease to propagate at unprecedented speed, global networks also played a central role in allowing scientists to mount an effective response. International scientific exchange facilitated the sharing of information about treatment options and allowed the development and production of vaccines in record time.

Connectivity has changed radically in the last century and even in the last few decades. Prior to the 2019 coronavirus outbreak, Microsoft founder and philanthropist Bill Gates funded research on how a disease such as the Spanish flu of 1918 would spread in today's highly interconnected world. "Within 60 days it's basically in all urban centers around the entire globe," he notes. "That didn't happen with the Spanish flu."[15] In 2018, people took 4.2 billion flights compared to 310 million in 1970.[16] This connectivity means that "an outbreak can travel from a remote village to any major city in the world in less than 36 hours."[17] "We've created, in terms of spread, the most dangerous environment that we've ever had in the history of mankind," Gates concluded.[18]

Globalization plays a key role in explaining how viruses spread and why no country is safe until every country is safe. "The virus is spreading like wildfire, and is likely to move swiftly into the global south, where health systems face constraints, people are more vulnerable, and millions live in densely populated slums or crowded settlements for refugees and internally displaced persons," explained the UN secretary general early in the coronavirus pandemic. "Fuelled by such conditions, the virus could devastate the developing world and then re-emerge where it was previously suppressed." Ending the pandemic everywhere is thus "both a moral imperative and a matter of enlightened self-interest" because, in our interconnected world, "we are only as strong as the weakest health systems."[19] The emergence of more contagious and potentially vaccine-resistant variants has underscored the reality that humanity can only overcome the virus collectively.

The recognition that the coronavirus pandemic was a global problem and would ultimately require a global solution did not stop governments from focusing first and foremost on how they could protect their own populations and safeguard their own countries' economic fortunes. Politicians all over the world, from ardent advocates of globalization to long-time skeptics of international integration, had to confront the question of how to reconcile the reality of economic globalization with the need to make their economies and societies more resilient. The resulting resilience narratives emphasize the values of self-reliance over interdependence, of diversification over concentration, and of redundancy over efficiency, or advocate, at a minimum, a better balance between these opposing goals.

Interdependence versus Self-Reliance

When the coronavirus pandemic hit, many countries found that they did not have enough masks and ventilators. Worse still, many of them had largely outsourced the production of these essential medical items to low-cost manufacturers in other countries, including China, Malaysia, and India, leaving them unable to quickly scale up production. From the establishment narrative's perspective, it was efficient to leave manufacturing to countries that were able to produce high-quality items at low cost. But when those international supply lines froze up—either because of excessive demand, because the producing countries imposed export bans on medical supplies, or because suppliers were impacted by coronavirus shutdowns—importing countries found themselves without adequate medical supplies and without the capacity to manufacture them domestically.[20]

"This crisis teaches us that on some goods, materials, the strategic character imposes having a European sovereignty, produce more on the national territory to reduce our dependence and equip us over the long run," said French president Emmanuel Macron while announcing an increase in domestic production of masks and respirators during the crisis. "The world has changed over the past few weeks," Macron said. "The past choices were built on a certainty that we could import these masks very easily. . . . [But] our priority today is to produce more in France and to produce more in Europe."[21] Likewise, German chancellor Angela Merkel explained that an important lesson to learn from the pandemic was that when it came to personal protective equipment, "we need a certain amount of sovereignty or at least a pillar of domestic production here."[22]

Across the Atlantic in Canada, the premier of Ontario, Doug Ford, announced an initiative to partner with the private sector to develop medical items after suffering international supply failures. "As long as I am Premier," he promised, "I will never, ever let this happen again to the people of our province or our country."[23] As David McKay, chief executive of Royal Bank of Canada, explained: "We've been able to take for granted the free flow of critical supplies, from medical equipment and drugs to food and agriculture products. That may not be so true in the next normal. Our governments, leading enterprises and academic institutions need to determine how to best develop and protect more resilient Canadian supply chains" even while recognizing that a "more self-reliant Canada could become a more expensive Canada."[24]

The resilience narrative differs from the geoeconomic narrative in that it does not focus attention on the dangers of interdependence only with a potentially hostile adversary that might intentionally weaponize that interdependence. The coronavirus crisis gave rise to a much more general concern about being reliant upon others—both friends and foes—who may fail to supply, for selfish or malicious reasons or through no fault of their own. The resilience narrative is not motivated by the danger caused by a rival so much as by the imperative for countries to be able to take care of themselves. In light of their experiences during the pandemic, many governments drew the same conclusion as President Trump, namely, that "we should never be reliant on a foreign country for the means of our own survival."[25] Those who had been arguing for increased self-reliance all along felt vindicated by the pandemic. "In crises like this, we have no allies," Peter Navarro declared.[26]

Concentration versus Diversification

Whereas some reacted to the coronavirus by calling for greater self-reliance, others drew attention to the dangers of concentration and the need for more diversification. In this view, only a well-diversified supply is a resilient supply, since a highly concentrated domestic supplier is just as vulnerable to shocks as a highly concentrated foreign supplier—a point that was illustrated by the temporary failure of domestic meat supply chains as a result of coronavirus outbreaks in meatpacking plants in several countries. Any failure of a single, highly connected central node can have outsized effects within a network, and any individual actor is vulnerable when it is overexposed to the fortunes of a single buyer or seller. Diversification minimizes these risks.

At a network level, concerns about concentration focus on the role that heavily connected central nodes can play in propagating risks throughout the network. In the global financial crisis, the failure of key nodes in the US economy, such as Lehman Brothers, set off a cascade of knock-on effects. The idea that certain companies or banks are "too big to fail" captures the concern that some nodes are so central and highly connected that their failure would have a large-scale effect on the wider network. Several global cities—including New York and London—play a similar role as central nodes in the world economy.[27] The fact that China had become the manufacturing workshop of the world meant that the initial lockdowns following the coronavirus outbreak had a significant impact on global supply chains. As a *New York Times* headline put it: "China Stopped Its Economy to Tackle Coronavirus. Now the World Suffers."[28]

According to economists Richard Baldwin and Beatrice Weder di Mauro, the coronavirus was as contagious economically as it was medically. In the early days of the crisis, the coronavirus spread from China to South Korea and Japan, two other highly connected economies that form part of the manufacturing hub of Asia. By early March 2020, the United States, China, Japan, Germany, Britain, France, and Italy were among the ten countries most affected by the disease. These countries account for the majority of world supply and demand, as well as of manufacturing and manufacturing exports. A seizure of supply in these countries produced a "supply-chain contagion" that affected virtually all countries: when these central "economies sneeze, the rest of the world will catch a cold."[29]

The coronavirus pandemic not only revealed the danger of overreliance on specific suppliers in the goods sector but also highlighted the risks of being highly dependent on a single source of demand in the service sector. For instance, when Australia decided to halt flights from China after the coronavirus broke out, it prevented tens of thousands of Chinese students from arriving to study. This decision brought into focus the Australian higher education sector's heavy reliance on Chinese students for generating income, with Chinese student fees making up over 70 percent of foreign student fees and over 20 percent of the total budgets of some Australian universities. The coronavirus crisis led to calls for greater diversification in the university sector and beyond.[30] If there is one lesson that people are drawing from the coronavirus pandemic, says Jörg Wuttke, president of the EU Chamber of Commerce in China, it is that "single source is out and diversification is in."[31]

Efficiency versus Redundancy

Global supply chains are highly efficient because they ensure that goods and components are made in the countries where they can be produced most economically. Likewise, just-in-time manufacturing processes—where component parts are delivered just before products are assembled, meaning that manufacturers do not need to rely on large stocks of inventory—have proven to be cheap and efficient. But what is economically efficient may create fragility that is disastrous in the face of a shock. In order to be able to absorb shocks and permit surges in capacity when required, resilience narratives focus on the importance of maintaining slack and including redundancies in a system. "Building resilience means building buffers," explains Mark Carney, former governor of the Bank of England.[32]

Lean supply chains have been a hallmark of globalized manufacturing, particularly in the auto industry. Toyota spearheaded an approach to production that reduced delay, overlap, and waste to an absolute minimum. This "Toyota Way" led to enormous efficiency and financial gains and came to be embodied in the idea of lean management that was globalized through MBA programs.[33] But the leanness of these supply chains proved to be an acute vulnerability during the coronavirus crisis. The average automobile contains about 30,000 parts, with one analysis finding that Toyota relied on 2,192 distinct firms (both direct and indirect suppliers) in its production process.[34] When China shut down its factories, global supply chains were thrown into disarray, with carmakers from Italy to America and South Korea to Japan sitting idle awaiting parts from China.[35]

ovides wide-open spaces
ological economics posits
e produce must be within
nd, indeed, our species—
ed with nature, whether we
n director Inger Andersen.
e care of ourselves."[47]

aceship Earth

) showed a tiny and fragile
e on it made possible by a
r Mitchell explained, "In
sciousness, a people orien-
of the world, and a compul-
"Spaceship Earth" together,
on, along with that of all
usly in the balance. Recog-
e planet and the increasing
nability narrative.
ibald MacLeish recounted:
en the Earth . . . whole and
lonely, floating planet, that
his sense of the fragility of
rlies the force of the Space-
e Economics of the Coming
linary philosopher Kenneth
nomy of apparently unlim-
nomy in which the earth ap-
ited reservoirs of anything,
which, therefore, man must
."[51]

he frequent use of words like
pecies and *planet* by propo-
d to be reacting as we would
g towards Earth," says Jem
hip.[52] "We forget that we are
na Shiva, who is an environ-
r. "There is no planet B. This
ies."[53]

ta
" he
l live
years
s de-
stra-
et."[41]
digs
of its
Aus-
l and
mine
t vul-

n also
re not
rative,
r also
rth."[42]
atten-
eemed
world
l failed
ability
lure.[43]
at have
sely the
has fu-
rty, but
l us into
r goods
world,
easingly
hockey
keting
te
cal
s a
osph

undancy appear
ls struggled to co
relentless quest fo
etched, fragile, and
itals had previously
t in the decade be-
res forced hospitals
5 percent capacity.
sult is little, if any,
ins Anita Charles-
[36] "Any disaster
dea of resilience—a
concludes commen-
agile state."[37]
ilience could be achieved
rdependence and greater
cy (such as government-
t in the coronavirus crisis,
ents to stockpile rather than
or a dearth of domestic man-
oning global supply chains" by
he Council on Foreign Relations,
focus on making them more re-
ventory might make global manu-
ent, but these redundancies will in-
enefiting countries, companies, and

of resilience that is commonly found in
s in *Anti-Fragile*: "Layers of redundancy
t property of natural systems. We humans
are parts, and extra capacity in many, many
sign tends to be spare and inversely redun-
private actors in a market are unlikely to pro-
dancy, as this is economically less efficient for
rofit margins can entail razor-thin margins for
. "Redundancy is ambiguous because it seems like
nusual happens. Except that something unusual
What seems efficient today may be neither resilient
r time.

Instead of assuming that the natural world p
from which people can take as they please, ec
that the resources we consume and the waste w
natural boundaries if we want our systems—a
to be sustainable. "We are intimately interconnec
like it or not," says UN Environmental Progran
"If we don't take care of nature, we can't tak

Interdependent and Precarious: Sp

The iconic 1968 image of Earthrise (Figure 8.2
planet in the vast emptiness of space, with lif
thin layer of atmosphere. As astronaut Edga
outer space, you develop an instant global con
tation, an intense dissatisfaction with the state o
sion to do something about it."[48] We are all on
and the continued existence of our civilizati
living creatures on our planet, hangs precario
nizing the interconnectedness of people and th
precariousness of both is central to the susta

Reacting to the Earthrise image, poet Arch
"For the first time in all of time, men have se
round and beautiful and small . . . that little,
tiny raft in the enormous, empty night."[49] T
life and the need to preserve our life raft und
ship Earth metaphor.[50] In his 1966 essay "Th
Spaceship Earth," economist and interdiscip
Boulding compared the open "cowboy" eco
ited resources with a closed "spaceman" econ
pears as "a single spaceship, without unlim
either for extraction or for pollution, and in
find his place in a cyclical ecological system

This Spaceship Earth imagery results in t
we, humanity, and *civilization* as well as *s*
nents of the sustainability narrative. "We nee
if an Armageddon-sized meteor was hurtlin
Bendell, a professor of sustainability leaders
one humanity on one planet," writes Vanda
mental activist and anti-globalization schola
is where we will live, or go extinct as a spec

Fig. 8.2: Earthrise
Note: This photo was taken by astronauts Commander Frank Borman, Command Module Pilot Jim Lovell, and Lunar Module Pilot William Anders during the first manned mission to the moon. The image depicts the earth and the moon from their spacecraft.
Credit: NASA.

A Global Emergency

"Our house is on fire," environmental activist Greta Thunberg warned when she spoke about climate change at the World Economic Forum. "I'm here to say, our house is on fire." Thunberg sought to awaken her audience to a crisis—a sense that something momentous and terrible is happening that requires immediate action. No more time for looking away and carrying on with business as usual. No more time for talking about small, clever market solutions to specific, isolated problems. Time for action, and bold action at that. In Thunberg's words: "I want you to panic. I want you to feel the fear I feel every day. And then I want you to act. I want you to act as you would in a crisis. I want you to act as if our house is on fire. Because it is."[54]

The past five years have been the hottest recorded in the history of the planet.[55] Icebergs are melting; sea levels are rising. Hurricanes are becoming more ferocious, wildfires more devastating. Since the last ice age 12,000 years ago, the climate has been stable enough for human civilization to flourish in an epoch known as the Holocene. But our addiction to fossil-fuel-powered economic growth, unsustainable consumption, and reckless disregard for the environment have had such a profound effect on the planet that we have now entered a new ecological age, the Anthropocene, in which human activity has been the dominant influence on the climate and environment.[56]

The invocation of the notion of an Anthropocene reflects a more radical take on the sustainability narrative. In the view of some proponents of the Anthropocene language, the notion of sustainability has been co-opted by status quo powers and has become an empty formula, a perpetually unfulfilled promise. From the 1980s onward, sustainability became the mantra of many international organizations, governments, and businesses that suggested it was possible to have it all—a win-win outcome of sustainable, inclusive, and green growth. Invocation of the Anthropocene concept signals a rejection of this rhetoric of reassurance—a move from unfulfilled hope to merciless diagnosis, from a term that has been co-opted by the powers that be to a concept that challenges them.[57]

The Anthropocene terminology also reflects a growing sense of alarm and of the need to communicate the severity of the crisis. Wallace-Wells's book *The Uninhabitable Earth* is a prime example. "It is worse, much worse, than you think," Wallace-Wells begins. The book abounds in metaphors and arresting language. The climate system that raised us "is now, like a parent, dead." Human actions have turned the planet into an "angry beast" and a "war machine." Climate change is more dramatic than the "Cold War prospect of mutually assured destruction." We "shiver in fear" at the "unending menace" even though we have managed only to process the threat in part.[58]

Narratives about climate change take as their starting point the world's skyrocketing levels of carbon emissions and the projected temperature rises and disastrous consequences that are likely to follow. According to the activist organization Extinction Rebellion: "We are facing an unprecedented global emergency. . . . We face floods, wildfires, extreme weather, crop failure, mass displacement and the breakdown of society. The time for denial is over. It is time to act."[59] Similarly, Klein argues that climate change constitutes a "clear and present danger to civilization": our economic system and our planetary system are now at "war"; we are embroiled in a "battle between capitalism and the planet."[60]

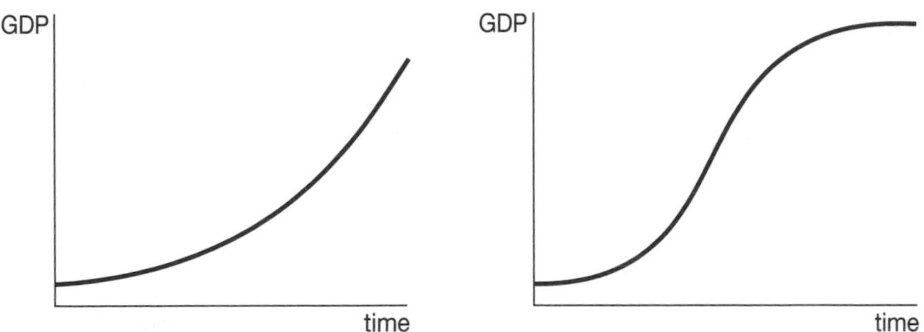

Fig. 8.3: From Exponential Economic Growth to a Steady-State Economy
Note: The exponential growth curve (left) and the S growth curve (right). Unlike the constant upward shape of the L curve, the S curve reflects the idea that economic growth should occur for a period but should then level off.
Credit: Reformatted from Kate Raworth, Doughnut Economics: Seven Ways to Think Like a 21st-Century Economist *(White River Junction, VT: Chelsea Green Publishing, 2017), 210 and 214. Used by permission of Chelsea Green Publishing and Penguin Random House, UK.*

Sustainable Orbits and Changing Goals

Another metaphor employed by the sustainability narrative is the notion of a sustainable orbit that we should follow, instead of our ever-expanding, onward-and-upward model of economic growth. This idea of circularity is also reflected in economist Kate Raworth's model of "doughnut economics," which expresses the goal of progressing to a "steady-state" economy that maintains economic activity at an ecologically sustainable equilibrium.[61] "Our economies have come to expect, demand and depend upon growth never ending," explains Raworth. In nature, however, nothing grows forever. Nature's growth curve is S-shaped: growth happens for a period and then flattens out (Figure 8.3). Anything that tries to grow forever will end up destroying itself or the system on which it depends, like a cancer. The same is true for economies: we should expect them to grow for a period but then flatten out, lest we destroy the planetary resources on which our economies are based.[62]

"Today we have economies that need to grow, whether or not they make us thrive," Raworth notes. "What we need are economies that make us thrive, whether or not they grow."[63] This small switch in word order reflects a big switch in mindset. It requires us to reformulate the aim of our economies so as to answer the question of how we can survive and thrive within the limits of our planet. According to environmental health professor Anthony McMichael: "Humankind is now using up Earth's capacity to supply, regenerate, restore, and absorb our effluent much faster than the planet can keep up with. To an increasing extent we are living off nature's capital rather than doing as all other species must do—live off nature's dividends."[64] The problem, health equity professor Sharon Friel indicates, is that our economy's addiction to growth has created a "consumptagenic system" that fuels unhealthy, inequitable, and environmentally destructive production and consumption.[65] Raworth concludes that we need to move from economies that are "degenerative, divisive and addicted to growth" to ones that are "regenerative, distributive and able to thrive beyond growth."[66]

Raworth's doughnut metaphor is designed to illustrate "humanity's 21st century challenge," which is to meet the needs of all within the means of the planet (Figure 8.4). Specifically, we must ensure that no one falls short on life's essentials, while remaining within the limits of Earth's life-supporting systems, on which we fundamentally depend.[67] Raworth argues that humans have various basic needs—food and health, for example—that we can either fail to meet (leaving us in the empty space in the hole in her metaphorical doughnut) or pursue recklessly (in which case we overshoot into the empty space outside the doughnut by exceeding our planetary boundaries). In between is the "sweet spot"—a safe and just space for humanity.

To achieve this reorientation, we must not only set different goals but also create different metrics. Thunberg argues that "we should no longer measure our wealth and success in the graph that shows economic growth, but in the curve that shows the emissions of greenhouse gases." The implications are clear: "We should no longer ask: 'Have we got enough money to go through with this?' but . . . 'Have we got enough of the carbon budget to spare to go through with this?' That should and must become the center of our new currency."[68]

According to other proponents of the sustainability narrative, governments should be aiming at maximizing people's well-being, of which income levels represent but one element. Many of the benefits of increased health and happiness correlate strongly with GDP growth at early stages of economic development but then level off. As countries become developed, their goals should change.[69] A few countries have moved in this direction in formulating government policies, with Bhutan taking the lead. In 2012, a UN high-level meeting launched the first World Happiness Report, which measures happiness across countries on the basis of GDP per capita, social support, health, life expectancy, freedom to make life choices, generosity, and freedom from corruption. In the West, New Zealand adopted

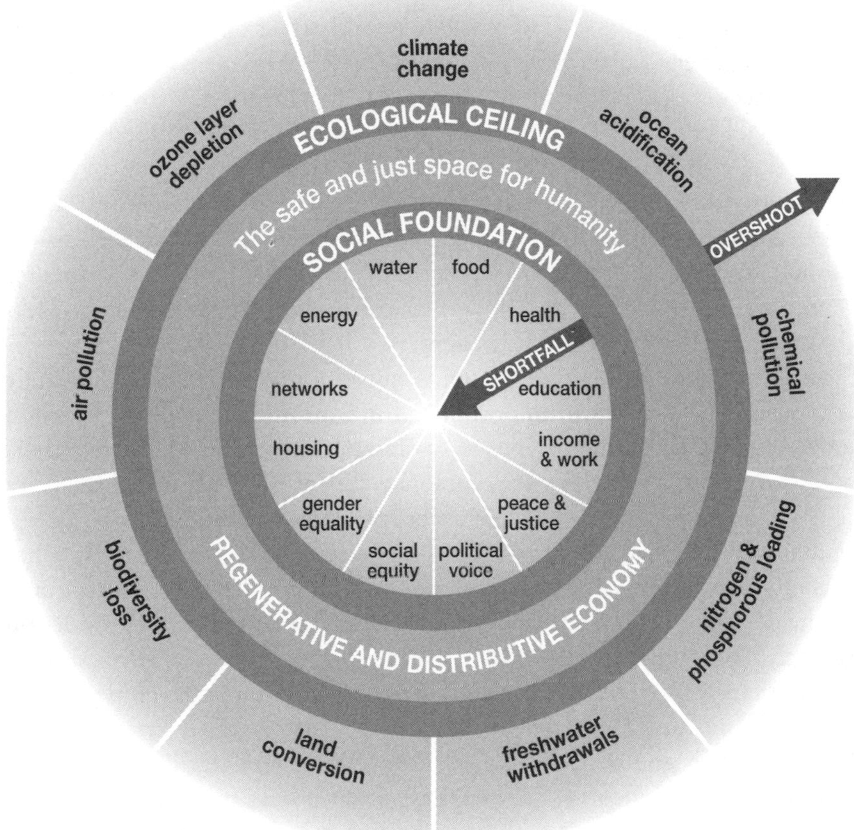

Fig. 8.4: The Doughnut of a Sustainable Economy

Note: The "doughnut" has an inner ring—the "social foundation"—which represents the basics of human well-being that every person should have. The outer ring represents an "ecological ceiling," which reflects the earth's ecological boundaries. In between the two rings is the "safe and just space for humanity."

Credit: Kate Raworth, Doughnut Economics: Seven Ways to Think Like a 21st-Century Economist *(White River Junction, VT: Chelsea Green Publishing, 2017), 38.*

a "wellbeing budget" in 2019, which focuses on improving the prosperity of local communities instead of maximizing GDP.[70]

Economic Globalization and Carbon Emissions

Klein charges that the links between increased trade and investment, on the one hand, and climate change, on the other, were largely ignored during the 1990s and 2000s. Few people asked how the vastly increased distances that many goods now travel would affect the carbon emissions that climate negotiators were seeking to reduce. And even fewer explored the indirect effects of the more obscure legal protections provided by international trade and investment agreements on the climate: would "granting companies like Monsanto and Cargill their regulatory wish list—from unfettered market access to aggressive patent protection" allow them to "entrench and expand the energy-intensive, higher-emissions model of industrial agriculture around the world," as Klein suspects? And would protections for foreign investors be used to challenge laws designed to promote renewable energy?[71]

International trade raises complex questions about who is ultimately responsible for the emissions produced in a particular country. Carbon emissions are typically attributed to the country where they are generated. European countries have employed this production-based measure to take credit for reducing their carbon emissions while faulting developing countries such as China for rapidly increasing their emissions. What this metric obscures, however, is that, through international trade, many of the developed countries have simply outsourced their dirty production overseas. Tracking emissions based on where goods are used or consumed, rather than where they are produced, reveals that most developed countries run substantial "carbon-trade deficits": the carbon emissions embedded in the goods and services they export are significantly lower than the carbon footprint of the goods and services they import.[72]

"When China became the 'workshop of the world,'" Klein notes, "it also became the coal-spewing 'chimney of the world.'" Developed countries pass regulations for clean energy at home at the same time as their companies take advantage of dirty energy rules abroad. Klein argues that the result is a "free trader's dream . . . and a climate nightmare." She finds it disingenuous when developed countries point to China's rapidly rising emissions "as if we in the West are mere spectators to this reckless and dirty model of economic growth," given that it was "our governments and our multinationals that pushed a model of export-led development that made all of this possible."[73]

The big black machine may produce wonderfully cheap consumer goods, but it encourages people to consume too much and generates considerable pollution in the process. Moreover, emissions from the transport of goods across borders are not formally ascribed to any country, even though container ship traffic has increased more than 400 percent during the past twenty years and shipping emissions are set to double or triple by 2050.[74] Sweden is often referred to as a leader in moving toward a zero-carbon economy, Thunberg notes, but if we include all of Sweden's emissions, including from foreign-produced goods, shipping transport, and air miles, Sweden registers as one of the top ten countries in the world for emissions per capita.[75]

Distributive Justice

Climate change may be a global threat in which all people and all countries are at risk of losing, but it also raises strong concerns about distributive justice. In terms of *responsibility,* carbon emissions to date have predominantly been caused by developed countries and rich people, including past and particularly current generations. In terms of *vulnerability,* climate change is likely to have a disproportionate impact on poor countries and poor people, as well as the young and future generations. And in terms of *capability,* rich countries, people, and multinational corporations are the ones best placed to avert the climate disaster. As economist Lucas Chancel explains, socio-environmental injustice arises because "the biggest polluters are typically the ones who are least affected by the damages they cause."[76]

Only a very small proportion of the world's population is responsible for the bulk of consumption and hence of global carbon emissions. According to a 2015 Oxfam report, the richest 10 percent of people produce almost 50 percent of global carbon emissions, while the poorest 50 percent contribute only about 10 percent (Figure 8.5).[77] An average person among the richest 1 percent emits 175 times more carbon than an average person among the bottom 10 percent. Similarly, developed countries typically have much higher per capita emissions than developing ones, both at current levels and especially if one takes into account their cumulative historical emissions. At the same time, it is often developing countries and their poorest citizens which are likely to be the worst hit by climate change.

Developed countries are also better placed to make meaningful changes that would merely involve lifestyle adaptations rather than curbs on the ability to develop, as would be the case for developing countries. In the words of philosopher Henry Shue: "Poor nations ought not be asked to sacrifice . . . their own economic development in order to help prevent the climate changes set in motion by the process of industrialization that has enriched others. Even in an emergency one pawns the jewelry before selling the blankets. . . . Whatever justice may positively

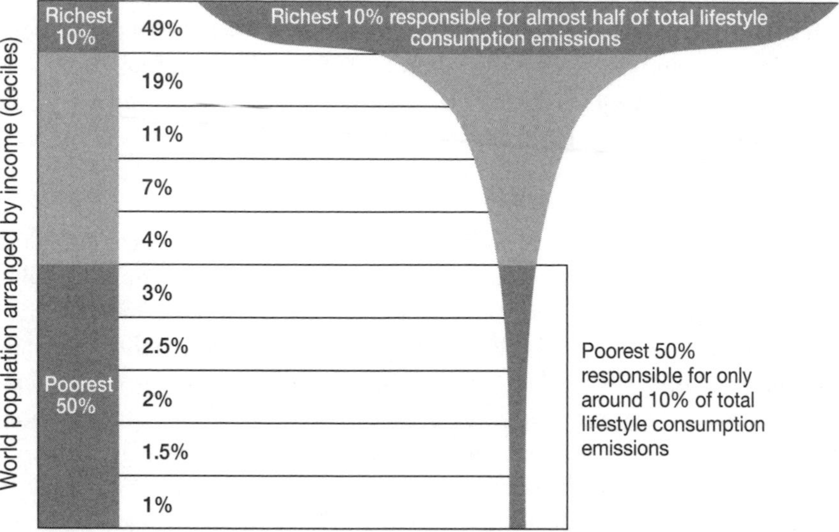

Fig. 8.5: Guess Who Is Responsible for Most Carbon Emissions
Note: This chart shows that the richest 10 percent of the world's population is responsible for almost half of global carbon emissions, while the poorest 50 percent contribute only about 10 percent.
Credit: Reformatted from Timothy Gore, "Extreme Carbon Inequality," Oxfam Media Briefing, *December 2, 2015, figure 1, by permission of Oxfam.*

require, it does not permit that poor nations be told to sell their blankets in order that the rich nations keep their jewelry."[78] This is also true of rich people, who could reduce their extravagant consumption without cutting back on the basics.

Writes economic anthropologist Jason Hickel: "Bringing our civilization back within planetary boundaries is going to require that we liberate ourselves from our dependence on economic growth—starting with rich nations." The problem for the world is not that we do not produce enough; it is that what we produce is not distributed equitably. To meet the needs of everyone within the confines of our planetary health, we must take from the haves (rich people, rich companies, and rich countries) and give to the have-nots (poor people and poor countries). "We can improve people's lives right now simply by sharing what we already have more fairly, rather than plundering the Earth for more."[79] According to Hickel, this means degrowth for some and growth for others.[80]

Climate change also has important distributive effects from an intergenerational perspective. The climate crisis has been created by the world's adults, but the main impact will be felt by their children and grandchildren. In 2018, then fifteen-year-old Thunberg began protesting global warming by engaging in a school strike to bring attention to the impending climate crisis. "Some people say that we should be in school instead, but why should we be studying for a future that's soon to be no more? And when no one is doing anything whatsoever to save that future?"[81]

Conclusion

Global threat narratives encourage people to think about threats to the system as a whole and how to make our economies and societies more resilient and sustainable. Instead of pitting winners and losers against each other, these narratives portray all people and all countries as potential losers and emphasize the need to address common threats to people and the planet in a cooperative fashion. Unless we make it the goal of our economic systems to survive and thrive within the limits of our planet, instead of fixating on maximizing economic growth, everyone is at risk of losing, proponents of these narratives warn.

PART III

WORKING WITH GLOBALIZATION NARRATIVES

IN PART II, WE PRESENTED THE NARRATIVES as (more or less) coherent constructs. By focusing on the logic of the narratives themselves rather than on the motivations of those who promote them, we tried to reflect the fact that these narratives are now part of the general Western political discourse in a way that escapes the control of any individual actor. While the different story lines that make up the narratives were originally created by concrete actors in specific circumstances, the narratives are not, or at least no longer, tied exclusively to any particular actor. In that sense, they have an existence above and beyond the motivations and actions of their individual proponents.

Although we invoke the texture and feel of these narratives by drawing primarily on the public debates of recent years, we do not believe that these narratives will lose their relevance anytime soon. Instead, arguments tracking the basic analytical structure of these narratives are likely to be with us long after their prominent contemporary proponents have left the scene. When stripped of their present particulars, the six faces of globalization differ in core ways: the level of analysis that they adopt (e.g., national, international, or transnational); the units of analysis that they focus on (e.g., class, communities, countries, or corporations); whether they direct attention to absolute or relative gains; and the direction of those flows (e.g., gains flowing upward to the elite or sideways to foreigners). We provide a table summarizing the main features of the narratives on the following pages (Table III.1).

Table III.1 Key Elements of the Rubik's Cube Narratives about Economic Globalization

	Level of Analysis	Unit of Analysis	Absolute vs. Relative Gains	Winners vs. Losers	Distributive Flows	Concepts, Language, Metaphors	Illustrative Proponents
Establishment	Global economy	Countries	Absolute gains Win-win	Everyone wins or winners can compensate losers and still be better off	Everyone wins in an absolute sense; little focus on distributional consequences	Rising tide that lifts all boats, growing the pie so that everyone gets a bigger slice, hockey stick, economic growth, GDP growth, efficiency, comparative advantage, economies of scale, technological improvement, innovation	World Bank, World Trade Organization, IMF, Thomas Friedman, Richard Baldwin, Kimberly Clausing, Angela Merkel in Germany, European Union
Left-Wing Populist	National level	Classes	Relative gains Win-lose	Winners = rich, upper middle class, college-educated Losers = poor, working class, middle class, non-college-educated Different divisions (e.g., 1% vs. 99% or 20% vs. 80%)	Vertical (upward), transfer from lower and middle classes to the rich or professional classes	Rigged economy, looting, leeching, inequality, unfair, unjust, class, exploitation, hourglass, hollowed-out middle class, dual economy, redistribution, predistribution, billionaires and billionaire class	Elizabeth Warren, Bernie Sanders, and Alexandria Ocasio-Cortez in United States, Jeremy Corbyn in United Kingdom, Syriza in Greece, Podemos in Spain, Five Star Movement in Italy, Die Linke in Germany

Right-Wing Populist	International level	Individuals, families, communities	Relative gains Win-lose	Winners = workers in developing countries; countries like China and Mexico; international organizations and international bureaucrats (e.g., in Brussels and the European Union) Losers = workers, families, and communities in developed countries	Horizontal (sideways), transfer from working-class communities in developed countries to working / middle classes in developing countries Also, vertical (upward) hostility against domestic and international elites	Protectionism, anti-immigration, Rust Belt, decay, family, community, nation, patriotism, values, loyalty, stability, tradition, jobs shipped offshore, giant sucking sound, influx of immigrants, Polish plumbers, Somewhere vs. Anywhere people, globalists vs. patriots, sovereignty, faceless international bureaucrats	Donald Trump, Peter Navarro, and Stephen Bannon in United States, UKIP and Nigel Farage in United Kingdom, Marine Le Pen in France, Matteo Salvini in Italy, AfD in Germany, Michael Lind, Oren Cass, J. D. Vance
Corporate Power	Transnational level	Corporations, particularly multinational ones	Relative gains Win-lose	Winners = transnational corporations Losers = workers, communities, countries, home country, transnational working class	Vertical (upward), from workers, communities, and countries to corporations, particularly multinational ones	Rent seeking, corporate power grab, asset protection, tax dodging, tilting the playing field, footloose multinationals, corporate concentration, lack of loyalty	Dani Rodrik, AFL-CIO, Unifor, Ralph Nader, Battle in Seattle protesters, TTIP protesters, Corporate Europe Observatory, Michael Lind, Lori Wallach, Joseph Stiglitz, Gabriel Zucman, Jeffrey Sachs, Lina Khan, Tim Wu, Rana Foroohar, Elizabeth Warren, Thilo Bode

(*continued*)

Table III.1 (continued)

	Level of Analysis	Unit of Analysis	Absolute vs. Relative Gains	Winners vs. Losers	Distributive Flows	Concepts, Language, Metaphors	Illustrative Proponents
Geoeconomic	International level (primarily interstate)	Countries, particularly the United States and China as great-power rivals	Relative gains Win-lose	Winners = China, which has closed the gap on the United States and other Western countries Losers = the United States and Western countries that have declined in relative terms	Horizontal (sideways), from the United States and other Western countries to China	Battle, war, weapons of job destruction, cold war, decoupling, great powers, rivalry, security, theft, cheating, competition, strategic, weaponized interdependence	Peter Navarro, Marco Rubio, Robert Spalding, Tom Cotton, Mike Pence, and Christopher Wray in the United States, Reinhard Bütikofer and Theo Sommer in Europe, Henry Farrell and Abraham Newman, Mark Leonhard
Global Threats	Global level (not just the economy)	People and planet	Absolute losses Lose-Lose	Everyone loses, the people and the planet	Everyone loses, including the rich and the poor, developed countries and developing countries, the people and the planet. Some focus on distributional issues (i.e., poor people and poor countries will often lose first or worst)	Interdependence, interconnection, networks, resilience, self-sufficiency, redundancy, diversification, sustainability, spaceship earth, sustainable orbit, doughnut, steady-state economics, survive and thrive, ecological limits, human well-being and flourishing, degrowth	On resilience: many Western government officials, officials from international organizations (e.g., UN secretary general and UN high commissioners for human rights and refugees), Ian Goldin, Mike Mariathasan, Roger Martin, Anne-Marie Slaughter, Yossi Sheffi. On sustainability: Greta Thunberg, Kate Raworth, Extinction Rebellion, Naomi Klein, David Wallace-Wells, Jason Hickel, Alexandria Ocasio-Cortez, proponents of Green New Deal, Commission for the Human Future

Understanding the analytical structure underlying these narratives not only allows us to see how they will endure beyond the current political moment but also can help us to gain a better grip on current debates by giving us the analytical tools to trace how specific actors invoke the different narratives to promote their own perspectives, values, and interests. In this part, we shift gears from a narrative approach to a more analytical one, moving the focus from the narratives themselves to some of the ways in which they are deployed by actors in public debates, international negotiations, and policymaking. Specifically, we use our conception of the analytical structure underlying the narratives to show how actors switch between different levels and units of analysis, which values policymakers see and trade off, and which perspectives this collection of narratives tends to overlook or downplay.

Chapter 9 tracks how actors try to switch narratives in order to steer public debate in a direction that suits their perspective or interests. These attempts to (re)frame the problem can be undertaken in good faith, when an actor genuinely believes in the utility of a particular narrative, or opportunistically, when an actor believes that a particular framing will better suit that actor's interests regardless of the narrative's veracity. We do not seek to parse the internal motivations of actors, but instead highlight the existence and consequence of actors strategically invoking and switching narratives in public debates.

Chapter 10 explores the implications of overlaps among narratives. Even if an actor has a primary commitment to a particular narrative, that actor often has to seek common ground with others who embrace different narratives in order to find sufficient support for particular proposals. Overlaps among narratives allow proponents of different narratives to form coalitions in favor of a policy even when they disagree on why they support that proposal. Although these overlaps can generate consensus around policies at a particular point in time, they can also present a source of political conflict and instability when disagreements about the underlying rationales come to the surface.

Chapter 11 brings into focus the trade-offs that policymakers confront when they attempt to reconcile different narratives. Actors often face difficult decisions on how to weigh incommensurable goals, such as economic gains, community cohesion, national security, and environmental protection, and different underlying probability models. Any actors wishing to mix and match different narratives need to be conscious of the trade-offs that are required to bring together different narratives.

In Chapter 12, we turn our attention to the blind spots and biases of the six Rubik's cube narratives. We do so by considering additional narratives that are more prominent outside the West and that shed light on aspects and experiences of economic globalization that receive little attention in Western debates about economic globalization. In doing so, we recognize that there are many faces of globalization, not just six.

CHAPTER 9

Switching Narratives

When Mark Zuckerberg testified at a US Senate hearing in 2018, a journalist snapped a photo of his notes. If he was asked any questions about whether Facebook should be broken up, his notes prompted: "US tech companies key asset for America; break up strengthens Chinese companies." Law professor Tim Wu calls this Facebook's China argument. When confronted with criticisms of their monopolistic market position, anti-competitive practices, and privacy violations, US tech companies essentially warn: "Don't you realize that if you damage us, you'll just be handing over the future to China? Unlike America, China is standing behind its tech firms, because it knows that the competition is global, and it wants to win."[1]

Facebook's China argument reflects a strategic attempt to change narratives, deflecting criticism under one narrative by invoking a different framing in which the actor appears in a better light or the policy prescriptions better suit the actor's agenda. Switching narratives often means changing the level of analysis (e.g., from national to international), the units of analysis (e.g., from corporations to countries), and the perceptions of winners and losers (e.g., reframing a win for a corporation as a win for the corporation's home country). Sophisticated actors can quite literally change the story; they redirect the focus of attention and redefine who counts as "us" in a fight between "us and them." In this chapter, we show how actors strategically invoke or switch narratives to in effect declare: "*that's* not the problem, *this* is." These moves are important because the first step in problem-solving is problem-framing.

From Horizontal to Vertical Hostility

In 2016, Trump campaigned by appealing to America's "left-behind" and "forgotten" people. In 2020, Elizabeth Warren tapped into the same outrage but offered a different explanation. "Here's the difference," Warren explained. "Donald Trump says, 'Your life isn't working, and the reason is all those people who don't look like you. They're not the same race as you, they don't worship like you, they don't talk like you. So blame them.' His answer is: divide working people. It's racist. And, ultimately, it makes everyone poorer."[2] Warren, for her part, attempts to redirect blame at the wealthy, who she says have rigged the system to serve their own interests.

Warren was attempting to reframe the problem faced by America's poor and middle classes by switching from the right-wing populist narrative, which directs hostility horizontally against a foreign other, to the left-wing populist narrative, which directs the hostility vertically against America's rich. Redirecting hostility in this way can be an effective political move because, as one of Warren's campaign staffers explained: "You have to inspire and fight for something. You have to name a villain."[3] By switching narratives, Warren is attempting to redefine what the problem is represented to be and, thus, who is to blame and what should be done in response.[4]

Warren's attempt to switch narratives in this way is common among left-wing populists. Alexandria Ocasio-Cortez made the same move in response to heckling by parents at an education town hall in New York. She expressed concern that this sort of infighting was "exactly what happens under a scarcity mindset." "This should not be the fight," Ocasio-Cortez explained, gesturing horizontally backward and forward between herself and the audience. "This should be the fight," she exclaimed, gesturing vertically up and down. "We are in this together."[5] Ocasio-Cortez was redefining the "we" and redirecting hostility upward.

The German left-wing politician Gregor Gysi used the same idea when an upset constituent confronted him about the funds that the German government was spending to help refugees and people on welfare. The mistake, Gysi explained, was that he was "looking to the people next to" him, which was the "wrong direction." "If you want to change something, if you want more social justice, we need to look upward; we have to address the relationship between the rich and poor in our society and in other societies."[6]

Left-wing populists attempt to change whom people perceive as the source of their problems—it is not the people who are across from them who are winning at their expense, it is the people who are on top who are unfairly exploiting those in the middle and at the bottom. As Matthew Klein and Michael Pettis diagnose the situation in *Trade Wars Are Class Wars:* "A global conflict between economic classes *within* countries is being misinterpreted as a series of conflicts *between* countries with competing interests."[7] But it is not just the rich who are on top; it is also large companies that have excessive corporate power, which leads into conversations about antitrust.

Rethinking Approaches to Antitrust

Antitrust or competition law in the United States and Europe is one area in which this narrative switching is playing out in regulatory actions and public discourse. For proponents of the left-wing populist and corporate power narratives, the failure of US authorities to impose robust antitrust limits on Big Tech's enormous market power has effectively and problematically allowed these companies to become monopolies, duopolies, and oligopolies.[8] The companies' level of market dominance has led to demands by publications such as *The Economist,* politicians such as Warren, academics such as Tim Wu, and others, including one of Facebook's founders, that the US government break up the Big Tech companies to better protect privacy and democracy, and to promote competitive markets. "To restore the balance of power in our democracy, to promote competition, and to ensure that the next generation of technology innovation is as vibrant as the last, it's time to break up our biggest tech companies," demands Warren.[9]

Implicit in this approach is the use of a domestic level of analysis: it centers on the American market and polity. The US government is cast as the actor that needs to regulate these big companies properly so as to protect the little guy. The crucial move in Facebook's China argument is to shift to the geoeconomic narrative and, in so doing, change the level of analysis from the domestic to the international, and the unit of analysis from corporations to countries. Suddenly, the battle becomes one between China and the United States in which America is fighting to protect its technological supremacy and market dominance against incursions by China and Chinese companies. Along these lines, authors Robert Atkinson and Michael Lind argue that "'big is ugly,' 'competition is king' thinking might make sense in closed national markets where the loss of a major firm is not a problem, because other national firms will come in to take market share. But in a deeply integrated global economy, particularly one where other nations are engaged in predatory state capitalism, such an approach is economic suicide."[10]

When it comes to competing against China, US security commentators typically assume that the Chinese government and Chinese companies play on the same side: they are "team China." The implication is that the US government, US corporations, and US citizens should be playing on the other side in this international game as "team USA." According to the geoeconomic narrative, privacy and competitive domestic markets may be worthwhile objectives, but they may need to be compromised to fight a more serious external economic and security threat. In an international confrontation, sacrifices have to be made on the domestic front, and everyone needs to pull together for the collective good of the nation. It appears, however, that the Biden administration is attempting to switch the terms of the discussion about Big Tech back to the corporate power framing; the administration has recruited or nominated for appointment prominent Big-Tech critics Wu and Lina Khan, signaling a much more robust approach to antitrust enforcement.[11]

Similar debates among proponents of different narratives are taking place in Europe. Unlike the United States, the European Commission has taken a strict approach to antitrust regulation, regularly refusing mergers and acquisitions that would create companies with outsize market share and penalizing companies for anti-competitive behavior. Instead of focusing narrowly on increased prices for consumers, as has been typical in the United States under the influence of Robert Bork, the Commission takes a broader view; it is sensitive to ensuring competitive opportunities for small and medium-size firms and pursuing general notions of fairness. On this basis, the European Commission has imposed fines on tech companies and prohibited certain acquisitions. The European Union has also led the field in protecting digital privacy through the General Data Protection Regulation.

Applying the same antitrust logic, the European Commission rejected German manufacturing giant Siemens's proposed acquisition of France's Alstom, a manufacturer of high-speed trains, in February 2019. The companies had argued that they needed to merge so they could create a company with enough market power to compete with Chinese rivals in building high-speed trains and railway systems, particularly in view of China's expansion of railways under its Belt and Road Initiative. The European Commission, however, was concerned that the merger would increase costs for European consumers and stifle innovation. The Commission did not consider the threat from Chinese competitors imminent since those companies operated primarily in the Chinese market.[12]

Geoeconomic reactions to this decision were swift. Noting that only five of the top forty biggest companies in the world were European, the French and German governments decried the decision as preventing the creation of European champions that could compete effectively with Chinese and US companies. Whereas the European Commission's approach adopted the regional level of analysis, which is equivalent to the domestic level of analysis in the US context, France and Germany were calling for an international level of analysis. The two governments argued for the adoption of a more ambitious industrial policy and a revised approach to antitrust to ensure that "team EU" could compete more effectively with other great powers and their companies in the twenty-first century.[13]

Whom Are You Afraid Of?

The level of analysis adopted by different narratives is instrumental in identifying who the bad guys are and what we need to be afraid of. For the left-wing populist and corporate power narratives, the villains are the big US technology companies, and it is surveillance capitalism that we need to be scared about. In the geoeconomic narrative, the villains are China and Chinese companies that aid and abet their government or might do so in the future, and we should be afraid of the power and spread of the (Chinese) surveillance state. Each narrative identifies a risk but often exhibits a blind spot concerning the risk identified by the other narrative or narratives.

Business school professor Shoshana Zuboff's work on surveillance capitalism is a case in point. Zuboff is extremely concerned about the power of US Big Tech. Like proponents of the corporate power narrative, she focuses attention on corporations rather than the rich. However, her analysis, like the left-wing populist narrative, tends to be predominantly domestic, paying primary attention to how Big Tech companies extract value from their users and less attention to the benefits they might receive from transnational opportunities and international arbitrage. Zuboff argues that in their search for revenue, these companies have created a new type of capitalism that feeds off the data revealed by individuals in their online searches, purchases, and social media use. Invoking Karl Marx's image of capitalism as a vampire that feeds off labor, Zuboff warns that "surveillance capitalism feeds on every aspect of humans' experience."[14]

Zuboff clearly invokes an us-versus-them framing. In her telling, "Surveillance capitalism operates through unprecedented asymmetries in knowledge and the power that accrues to knowledge. Surveillance capitalists know everything *about us,* whereas their operations are designed to be unknowable *to us.* They accumulate vast domains of new knowledge *from us,* but not *for us.* They predict our futures for the sake of others' gain, not ours."[15] Far from protecting people from being preyed upon by this rapacious beast, the US government has been ineffective in stopping the onslaught. It has been behind the times in understanding the new technology and stymied in its ability to regulate by the power and financial leverage of surveillance capitalists.

By contrast, China and Chinese companies are almost absent from Zuboff's analysis. Zuboff explains that she focuses on Google, Facebook, and Microsoft because surveillance capitalism was invented in Silicon Valley, even though she acknowledges that it has since become a "global reality." China makes a cameo appearance in her book in the context of explaining its "social credit" system, which Zuboff cautions might be the terrifying Orwellian end point of some of the practices being developed in America. The patterns of surveillance are the same, she notes, but in America it will be a market project, whereas in China it will be a political one.[16] Apart from this brief discussion, her framing misses the geoeconomic reading of the relationship between China and the United States in which US companies appear as vital actors in the competition for technological supremacy.

Whose Side Are You On?

Under the geoeconomic narrative, the villain is China, which is ruthlessly seeking to extend the surveillance state, within and beyond mainland China. The hero is the United States, which is trying to save itself and others from falling victim to the global threat of China's techno-authoritarianism. This geoeconomic story contains multiple subplots. One focuses on China's state surveillance as part of the narrative that sees China as an illiberal, authoritarian country that poses a threat to liberal democracies like the United States. Another emphasizes how allowing Chinese companies, such as Huawei, to build critical infrastructure in America or its allied countries will make them more vulnerable to cyberattacks and espionage. A third highlights what the collection of huge amounts of data by China and Chinese companies may bode for a US-China arms race regarding AI. The fourth focuses on China's censorship of its internet and how it is seeking to affect international internet governance to create a safe space for that approach. The fifth turns attention to the battle over third-country markets, where China is portrayed as exporting tools of techno-authoritarianism through Chinese companies' international marketing of digital technology.[17]

As with any narrative, by focusing on one story, proponents miss or downplay others. In this us-versus-them framing, the danger that China is operating a surveillance state and conducting cyberattacks and espionage takes center stage. The United States' own history of surveillance, particularly of foreigners, and the significant cyberattacks that it has leveled against foreign countries are rarely mentioned. Another salient aspect of this narrative is that it describes Chinese companies as untrustworthy because they are subject to national security and cybersecurity laws that require them to hand over data to the Chinese state. However, US companies are subject to American laws that are arguably similar, and US technology companies turned over reams of such data under programs exposed by Edward Snowden.

The geoeconomic narrative assumes that Chinese companies play on the same team as the Chinese state, whether they are state-owned or privately owned. No matter how much Huawei protests that it is not state-owned, has never spied for the Chinese government, and would never do so, many US commentators conclude that the risk that it might is simply not worth taking. Even when studies find, for instance, that Chinese companies do not necessarily export Chinese censorship approaches when they operate in third countries, the Chinese government's use of censorship at home creates concern that it might require similar compliance abroad in the future. Such concerns are heightened in the Chinese case by the strong integration of China's triple helix of the state, market, and universities accomplished through doctrines such as civil-military fusion, which, for instance, has inspired the recruitment of Chinese technology companies as AI champions for the "national team."[18]

US officials tend to decry the state-led China Inc. model, but at the same time they often evidence frustration with US tech companies for not being sufficiently loyal players for their home team.[19] For example, Marine Corps Gen. Joseph F. Dunford Jr. has lambasted US technology companies for refusing to work with the Pentagon but partnering with Chinese companies, even though those companies are subject to the civilian-military fusion doctrine, and thus innovations developed jointly might find their way into the hands of the Chinese People's Liberation Army.[20] In a similar vein, former US secretary of defense Ashton Carter complained that it was "ironic to be working with Chinese companies as though that is not a direct channel to the Chinese military and not to be willing to operate with the US military, which is far more transparent and which reflects the values of our society. We're imperfect for sure, but we're not a dictatorship."[21]

One of the ironies of this approach is that US officials object to China's state capitalism but often counter by effectively calling for something akin to "patriotic capitalism."[22] For example, in 2018, Google's plans to secretly reenter China with a censored search engine that would comport with the requirements of China's firewall were leaked. US vice president Mike Pence subsequently called on American companies to think "beyond the next quarter" and to think twice before "diving into the Chinese market." By way of example, he declared: "Google should immediately end development of the 'Dragonfly' app that will strengthen Communist Party censorship and compromise the privacy of Chinese customers."[23] Peter Navarro likewise rebuked US companies as "corporate turncoats": "There is no honor among thieves—and no patriotism among American corporations."[24]

Changing the narrative can invert the story about what is good and what is bad. In the left-wing populist and corporate power narratives, what is bad is that the US Big Tech companies have achieved market dominance and violate their users' privacy by collecting large quantities of data. In the geoeconomic narrative, by contrast, these vices become virtues. The battle against Chinese companies requires that US companies have market power and as much data as possible on which they can train AI algorithms.[25] Of course, these arguments are open to debate. The possession of overly large market shares by US companies might stifle innovation, undermining US technological competitiveness in the long term.[26] Collecting lots of data from users might fuel US efforts in AI but may turn America into a surveillance state uncomfortably close to what America objects to in China. The point is not that arguments within a particular narrative are preordained. But those who operate within particular narratives often display relative blindness to points that have traction under other narratives.

Who or What Is the Enemy?

Facebook might be attempting to switch from the left-wing populist and corporate power narratives to the geoeconomic narrative, but other actors are attempting the opposite move, redirecting hostility from China toward US multinational companies and from external threats to domestic ills.

A good example of the latter switch is the economist Jeffrey Sachs's argument that "China is not an enemy" but rather is used as "a scapegoat for rising inequality in the United States." In Sachs's telling, China is simply a developing country that is trying to raise the standards of living of its people through education, international trade, infrastructure investment, and improved technologies. Sachs concedes that some US workers have lost their jobs as a result of offshoring to China; however, he argues that "instead of blaming China for this normal phenomenon of market competition, we should be taxing the soaring corporate profits of our own multinational corporations" and using those revenues to help those who have been left behind and to rebuild America's crumbling infrastructure.[27]

Sachs makes two moves. First, at the international level of analysis used by the protectionist and geoeconomic narratives, he seeks to contextualize and normalize China's conduct. China, he claims, has roughly followed the same development strategy as Japan, South Korea, Taiwan, Hong Kong, and Singapore before it. From an economic standpoint, China is not doing anything unusual for a country playing catch-up. It is normal for such countries to seek to upgrade their technologies in a variety of ways, including through study, imitation, purchases, and copying. Indeed, he points out, the United States adopted exactly this approach when it attempted to close the technology gap with the United Kingdom in the nineteenth century.

Second, Sachs argues that the real ill plaguing America is corporate greed. Because free trade increases the size of the pie, it works for everyone *if* the winners compensate the losers. The problem with US capitalism, he concludes, is that "today's winners flat-out reject sharing their winnings." "The real battle," Sachs submits, "is not with China but with America's own giant companies, many of which are raking in fortunes while failing to pay their own workers decent wages." These companies push for tax cuts for the mega-rich, monopoly power, and freedom to offshore while rejecting policies to make US society fairer. China is simply a scapegoat for the resulting problems.

Sachs seeks to shift from a geoeconomic narrative to the corporate power and left-wing populist ones. In so doing, he implicitly moves from an international level of analysis to a domestic one and from horizontal hostility among countries to vertical hostility within a country. Sachs is not alone in making such a move. The commentator Cody Cain likewise argues that China merely accepted the "gift" of manufacturing jobs that was offered to it by US corporations: "Corporate America decided to close their American plants and open new plants in China. Corporate America decided to lay off multitudes of American workers and ruin entire American communities." Cain accuses Trump of misleading US workers: "Focusing all the ire on China is a grand misdirection that conceals the true culprit, namely, the super-rich corporate executives and shareholders in America."[28]

In his book *Blaming China: It Might Feel Good but It Won't Fix America's Economy,* author Benjamin Shobert makes a similar claim. Watching Trump campaign in 2016, Shobert was worried that Trump was directing US insecurities toward an outside actor, China. He feared that American citizens might become convinced that China was at fault for problems for which America had only itself to blame and that this mindset might spiral out of control, taking both countries on a path toward war. In Shobert's view, blaming China is a cheap answer to an expensive problem. Instead of looking for an external enemy, America needs to look in the mirror and face some of the structural challenges that have got it into its current predicament.[29]

Narratives play an important part in the construction of the "us" and "them" in competitive relationships. Social psychologists have demonstrated the significance of "othering" in identity formation for individuals, and research has shown this process is equally at work in relation to countries.[30] Having a clear sense of who is not on their team ("them") helps people feel closer to those who are on their team ("us"). Indeed, some US scholars have explicitly called on the United States to "other" China as a way of overcoming some of the deep divisions within American society. In this vein, political scientists Jeff Colgan and Robert Keohane argue that "Washington should nurture a uniquely American social identity and a national narrative. That will require othering authoritarian and illiberal countries . . . such as China. . . . Done properly, that sort of othering could help clarify the American national identity and build solidarity." Of course there are costs to this approach, they acknowledge, but the gains are worth it. "It might at times constrain commercial relationships. However, a society is more than just an economy, and the benefits of social cohesion would justify a modest economic cost."[31]

Making Common Cause

One of the conundrums of the geoeconomic narrative is that it might become a self-fulfilling prophecy. “If you treat China as an enemy, China will become an enemy,” warns the former US assistant secretary of defense Joseph Nye Jr.[32] That would not only increase the risk of trade wars and military confrontations but might also get in the way of the two nations finding common ground in fighting a global threat: climate change.

The historian Stephen Wertheim attempts to make this strategic shift from the geoeconomic narrative to the global threats narrative. He argues that descending into a new Cold War is unnecessary and dangerous, not least because it risks undermining the cooperation that is needed to tackle a more existential external threat. Speaking of then US president Trump, Wertheim has noted: “It is no coincidence that a president who denies climate change is leading the charge against China, the top emitter of greenhouse gases. Arresting climate change requires America and China to cooperate and channel their competition into salvaging the planet rather than seizing its resources. The American people can live with an authoritarian China. They cannot live on an uninhabitable Earth.”[33]

Along similar lines, the political scientist Stephen Pampinella laments that US national security policymakers cannot recognize that “the greatest dangers faced by US citizens are non-state economic and ecological global processes that shape domestic politics from the inside-out, and not rival sovereigns.”[34] Former US president Jimmy Carter exhorts the two great powers to work together in the “epic struggle against global warming” in order to “build their futures together, for themselves and for humanity at large.”[35] If the two superpowers do not make peace and focus on human salvation, the professor of peace and world security studies Michael Klare warns, perhaps the greatest victim “will be planet Earth itself and all the creatures, humans included, who inhabit it.”[36]

These arguments involve a shift both in the metrics of analysis and in the underlying assumption of zero-sum or positive-sum relations. The geoeconomic narrative uses countries as the unit of analysis and adopts a zero-sum mentality (China versus America in conflict and competition), whereas the global threats narrative treats the world as the unit of analysis and adopts a positive-sum mentality (China and America in cooperation to save people and the planet). The “us” versus “them” becomes a “we”; nationalism dissolves into invocations of our common humanity in the face of an existential threat.

Whether for genuine or calculated reasons, a clear proponent of this narrative is China's president, Xi Jinping: "Tackling climate change is a shared mission for mankind," so "we should create a future of win-win cooperation, with each country making [a] contribution to the best of its ability" while rejecting the "narrow-minded mentality of 'zero sum game[s].'"[37] Other Chinese officials make a similar case. China's ambassador to the United States, Cui Tiankai, has warned against seeing the competition between the two countries as a zero-sum and winner-takes-all game, particularly as the two countries "have so many global issues that we have to work together on," including climate change, terrorism, poverty, pandemics, and natural disasters.[38]

Instead of switching the framework for the relationship between China and the United States back from a (competitive) geoeconomic to a (cooperative) global threats framing, the Biden administration is trying to combine the two narratives. Biden plans "to confront China's abusive behaviors and human rights violations, even as we seek to cooperate with Beijing on issues where our interests converge, such as climate change, nonproliferation, and global health security." The key, according to national security advisor Jake Sullivan, is to find a way for the United States and China to manage their relationship in a way that reconciles competitive and cooperative elements and ensures that the situation does not spiral into conflict or end in catastrophe.[39]

International Research and Cooperation

The contest between the competitive and conflictual geoeconomic narrative and the cooperative establishment and global threats narratives plays out on many levels, including with respect to scientific research and international cooperation. The geoeconomic narrative suggests that countries must be careful about foreign students, scholars, and research collaborations, particularly Chinese ones in science and technology, lest important technological developments leak to rival countries. For example, Alex Joske, an analyst at the Australian Strategic Policy Institute, warns that since 2007, the Chinese People's Liberation Army has sponsored more than 2,500 military scientists and engineers to study abroad and has developed relationships with researchers and institutions across the globe—something that may jeopardize the West's technological lead.[40] In the establishment and global threats narratives, by contrast, open international scientific collaboration is desirable because it maximizes the chance of innovations that will help to fuel economic growth, solve the sustainability challenge, and cure global health problems.

Nowhere is this divide more evident than in responses to the coronavirus. The US deputy national security advisor for strategy under the Trump administration, Nadia Schadlow, argued that the coronavirus vindicated Trump's geoeconomic agenda. Listing problems ranging from China's initial attempt to cover up evidence about the virus to its undue influence over the WHO, her message was clear: China is a grave security threat to the United States, not a vital cooperative partner in dealing with global threats.[41] By contrast, the US ambassador to the United Nations under the Obama administration, Samantha Power, adopted a cooperative framing, arguing that "the coronavirus must do the work of that alien invader, inspiring cooperation both across borders and across the aisle."[42] "The coronavirus pandemic pits all of humanity against the virus," Bill Gates likewise explained. "This is like a world war, except in this case, we're all on the same side."[43] This global threat perspective has also been embraced by many scientists around the world who have worked across borders in a truly international effort to develop treatments and a vaccine. The geopolitical rivalry is "absolutely ridiculous," according to one researcher. "I never hear scientists—true scientists, good quality scientists—speak in terms of nationality," explained another.[44]

Conclusion

Changing the framing of a story in a way that chimes with one's perspective or promotes one's interests is the essence of politics. Identifying the different narratives and tracking how they vary across multiple dimensions helps to understand the consequences of actors strategically switching narratives. Whether done cynically or in good faith, this sort of (re)framing has important implications for what we perceive the problem to be and which policies we are inclined to pursue.

CHAPTER 10

Overlaps among Narratives

Proponents of a particular narrative will often not have sufficient strength to be able to win out in policy battles or international negotiations on the basis of a single narrative. They will hence look for overlaps with other narratives in order to form coalitions with respect to particular proposals, even though the partners in the coalition may not share the same ultimate objectives. Law professor Cass Sunstein has described such overlaps as "incompletely theorized agreements," in which different actors support a particular policy or result even though they cannot agree on fundamental principles.[1] However, overlaps among narratives can also give rise to conflicts, where actors advance different interpretations of the same measure, and even result in sabotage, where the different narratives that can serve as rationales for a policy undermine each other. In this chapter, we illustrate these dynamics by analyzing the overlapping narratives that shaped the Trump administration's approach to trade policy and by sketching the interplay between different narratives in the renegotiation of the NAFTA among the United States, Mexico, and Canada between 2017 and 2019.

The Trump Administration's Trade Policies

The Trump administration's trade policies were a source of widespread confusion, as US trading partners and observers tried to make sense of conflicting signals about the rationales for different policies. Consider the measures that the Trump administration took against Chinese imports and companies. Were these measures intended to build up leverage to incentivize China to change its market-distorting ways—a perspective that chimes with the establishment narrative? Or were the administration's policies driven by concern about the strategic vulnerabilities that

Fig. 10.1: A Venn Diagram of the Trump Administration's Trade Policies
Note: This diagram shows how different narratives can be used to explain trade measures taken by the Trump administration and how some policies exist in the areas of overlap between two narratives.
Credit: © Anthea Roberts and Nicolas Lamp.

arise from economic and technological interdependence—a geoeconomic perspective? Or was President Trump simply indulging his long-declared love of "beautiful" tariffs—the protectionist explanation that accords with the right-wing populist narrative?[2] In Figure 10.1, we map the various trade policies adopted by the Trump administration onto these three narratives.

Some of the Trump administration's measures could be straightforwardly explained from the perspective of a single narrative. In January 2018, for instance, the administration began levying tariffs on imports of washing machines and solar panels.[3] The opening to impose these tariffs was created by the independent US International Trade Commission, which had found that increased imports of washing machines and solar modules during the preceding years had been "a substantial cause of serious injury" to the domestic industry.[4] These findings provided a legal basis for the imposition of so-called safeguard tariffs, and the Trump administration leapt at the opportunity. Nobody argued that these safeguards served any purpose other than the protection of domestic producers.[5] While the legality of the safeguards imposed by the Trump administration was challenged by other countries in the WTO, the purpose of the measures was not contested.[6]

Other measures adopted by the Trump administration squarely addressed what the administration saw as China's market-distorting policies in the way that proponents of the establishment narrative would typically advocate. The administration's attempt to put pressure on China for its use of market-distorting subsidies by presenting a united front with the European Union and Japan falls into this category, as did the administration's decision to challenge at the WTO China's failure to adequately protect US intellectual property.[7] These measures align with the establishment narrative both with respect to their objective (getting China to liberalize its market and to adhere to WTO rules) and with respect to the means chosen to pursue that objective (relying on international cooperation and legal procedures). The close correspondence of these measures with the establishment narrative helps explain why they enjoyed bipartisan support in the United States, as well as the backing of US allies.[8]

A final measure that is explicable by a single narrative is the 2019 Executive Order on Securing the Information and Communications Technology and Services Supply Chain. The executive order declares a "national emergency" on the basis that "foreign adversaries are increasingly creating and exploiting vulnerabilities in information and communications technology and services" in order to commit "malicious cyber-enabled actions, including economic and industrial espionage." The explanation for the executive order clearly embodies the geoeconomic narrative: it focuses on information and communications technology and the threat posed by service suppliers who might be controlled by "foreign adversaries." It warns that these could create and exploit vulnerabilities with potentially catastrophic effects, constituting a national security threat.[9]

In sum, some of the Trump administration's trade measures could clearly be explained by a single narrative. Whether specific actors supported those policies typically depended on whether they subscribed to the narrative in question.[10] The dynamics become more interesting when a government measure or policy falls in an area of overlap among different narratives. Depending on the context, the ability to explain these measures from the perspective of more than one narrative can mean that they enjoy broad support, are the subject of heated contestation, or cannot achieve the purpose envisaged by any one of the narratives because another narrative undermines its effectiveness.

Coalitions: The Overlapping Consensus in Favor of "Getting Tough" with China

In 2018, the Trump administration initiated an investigation into "unreasonable" practices by China that were harming US economic interests: intellectual property theft, forced technology transfer, cyberespionage, and aggressive industrial policies.[11] In response to the investigation's findings, the Trump administration began imposing tariffs on Chinese imports, under the authority of Section 301 of the Trade Act of 1974. Initially, these measures were widely interpreted as an attempt to persuade China to modify its practices. The sustained efforts by US government officials to negotiate a deal with China under which China would implement reforms supported this reading. On this interpretation, even proponents of the establishment narrative could support the measures, since their ultimate aim was a more market-based and rule-conforming Chinese economy. Although the means used by the Trump administration were unconventional, they could be understood as an attempt to vindicate the promise of China's accession to the WTO.

Yet as the months went by, no deal between the United States and China materialized, and the Trump administration continued to escalate its tariffs, a different interpretation of the measures started to gain plausibility. Some observers began to suspect that a protectionist motivation, rather than the establishment one, might have been the driving force behind the measures. As Ana Swanson wrote in the *New York Times:* "President Trump's tariffs were initially seen as a cudgel to force other countries to drop their trade barriers. But they increasingly look like a more permanent tool to shelter American industry, block imports and banish an undesirable trade deficit." Similarly, Shawn Donnan at Bloomberg observed: "Increasingly . . . Trump's tariffs are looking like an end-goal rather than a tool and more tangible than any of the deals the president has promised."[12]

There was a clear shift in perspective from understanding the tariffs as leverage to seeing them as examples of protectionism, pure and simple. Still, the ambiguity of purpose of the Section 301 tariffs did little to erode political support for them. The fact that the Section 301 measures fell into an area of overlap between two narratives was not a source of contention as much as a source of strength: different segments of the US political class supported them for different reasons.

What made this incompletely theorized agreement possible was the fact that as long as there was no deal with China that satisfied the trade establishment's concerns, the two motivations did not conflict: some political actors would maintain the measures to keep up the pressure on China, while others would be happy about the protection to domestic producers that the tariffs provide. Only if a Chinese offer materialized that would satisfy the underlying establishment concerns in return for abandoning the tariffs would the conflict between the two motivations break into the open. The "Phase 1" deal concluded in December 2019 did not force such a decision: its limited scope meant that the US administration only had to suspend further scheduled tariff increases in exchange for China's commitment to purchase $200 billion worth of US goods. In fact, it appears doubtful that China will ever offer a deal that would address all the United States' concerns about its economic model; as a result, a broad cross-section of the US political class—from both the establishment and protectionist camps—could potentially support maintaining tariffs against Chinese imports for the foreseeable future. When the Biden administration took over in January 2021, it showed no inclination to quickly rescind the tariffs; instead, it treated them as a potential tool in a "comprehensive strategy to confront the China challenge."[13]

Conflict: The Contested National Security Rationale for Tariffs on Steel and Aluminum

Yet another set of tariffs imposed by the Trump administration suffered a different fate. In January 2018, US secretary of commerce Wilbur Ross delivered reports to President Trump finding that steel and aluminum articles were "being imported into the United States in such quantities and under such circumstances as to threaten to impair the national security of the United States." The basis for these findings was not that the imported steel and aluminum itself posed a danger; rather, the reports reasoned that the imports were weakening the US domestic steel and aluminum industries, which would impair America's "ability to meet national security production requirements in a national emergency." These findings served as the basis for Trump to impose tariffs on steel and aluminum imports from a range of US trading partners, including close allies such as Canada, the European Union, and Japan, under the authority of Section 232 of the Trade Expansion Act of 1962.[14]

Like the Section 301 tariffs discussed in the previous section, these Section 232 tariffs on steel and aluminum were susceptible to different interpretations, as they fell within the overlap of the protectionist and geoeconomic narratives. The Trump administration invoked the geoeconomic narrative as a justification for the measures, taking the position that the United States needed to strengthen its industrial base even if that came at the expense of economic efficiency. Yet virtually all US trading partners interpreted the steel and aluminum tariffs as purely protectionist measures taken without a valid national security rationale. The national security justification for the tariffs was also met with disbelief within the United States—many US lawmakers questioned how steel imports from countries such as Canada could conceivably constitute a national security threat. In contrast to the Section 301 measures against China, the fact that the steel and aluminum tariffs were open to different interpretations created a dynamic of domestic and international conflict.[15]

In the public debate about the steel and aluminum tariffs, the plausibility of the "national security" rationale for the tariffs immediately assumed central importance, as it was key to both the international legal justification and the domestic political legitimacy of the measures. To explain why it was within its rights in imposing the tariffs, the United States relied on a rarely used exception in international trade law that allows a member of the WTO to take "any action which it considers necessary for the protection of its essential security interests" if certain prerequisites are met. Other WTO members disbelieved this justification and accused the United States of abusing the exception; many imposed retaliatory tariffs in response, which in turn heightened political pressure in the United States to abandon the tariffs.[16] The fact that many outside of the US administration regarded the professed rationale for the steel and aluminum tariffs as contrived thus had almost immediate legal and political consequences.

The comparison of the Section 232 and Section 301 measures can shed light on the question of whether measures that fall into an area of overlap between two narratives will enjoy the support of proponents of both narratives or will cause conflicts about how the measure should be understood: the answer depends on the political and legal relevance of the rationale for adopting the measure. As long as the rationale for the measure has little import, proponents of both narratives can reach an incompletely theorized agreement in support of the measure; by contrast, where the rationale has legal or political importance, the ambiguous purpose of the measure can become a source of conflict.

Sabotage: When Different Narratives Undermine Each Other

Despite the different interpretations proffered by the United States and its trading partners of the purpose of the US Section 232 measures, the tariffs were still able to fulfill their purpose under either interpretation. If the purpose was to afford protection to the steel and aluminum industries, the attempt by the United States to sell the measures as motivated by national security did not take away from that protectionist effect. Similarly, if the measures were intended for national security purposes, the security gains they achieved were not lessened by other countries' interpretation of them as protectionist. Whether the protection afforded by the tariffs was interpreted as a means to another end (national security) or as an end in itself made all the difference in determining whether they were legally justified, but had no implications for the measures' ability to achieve either objective. The same cannot be said for measures that fall into the area of overlap between the geoeconomic and establishment narratives, such as the decision to prevent American companies from buying from or selling to Huawei. Here, the narratives sabotaged each other, both conceptually and practically.

At the conceptual level, the geoeconomic narrative suggested that the measures were essential to safeguarding national security, which is such a high value that the measures would normally be expected to be non-negotiable. In the establishment narrative's interpretation, however, the entire purpose of the measure was to serve as a bargaining chip to force more market-conforming behavior by China. The explanation offered by the establishment narrative thus runs directly counter to the geoeconomic justification. Indeed, when Trump suggested that America's treatment of Huawei could be used as a bargaining chip in the trade negotiations with China, those who viewed Huawei as a genuine national security threat reacted in horror, arguing that treating the measures as negotiable "surrenders the moral high ground" and destroys US credibility in national security matters.[17]

On a practical level, this sort of security measure created an incentive for China to become more self-reliant in technology by doubling down on state support for the development of its indigenous capabilities. This result, however, was exactly the opposite of what the United States was seeking to accomplish under the establishment narrative's interpretation, where the ban served as a bargaining chip to pry open China's market and reduce the role of the state.[18] The result was an example of what political scientists Darren Lim and Victor Ferguson have called the "decoupling dilemma": although decoupling may make sense on national security grounds, it runs counter to the objective of integrating China more closely into the world economy by opening up the Chinese economy to

Western investment and exports. The more successful the United States is in effecting decoupling, the less successful it will be in expanding economic integration, as China will not trust that it can retain access to the US market and will be more likely to resort to the very state-led methods of achieving self-reliance that unsettled America in the first place.[19]

The Trump administration did not find an answer to this dilemma. As political scientist Geoffrey Gertz put it bluntly: "Trump can't decide what he wants from China. Some of his policies point to deeper integration, some to decoupling. He'll need to pick one—or fail at both."[20] Biden has now inherited the stark choice that the dilemma presents: his administration has to decide whether to prioritize economic integration with China (which would require flexibility on national security measures, thereby casting doubt on how genuine the security concerns advanced by proponents of the geoeconomics narrative were in the first place) or put national security first (which would undercut any incentives that China may have had to accede to US demands to reform its economic system—the establishment narrative's priority). If the Biden administration tries to have it both ways and adopts measures that fall within the area of overlap between the two narratives without clearly settling on *one* of the narratives, it may end up with measures that are neither credible security measures nor effective bargaining chips.

The Renegotiation of NAFTA

During the presidential election campaign in 2016, Trump decried the NAFTA treaty between the United States, Canada, and Mexico as the "worst trade deal maybe ever signed anywhere, but certainly ever signed in this country."[21] He vowed either to renegotiate it or to withdraw from it if he became president. Once Trump assumed office, his obvious aversion to NAFTA quickly brought the other parties to the negotiating table. In November 2018, the three parties finalized a revision of the agreement, which the US negotiators decided to call the United States–Mexico–Canada Agreement (USMCA).[22] How can the narratives shed light on the negotiating dynamics between the parties and on the agreement that they ultimately reached?

The original NAFTA, negotiated in the early 1990s, largely reflected the prescriptions of the establishment narrative. The agreement liberalized all trade in goods, included extensive protections for investments, and enshrined high levels of intellectual property protection in the three countries. The NAFTA also provided for limited free movement of people: members of certain professions could gain "temporary entry" into other NAFTA parties without having to meet the usual immigration requirements. To be sure, the agreement also contained elements that were motivated by other narratives. A protectionist motivation best explains why the Canadian government insisted on maintaining high barriers to imports of some agricultural products: Canada hoped to protect its farmers and the rural communities who depend on farming for their survival. Similarly, Canada's fear that its cultural industries would not be able to withstand an onslaught of their better-resourced US competitors was accommodated by a "cultural exception" that allowed Canada to take virtually any measures it saw fit to shield its cultural sector from US competition. The agreement also contained traces of the corporate power narrative: President Clinton agreed to go forward with the agreement only after the addition of two side agreements that were meant to ensure that the parties did not lower their labor and environmental standards. Overall, however, it was the establishment narrative that shaped NAFTA.

The Establishment View: Don't Fix What's Not Broken

In 2017, when the Trump administration triggered the renegotiation of the agreement, large sections of the business community in the three countries, as well as the Canadian and Mexican governments, would have been content to continue in the same vein. In setting out Canada's objectives for the renegotiation, Minister of Foreign Affairs Chrystia Freeland described NAFTA as an "extraordinary success story" and noted that Canadians overwhelmingly believed that "NAFTA has been good for Canada." But Freeland was not oblivious to the challenges to continuing with business as usual, warning that "Canadians may lose faith in the open society, in immigration and in free trade" if issues such as income inequality and precarious working conditions were not addressed. Her prescriptions for dealing with these challenges, however, remained firmly rooted in the establishment narrative. Freeland implored her counterparts to "avoid scapegoating the 'other'" and to recognize that "although economic globalization has put pressure on some of our jobs, automation and digitization have been far greater factors." The key challenge was to make sure that "the gains of trade are fairly, broadly shared." Free trade had to be tied to "equitable domestic policy: If the second is missing, the first breaks down. And if the first is missing, the second is unaffordable."[23] But Freeland also embraced some tenets of the corporate power narrative, urging the inclusion of chapters on labor rights, environmental protection, indigenous rights, and gender, as well as amendments to ISDS.

Proponents of the establishment narrative, though generally happy with NAFTA, thought Trump's renegotiation might at least provide an opportunity to modernize the agreement. The US Chamber of Commerce highlighted the need for rules on digital trade, and the Canadian government proposed updating the list of professions eligible for temporary entry. The wish list of the US business community also featured a further extension of intellectual property protections, especially for highly innovative drugs, so-called biologics. In addition, the US Chamber of Commerce pointed out opportunities for further liberalization. Whereas the original NAFTA had already eliminated almost all tariffs, its definitions of when a product counted as a product *from* a NAFTA country and hence qualified for duty-free treatment were relatively restrictive: for instance, a car could be shipped from one NAFTA country without the payment of a tariff only if at least 62.5 percent of the value of the car had been added in a NAFTA party. In more recent trade agreements, these so-called rules of origin had tended to be much more lenient. The NAFTA parties therefore had significant scope for further liberalization in a renegotiated version of the agreement (Figure 10.2).[24]

The Protectionist Goal: Bring Back US Manufacturing Jobs

For the Trump administration, merely tinkering with the original NAFTA was a nonstarter. The proponents of the protectionist viewpoint in the administration viewed NAFTA as nothing short of a disaster, primarily because they blamed it for the exodus of manufacturing jobs to Mexico. At the opening of the renegotiations, the US trade representative at the time, Robert Lighthizer, stated: "The numbers are clear. The US government has certified that at least 700,000 Americans have lost their jobs due to changing trade flows resulting from NAFTA. Many people believe that number is much, much bigger than that. In 1993, when NAFTA was approved, the United States and Mexico experienced relatively balanced trade. However since then, we have had persistent trade deficits."[25]

For the Trump administration, the implications of this diagnosis were clear: the renegotiated NAFTA had to bring jobs—especially auto manufacturing jobs—back to the United States. But this reversal was not easy to achieve. Over the course of twenty-five years of free trade in autos and auto parts under NAFTA, the auto manufacturers had built up dense supply chains across the three countries. Car parts at various states of

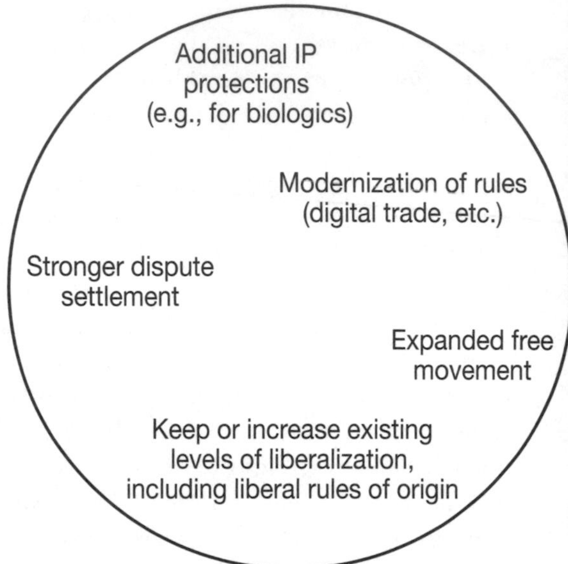

Fig. 10.2: What Proponents of the Establishment Narrative Wanted in the NAFTA Renegotiations
Note: This diagram shows some of the key objectives that proponents of the establishment narrative pursued during the NAFTA renegotiations. These objectives reflect the views of the business community in the three countries and of most US Republicans (based on their positions in previous negotiations, such as the TPP). They were supported in part by the governments of Canada and Mexico, with the exception of the proposal for increased intellectual property protection.
Credit: © Anthea Roberts and Nicolas Lamp.

assembly typically crossed the borders between the NAFTA parties several times before they found their way into the finished car. Even the Trump administration was not willing to fracture these supply chains by simply withdrawing from NAFTA and imposing tariffs, since doing so would have massively disrupted production and led to spiraling costs. Instead, the Trump administration set out to use the rules of origin in the agreement to incentivize car manufacturers to produce more of their vehicles in the United States. And it initially tried to do so in the bluntest way possible: by adding a US domestic content requirement of 50 percent to those rules. That is, the United States demanded that cars should qualify for duty-free entry into the United States only if at least 50 percent of the value of the car had been manufactured in the United States. The message to car manufacturers could not have been clearer: if they wanted to continue enjoying the benefits of NAFTA, they would need to bring at least half of their production (by value added) back to the United States.[26]

This proposal went hand in hand with three others that were designed to discourage manufacturers from investing in production in Mexico. The first was to introduce a five-year sunset period for the agreement, after which it would have continued in force only if all three parties approved.

If this provision had been adopted, car manufacturers would not have been certain that they would still have access to the US market after the five-year period and thus would have thought twice before moving production to Mexico. The second proposal was to abolish ISDS, the mechanism that protects companies from government action that diminishes the value of their investment by allowing them to obtain compensation from governments through international arbitration. By removing this protection from investments in Mexico and Canada, the US negotiators similarly tried to encourage investment in the United States. Lighthizer told reporters: "I've had people come in and say, literally, to me, 'Oh but you can't do this, you can't change ISDS. . . . You can't do that, because we wouldn't have made the investment otherwise.' I'm thinking, 'Well then why is it a good policy of the United States government to encourage investment in Mexico?'"[27] Finally, US negotiators sought to gut the already-defunct state-to-state dispute settlement mechanism of NAFTA, which would have sowed doubt about the enforceability of the deal and discouraged investors from relying on its market-access guarantees. As Figure 10.3 shows, there was little overlap between the objectives of the Trump administration and proponents of the establishment narrative in the negotiations.

The Corporate Power Narrative: Making Bad Jobs in Mexico into Good Jobs in Mexico

As it turned out, the traditional proponents of the establishment narrative were not the protectionists' most formidable opponents in the negotiations. Historically, the chief defenders of the establishment narrative in the United States were found in the Republican Party, but given Trump's iron-clad hold on the Republican base, even the party's pro-business wing felt the pressure to fall in line with the Trump administration's priorities. And while the Canadian and Mexican governments tried to keep the deal as liberal as possible, they had much to lose, given how strongly their economies depended on access to the US market. As a result, proponents of the establishment narrative were in a weak negotiating position. The main countervailing force that US negotiators had to reckon with instead emerged in November 2018 in the form of the new Democratic majority in the US House of Representatives, which would have to approve the agreement. The Democrats wielded considerable leverage: they had little to lose politically from opposing a deal proposed by the Trump administration and hence no incentive to vote for an agreement

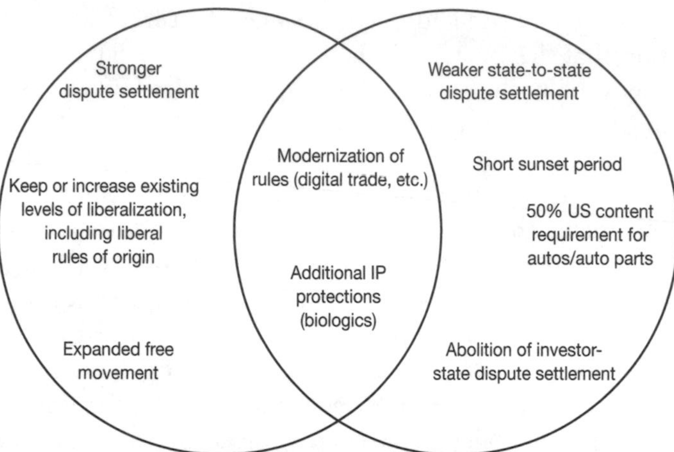

Fig. 10.3: Not Much Common Ground between the Protectionists and the Trade Establishment

Note: This figure juxtaposes the objectives of the proponents of the protectionist narrative with those of the establishment narrative. There was some common ground between the two camps about increased intellectual property protections (which would have largely benefited US firms) as well as the modernization of some rules; however, when it came to the rules governing access to the US market and the dispute settlement provisions of the deal, the positions of the two camps were diametrically opposed.

Credit: © Anthea Roberts and Nicolas Lamp.

that did not reflect their priorities. And those priorities were largely informed by the corporate power narrative.

The single most pressing issue for congressional Democrats in the NAFTA renegotiations was to strengthen labor standards in the agreement. In the view of US labor unions and their congressional allies, previous US trade agreements with provisions on labor standards had failed to make a difference on the ground. In particular, the unions had long complained that NAFTA provided no effective tools to raise wages. The AFL-CIO pointed out that since the conclusion of NAFTA, wages in Mexico had lost purchasing power, and the US-Mexico wage gap had increased. The AFL-CIO blamed NAFTA for "dragging down taxes, wages and standards towards their lowest level within the trade bloc," and emphasized that the income distribution in all three NAFTA countries had "become more unequal as capital captures an ever-larger share and workers an ever-smaller share."[28]

Previous attempts to use trade agreements to sanction developing countries for violating labor standards had produced disappointing results. In 2011, the United States had initiated dispute settlement proceedings against Guatemala, arguing that Guatemala had failed to enforce its labor laws, as required by a Central American trade accord to which both countries were parties. After years of litigation and delays, the dispute settlement panel finally published its ruling in 2017. Even though the United States had proved Guatemala's failure to effectively enforce its labor laws in several instances, the panel found that not enough of those instances were "in a manner affecting trade" to satisfy the high bar for a violation set by the agreement.[29]

The Democrats in Congress were determined to use the renegotiation of NAFTA to design provisions that were aggressive enough to enable Mexican workers to bargain for higher wages and improved working conditions, which in turn would also ease competitive pressures on US and Canadian workers and rebalance the agreement in favor of workers. Other demands followed from this objective. Any provisions on labor standards in the agreement were worthless if they could not be enforced, so the Democrats insisted on fixing NAFTA's state-to-state dispute settlement system. Moreover, in light of the disappointing experience of the lengthy dispute settlement proceedings against Guatemala, the Democrats demanded a mechanism that would allow the United States to react quickly to the violation of key labor rights by specific producers.

The Democrats also sought to rebalance the agreement by eliminating giveaways to corporations. Specifically, they opposed granting pharmaceutical companies additional protection for biologic drugs because they feared that such protection would stymie attempts to lower drug prices in the United States. They also cheered the US negotiators' willingness to eliminate ISDS from the agreement—though not for the same reason as proponents of the protectionist narrative. Lighthizer wanted to abolish ISDS to dissuade companies from investing in Mexico. Proponents of the corporate power narrative, by contrast, were just as worried about the opportunities that ISDS gave corporations to sue the US and Canadian governments over regulatory measures. In other words, Lighthizer disliked ISDS because of the protection it afforded US corporations *in developing countries,* whereas proponents of the corporate power narrative rejected ISDS because the governments *of developed countries* might have to compensate companies for losses or might fail to enact socially beneficial measures for fear of being sued. These differences produced

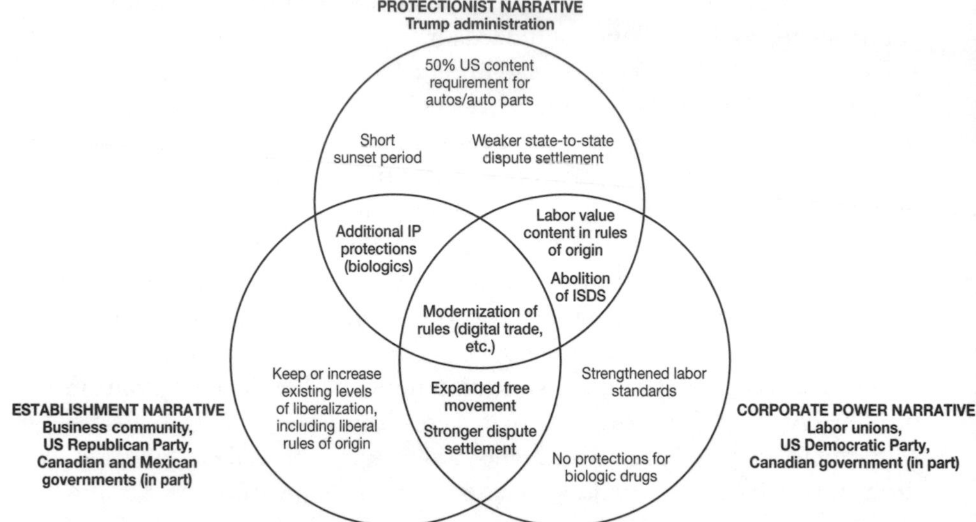

Fig. 10.4: Negotiating Positions at the Start of the NAFTA Renegotiations
Note: This diagram shows the objectives of proponents of the protectionist, establishment, and corporate power narratives at the outset of the NAFTA renegotiations.
Credit: © Anthea Roberts and Nicolas Lamp.

an incompletely theorized agreement between proponents of the protectionist and corporate power narratives on the desirability of abolishing ISDS. Figure 10.4 maps the preferences of the three narratives.

Buenos Aires 2018: An Agreement with the Imprint of the Protectionist Narrative

After more than eighteen months of tense negotiations, US president Trump, Canadian prime minister Justin Trudeau, and Mexican president Enrique Peña Nieto signed a first version of the new trade pact between their three countries at the G20 summit in Buenos Aires in November 2018. The changes that the agreement made to the original NAFTA reflected the predominant influence of the protectionist narrative championed by the Trump administration: although the key components of the changes to the NAFTA lay within the areas of overlap between the protectionist narrative and the other narratives, no proposal outside the protectionist circle was adopted (see Figure 10.5). In view of the power of the United States compared with its trading partners, this was not a surprising result. It is instructive, however, to examine how

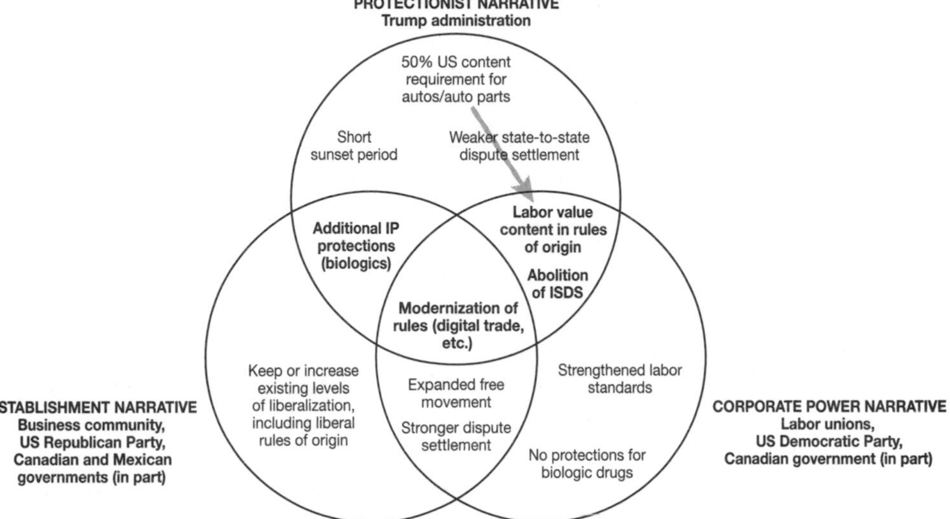

Fig. 10.5: The First Version of the USMCA Reflects Protectionist Priorities
Note: This diagram shows the changes—highlighted in bold—that the USMCA, as signed on November 30, 2018, made to the original NAFTA. All changes were within the protectionist circle, though in areas of overlap with other narratives.
Credit: © Anthea Roberts and Nicolas Lamp.

some of the US administration's protectionist proposals were adapted to bring them into the areas of overlap with the other narratives.

The Trump administration's proposal to require 50 percent US domestic content immediately became the subject of heated discussions—it left Canadian and Mexican negotiators "stunned." The blatant favoritism toward the United States as a production location went against the very idea of a free trade agreement: if businesses were not allowed to organize their supply chains in the way they saw as most efficient, they could not realize the gains from trade. In its original form, the proposal was deemed "not negotiable" by Canadian and Mexican trade officials.[30]

But over time the negotiators found a way to reformulate the US proposal so as to build a bridge to proponents of the corporate power narrative: instead of requiring 50 percent US content, the new rules would mandate that a certain percentage of the value of the product had to be added by workers making the equivalent of at least $16 an hour in any of the three countries. Rather than openly incentivize companies to produce in the United States, this proposal would reward them for paying their workers decent wages. Of course, the US negotiators hoped that the two versions of the rule would have the same effect in practice. Nonetheless, by presenting their concern about production location as a concern about wages, the protectionists were able to reach another incompletely theorized agreement with proponents of the corporate power narrative. The latter could support the proposal because, at least in theory, it would give companies an incentive to raise the wages of Mexican workers, which would ease pressure on wages in the United States and Canada and raise the share of the gains from trade that would accrue to workers.[31]

As Figure 10.5 shows, the dominant role of the protectionist narrative espoused by the Trump administration was also reflected in the omission from the new agreement of any of the elements that proponents of the narrative did not support. That applied even to proposals that enjoyed backing from proponents of both of the other narratives. Neither the Canadian government's proposal to update and expand the list of professions eligible for temporary entry nor the Canadians' and Mexicans' ideas for strengthening the state-to-state dispute settlement procedures were adopted. Expanding the free movement of workers collided with the anti-immigration sentiment of the right-wing populist narrative. As the US administration was not willing to contemplate this proposal, the outdated list of professions remained in place. And even though Canada and Mexico were able to beat back US attempts to further undermine the dispute settlement system, the uneasy compromise was to leave the (dysfunctional) system unchanged.

Mexico City 2019: The Center of Gravity Shifts to the Corporate Power Narrative

When Trump, Trudeau, and Peña Nieto signed the revised NAFTA in Buenos Aires in November 2018, the new congressional majority, elected earlier that month, had not yet been seated. Over the course of the year 2019, Lighthizer was forced to renegotiate the agreement with Canada and Mexico to win the Democrats' approval in Congress. The Democratic majority insisted on, and obtained, three major changes to the renegotiated agreement. As a result of these amendments, the center of gravity of the changes to NAFTA shifted from the protectionist narrative to the corporate power narrative (see Figure 10.6).

The first change required extensive and delicate negotiations with Mexico. It imposed a much more aggressive mechanism for the enforce-

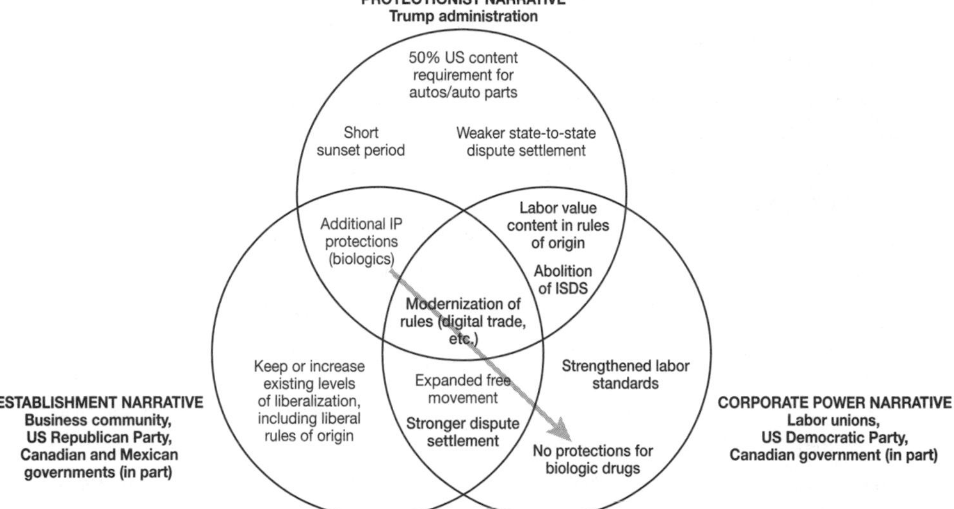

Fig. 10.6: The Center of Gravity Shifts to the Corporate Power Narrative
Note: This diagram shows key elements—highlighted in bold—of the USMCA, as amended on December 10, 2019. The center of gravity of the changes that the USMCA makes to the original NAFTA shifted from the protectionist to the corporate power narrative. All changes are now within the corporate power narrative's circle, though in areas of overlap with other narratives.
Credit: © Anthea Roberts and Nicolas Lamp.

ment of labor standards, which allowed independent inspectors to visit Mexican factories and authorized the United States and Canada to ban imports from facilities that deny their workers the right to free association and collective bargaining.[32] The second major change eliminated the additional protections for biologic drugs on which US negotiators previously had insisted. Finally, the revised agreement strengthened the state-to-state dispute settlement procedures by closing procedural loopholes that previously had allowed a party to effectively block dispute settlement proceedings.

These changes were all demanded by proponents of the corporate power narrative. The extent to which the changes to the renegotiated NAFTA conform to the priorities of this constituency is evidenced by it being the first US trade agreement since 2001 to be endorsed by the powerful AFL-CIO, which argued that the new USMCA was an "agreement that working people can proudly support." As the AFL-CIO's president told its

12.5 million members: "President Trump may have opened this deal. But working people closed it."[33] The leader of the Democratic House majority, Nancy Pelosi, was similarly convinced that she had outmaneuvered the Trump administration, telling her colleagues, "We stayed on this, and we ate their lunch."[34]

Despite the concessions to the Democratic House majority, the USMCA passed with broad bipartisan support, which has also carried over into the Biden administration. Biden's US trade representative Katherine Tai, who had worked on the agreement, declared that it would be her priority to "implement and enforce" the accord, which she described as a "uniquely bipartisan accomplishment."[35] Tai's confirmation hearing, which concluded with the US Senate voting unanimously to confirm her, was interpreted by many observers as marking a profound and permanent shift in US trade policy away from the establishment narrative's strong support for free trade and toward a more skeptical and nuanced perspective informed by the protectionist, corporate power, and geoeconomic narratives.[36]

Conclusion

Different conceptions of the winners and losers from international trade have been among the principal drivers of the attack on the establishment narrative by proponents of the protectionist, geoeconomic, and corporate power narratives in recent years, especially in the United States. In this chapter, we have shown how the narratives underpinning the six faces of globalization can illuminate those debates and how overlaps between the narratives can explain coalitions, contestation, and conflict over international trade policies both within and among countries.

CHAPTER 11

Trade-offs among Narratives

"We're not going to put a dollar figure on human life," Governor Andrew Cuomo of New York declared as the coronavirus epidemic was reaching its peak in his state. "My mother is not expendable, your mother is not expendable and our brothers and sisters are not expendable. . . . The first order of business is to save lives, period. Whatever it costs."[1] Cuomo's refusal to trade off lives against money contrasted with Trump's warning that the "cure" (the lockdown that had brought public life to a halt) must not be "worse than the problem" (the virus itself).[2] As uncomfortable for many as it was, the coronavirus pandemic brought into sharp relief the reality that policymaking often involves trade-offs among different values.[3]

One of the main fault lines among the narratives lies in whether and how they are willing to trade off different values. The establishment narrative's core proposition—that we should focus on growing the pie so that everyone can get a bigger piece—rests on the idea that all we could ever want takes the form of a single pie, and that we can therefore fully compensate anyone who loses one part of the pie with another, larger piece of that same pie. The narrative assumes that what is lost and what is gained are perfectly commensurable. Proponents of the other narratives dissent. They either set other values as absolute or disagree with the way the establishment narrative balances economic efficiency with those other values.[4] In this chapter, we foreground the difficulties that arise when values conflict, as these present some of the toughest obstacles to reconciling or combining different narratives.

Understanding Conflicts between Different Values

Consumption versus Production

In the run-up to the 2016 US presidential election, Trump's claim that China had been "stealing" US jobs became one of the hallmarks of his campaign. The claim's empirical merits have been widely debated; what has attracted less attention is the normative proposition implied by the claim, namely, that the movement of jobs from one country to another is akin to theft. Yet this characterization marks the most significant dividing line between the protectionist strand of the right-wing populist narrative and the establishment narrative. The establishment narrative does not deny that some work previously carried out in the United States is now done in China and other developing countries, but it regards that reshuffling of the international division of labor as entirely unobjectionable. For Trump and his allies, by contrast, such movement of jobs was tantamount to someone stealing your watch or car.

In likening the loss of manufacturing jobs to thievery, Trump suggested that US manufacturing workers were entitled to their jobs as though they had a property right to them. It is not hard to understand why this jobs-as-property metaphor has emotional purchase. Many workers, especially those who have held jobs in an industry for many years, sometimes going back for generations, feel as if these jobs belong to them: their jobs are bound up with their history, their identity, and their status in the community. To these workers, their jobs amount to much more than simply a means of earning a living. Trump evoked this emotional connection when he talked about "skilled craftsmen and tradespeople and factory workers" who have "seen the jobs they love shipped thousands and thousands of miles away," or about steelworkers and coal miners who saw their "way of life destroyed" when their mills and mines closed: "Their fathers were in the mines, their grandfathers . . . that's what they do."[5]

Apart from capturing the sense of loss that manufacturing workers feel when their jobs disappear, the jobs-as-property metaphor also sends a clear message to those who suggest that workers should be expected to give up their jobs for the greater good: property owners cannot be required to relinquish their property even if it creates opportunity costs for others.[6] As the flip side of treating manufacturing workers' jobs as an almost sacrosanct entitlement, the jobs-as-property metaphor implies that the access to cheaper products that consumers gain through trade liberalization is normatively insignificant. "Maybe a person will buy fewer cars over the course of a lifetime. Who cares?" was Trump's response when asked whether his proposed trade restrictions would make goods more expensive. Trump and his allies considered the protection of manufacturing jobs as an absolute, almost sacred value and rejected any suggestion that a government should sacrifice those jobs in the interest of overall economic prosperity.[7]

Other proponents of the protectionist narrative elaborate on why the establishment narrative's focus on overall economic prosperity at the expense of other values is misguided and can even have catastrophic consequences. According to some, the narrative's fixation on growing the pie reflects an assumption that people are primarily consumers rather than producers. J. D. Vance, who became famous for describing the travails of blue-collar America in his memoir *Hillbilly Elegy,* faults his fellow conservative Milton Friedman for ignoring the social cost of opening US markets. Friedman had asked in the 1970s whether anyone could think of a "better deal . . . than our getting fine textiles, shiny cars, and sophisticated T.V. sets for a bale of green printed paper." Conservatives in the 2020s, Vance suggests, would answer that "a better deal might include millions of men in the South and Midwest with jobs instead of pill bottles and iPhones. How about communities with more steady father figures than opioids?"[8]

The answer to the question of what kind of country the United States wanted to be "used to be obvious," the Fox News host Tucker Carlson has argued: the "overriding goal for America" was "more prosperity, meaning cheaper consumer goods." "But is that still true?" he asks. "Does anyone still believe that cheaper iPhones, or more Amazon deliveries of plastic garbage from China are going to make us happy? They haven't so far. A lot of Americans are drowning in stuff. And yet drug addiction and suicide are depopulating large parts of the country. Anyone who thinks the health of a nation can be summed up in GDP is an idiot. . . . We do not exist to serve markets. Just the opposite. Any economic system that weakens and destroys families is not worth having. A system like that is the enemy of a healthy society."[9]

It is not entirely fair to criticize the establishment narrative for focusing exclusively on people as consumers: the narrative does not favor consumption over production, but simply treats income gains derived from remunerated work and from access to cheaper products as fungible. "Fungibility," the economist Richard Thaler explains, "is the notion that money has no labels."[10] In this view, the source of income has no bearing on how we feel about it or conduct ourselves with respect to it: rising "real" incomes—one of the professed goals of the multilateral trade regime—can mean either that people earn more or that they need to spend less on the same basket of goods. But protectionists reject the assumption that income gains through higher pay or lower prices are fungible. They argue that proponents of the establishment narrative forget that "people care more about their identities as producers than . . . as consumers."[11]

Oren Cass articulates the key implication of this insight: instead of seeking to maximize how much everyone is able to consume, economic policy should be directed toward ensuring that all people have decent jobs and are able to sustain themselves, their families, and their communities, even if pursuing these objectives results in lower efficiency overall. Automation and offshoring might improve the bottom lines of multinationals and boost countries' GDP, but they deprive large swaths of the non-college-educated population of productive employment, as well as of self-respect and the ability to form stable families and thriving communities. Cass argues that "economic piety"—the fixation on increasing the size of the economic pie—represents a truncated and self-undermining concept of prosperity: "Workers have no standing, in this view of the economy; neither do their families or communities."[12] Instead of attending only to society's economic gains, we must heed our society's and economy's social foundations; otherwise short-term economic growth will come at the expense of longer-term well-being. "If work is foundational to our society, then we have a duty to make the changes and trade-offs necessary to support it," says Cass. He argues for a "productive pluralism," which recognizes that there are many productive pursuits—in the market, the community, and the family, both paid and unpaid—that support thriving families and communities. Prioritizing some of these goals may seem economically inefficient in the short term but will contribute to greater well-being in the long term.[13]

Present-day protectionists such as Cass and Vance are fighting a rearguard action, as many manufacturing communities have been irreversibly damaged by the decline of manufacturing employment in the United States and other Western countries. However, in another sector—agriculture—the argument that economic policy should take account of values other than economic efficiency has long been accepted by Western governments. Even as trade restrictions on manufactured goods tumbled in the decades following World War II, many Western countries doggedly maintained high barriers to imports of agricultural goods ranging from meat and dairy products to rice and sugar, and simultaneously supported their agricultural producers with tens of billions in subsidies.

Western governments' policy decision to protect agricultural producers has been consistently decried by economists as wasteful and by developing countries as hypocritical. To some extent this policy of protection is due to the often disproportionate political power that agribusiness and rural constituencies wield in Western countries. But the policy also reflects a conviction that agriculture implicates objectives other than delivering goods to consumers at the lowest possible prices. These objectives include ensuring that the country produces a sufficient supply of food while maintaining rural landscapes, sustaining farming communities, safeguarding the welfare of animals, and protecting the environment. Trade negotiators often refer to these "non-commodity outputs" of agricultural production by saying that agriculture is "multifunctional": it serves more than one objective.[14]

One example of this approach is Canada's system of supply management. In products ranging from dairy to poultry to eggs, Canada does not allow a free market. Farmers are permitted to sell their product on the market only if they have been allocated a quota by a government agency. The quotas are meant to prevent overproduction and price competition. The resulting high prices result in substantial transfers from consumers to producers of agricultural products, which ensures a decent living for farmers. The Canadian government prevents price competition from imports by imposing very high tariffs—often exceeding 200 percent—on supply-managed agricultural products. So far, Canada's agricultural interests have successfully resisted trade-liberalizing reforms that, in the words of the Canadian National Farmers Union, would put "markets and competition before livelihoods and community."[15]

In effect, the protectionist narrative is arguing that agriculture is not the only sector that is multifunctional and produces "non-commodity" outputs. Proponents of the narrative urge governments to recognize that work in general, and manufacturing employment in particular, serve psychological and social ends that are not fully captured by their contribution to a country's GDP, and the loss of which cannot be compensated through welfare payments. Recognition of this critique is now sounding in policy statements by the Biden administration. For instance, US trade representative Katherine Tai stated at her confirmation hearing: "we must pursue trade policies that advance the interests of all Americans—policies that recognize that people are workers and wage earners, not just consumers."[16] On this account, economic efficiency is not the only value worth maximizing; it needs to be traded off against other values.

Efficiency versus Equality, Rights, and Democracy

At first sight, the left-wing populists' views are more compatible with the establishment narrative's two-step approach to organizing economic life than the protectionists' approach. Left-wing populists are happy to maximize economic growth if it is accompanied by effective redistribution to ensure greater equality. However, the main disagreement between the establishment narrative and the left-wing populist narrative nowadays is not about whether to prioritize economic growth or economic equality; it is about whether the two values are in conflict at all.

Mainstream economists have long held that there is a trade-off between economic growth and equality, and they have insisted on maximizing the former.[17] Some proponents of the left-wing populist narrative contest the view that there is such a trade-off, arguing that the pathologies of Western economies—rising inequality, lack of social mobility, and financialization—actually represent a drag on growth.[18] Similarly, proponents of some strands of the corporate power narrative complain that we do not even know what the distributive effects of international economic agreements are, and we are therefore unable to make informed choices, including about issues such as intellectual property protection, regulatory harmonization, and ISDS. They argue that proponents of the establishment narrative should abandon their "default attitude" of support for trade agreements and instead demand positive evidence of the benefits of these provisions.[19]

Apart from this general debate, there are specific issues in relation to which proponents of the left-wing populist and corporate power narratives do set certain values as absolute and refuse to trade them off in the name of increasing economic efficiency. These arguments are typically founded on ideas about the protection of individual rights, such as the rights to health, education, and decent working conditions, or about the protection of collective goods, such as democracy and regulatory autonomy. For example, Bernie Sanders's long-standing campaign for "Medicare for all" is framed as an attempt to guarantee healthcare to all people as a human right as part of an "Economic Bill of Rights."[20] This framing reflects the same absolutist approach that informed Cuomo's stance on the coronavirus epidemic—though Sanders and his allies would add that eliminating profiteering from the healthcare and education sectors would, as an added benefit, also increase efficiency.

Proponents of the corporate power narrative often invoke rights such as the right to health to oppose the types of trade-offs that lie at the heart of international economic agreements. In these agreements, developing countries typically promise to exchange increased intellectual property protections for export opportunities to developed countries' markets. Proponents of the corporate power narrative argue that such horse-trading must not come at the expense of developing countries' ability to provide essential medicines to their populations, since to do otherwise would imperil their citizens' right to health. In the WTO, developing countries and health advocates have had some success in reframing the scope of intellectual property protection as an issue that implicates the right to health. The TRIPS agreement, for example, was amended to facilitate developing countries' access to essential medicines through "compulsory licensing" during public health crises.[21]

In other instances, proponents of the corporate power narrative invoke rights primarily as a means to achieve their distributive ends. These proponents advocate including labor rights in trade agreements partly because they expect that improved rights protection for workers in developing countries will redound to the benefit of workers in developed countries as well, who will face less competitive pressure if their counterparts in developing countries enjoy better wages and working conditions. This link may explain why the protection of no other set of individual rights in *developing* countries enjoys as much support among politicians in *developed* countries as the protection of labor rights. These individual rights are invoked partly for their instrumental effect, not just their intrinsic value; if their proponents could get their distributive concerns met in another way, they might be willing to trade off their stated concern.

As regards the protection of collective goods, Dani Rodrik argues that the last few decades of what he calls "hyperglobalization" have pushed us in the wrong direction. Global rules inevitably confront us with a "central trade-off." On the one hand, they "increase efficiency, reduce transaction costs, and multiply the benefits of scale." On the other hand, they reduce autonomy, diminish democracy, and limit the scope for policy experimentation. To a mainstream economist, national sovereignty is often a problem to be overcome because inconsistent domestic rules slow down economic integration and limit efficiency. To Rodrik, by contrast, the ability of national governments to develop policies that suit their specific circumstances and to engage in policy experimentation are significant goals. Rodrik argues that a "well-crafted globalisation regime would pursue an appropriate mix of global efficiency and policy diversity, not simply maximise one at the expense of the other."[22]

Efficiency versus Security

Should the United States and China decouple in certain technology fields, such as 5G infrastructure, and work for greater self-sufficiency in essential items, such as medical supplies? If the only concern were economic efficiency, the answer to these questions would be an unequivocal no, since decoupling and increased self-sufficiency entail substantial economic costs. For proponents of the geoeconomic narrative, however, the economic cost is worth paying to safeguard their country's security. Whether you think that the United States is rightly or wrongly concerned about Huawei, you will not find the answer by reading David Ricardo on comparative advantage, notes economist Tyler Cowen.[23] That is because the debate involves a clash of competing values: prosperity-enhancing efficiency and economically costly security.

This conflict reflects the foundational guns-versus-butter questions that have preoccupied realist scholars of international relations for decades. The realist school sees international politics as "a recurring struggle for wealth and power among independent actors in a state of anarchy."[24] In this environment, each country needs to decide how to divide its resources between guns (defense goods) and butter (civilian goods).[25] In the long term, of course, security goals and wealth maximization are interdependent: reliable wealth maximization depends on having a secure country, and a secure country relies on having sufficient funds for an effective defense. In some concrete cases, however, a given policy choice presents a clear trade-off between the two.

The rise of China has left policymakers in various Western countries trying to work out how to integrate these different, and sometimes incommensurable, values in defining the national interest. The choices that the West faces in its relationship with China are much more complex than they ever were in its relationship with its primary geopolitical rival in the twentieth century, the Soviet Union. The Soviet Union reached its superpower status during the 1930s and 1940s, a period of international economic retrenchment and war; moreover, it followed its own economic model, in which trade with the West played a minor role. By contrast,

China's rise since the 1980s coincided with a period of high globalization, and its breakneck industrialization was powered in no small part by trade with and investment from the West. As a result, the level of economic integration and interdependence between the West and China is much deeper than it was with the Soviet Union.

The choices that the West confronts in its relationship with China are uncommonly complex not only because of the *depth* of its economic interdependence with China; the technological developments of the past decades have also vastly expanded the *breadth* of economic activity that is seen to pose potential security risks, as the ubiquity of digital technologies and data in modern economies multiplies opportunities for espionage, sabotage, and other nefarious activities. When China was mainly an exporter of plastic toys, furniture, and other simple manufactured goods, deep trade ties raised few security concerns. It was only when Chinese companies began to master and in some cases dominate cutting-edge technology, as well as the production of critical goods such as medicines and rare earth metals, that interdependence with China came to be viewed with more suspicion.

However, neither the deep economic integration between China and the West nor China's increasing technological prowess would, on their own or even when taken together, necessarily have created the perception that the West has to trade off the economic gains of its relationship with China against its security risks. Instead, a key factor that has brought this trade-off to the fore has been the changing perception of China's intentions. When Western governments and corporations embarked on their single-minded pursuit of the economic benefits of deeper integration with China, they did so on the assumption that interdependence would further their security interests as well—not only by escalating the costs of an all-out military confrontation but also by transforming China's economy and political system in a more market-friendly and democratic direction. It was the gradual realization that this expectation was unfounded—Xi Jinping's China was instead doubling down on its own economic and political path—that brought the trade-off into sharp relief, prompting commentators and politicians in the United States and increasingly in other Western countries to sound the alarm bells.[26] The West's growing perception that China's intentions may be hostile has made China's increasing capabilities appear in a new, more threatening light. As a result, attention has shifted from the absolute gains that both countries derived from their relationship to changes in their relative positions.[27]

This dynamic is particularly striking in the case of technological power, notably dual-use technologies such as artificial intelligence and quantum computing. When the United States held a clear technological lead over China, it was hardly troubled that Chinese researchers were studying in its universities and US companies were handing over their intellectual property in exchange for market access. Instead, these relationships were seen as positives, since innovative capacity is often aided by immigration flows and wider markets, and the United States did not view China as a threat at the time. As the technological capacity gap between the two countries has narrowed, however, the United States has focused less on its absolute position (how much and how fast is the United States innovating?) and more on its relative position (how can the United States retain its technological lead over China?). Since technology transfers help advance China's technological catch-up game, this shift is generating more concern in the United States about such transfers, and the concern reverberates in policies ranging from restrictions on Chinese science and technology students to export controls and investment screening.[28]

Political scientists have created more general models of the trade-off between absolute and relative gains in collaborations involving advanced technology. For instance, Jonathan Tucker has created a model for understanding the trade-offs that a technological leader must make in deciding whether to collaborate with a rising technological player. In terms of absolute welfare, collaboration generally yields a positive payoff for both parties because it permits better technology to be developed faster. Yet because more know-how typically flows from the stronger technological power to the weaker one, the positional payoff means that the weaker party gains ground. For the weaker party, technological collaboration thus involves absolute and relative gains. For the stronger party, however, it may involve absolute gains but a relative positional loss; determining the leader's net interest requires weighing the two (Figure 11.1).[29]

Are there any general lessons here for when trade-offs between economic efficiency and security will appear? Proponents of the establishment narrative argue that deepening economic integration diminishes the incentive for each side to engage in hostile actions, as they come to rely on the other more. This mutual reliance does not remove vulnerability so much as reduce the likelihood of hostile intentions existing or being acted upon. But this reasoning requires several qualifications.

First, interdependence engenders fewer concerns about vulnerability where it is symmetrical, as both sides have an equal incentive to preserve

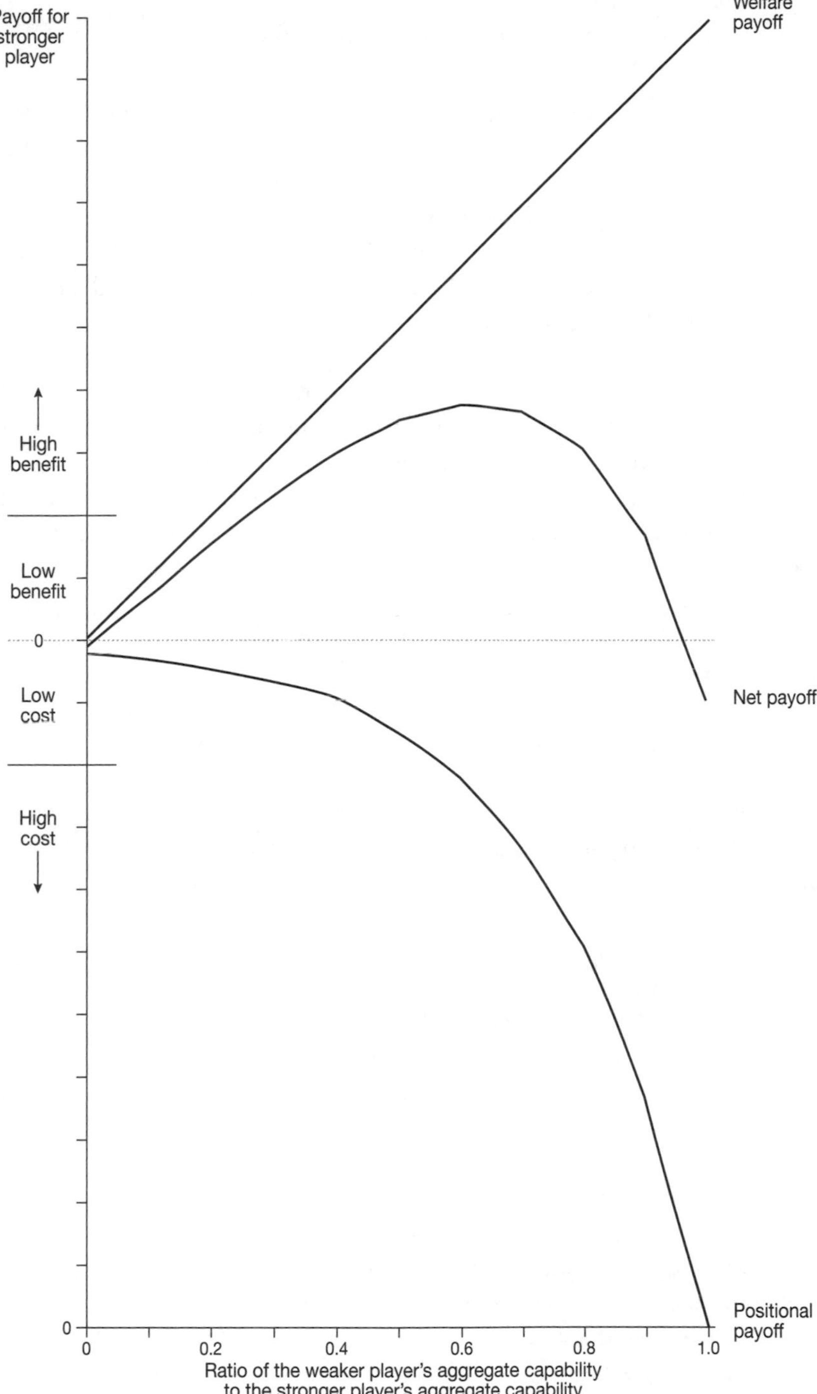

Fig. 11.1: How to Determine the Net Payoff When Cooperating with a Weaker Party

Note: This diagram shows the trade-off between absolute gains ("welfare payoff") and relative losses ("positional payoff") that a stronger party experiences in engaging in technological cooperation with a weaker party. At some point, the latter may outweigh the former.

Credit: Reformatted from Jonathan B. Tucker, "Partners and Rivals: A Model of International Collaboration in Advanced Technology," International Organization *45, no. 1 (Winter, 1991), 83–120, figure 1.*

the relationship. However, in cases where the interdependence is asymmetrical—for instance, where a small country is much more reliant on trade flows with a large country than vice versa, or a seller has access to alternative buyers whereas the buyer is dependent on the seller—one interdependent party is more vulnerable than the other. As political scientists Robert Keohane and Joseph Nye explain, the less dependent actor can use the interdependent relationship as a source of power in bargaining.[30]

Second, even though two deeply and symmetrically interdependent economies may have little incentive to exploit each other's vulnerabilities, the consequences of disruptions are all the more devastating the deeper the interdependence is. The same interdependence that drives down the probability of conflict (by reducing intent) also magnifies the consequences (by worsening the potential fallout). Since risk is a product of probability and consequences, increased interdependence plays an ambiguous role. That ambiguity means that the policy merits of increased interdependence are often interpreted in diametrically opposed ways by economists, who focus on the reduced probability of conflict, and security specialists, who are wary of the heightened consequences of disruptions.

As risk depends on a combination of probability and consequences, risk levels will vary among activities and sectors. Digital and economic connectivity represents a case in point. The 5G issue is often styled as a concern about low-probability, high-impact events. Even if there is a low probability that Huawei or the Chinese government would weaponize 5G networks by, for instance, cutting off digital communications, some countries may still judge it not worth the risk as the consequences could be catastrophic. By contrast, the same dire consequences do not exist for most trading relations, where disruptions would be costly but would not endanger a country's critical infrastructure. This difference helps to explain why we are seeing stronger moves toward the bifurcation of 5G than we are with economic relations in general.[31]

Finally, interdependence can create risks even in the absence of hostile intentions, as demonstrated by the coronavirus outbreak. The export bans on medical supplies imposed by various countries in response to the pandemic show that a country may refuse to export medical supplies to another country simply in an effort to ensure that it can meet the demands of its own population rather than because it bears any ill will toward the other country.

Trade-offs Involving Different Probabilities

One of the difficulties in weighing economic and security interests is that they do not simply involve different values but also often involve different underlying probabilities. This observation applies as well to global threats, such as climate change and pandemics. Any framework for integrating insights from these different narratives must thus be mindful of both differences.

Economics versus Security

In many cases that pit economic and security interests against each other, decision-makers are asked to weigh high-probability economic gains against low-probability but high-impact security risks, as in the case of 5G connectivity. Decision-makers often struggle to assess low-probability, high-impact events rationally. When very unlikely events or "tail" risks are not discussed, people often underestimate the likelihood of their occurrence; they focus on what happens when everything is normal, not what might happen at the outer limits of probability.[32] For instance, in insurance contracts, people typically neglect improbable events, even if they would have a high impact. They would rather insure against probable small losses than improbable large ones. When tail risks are discussed, however, the opposite occurs: people are likely to overestimate that the risk will come to pass. People asked to assess the probability of death from a plane crash tend to exaggerate its likelihood because the very question turns their mind to the possibility of disaster.[33]

The establishment narrative frequently deals with economic risks and rewards that are relatively probable—that is, that typically occur within one or two standard deviations from the mean (most likely) outcome. The basic mental model adopted is a bell curve where most outcomes, good or bad, will fall within a few standard deviations of the mean, whereas highly positive and highly negative outcomes are not only unlikely but will balance each other out. The geoeconomic narrative, by contrast, often involves a greater focus on tail risks, particularly of events that might be improbable but would have a high impact. One problem with tail risks is that there is no rational way to evaluate them, as Nassim Taleb argues. When probability goes to zero but the consequences approach infinity, there can be no rational risk calculation because zero multiplied by infinity is mathematically undefined.[34] Faced with this sort of impossibility, economists have often defaulted to focusing on the low probability, while security specialists have often focused on the infinite harm.

It is not just that some events are more likely than others; the shape of the underlying probability curves may be different for economic and security gains and risks, respectively. Some of the risks that proponents of the geoeconomic, corporate power, and global threats narratives are worried about are better understood by using a power law curve, which is asymmetrical, rather than a bell curve (Figure 11.2). For example, digital connectivity often leads to a power law curve where a handful of companies service the vast majority of users due to the operation of network effects and preferential attachment, creating concerns about both corporate concentration and security risks. Hazards like earthquakes and pandemics often also follow power law curves where modest events are relatively common, but extreme events are very rare. Small disruptions in international supply chains may be common, but large ones (such as the one arising from the coronavirus) are rare. Unlike the bell curve model, the power law model provides no counterbalancing risk of an extremely good event for the risk of an extremely bad event. There is no equal and opposite good to the coronavirus, for example. Bell curves teach us for the most part to exclude outliers from our considerations because they are infrequent and cancel each other out, but that approach cannot be adopted for risks that exhibit power law characteristics.

Complex systems that do not follow a bell curve distribution often arise in networked and collective settings where contagion shapes behavior, like runs on a bank or the financial failures that led to the global financial crisis. In such systems, the probability distribution for possible events is frequently fat-tailed, which means that there is a higher probability of extreme events occurring, such as a massive increase in infections or the failure of a single, central node causing contagion within a networked system. Complex systems are often bursty, which means that they can rapidly tip out of control due to a handful of outlier events. In these systems, markers like the average rate at which people transmit an infection may be considerably less important than the occurrence of a small number of superspreader events. Although these outlier events are still unlikely, they occur more frequently than would be expected under normal bell curve distributions. And once a low-probability but high-impact tail event takes place, it raises the probability of further tail events, like earthquake aftershocks. These nonlinear and unpredictable dynamics further complicate efforts to weigh economic and security interests.[35]

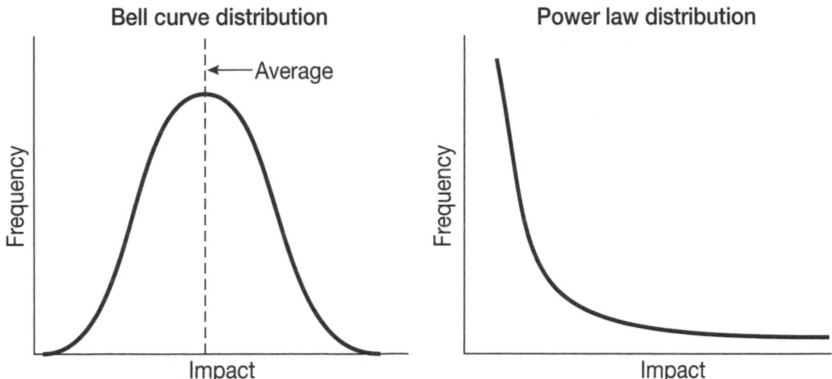

Fig. 11.2: Different Distribution Curves Often Underlie Economic and Security Thinking

Note: The bell curve distribution often underlies the economic perspective: the low risk of very high losses is balanced out by the low risk of very high rewards, with most events clustering around the average point. The power law distribution often underlies the security perspective: there is no positive counterpart for the low risk of a catastrophic security failure.

Economics versus Environmental Risks

A similar difficulty of integrating or trading off different probability profiles arises in the climate change debate. In climate modeling, scientists have often focused on the most likely outcomes of different climate change scenarios. Yet some are turning their attention to worst-case scenarios that are lower in probability but higher in consequence.[36] They recognize that although some of these outlier scenarios might be unlikely, their effects would be devastating, and the advent of tipping points—where a small shift might set in motion large-scale, irreversible changes—may make these extreme events more likely to occur and harder to predict. The decision to include modeling based on abrupt change in the 2021 report of the Intergovernmental Panel on Climate Change acknowledges the cogency of this thinking.[37]

There is also an expanding critique that the economic modeling of the effects of climate change radically underestimates the potential costs. Although climate scientists are increasingly alarmed about the physical impact of climate change, most economists seem to be comparatively blasé about its potential economic costs. One reason they differ may be the lack of commensurability of different values. Economic modeling typically focuses on the impact of climate change on GDP. Yet, as the Intergovernmental Panel on Climate Change notes, many impacts, such as loss of human life, cultural heritage, and ecosystem services, are difficult to value in monetary terms. As with security risks, it can be hard to capture the value of environmental preservation or destruction in economic models, which leads to significant underestimation of their impact on human lives and livelihoods.[38]

The standard economic models also have trouble accounting for low-risk but high-probability events that are unprecedented in human history, cascading risks where the compounding of different factors makes them much worse than they would be in isolation, and tipping points where small changes cross thresholds that result in fundamental and irreversible shifts. As many estimates do not adequately take into account factors such as catastrophic changes and tipping points, the models have been criticized for "grafting gross underestimation of risk onto already narrow science models," as the economist Nicholas Stern has put it.[39] "These uncertainties mean that the impacts are difficult to represent in terms of costs and benefits and are therefore often ignored or omitted from economic models. In essence, they are assigned a probability of zero even though it is understood that to do so is incorrect."[40] There have been calls to improve how the models cope with the uncertainty and risk inherent in climate change.[41]

As the world becomes more connected and more uncertain, both geopolitically and ecologically, risk assessments may come to focus increasingly on low-probability but high-impact events, either because they are now more likely to occur or because probability is harder to assess in complex and unpredictable environments. As geopolitical tensions rise, events that may once have looked like unlikely tail risks may begin to be perceived as more likely. China has a history of imposing trade sanctions on countries that have displeased it over the years, such as banning Norwegian salmon in 2015 and punishing South Korea in 2017 for installing a US anti-missile shield. But the scale of sanctions by China that Australia experienced in 2020 was unprecedented, targeting more than a dozen sectors and impacting over 10 percent of Australia's exports.[42] In the environment, extreme weather events, such as the massive pyrocumulonimbus storm clouds that can form over the most intense fires, are becoming more common. Such firestorms are historically rare, but dozens ravaged Australia in the 2019–2020 summer of fire. To deploy their resources to maximum effect, firefighters must rely on models to predict how fires will unfold, but the progression of the now more commonly seen megablazes does not fit the current models, which are based on previous observations of smaller fires.[43]

Some authorities are responding to changing realities by adjusting their approach to risk management. For instance, one reason the 2019 Australian New Year's Eve inferno caused so much damage and disruption was that its spread, instead of conforming to the most likely scenario, followed the worst-case scenario. Recognizing this pattern, the fire services subsequently stopped basing their projections of fire zones on the most likely scenario and circulated the worst-case scenario instead. Similarly, Mark Carney, former governor of the Bank of England, explains that insurers are starting to recognize with respect to climate change risks that "the past is not prologue and . . . the catastrophic norms of the future can be seen in the tail risks of today." The devastating effects of other low-probability, high-consequence events like the coronavirus pandemic are also making governments around the world rethink the balance between efficiency and resilience in their supply chains. Building more redundancy into supply chains and ensuring some level of domestic manufacturing capacity or stockpiling will be more expensive, but governments may be more willing to pay that price, especially if risks like pandemics become more frequent in the age of global connections and the Anthropocene.[44]

Conclusion

In some ways, the six faces of the Rubik's cube are complementary in that they describe different parts of the same reality. In other ways, the different narratives express normative commitments to different values. Once we move past the establishment narrative, the question no longer is just how to maximize economic gains but how to weigh efficiency against other values, such as family and community stability, equality and rights, national security, and environmental protection. Integrating different values and probabilities into common frameworks is difficult and requires policymakers to make normative choices about which values to recognize, what risks to tolerate, and how to trade off competing goals.

CHAPTER 12

Blind Spots and Biases

Nassim Taleb is famous for popularizing the concept of the black swan, which refers to an unforeseen event of major impact. Before 1690, only white swans had been observed in the Northern Hemisphere and thus people from the West assumed that black swans did not exist. This assumption was proven wrong when a Dutch explorer observed black swans; it was an unforeseen event that changed how people viewed swans. But from the perspective of Aurora Milroy, an indigenous woman raised in Noongar country in Australia, the black swan theory "highlights the arrogance of Western knowledge systems." For her mob, a black swan was not unforeseen—"Noongars had this knowledge all along." The black swan anecdote illustrates the need to interweave Western and non-Western knowledge and perspectives to create a more rounded understanding.[1]

What holds true for swans also applies to economic globalization. Many in the West still treat Western experiences as universal. We do not want to make this mistake. The narratives that we have reconstructed in this book dominate debates about economic globalization in the West, but they do not reflect the experiences of many outside the West. For instance, even as the backlash against globalization was brewing in the West, the Singaporean public intellectual and former diplomat Kishore Mahbubani noted that "for the majority of us, the past three decades—1990 to 2020—have been the best in human history," as hundreds of millions were lifted out of poverty and living standards soared across much of the developing world. Parag Khanna, the author of the book *The Future Is Asian,* concurs: "Western populist politics from Brexit to Trump haven't infected Asia, where pragmatic governments are focused on inclusive growth and social cohesion. . . . Rather than being backward-looking, navel-gazing, and pessimistic, billions of Asians are forward-looking, outward-orientated, and optimistic."[2]

This is not to say that the narratives that dominate debates about economic globalization in the West have no currency elsewhere. Proponents of the establishment narrative occupy influential positions in many non-Western countries; indeed, many developing countries that used to be skeptical about economic globalization later became staunch advocates for it.[3] China's president Xi, for example, declared at the World Economic Forum in Davos in 2017: "We must remain committed to developing global free trade and investment, promote trade and investment liberalization and facilitation through opening-up and say no to protectionism."[4] India is the birthplace of numerous prominent international economists, including Jagdish Bhagwati, Raghuram Rajan, and T. N. Srinivasan, all of whom are strong proponents of the establishment narrative. Yet, just as in the West, no single narrative predominates in non-Western countries. In China, New Left and neo-Maoist groups have objected to the country's market transformation, framing the WTO as the tool of a "'soft war' waged by Western powers, particularly the United States and the United Kingdom, to pry open China's markets for the benefit of Western corporations."[5] And India is home to influential public intellectuals who decry global capitalism, imperialism, and environmental destruction, such as Pankaj Mishra, Sunita Narain, Vandana Shiva, and Arundhati Roy.[6]

Other Rubik's cube narratives also play out beyond the West. Indian prime minister Narendra Modi's promotion of Hindu nationalism is reminiscent of Trump's nativism.[7] For Russia, national security considerations have become central to its relationship with the West, especially since the latter's imposition of crippling financial sanctions after the Russian annexation of Crimea. Brazil's president, Jair Bolsonaro, combines elements of different narratives; he embraces neoliberal economic orthodoxy while rejecting climate science and calling for more of the Amazon rainforest to be cleared for farming, mining, and logging. Many of the most vocal proponents of the global threats narratives also come from outside the West, including the leaders of various Pacific Island countries endangered by climate change.

These examples—and there are many more—reveal considerable overlap between debates in the West and elsewhere, as well as much variation within and between countries. In the remainder of the chapter, however, we focus on some non-Western perspectives that are absent from or downplayed in the Western debates. Some of these reflect blind spots related to the specific historical role of the West: its subjugation and exploitation of non-Western peoples still color the perspective of many developing countries on economic globalization but do not register significantly in Western mainstream narratives. Some other non-Western perspectives reflect biases derived from a particular geographical vantage point: whereas right-wing populists in the West see the movement of manufacturing jobs to the developing world as a story of loss and decline, for workers in emerging economies in Asia that same movement feeds uplifting narratives about Asia's rise. Moreover, Western narratives often share certain unquestioned assumptions about the superiority of Western values and forms of political and market organization that some non-Western governments reject as hegemonic impositions. And those in the poorest countries of the world who are truly left behind by globalization rarely feature in Western narratives about economic globalization.

Although not exhaustive, these alternative perspectives help to highlight some of the blind spots and biases of the six faces of globalization on which we focus. They remind us that what is omitted or treated as a side issue in one story line may be central to another. In sketching the following non-Western narratives, we have had recourse to a variety of local and foreign sources. As Western scholars almost exclusively educated and employed in Western countries, our ability to identify and articulate these narratives is necessarily limited. We have benefited greatly from suggestions by colleagues all over the world who have broadened our understanding, but our perspectives nevertheless remain partial on account of our own positionality. We hope that others with different experiences will supplement and qualify our understanding of how various narratives from outside the West confirm, run counter to, or extend the six faces of globalization that we have discussed in detail.

The Neocolonial Narrative

The longest-standing narrative from outside the West, the neocolonial narrative, maintains that Western countries fashioned the rules of economic globalization to suit the interests of their citizens and the transnational capitalist class at the expense of developing countries. According to this narrative, the developed countries have used international law and international institutions to perpetuate the quasi-colonial domination of developing countries in the spheres of international trade, investment, and finance.

Since 1945, the neocolonial critique of the multilateral trading regime has been most clearly articulated in three contexts. First, when the regime was established in the 1940s, countries such as India and Cuba raised concerns that the Anglo-American designs would stifle the development of newly independent countries and prolong the disadvantageous international division of labor. As the Cuban representative put it during negotiations in 1947, developing countries feared that by adopting the trade obligations suggested by the United States, they would be "freezing the actual economic status of the different countries of the world. The agricultural countries would continue to be agricultural. The monopoly countries would continue to be monopolies, and the more developed countries would continue selling typewriters and radios, etc. to those nations that were trying to produce the primitive tools."[8] This argument would later be developed into dependency theory, which was originally formulated by economists in Latin America but also embraced as applicable to other developing regions.[9]

A second, related target of the neocolonial critique of the multilateral trade regime was the hypocrisy of the developed countries in pushing for trade liberalization in sectors where they held the comparative advantage, while maintaining high barriers to agricultural products and textiles, the primary exports of most developing countries.[10] While the developed countries used the multilateral trade regime with remarkable success to reduce tariffs on industrial products, they left barriers on agricultural products virtually untouched, and even expanded subsidy programs for their farmers to a degree that left developing-country farmers unable to compete. And when developing countries became competitive in some manufacturing sectors formerly dominated by developed countries, such as in textiles and clothing in the 1950s and 1960s, the developed countries responded by citing the danger of "market disruption" and erecting new import barriers to protect their domestic industries.[11]

A third prong of the neocolonial critique took aim at the exclusionary negotiating tactics employed by the developed countries to further their interests and disempower the developing countries in the multilateral trade regime. The GATT, adopted in 1947, was seen by many as a "rich men's club," where "the leading countries could go off to do business by themselves." Most agreements were formulated by the so-called Quad (the United States, the European Union, Japan, and Canada) before being presented as a fait accompli to the broader membership. This procedure left developing countries with few means to ensure that multilateral trade negotiations addressed their concerns and little leverage to prevent skewed outcomes.[12] These issues came to a head during the Uruguay Round of trade negotiations in the late 1980s and early 1990s, when the United States and Europe pushed for more effective protection of intellectual property despite fierce objections by developing countries.[13] The developed countries ultimately managed to compel developing countries to accept these new obligations by creating the WTO and making acceptance of intellectual property rights a precondition for membership. Developing countries faced the choice of either joining the WTO—an organization armed with a compulsory dispute settlement system—or being shut out of the multilateral trade regime. Even some US commentators described the outcome of the Uruguay Round as a "contract of adhesion" (meaning a contract in which the powerful side drafts all the terms and the less powerful side is left in a "take-it-or-leave-it" position).[14]

The results of the Uruguay Round remain a sore point for many developing countries. From their perspective, the Doha Round of trade negotiations, launched in 2001, was supposed to "rebalance" the trade regime after the skewed results of the previous round by focusing on rules that would promote development. But the Doha Round ultimately folded, in part because the United States and the European Union refused to reduce support for their agricultural sectors if they did not receive significant additional concessions from developing countries in return. From the neocolonial perspective, the collapse of the Doha Round marked a failure of the multilateral trade regime to deliver for developing countries, whereas the existing rules continue to reflect and protect the interests of the developed countries and their corporations.[15]

The neocolonial narrative tells a similar story of exploitation and hypocrisy about international investment protection. During colonial times, investors from the colonial powers would frequently be granted ownership or concession agreements to extract resources in the colonial territory. Prior to decolonization, these investments were generally protected by the extraterritorial application of colonial law. After the colonies gained independence, Western governments needed to find a way to safeguard the investments of their nationals in the new countries. However, having just achieved their freedom, these developing countries asserted their entitlement to exercise permanent sovereignty over their natural resources and to expropriate these investments for the benefit of their people.[16] The newly independent countries' desire to "recover control over vital sectors of their economies from foreign investors" led to a wave of nationalizations.[17]

These conflicting interests led to significant confrontations between developed and developing countries over the obligations owed to foreign nationals under international law. As developing countries gained a numerical advantage in the United Nations General Assembly, they pushed through a series of resolutions that would enshrine the principle of permanent sovereignty over natural resources and establish a New International Economic Order. Developed countries responded by shifting form and forum. They started entering into what would ultimately become thousands of bilateral investment treaties, many of which had compulsory arbitration provisions. Although developing countries had been able to hold the line when they were acting as a group in the United Nations, the bilateral approach allowed developed countries to play a game of "divide and conquer" by making the developing countries compete with each other to attract capital.[18]

Developing countries started to feel the bite of these bilateral investment treaties in the early 2000s when investors initiated a growing number of arbitral claims against developing countries, particularly in Latin America. Argentina was the hardest hit, facing more than thirty claims worth billions of dollars after its financial crisis in 2001–2002. Yet developed-country governments remained unmoved by the plight of developing countries and often sided with their multinational corporations. Only when developed countries themselves were sued by investors and faced public protests, which were motivated by the corporate power narrative's concerns about investor-state dispute settlement, did some reconsider their stance.

The neocolonial narrative also accuses international financial institutions, such as the World Bank and the IMF, of wielding their financial leverage over developing countries to impose neoliberal policies that ultimately come at the expense of developing countries and their populations.[19] For instance, African commentators often criticize the structural adjustment programs overseen by the international financial institutions, which required many African countries to adopt neoliberal market principles in return for debt assistance. According to former Ghanaian president Kwame Nkrumah: "The essence of neo-colonialism is that the State which is subject to it is, in theory, independent and has all the outward trappings of international sovereignty. In reality its economic system and thus its political policy is directed from outside." The Ghanaian political scientist Kwame Ninsin agrees: "African governments no longer sovereign in making public policy . . . have been reduced to virtual recipients and implementers of policies" issued by the "dictatorship of the Bretton Woods institutions."[20]

To proponents of the neocolonial narrative, this form of economic imperialism by Western countries and corporations and international institutions has often been facilitated by the elite in developing countries themselves, both because it suits their individual economic interests and because many have used their privilege to study and work in the West, which often imbues them with Western ideas. Notable examples include the "Chicago Boys" in Chile, the "Vanderbilt Boys" in Brazil, and the "Berkeley Mafia" in Indonesia—all of them US-trained economists who subsequently occupied positions of power in their home governments and applied their neoliberal training in redesigning their countries' economic policies.[21] By highlighting the impact of international economic law and institutions on developing countries, which often had little say in creating them and much less influence on their operation than Western countries, the neocolonial narrative illuminates a significant blind spot in the Western narratives about economic globalization.

Narratives on the Rise of Asia

Bucking the idea that all developing countries are losers in a game shaped by neocolonial Western domination, many Asian countries have leveraged their comparative advantage in cheap and abundant labor to integrate into the world economy and to fuel their own development. This strategy has enabled Asia in general and China in particular to become the factory of the world. The economic gains many countries have reaped as a result have engendered a range of positive narratives about economic globalization in Asia. Asian countries may not have created the rules, the story goes, but hard work and proactive government policies have made them the game's unexpected winners (Figure 12.1). The upswing has spawned several narratives about Asia's rise that are broadly similar but differ in the actors they focus on, the levels of analysis they adopt, the explanations they favor, and the time period in which they came to the fore.

An early version, the East Asian miracle narrative, took its name from a widely read, though controversial, 1993 World Bank report.[22] From 1965 to 1990, the twenty-three economies of East Asia grew faster than those in all other regions of the world, having rapidly industrialized by focusing on exports. Japan was first, followed by the Four Tigers (Hong

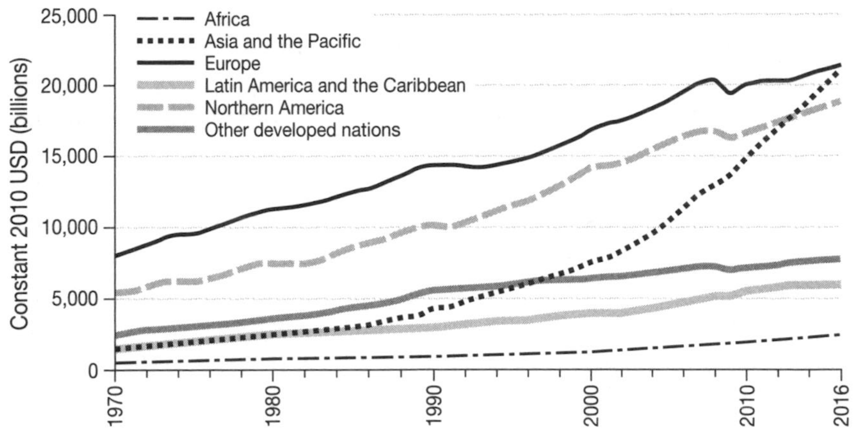

Fig. 12.1: Asia Is Rising
Note: This graph shows GDP by region in constant 2010 US dollars from 1970 to 2016.
Data source: United Nations Statistics Division and the Food and Agriculture Organization.

Kong, the Republic of Korea, Singapore, and Taiwan), and then China and the three newly industrialized economies of Southeast Asia (Indonesia, Malaysia, and Thailand). The latter eight countries grew more than twice as fast as the rest of East Asia, roughly three times as fast as Latin America and South Asia, and five times faster than sub-Saharan Africa. The combination of high growth and relatively equal income distributions within those countries prompted the "miracle" moniker, though debates continue about what caused it.

Another story line, which focuses more on China and India, could be called the awakening-giants narrative. According to this narrative, both countries were once "great empires in their own right," and both "awoke" after a "long sleep,"[23] like "giants shaking off their 'socialist slumber'" or "'caged tigers' unshackled."[24] Whereas the East Asian miracle narrative emphasizes economic models, this narrative looks more to economic fundamentals, such as population size, and their implications not just for growth but also for the global balance of economic power.

Of the two countries, China began its rapid expansion first. After deciding to reintegrate into the world economy in 1978, the country experienced unprecedented growth for more than three decades, making China the world's second-largest economy (the largest in purchasing power parity terms) and in the process lifting more than 700 million people out of poverty. Those achievements have turned its leaders into vocal advocates of economic globalization. "Economic globalization has powered global growth and facilitated movement of goods and capital, advances in science, technology and civilization, and interactions among peoples," President Xi has marveled.[25]

India followed suit after decades of nationalist economic policies failed to remedy its poor economic performance. As Jagdish Bhagwati recounts: "From the 1960s to the 1980s, India remained locked in relatively autarkic trade policies; the Far Eastern countries . . . shifted to outward orientation dramatically. The results speak for themselves: exports and income grew at abysmal rates in India, at dramatic rates in the Far East. India missed the bus. No, it missed the Concorde!"[26] India reversed course in 1991 and adopted a series of economic reforms with the aim of liberalizing its markets, which led to a sustained period of strong economic growth and a significant drop in poverty rates.[27]

The awakening-giants narrative portrays the rise of these enormous countries as a return to their rightful place as titans on the world stage.[28] In the two millennia prior to 1820, China and India were the two largest economies in the world (Figure 12.2). After that, the Industrial Revolution propelled western Europe, followed by the United States, into a 200-year period of dominance in global production that saw Western living standards soar.[29] But the narrative sees those two centuries as an aberration that is now coming to an end. "By 2050 or earlier," Mahbubani claims, India and China will once again become the two largest economies in the world, and "we will return to the historic norm of the past 2000 years."[30]

Another narrative focuses less on China and India as great powers and more on the importance of the region as a whole. According to Indian prime minister Narendra Modi, the Asian continent now "finds itself at the centre of global economic activity": in this view, we are living through the "Asian Century." Wang Huiyao, president of the Beijing think tank Center for China and Globalization, describes Asia as "the center of global gravity"; in terms of purchasing power, Asian economies were projected to outperform the rest of the world combined in 2020 (Figure 12.3). As Khanna tells it: "In the 19th century, the world was Europeanized. In the 20th century, it was Americanized. Now, in the 21st century, the world is being irreversibly Asianized."[31]

Proponents of the various Asia-rising narratives suggest that, far from being on the receiving end of Western wisdom and power, Asian countries have lessons to offer the world about "Asian style" capitalism in

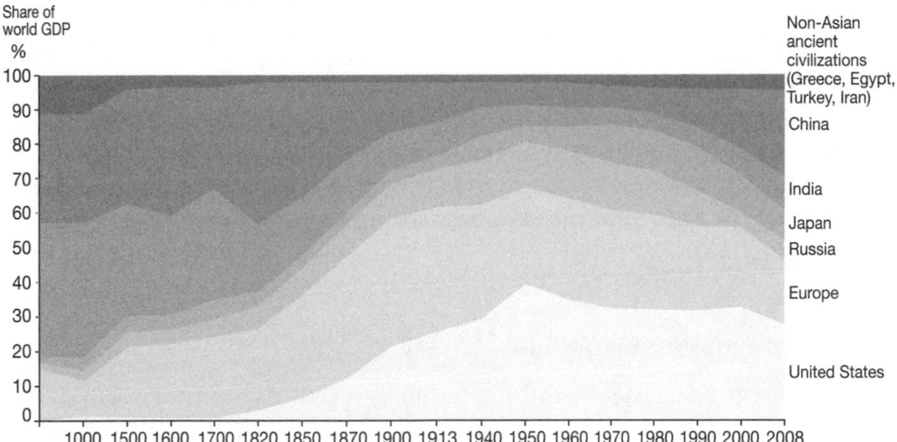

Fig. 12.2: China's and India's Share of the World Economy Is Returning to the Historical Norm

Note: This graph shows different countries' share of world GDP over the past 2,000 years.

Credit: Reformatted from Derek Thompson, "The Economic History of the Last 2,000 Years in 1 Little Graph," Atlantic, *June 19, 2020, figure: "Economic history of China and other major powers."*

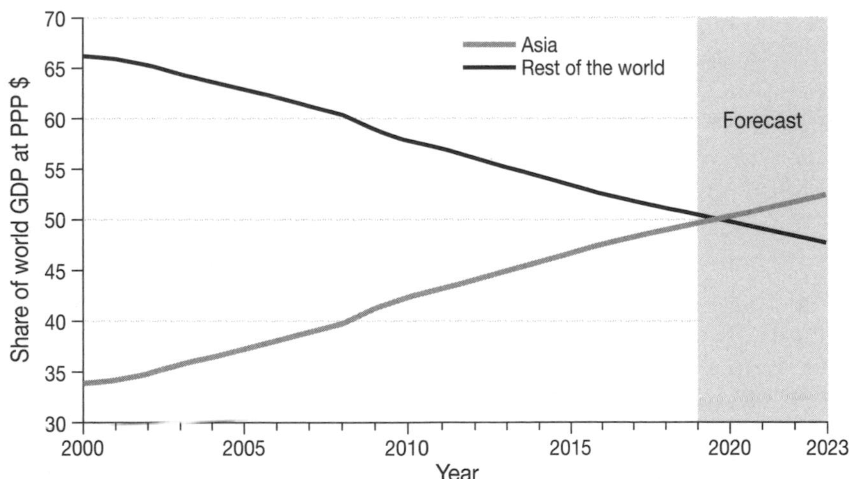

Fig. 12.3: The Beginning of the Asian Century

Note: This graph shows the trajectories of Asia's share of world GDP (in gray) and of the share of the rest of the world (in black) in purchasing parity terms. Asia's share of world GDP was forecast to surpass the rest of the world's share by 2020.

Credit: Reformatted from Valentina Romei and John Reed, "The Asian Century Is Set to Begin," Financial Times, *March 25, 2019, figure: "The Asian century is about to begin," by permission of the Financial Times.*

which governments take a stronger hand in steering economic policies than in the West, seeing the market as a partner, not a master.[32] By highlighting the policy choices that Asian governments have made and the resources they have mobilized to raise their populations out of poverty, these narratives decenter the West and bring the agency of Asian countries to the fore.

Narratives against Western Hegemony

In a different vein, Russia and China charge that the West is trying to use globalization to universalize its model of liberal democracy and market-led capitalism. Like the neocolonial narrative, the narratives against Western hegemony accuse the West of hypocrisy, pointing out that Western countries wrote the rules and expect other countries to follow them while often exempting themselves. But the thrust of the narratives against Western hegemony is directed against efforts to enforce a one-size-fits-all model of political and economic organization. Their proponents insist that different models must be respected, and that multipolarity, not hegemony, must be the global organizing principle.

Russian Narratives against Western Hegemony

Russia has experienced economic globalization very differently from Asian countries such as China and India. It faced multiple horrors in the decade following the collapse of the Soviet Union: decreased GDP *and* increased poverty *and* an extraordinary rise in inequality, particularly at the top end, which bulges with an exceptional concentration of wealth among billionaires. These events have been interpreted in radically different ways by the West, which has emphasized the wrong of extreme domestic inequality, and by Russia, where many have concluded that the Western model of political organization does not work for them.

The Western story starts with the observation that prior to the dissolution of the Soviet Union, the communist system had the effect of suppressing wage differences while providing many public goods, such as education, housing, health care, and childcare services. Although economic growth was not strong, it was more or less evenly apportioned. After Russia transitioned to capitalism, however, those in the bottom 50 percent of the income distribution saw their fortunes deteriorate, whereas the income of the top 10 percent skyrocketed by almost 200 percent. The most striking disparity appeared at the billionaire end

Table 12.1 Differences in Income Growth across Countries Show the Relative Explosion of Inequality in Russia

Income Group (distribution of per-adult pretax national income)	China (%)	Europe (%)	India (%)	Russia (%)	US and Canada (%)	World (%)
Full Population	**831**	**40**	**223**	**34**	**63**	**60**
Bottom 50%	417	26	107	–26	5	94
Middle 40%	785	34	112	5	44	43
Top 10%	1,316	58	469	190	123	70
Top 1%	*1,920*	*58*	*469*	*190*	*123*	*70*
Top 0.1%	*2,421*	*76*	*1,295*	*2,562*	*320*	*133*
Top 0.01%	*3,112*	*87*	*2,078*	*8,239*	*452*	*185*
Top 0.001%	*3,752*	*120*	*3,083*	*25,269*	*626*	*235*

Note: This table shows real income growth from 1980 to 2016 for different parts of the income distribution in various countries, regions, and the world. The income of the top 0.001 percent in Russia rose by over 25,000 percent, while the income of the bottom 50 percent of Russians fell by 26 percent.

Source: Facundo Alvaredo et al., "The Elephant Curve of Global Inequality and Growth" (World Inequality Database World Working Paper Series No. 2017/20, December 2017), Table 1.

of the spectrum, where a 25,000 percent increase in income of the top 0.001 percent between 1980 and 2016 produced a class of powerful oligarchs (Table 12.1).[33] These astounding levels of inequality resulted primarily from the rushed privatization of Russia's economy; instead of opting for a gradual transition to capitalism, the government engaged in a fire sale of its state-owned assets at massively undervalued prices.

Proponents of this narrative blame this debacle not just on the Russian government but also on Western advisors and international institutions that encouraged the "shock therapy" approach. According to Joseph Stiglitz, for instance, "The IMF told Russia to privatize as fast as possible; how privatization was done was viewed as secondary."[34] This approach was intended to ensure that Russia did not fall back into communism; it rested on optimistic assumptions that the market would ensure an efficient allocation of resources. But the bargain-basement prices of many assets enabled corrupt officials to snag exorbitantly good deals for themselves and their contacts. An enormous amount of wealth was transferred from the public to private individuals. Moreover, the newly rich did not push for the rule of law to protect their money, as Western advisors had predicted. Rather than fight for the rule of law in their own country, the oligarchs found it much easier to send their money to a tax haven or another jurisdiction that already practiced the rule of law.[35]

While the Western narratives about Russia continue to focus on the injustices of the country's astounding levels of inequality, the narratives more commonly found in Russia itself draw different lessons from the economic hardship and lawlessness that accompanied the transition to capitalism, as well as from the country's diminished international standing after the dissolution of the Soviet Union. The Western and Russian narratives already part company in the way they interpret the events of the 1989–1991 period. From the perspective of the West, the end of the Cold War often appears as a single political and ideological triumph; from Russia's perspective, however, it involved three developments of radically different—and in some ways very negative—historical significance.

The first development was the conclusion of the international confrontation with the West, which manifested itself in the reunification of Germany, the exit of the eastern European satellite states from the Soviet Union's orbit, and the eventual dissolution of the Warsaw Pact, a development that few Russians begrudge.

The second was the end of communism and the transition to capitalism, which was welcomed by many Russians at the time, but only because they expected that their material conditions would quickly improve. Yet, as Russian president Vladimir Putin has noted, "Life became worse for very many people, especially at the beginning of the 1990s when the social protection and healthcare systems collapsed and industry was crumbling." He admitted that the old system could be ineffective, but "at least people had jobs. After the collapse, they lost them." The deterioration of socioeconomic conditions that accompanied the transition to capitalism manifested itself in a stark increase in suicides and drug- and alcohol-related deaths and a sharp drop in average life expectancy—Russia's own version of deaths of despair.[36] In the view of many Russians, the liberal economic reformers were to blame for the "damned nineties."

But it was the third development that proved to be the most politically traumatic: the dissolution of the Soviet Union, an event that Putin would later describe as the "greatest geopolitical catastrophe of the century." The surprise with which Putin's assessment was greeted by many in the West illustrates the disconnect between Western and Russian perceptions of the end of the Cold War. For Russians, the dissolution of the Soviet Union came not only with economic hardship and political disorientation but also with a "harrowing loss of territory and population."[37]

It took time for a new narrative about Russia's role in the world to emerge. After the chaos of the transition years, Boris Yeltsin picked Putin as his successor in 1999. Putin went on to win the presidential election in 2000 and quickly moved to rein in the oligarchs who had run rampant under Yeltsin, reestablish state control over key industries, and restore a semblance of order in public life. In his first term, Putin oversaw the doubling of Russia's GDP and an even faster rise in real incomes.[38] "Russia has returned to the global stage as a strong state," he declared triumphantly in 2008, noting that "the main thing we achieved is stability."[39]

The lesson that Putin—and many Russians—derived from the 1990s was the need for strong leadership.[40] At the same time, Putin professes to have learned from the fall of the Soviet Union that stable leadership ultimately depends on popular support: "The internal reason for the Soviet Union's collapse was that life was difficult for the people. . . . The shops were empty, and the people lost the intrinsic desire to preserve the state. . . . One of the things we must do in Russia is never to forget that the purpose of the operation and existence of any government is to create a stable, normal, safe and predictable life for the people." For Putin, the Western emphasis on individual rights is simply not suited to achieving these objectives; the populist backlash against globalization and liberalism in the West shows that the "ruling elites" in Western countries have "broken away from the people" and that the liberal idea has "outlived its purpose" and is now "obsolete."[41]

Whereas the Russian establishment rejects criticism of domestic policies as "interference" in Russia's domestic affairs, it is the West's conduct in international relations that is at the center of Russian allegations of hypocrisy and double standards. In this telling, the West insists that others comply with international legal rules but disregards those rules when they do not suit its own interests. The West's differential treatment of Kosovo and Crimea is Russia's Exhibit A in this regard.[42] More recently, the Russian government has extended this narrative to the international economic order. Putin accuses "the states that previously preached the principles of free trade and honest and open competition" of now dealing in trade wars and sanctions, and resorting to "undisguised economic raids with arm[-]twisting, intimidation and the removal of rivals by so-called non-market methods."[43] Russian political scientists Sergei Karaganov and Dmitry Suslov concur, referring to the "so-called liberal world-order" as the era of the "law of the jungle," and celebrating the decline of Western dominance as giving rise to a new and fairer world order.[44]

Chinese Narratives against Western Hegemony

Although China's leaders have embraced economic globalization in language that reflects the establishment narrative, the Chinese government has long pushed back against the universalization of Western forms of political and economic organization. China undertook substantial market reforms in the process of transforming its economy and opening up to the world, including to gain entry to the WTO, but it retains a strong state-capitalist orientation. Every state should be permitted to chart its own path to development, Chinese officials regularly declare. Thus, President Xi states: "No country should view its own development path as the only viable one, still less should it impose its own development path on others." As the US government under the Trump administration escalated its pressure on China to embark on far-reaching economic reforms, Chinese officials insisted that the state would not compromise its "core interests" or its model of development and would "struggle" against those that sought to contain its rise.[45]

The need to "struggle" against Western oppression has special resonance in China because of the perception that the ancient civilization suffered a "Century of Humiliation" at the hands of Western oppressors, beginning with the Opium Wars, when Britain forced China to open up to British trade. According to Xi: "With a history of more than 5,000 years, our nation created a splendid civilization, made remarkable contributions to mankind, and became one of the world's great nations. But with the Opium War of 1840, China was plunged into the darkness of domestic turmoil and foreign aggression; its people, ravaged by war, saw their homeland torn apart and lived in poverty and despair." The country was desperately poor at the time, but China's government and people are said to have worked heroically to restore national power and prosperity. Decades after reforming and opening up, Xi explains, China has "stood up, grown rich, and is becoming strong"; it is finally "moving closer to center stage." No longer the sick man of Asia, the "Chinese nation, with an entirely new posture, now stands tall and firm."[46]

Yet instead of celebrating China's hard-earned success, proponents of this narrative claim, the West has reacted by inventing a "China threat theory" to justify taking geoeconomic measures to contain China's rise.[47] These actions have led to calls within China to decouple from the West economically and technologically in everything from the internet and information flows (where decoupling already exists to a large degree) to payment systems and technology (where decoupling is suggested as a means of reducing Western leverage). Xi has endorsed a broad notion of "national security" or "big security" that encompasses "economic security," including "the security of important industries and key areas that are related to the lifeline of the national economy." He has increasingly invoked the importance of *zìlìgēngshēng* (self-reliance and sufficiency) and emphasized efforts at indigenization (e.g., Made in China 2025) to prevent the United States and other Western countries from exercising a chokehold over key technologies. "Advanced technology is the sharp weapon of the modern state," observes Xi. "We must make a big effort in key fields and areas where there is a stranglehold."[48]

Although some prominent Chinese thinkers view potential decoupling as "dangerous" and a "disaster for both China and the United States and the whole world," an increasing number of elite Chinese thinkers disagree, particularly given US geoeconomic actions with respect to key Chinese technology firms such as Huawei and ZTE.[49] This viewpoint has been affirmed by Xi who has pledged technological independence in key areas: "Only by holding these technologies in our own hands can we ensure economic security, national security and security in other areas." China's 14th five-year plan described technological development as a matter of national security, not just economic development, marking a departure from previous plans. The government has also doubled down on pursuing self-sufficiency in core technologies, such as semiconductors, and emphasized the importance of China's dual circulation strategy, which aims to reduce the country's vulnerability to external shocks by increasing domestic production and consumption.[50]

Decoupling pressures are thus emanating from both the West and China, particularly in technology, as each becomes increasingly concerned about weaponized interdependence. Even so, for China, just as for Russia, decoupling has an additional attraction: it helps to guard against, and perhaps ultimately dismantle, the West's ideological hegemony with regard to forms of political and economic organization—a dimension of economic globalization that receives little attention in Western narratives.

Who Has Been Left Behind?

Proponents of the establishment narrative often cite the huge reduction in global poverty as evidence of the success of economic globalization. Yet almost all of this decrease has occurred in East and South Asia (Figure 12.4). By contrast, the absolute number of Africans living in poverty has risen in recent decades despite a slight drop in percentage terms. The divergent fates of the two continents undermine the claim that all countries win from economic globalization, at least in the short term.[51]

Africa's long and painful engagement with economic globalization harks back to the slave trade, when Arab and European powers sold Africans into slavery in the Middle East, North Africa, and the Americas. In the nineteenth and twentieth centuries, European powers imposed extractive colonialism on the continent, as they carved up the map and Africa's resources to suit their own purposes. After decolonization, Africans sought to reassert their independence but ended up having to rely on Western donor countries for economic support, which limited their economic sovereignty. Finally, and consistent with the neocolonial narrative, economic globalization left them dependent on multinational companies. In the face of these developments, African countries were left behind while Asian countries took off.[52]

Some commentators blame patterns of trade and investment for the continent's ongoing economic troubles. The West has not been alone in losing manufacturing jobs to Asia: a similar process took place in the developing countries of Latin America and sub-Saharan Africa. Once they opened themselves up to trade, they were outcompeted by Asian countries with a comparative advantage in manufacturing; the latter eventually drove domestic goods out of African markets by flooding them with cheap imported products. Many poor countries deindustrialized before they had a chance to reap the benefits of industrialization.[53] As for investment, the emphasis on resource industries has led to environmental degradation and a preponderance of poorly paid and dangerous jobs. Countries that are heavily reliant on natural resources fall prey to the resource curse, which makes it harder to develop alternative industries and move up the value chain. Because globalization also floods communities with influences from the outside, some have warned that African countries are "rapidly losing their cultural identity and therefore their ability to interact with other cultures on an equal and autonomous basis."[54]

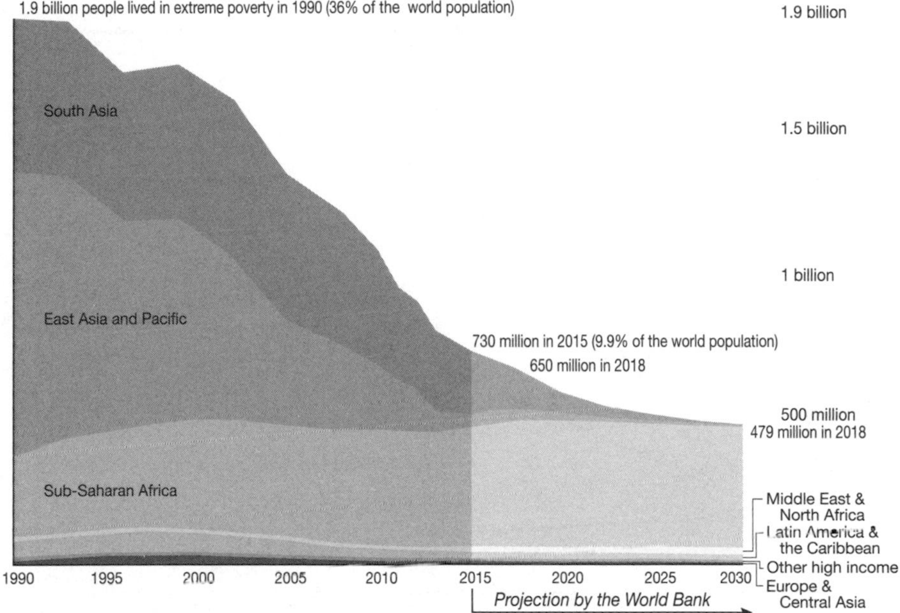

Fig. 12.4: The Persistence of Extreme Poverty in Sub-Saharan Africa

Note: This graph shows the number of people living in extreme poverty from 1990 to 2015 and projected forward up to 2030 for various regions. While poverty has dropped sharply in Asia, it has persisted and even grown in Africa.

Credit: Reformatted from Max Roser and Esteban Ortiz-Ospina, "Global Extreme Poverty," Our World in Data *(2013), figure: "The number of people in extreme poverty—including projections to 2030," https://ourworldindata.org/extreme-poverty, based on data from the World Bank.*

In contrast with this depressing historical perspective, in the past decade a new Africa-rising narrative has started circulating that suggests that Africa might be at a turning point in its economic development, and that newly industrialized countries might help lead the way.[55] President Uhuru Kenyatta of Kenya proclaims: "The narrative of African despair is false, and indeed was never true. Let them know that Africa is open and ready for business."[56] According to the Flying Geese paradigm of development, popularized by the Japanese scholar Kaname Akamatsu, industrialization arrived in European countries and America first, but as their living standards rose, the cost of production in those countries became too high. At that point, Japan became a major manufacturing hub, which sparked its economic miracle. When production became too

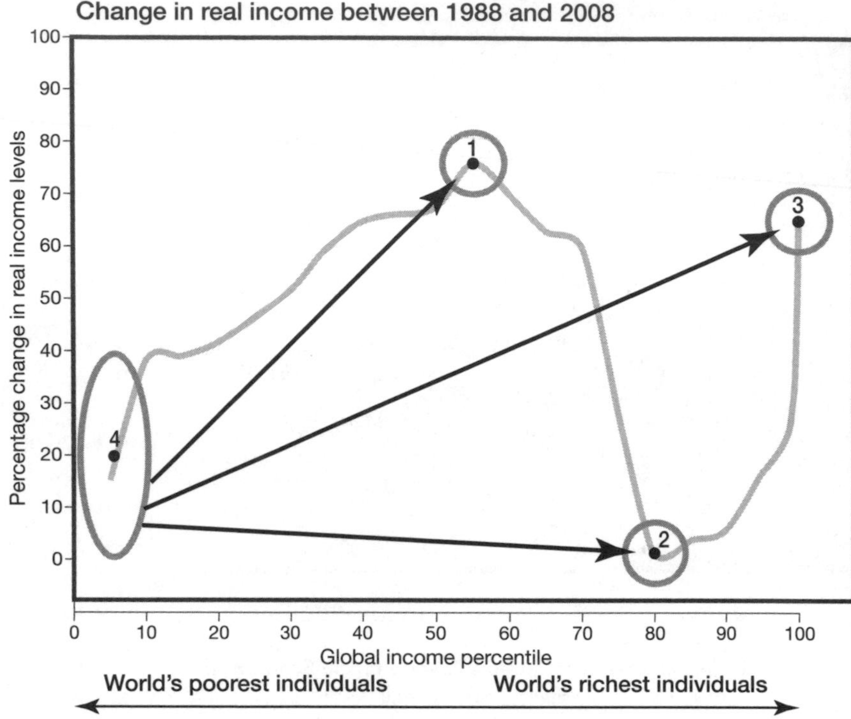

Fig. 12.5: The Elephant Graph and the Neglected Bottom Billion
Note: The arrows indicate whom the narrative sees as the winners (endpoints of the arrows at points 1, 2 and 3) and the losers (origin of the arrows at point 4) from globalization.
Credit: Data source: Branko Milanovic, Global Inequality: A New Approach for the Age of Globalization *(Cambridge, MA: The Belknap Press of Harvard University Press, 2016), 11.*

expensive in Japan, manufacturing industries shifted to the Asian Tigers, and so on. Country after country moved up the value chain, just like geese following in each other's slipstream. Africa may be next, and China may become a "leading dragon" for it and other developing countries.[57] In this vein, Chinese officials point to their own history of export-led and infrastructure-led development as a path for other countries—an approach they are promoting through the Belt and Road Initiative.[58]

All the same, this Africa-rising narrative has detractors. Some doubt that Africa can break its dependence on natural resources.[59] Others debate whether the increase in foreign investment is causing a "new scramble for Africa" that will effectively lead to recolonization.[60] Studies of domestic attitudes and narratives across Africa suggest that many believe that multinational companies and local elites have disproportionately captured the advantages of economic globalization, which has resulted in increasing inequality, few gains for the poor, and a relatively weak middle class.[61] Some people and some countries in the region may rise, but the poorest are likely to remain stuck at the bottom of the global economic system (part of the "bottom billion," in Paul Collier's words) because they are caught in conflicts or held back by the resource curse, weak governance, or unfavorable geography (such as being "landlocked with bad neighbors").[62] This bottom billion—the vast majority of whom live in sub-Saharan Africa—are often overlooked in discussions of the Elephant Graph (Figure 12.5). Most Western commentators focus on three points on the graph: the poor and working classes in the West that have been left behind and the Asian middle classes and global elite that have surged ahead. But they frequently neglect to discuss the tail of the elephant (point 4), which comprises individuals who have seen little growth in their incomes in either absolute or relative terms.

Conclusion

In a famous parable that originated in India, six blind men encounter an elephant for the first time. They seek to learn what the elephant is by touching it, but each man feels a different part of the animal. One feels the trunk and declares elephants to be like a snake, another feels its body and announces elephants are like a wall, yet another feels its tail and opines that elephants are like a rope, and so on. The men get into a quarrel about what an elephant is, each affirming his own experience and discounting the claims of the others as mistaken or untruthful. The moral of the story is that people have a tendency to understand reality based on their limited, subjective experiences, while ignoring that other people may have limited, subjective experiences that may be different but equally true. As with the blind men, proponents of different narratives tell distinct and partial stories about economic globalization. Only by integrating multiple perspectives can we begin to understand the elephant as a whole.

PART IV

FROM THE CUBE TO THE KALEIDOSCOPE

ONE OF THE MOST POPULAR PUZZLES OF ALL TIME, the Rubik's cube was invented in 1974 by Ernő Rubik, a Hungarian architect and professor of architecture, who wanted a model he could manipulate to help explain three-dimensional geometry to his students. He wired together some blocks, put colors on them, and began to twist. "It was wonderful," Rubik reflected in an unpublished memoir, "to see how, after only a few turns, the colors became mixed, apparently in random fashion. It was tremendously satisfying to watch this color parade. Like after a nice walk when you have seen many lovely sights you decide to go home, after a while I decided it was time to go home, let us put the cubes back in order. And it was at that moment that I came face to face with the Big Challenge: What is the way home?"[1]

As anyone who has tried to solve a Rubik's cube knows, the way home is complicated. In Rubik's case, it took him over a month to solve his own puzzle. But the thing about the Rubik's cube is, no matter how complicated, it can be solved. In fact, if you learn the right algorithms, it can be solved relatively quickly and easily. That is not the case when we deal with matters that are *complex* rather than *complicated.* A clock is complicated. It has many moving parts, but someone with the right skills can take it apart and put it back together again because it works in a predictable way. A cloud, by contrast, is complex. There is a lot we can do to analyze the weather, but it will always remain somewhat unpredictable because of the myriad of moving elements that interact in ways that cannot be fully anticipated. Clouds just do not work like clockwork.

Economic globalization is complex: the whole is more than the sum of its many interacting parts. The system's emergent properties are based on dynamic interactions among many actors, which cannot be fully predicted by examining their individual features in isolation. The system produces nonlinear effects, such as feedback loops and tipping points. Actors and the system constantly adapt and coevolve, organizing and reorganizing themselves in light of new information and changing conditions. These sorts of complex adaptive systems are unpredictable and beyond the control of any one actor. In seeking to understand and navigate such systems, scholars and policymakers are increasingly drawing lessons from complexity science in areas ranging from finance to macroeconomics to the global governance of economic regimes.[2]

No toy captures the full dynamism and unpredictability of complex phenomena such as economic globalization, but one comes close: the kaleidoscope. Invented in 1816 by the Scotsman David Brewster, the kaleidoscope consists of mirrors that reflect images of different colored pieces of glass in intricate patterns. Unlike the Rubik's cube, the kaleidoscope does not have a solution or an end point. The picture it produces can be changed endlessly by rotating the tube containing the loose fragments. With each turn, the pieces shift, new reflections are formed, and a new set of patterns emerges. We do not provide a full explanation of economic globalization from the perspective of complexity science. Instead, consistent with insights from how to navigate complex systems, we show how a variety of perspectives on complex issues can be overlaid to produce improved understandings and point the way to potential new alliances.

In Parts I and II, our objective was to map the competing narratives in debates about economic globalization in the West.

The Rubik's cube metaphor provided a useful way of organizing these debates: grouping together different arguments to identify relatively coherent narratives and understanding their relationship to each other is a bit like solving the Rubik's cube puzzle. In Part III, we moved from identifying the narratives to analyzing how they are used in practice—how actors switch between them, exploit overlaps among them, and trade their values off against each other. We also identified some blind spots and biases in the main Western debates by highlighting a variety of additional narratives about economic globalization that reflect distinct historical experiences and contemporary realities from outside the West.

In this part, we go beyond the Rubik's cube to show how one can use a multiplicity of narratives to better understand complex and contested issues, such as climate change and the coronavirus pandemic. Instead of treating these issues like puzzles to be solved, we try to understand them in their full complexity by using the narratives in the manner of a kaleidoscope: with each turn, we introduce a new perspective and show how the pieces of the phenomenon shift to create a new pattern. Although less ordered and predictable, this kaleidoscopic method allows us to get a better handle on the myriad dimensions and unpredictable dynamics of complex issues. By layering different narratives on top of each other and seeing where they overlap, we can also identify potential alliances to support particular policy proposals, providing a pointer toward possible future policymaking pathways.

CHAPTER 13

Kaleidoscopic Complexity

If the art of advocacy lies in convincing others to view the world through the lens of your preferred narrative, the art of policymaking requires actors to examine an issue from diverse perspectives. In this book, we have so far adopted the policymakers' approach to explore the complexity of globalization. In this chapter, we show how this approach can help illuminate debates about two specific issues related to globalization: climate change and the coronavirus pandemic.

We are not the first to note the kaleidoscopic quality of these complex issues. For instance, climate change expert Mike Hulme has observed that despite the broad scientific consensus on climate change, there is "no comparable consensus—no single perspective or vantage point—that allows us to understand what this kaleidoscopic idea of climate change means for us and our descendants." Similarly, David Wallace-Wells introduces the notion of a "climate kaleidoscope" to capture our sense of being "mesmerized by the threat" of climate change without being able to "perceive[e] it clearly."[1]

Economist Larry Summers once declared that "the laws of economics are like the laws of engineering. One set of laws works everywhere."[2] Yet, complex issues like economic globalization, climate change, and the coronavirus pandemic mean "different things to different people in different contexts, places, and networks."[3] Since they are global issues, it helps to understand them through the lenses of a variety of narratives from within and beyond the West. In discussing climate change, we start with some influential non-Western perspectives and then move to the Western narratives; when we turn to the coronavirus, we reverse direction.

The Climate Kaleidoscope

What happens if we view climate change—the central concern of the sustainability narrative—through other narrative lenses? Each narrative directs attention to different facts and considerations. Each also offers its own way of understanding what the same facts mean and how we should evaluate them. By turning the kaleidoscope, we can get a sense of these multiple and sometimes intersecting perspectives. In some respects, the sustainability narrative and the others pull in the same direction; in other respects, they are in tension.

Sustainability Narrative—A Non-Western Perspective

Climate change is an issue on which leaders and commentators from many developing countries have been particularly vocal. They emphasize the deep inequalities and injustices produced or exacerbated by rising emissions and the environmental changes that they cause. Depicting climate change as a global threat can sometimes obscure its asymmetrical causes and effects: proponents of the sustainability narrative often point to the cruel irony that those who will "suffer worst and first . . . are often not those who caused the problem."[4] These concerns about distributive justice are of central importance to non-Western proponents of the sustainability narrative, who often place primary emphasis on inequality among countries.

These distributional problems have significant implications for the possibility of global cooperation, as they play into different perspectives about what is equitable and which actors can and should act. The 1992 United Nations Framework Convention on Climate Change called on all nations to protect the climate system on "the basis of equity and in accordance with their common but differentiated responsibilities and respective capabilities." Many developing countries interpret this formulation to mean that developed nations must take the lead in dealing with climate change by cutting their own emissions and providing financial and technical assistance to developing countries, especially those that are most vulnerable and least able to adapt by themselves.

On the question of who is responsible, developing countries give a clear answer: developed countries bear historical responsibility for climate change.[5] If one looks at cumulative emissions since the start of the Industrial Revolution, it is clear that the bulk of emissions has been generated by developed countries (Figure 13.1). To suggest that all countries

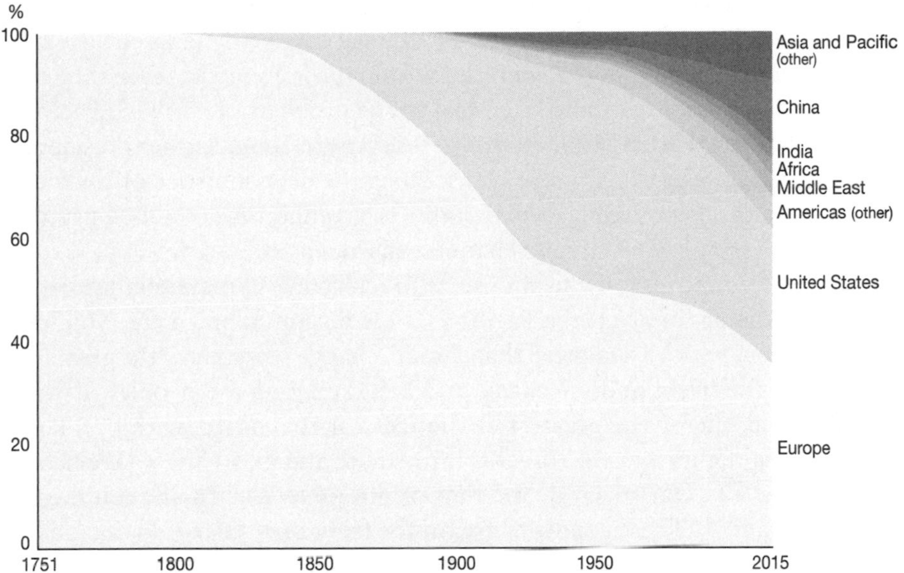

Fig. 13.1: The Developed Countries' Historical Responsibility for Carbon Emissions

Note: This graph shows the percentage of cumulative carbon dioxide emissions by region / country between 1751 and 2015.

Credit: Reformatted from Hannah Ritchie and Max Roser, "Cumulative CO_2 Emissions by World Region, 1751 to 2017," Our World in Data *(2017), figure: "Annual total CO2 emissions, by world region," https://ourworldindata.org/grapher/cumulative-co2-emissions-region, based on data from the Global Carbon Project and the Carbon Dioxide Information Analysis Centre.*

must now equally share the burden of reducing emissions is as if a well-fed man consumed a three-course meal, invited his hungry neighbor to have coffee, and then suggested they split the bill equally.

Non-Western proponents of the sustainability narrative argue that we should measure emissions on a per capita basis rather than a per country basis, to capture the fact that developing countries with large populations, especially China and India, still have much lower per capita emissions than developed countries. As a Chinese official stated at the Kyoto summit in 1997, "In the developed world, only two people ride in a car—and yet you want us to give up riding in a bus."[6] Some scientists from developing countries such as China have advocated basing climate change action on cumulative emissions per capita to ensure "carbon equity."[7]

When it comes to who is the most vulnerable, proponents of this narrative similarly point out that climate change disproportionately affects poor countries and poor communities within those countries, even though these actors have contributed the least to the problem.[8] Low-lying Pacific island countries are a prime example.[9] As Anote Tong, former president of Kiribati, explains: "There is no escaping the deep injustice of the fact that, despite our negligible contributions to greenhouse gas emissions, we are on the frontline of climate change consequences."[10]

Pacific countries led the way in characterizing climate change as a security threat. In 2013, the Pacific Islands Forum adopted the Majuro Declaration, which announced that climate change represents "the greatest threat to the livelihoods, security and well-being of the peoples of the Pacific and one of the greatest challenges for the entire world."[11] The Forum highlights that the threat is immediate and existential: "We need to act now. . . . Our survival, and that of this great Blue Pacific continent depend on it."[12] These countries are on the front line: "If we do not [act], we will lose. . . . We know this because we are experiencing loss already." But they warn that "our today in the Pacific is undoubtedly your tomorrow," as "no one country or individual will be spared."[13]

On the question of who is most capable of responding, developing countries point to the West. There is a "difference between the emissions of developing countries which are 'survival' emissions and those of developed countries which are in the nature of 'lifestyle' emissions," argues former Indian foreign secretary Shyam Saran. "They do not belong to the same category and cannot be treated on a par."[14] Moreover, developed countries should extend financial support and transfer technology to developing countries to help them curb their emissions.[15] In India's view, this is "not 'aid' but a discharge of responsibility by developed countries" based on their "historical responsibilities for climate change and the capabilities they have acquired thereby."[16]

Although developing countries tend to highlight developed countries' responsibility, the most vulnerable also make it clear that all major emitters must take action to halt the climate crisis. For instance, the Pacific countries have declared: "All countries, *with no caveats,* must agree to take decisive and transformative action to reduce global emissions, and ensure at scale mitigation and adaption support for those countries that need it."[17] That includes large developing economies such as China and India, whose emissions have grown significantly in recent years.

Establishment Narrative

When one turns the kaleidoscope to look at climate change through the lens of the establishment narrative, one sees little concern about global inequality. Instead, proponents of this narrative argue that we can use the very tools—market incentives and technological innovation—that have made globalization an economic success to make it an ecological one as well.[18] The establishment narrative rejects the idea that mitigating climate change requires "degrowth," or a reduction in the material consumption of rich countries and rich people.[19] Some proponents have described degrowth as the climate equivalent to abstinence education—telling societies to stop striving for growth is viewed as being about as effective as telling young people to abstain from having sex outside of marriage.[20] Instead they claim that we need to focus on sustaining growth while reducing its carbon intensity; the objective is "clean" or "green growth" (see Figure 13.2).[21]

To achieve this goal, the key prescription of the establishment narrative is to put a price on carbon, which can be done in one of two ways. The first option is to put a cap on total emissions for a particular economic sector, allocating permits for those emissions and allowing the owners to trade them. This approach would create an economic incentive to reduce emissions so as to be able to sell one's permits or avoid having to purchase one, which would lead to emissions reductions where they can be achieved most efficiently. A second option is to impose a carbon tax, ideally one that reflects the social cost of carbon emissions. Faced with a price on carbon emissions, market actors would find it in their own interest to reduce their emissions, which would pave the way for the adoption of more climate-friendly technology. On this view, there is no need to change the paradigm; environmental protection can be achieved within the framework of the establishment approach.

Left-Wing Populist Narrative

For the left-wing populist narrative, both the direct effects of climate change and some of the policy responses to it create new inequities between the rich and poor. The poor are least able to protect themselves against rising temperatures and extreme weather events; they do not have the means to move from flood-prone areas or pay for the air-conditioning that is turning from a luxury to a necessity in ever more parts of the world. Whereas the inequities of climate change are starkest between developed

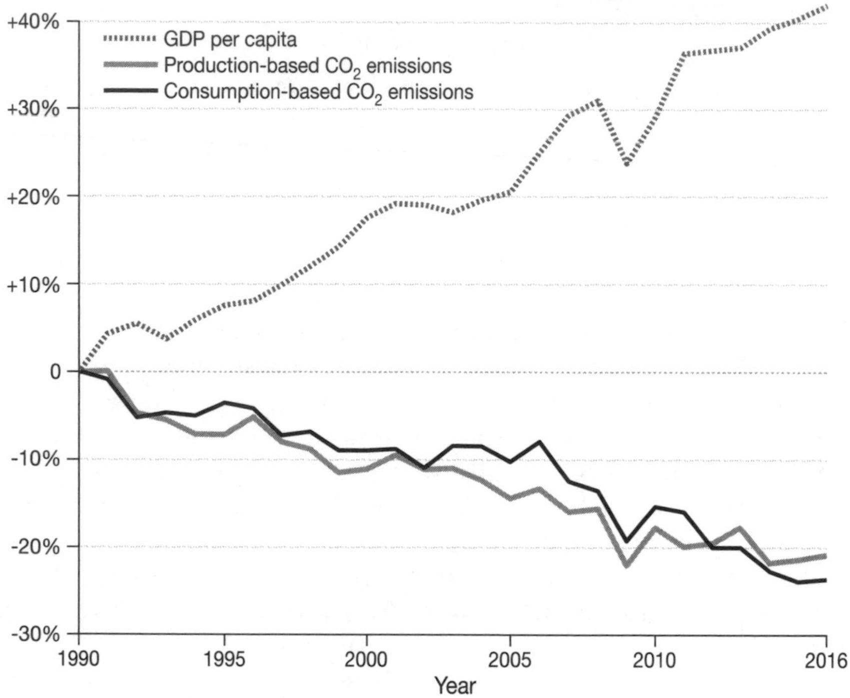

Fig. 13.2: Germany as an Example of "Clean Growth"?
Note: This graph shows that since 1990, Germany's GDP per capita (in dotted gray) has increased while production- and consumption-based CO_2 emissions (in gray and black, respectively) have decreased.
Credit: Reformatted from Hannah Ritchie and Max Roser, "CO_2 Emissions and GDP Growth," Our World in Data *(2017), figure: "Change in per capita CO_2 emissions and GDP, Germany," https://ourworldindata.org/grapher/co2-emissions-and-gdp?country=~DEU, based on data from the Global Carbon Project and the World Bank.*

and developing countries, they are also increasingly visible within the West, where construction workers and farmhands labor in sweltering heat while professionals work in air-conditioned offices.[22] In sun-drenched cities in the southern parts of the United States, shade is increasingly seen as a precious commodity mostly available to the rich. The wealthy Beverly Hills neighborhood of Los Angeles has tree-canopied avenues, whereas someone waiting for a bus in poorer South Los Angeles will struggle to find relief in the shade of a stop sign.[23] Shade is just one example of the metrics that climate change adds to the "index of inequality," together with access to air-conditioning and insurance for flood, fire, and damage to crops. Philip Alston, the UN's special rapporteur on extreme poverty, has warned that the vast discrepancies in our ability to protect ourselves against the effects of climate change could result in a "'climate apartheid' scenario where the wealthy pay to escape overheating, hunger and conflict while the rest of the world is left to suffer." Wallace-Wells invokes another terrifying political analogy: we are heading toward a "climate caste system" in which "the most punishing climate horrors" will hit those "least able to respond and recover."[24]

Right-Wing Populist Narrative

A different image appears if we turn the kaleidoscope to bring into focus the picture presented by the right-wing populist narrative. Its relationship with climate change is complex, though largely antagonistic. On the one hand, climate change raises a whole host of new threats to the sustainability of communities; traditional forms of life are threatened not just by immigrants or the exodus of manufacturing jobs, but also by environmental calamities.[25] Neverthcless, the predominant posture of proponents of this narrative toward worries about sustainability has been hostile. Most proponents of the right-wing populist narrative see the policy responses to climate change, not climate change itself, as the more important threat to their way of life.

The increase in the diesel tax in France, which was implemented to reduce carbon emissions from transport, provides an example. The tax provoked the "yellow vest" protests, which were driven by the white lower middle class, whose members often drive a long way to work and who would thus have been disproportionately hit by the tax. Their anger was compounded by the fact that President Macron did nothing to compensate them, nor did he seek a comparable sacrifice from the well-to-do city-dwelling elites who have shorter commutes and access to public transport, even though they generate more emissions in other ways, such as by air travel.[26]

Some right-wing populists do not just criticize the proposed policy responses to the climate crisis but go so far as denying the science on anthropogenic climate change. From Trump in the United States to the AfD in Germany and Vox in Spain, climate change denial seems to go hand in hand with a preference for old-style manufacturing jobs and opposition to immigration. Some have suggested that the common theme to these elements is that they pose threats to "industrial breadwinner masculinity,"[27] a masculinity that is "willing to think of natural resources as something that exist for humans to grab, use, and create value from."[28] The disappearance of manufacturing jobs undermines industrial breadwinner masculinity in the same way as suggestions that we should stop driving large, polluting pickup trucks or eat less meat. The arguments against these policies are often not primarily economic but visceral: in addition to its concern about the impact of a carbon price on German car manufacturers, the AfD has zeroed in on Greta Thunberg's Fridays For Future movement by promoting an alternative movement called Fridays For Hubraum (the German term for the cylinder capacity of an internal combustion engine).[29]

The right-wing populist narrative often has a gendered dimension.[30] Whereas its proponents are stereotypically older and male, some of the most prominent advocates of the sustainability narrative are young and female, with the latter frequently provoking the ire of the former.[31] Thunberg has been subjected to a torrent of abuse online.[32] Similarly, Canada's former minister of environment and climate change, Catherine McKenna, has been ridiculed as the "climate Barbie," and attacking Alexandria Ocasio-Cortez, the chief proponent of a Green New Deal in America, has become a pastime that is pursued with obsessive passion on the US right.[33] Not all climate change deniers are men and not all deniers use misogynistic language, but researchers of climate skepticism suggest that the most vociferous climate change skeptics tend to be older men who perceive the sustainability narrative as a threat to their livelihood, status, and worldview.[34]

Proponents of the right-wing populist narrative also have a ready response to the threat of social upheaval as a result of climate change—namely, to crack down on immigration and build walls to keep out climate-displaced people. Here, climate denialism transforms into climate protectionism and environmental nationalism, provoked by the external threat of the other.[35] For example, the gunman who targeted the Muslim community in Christchurch, New Zealand, in March 2019 identified as an "ethno-nationalist eco-fascist" and complained that immigration is "environmental warfare."[36]

Geoeconomic Narrative

The notion that climate change might pose an existential or national security threat unfolds at the intersection of the sustainability and geoeconomic narratives. Some proponents of the sustainability narrative encourage proponents of the geoeconomic narrative to leave their rivalry with China to one side so that China and the United States can work together on existential threats such as climate change and prioritize "humanity's common interest in sheer survival."[37] Such cooperation may require Western countries to swallow some of their concerns about China's economic practices: Chinese firms were able to scale up their production of renewable energy technology at unprecedented speed in part because of some of the very practices that Western countries have been complaining about, such as massive state subsidies. China's momentum in this area is unlikely to be matched by efforts from any other state within the time available for averting a climate catastrophe; the Chinese solar panels and wind turbines that are sold in Western markets at rock-bottom prices may harm domestic producers, but they are a boon for sustainability.[38]

Others see climate change itself as a threat to national security. These observers warn that climate change will create conditions, such as competition for scarce resources and mass migration, that aggravate existing stressors, including poverty, political instability, and social tensions. From this perspective, climate change functions as a "threat multiplier."[39]

Corporate Power Narrative

For proponents of the corporate power narrative, corporations play a central role in the climate crisis. Corporations knew that climate change was happening before virtually anyone else: scientists employed by companies such as ExxonMobil conducted cutting-edge research in the 1970s and 1980s that established the connection between increasing carbon concentration in the atmosphere and higher temperatures. Instead of changing their business models, these companies decided that the best strategy for their bottom line was to "manufacture uncertainty" about climate change by writing public-facing advertorials and funding scientists and think tanks that would sow doubt in the public mind.[40]

Only a small number of companies are responsible for most global emissions. A 2017 report pointed out that just 100 companies are responsible directly (via their production processes) or indirectly (via consumption of their products) for 71 percent of all carbon emissions.[41] More than half of global industrial emissions since 1988—the year the Intergovernmental Panel on Climate Change was established—can be traced to just twenty-five corporate and state-owned entities.[42] By focusing directly on companies rather than countries, the corporate power narrative draws attention to corporate responsibility for climate change. Moreover, the narrative highlights how intense lobbying by fossil fuel companies and their trade associations has played a key role in derailing national and international regulatory efforts to curb climate change.[43]

The Coronavirus Kaleidoscope

Major crises often provoke a political fight-or-flight response as proponents of different narratives, awash with adrenaline, double down on their preexisting political convictions. So it was with the outbreak of the novel coronavirus. For proponents of the right-wing populist narrative, the virus provided another reason to keep foreigners out. For left-wing populists, the crisis made it abundantly clear that governments need to guarantee healthcare and paid sick leave for everyone. Proponents of the geoeconomic narrative, long worried about the West's dependence on Chinese suppliers and customers, saw their decoupling agenda vindicated when the public health crisis exposed the vulnerability of supply chains. And climate advocates pointed to the bizarre fact that, due to the decrease in air pollution that followed the slowdown of industrial production in China, the virus may on balance have saved Chinese lives.[44]

None of these reactions was without merit. Though Trump's early ban on Chinese travelers was decried at the time by many on the left as just another xenophobic policy move, it turned out to have bought the United States valuable time (which it subsequently proceeded to squander) and was soon copied by many other countries. Providing testing and treatment to everyone exposed to the virus—the left-wing populist prescription—has been key to every successful effort to suppress the outbreak. The crisis also caused many countries to begin to rethink their dependence on foreign suppliers of essential medicines and equipment, as export restrictions and skyrocketing demand led to shortages. And the beneficial impact of the crisis on global carbon emissions was undeniable.

The validity of these different perspectives reveals the coronavirus pandemic as another issue with kaleidoscopic complexity: we can fully appreciate the pandemic's ramifications only if we refract it through multiple narrative lenses. While the narratives often differ in their prescriptions and are in some respects irreconcilable, each narrative highlights dimensions of the pandemic that the others miss, and each offers a different interpretation of the outbreak's implications and lessons.

Establishment Narrative

For proponents of the establishment narrative, the pandemic highlighted the need for global cooperation to address both the medical and economic challenges posed by the crisis. Instead of resorting to a "sicken-thy-neighbor" approach by banning exports of medical supplies or engaging in "vaccine nationalism," countries should encourage their scientists to work together to develop vaccines and treatments for the disease.[45] Moreover, they should do their utmost to keep their borders open and dismantle obstacles to the free flow of goods, people, and expertise. In fact, proponents of this narrative highlighted how a commitment to free trade would have helped in dealing with the coronavirus: economist Chad Bown noted how Trump's trade war with China increased the cost of medical supplies imported into America prior to the outbreak, warning that "President Donald Trump's misguided trade war with China . . . threatened to cripple the US fight against the COVID-19 pandemic."[46] Others pointed out the dangers that tit-for-tat "pandemic protectionism" posed for the economic recovery. In line with these concerns, a group of WTO members proposed a "trade and health" initiative in November 2020 to consider the need for new rules on trade in medical supplies to ensure that the world is "better prepared to fight both COVID-19 and future pandemics."[47]

Proponents of the establishment narrative also drew attention to the ways in which the coronavirus pandemic was likely to serve as a catalyst for innovation and productivity growth. From this perspective, the increasing importance of e-commerce and the mainstreaming of telecommuting as a result of lockdowns hold the potential to further deepen economic globalization. Work that can be done from home can also be performed on the other side of the planet. As economist Richard Baldwin points out, it is just a short hop, skip, and jump from flexible working arrangements to a new wave of globalization in the service sector.[48]

Right-Wing Populist Narrative

For right-wing populists, the coronavirus underscored the importance of protecting the country's borders and keeping foreigners—and their diseases—out. Right-wing nationalists were among the first to call for border controls and entry bans, measures that most governments ended up taking. As Aurélia Beigneux, a member of the European Parliament from France's right-wing National Rally, warned: "The free circulation of goods and people, immigration policies and weak controls at the borders obviously allow the exponential spread of this type of virus."[49] In Switzerland, Lorenzo Quadri, of the right-wing Lega dei Ticinesi, called for a "closed-doors" policy, noting that it was alarming that some considered the "dogma of wide-open borders" to be a priority. And Trump tweeted, "THIS IS WHY WE NEED BORDERS!" and "We need the Wall more than ever!"[50]

The coronavirus also highlighted the risks of living in a hyperconnected and dense global city—a lifestyle that many right-wing populists contrast unfavorably with the sense of place and community that they see as characteristic of the rural areas and former manufacturing cities that have been decimated by economic globalization. The fact that global cities served as entry ports for infectious diseases showed that living in a "flyover" state could also be an advantage, at least in the early days of a pandemic.

Left-Wing Populist Narrative

Left-wing populists focused less on the foreign threat (how the virus arrived in the country) and more on domestic problems (how socioeconomic inequality helped the virus to spread). One reason New York was so heavily affected by the virus was the hourglass shape of its economy: along with a well-off elite, New York is home to many poorly paid service workers, many of whom do not have paid sick leave or access to affordable healthcare. As a result, these workers were less likely to get tested early for the disease or to self-isolate when they showed symptoms, proponents of the left-wing populist narrative point out.[51]

Left-wing populists also emphasized the disproportionate impact of shocks such as the coronavirus on the already vulnerable. As Ocasio-Cortez explains: "COVID deaths are disproportionately spiking in Black + Brown communities. Why? Because the chronic toll of redlining, environmental racism, wealth gap, etc. ARE underlying health conditions. *Inequality is a comorbidity*."[52] Likewise, the rate of infections in working-class areas in and around Barcelona was nearly seven times higher than in upmarket areas, in part because many people from these areas could not physically distance by working remotely.[53]

Not everyone is equally at risk of catching the coronavirus, and its impacts differ significantly among socioeconomic classes. But because of the interdependence of people in society, failure to protect the most vulnerable poses risks to everyone. "If we work sick, then you get sick," workers from the Chipotle restaurant chain chanted during a protest.[54] According to Bernie Sanders, "We are only as safe as the least insured person in America."[55] On this point, the left-wing populist and global threat narratives meet: "We are in this together," says Sanders.[56]

Geoeconomic Narrative

The concern that was foremost on the minds of proponents of the geo-economic narrative was Western countries' dependence on China for the supply of essential items such as medicines and masks. More than 80 percent of the active pharmaceutical ingredients in US medicines is produced abroad, mainly in China and India, including over 97 percent of the antibiotics prescribed in the United States.[57] "When you control the supply of medicines, you control the world," observed healthcare expert and author Rosemary Gibson. "Medicines in the hands of an adversary can be weaponized. Supplies can be withheld. Medicines can be made with lethal contaminants or sold without any real medicine in them, rendering them ineffective."[58] For Canada, these dangers became a painful reality when high-level Chinese officials blocked the shipment of vaccine supplies for clinical trials to Canada in August 2020. The Chinese government's decision to block the export of the supplies, apparently for geopolitical reasons, left Canada's vaccination strategy in a shambles, as Canada had to join the back of the queue for alternative vaccines.[59] From the geoeconomic perspective, countries must develop greater self-reliance and limit interdependence with potential adversaries. "The coronavirus outbreak has made clear we must combat America's supply chain vulnerabilities and dependence on China in critical sectors of our economy," declared US senator Marco Rubio. For Trump, the pandemic "shows the importance of bringing manufacturing back to America."[60]

On this view, the coronavirus acted as an accelerant to geopolitical divisions and animosity, with the United States and other Western countries on one side, and China on the other, with both sides playing the blame game. The Trump administration insisted on calling the coronavirus the "Wuhan" or "Chinese" virus and blamed China for covering up the virus instead of immediately reporting it to the WHO. Chinese officials and commentators responded by accusing the United States of politicizing the virus to suit its own ends and of trying to deflect attention from its own poor handling of the outbreak domestically.[61] Australia's demand for an official investigation into the origins of the virus similarly provoked China's ire, contributing to China's decision to employ what many perceived to be a broad campaign of economic coercion against over a dozen Australian industries.[62]

Corporate Power Narrative

There are many losers from the coronavirus, but one set of winners will be Big Tech, warn proponents of the corporate power narrative. "When you have an industry leader, and something collapses, the industry leader, if it's well-managed, tends to emerge stronger a year later," observed former Google CEO Eric Schmidt.[63] The global financial crisis led to consolidation in various industries, from banking to airlines, and the coronavirus crisis has had a similar effect, in that it has strengthened the tech sector's position in the economy.

The coronavirus seemed tailor-made to play to Big Tech's strengths. Orders for people to shelter and work from home rapidly increased demand for deliveries by Amazon, teleconferencing by Zoom, and streaming by Netflix. Microsoft's corporate software packages, cloud-computing services, and video gaming were similarly sought after. "The firms that were the top dogs going into the crisis also happen to have the most resilient business models because they can do everything online," explains economist Thomas Philippon.[64]

The coronavirus also revealed some of the dangers of corporate concentration in other areas. For example, meat processing in North America has become highly concentrated among a few billion-dollar corporations that produce in a handful of massive plants. When some of these plants were forced to close down due to coronavirus outbreaks, severe disruptions ensued: closing one large beef-processing facility can result in the loss of over 10 million servings of beef a day. Meanwhile, farmers had to kill millions of animals that could no longer be processed.[65]

Global Threats: Western and Non-Western Perspectives

For proponents of the sustainability narrative, halting industrial production, grounding flights, and bringing public life to a standstill offered a glimpse of what degrowth might look like. In their view, the coronavirus slowdown showed that much economic activity is not essential for our survival—that we are perfectly fine without that extra flight or cruise. They hope that the experience will teach us that many of our trips are not necessary and much of what they achieve could be done via video conferencing with lower carbon emissions.

The consequences of the virus may even have been a net positive in terms of public health in countries such as China, according to some proponents of this narrative. One estimate suggested that because of the decrease in air pollution, the economic slowdown caused by the virus may have saved twenty times as many lives in China as were lost to the virus.[66] For some, this perverse result shows that the detrimental health effects of our obsession with economic growth have been "normalized."[67] Others worry that the immediacy of the coronavirus crisis and the economic downturn will take the focus away from the slower-moving climate crisis.

At the outset of the pandemic, non-Western proponents of the global threats narrative often noted that although the coronavirus hit China and many major developed countries first, it might ultimately have a more devastating impact in developing countries, which had neither the economic means to cushion the impact of a prolonged shutdown nor the state capacity to treat those who got infected. This prospect prompted calls for global solidarity and cooperation.

"Fragile and vulnerable at the best of times, African economies are staring at an abyss," explained Ethiopia's prime minister, Abiy Ahmed, at the onset of the pandemic. "Access to basic health services remains the exception rather than the norm." Although the coronavirus shone a spotlight on shortages of intensive care beds and ventilators in many developed countries, the shortfalls in developing countries were much starker. The United States had 33 ICU beds per 100,000 people, compared with 0.6 in Zambia, 0.4 in Gambia, and 0.1 in Uganda. "Everybody is talking about ventilators," stated former Nigerian finance minister and later director-general of the WTO Ngozi Okonjo-Iweala, but "I hear some countries have less than 100."[68]

Many of the physical distancing measures prescribed in developed countries were impossible to implement in developing countries and may not have struck the right balance between physical and economic health in those settings. "In shantytowns or townships people don't have the wherewithal to stockpile food and social isolation is physically impossible," noted Dele Olojede, a Pulitzer Prize–winning Nigerian journalist. As Abiy observed: "Even taking such common-sense precautions as washing hands is often an unaffordable luxury to the half of the population who lack access to clean water."[69] Many people also work in the informal sector and have no means of replacing their incomes if they were subject to lockdowns, which could lead to starvation, economic ruin, and civil unrest. As the pandemic progressed, it appeared that—for reasons that scientists have struggled to explain—sub-Saharan Africa would be spared the worst, whereas developing countries in South Asia and the Americas had among the highest death tolls.[70]

Given their greater resources, developed countries were uniquely positioned to help developing countries navigate this crisis. Some commentators called on them to do so as a matter of humanity. Others emphasized that, in view of the interconnected nature of global threats, it is in the self-interest of developed countries to help developing countries. If the virus is not defeated in Africa, it will bounce back to the rest of the world, warned Abiy. Because "health is a worldwide public good," it follows that fighting pandemics "requires global action guided by a sense of global solidarity."[71] The tendency of rich Western nations to horde vaccines for the benefit of their own populations rather than ensure that they were available to those in poorer countries came in for criticism on this account as both immoral and shortsighted.

Against Western Hegemony and Asia-Rising Narratives

While some established democracies—including the United States and the United Kingdom—flailed in response to the coronavirus, China was quick to point to the effectiveness of its authoritarian model in suppressing the outbreak in Wuhan.[72] More generally, some of the most effective efforts to contain it were made by Asian countries, such as Singapore, South Korea, Taiwan, and Vietnam. These successes reinforced various narratives about the advantages of Asian-style governance and the dangers of Western hubris, feeding into more general claims about Asia's rise and the West's decline.

This mood was well captured by Singaporean writer Tan Tarn How in a piece entitled "Why the West's Coronavirus Response Shows It Isn't Better than the Rest of Us." Tan credits the successful handling of the virus by various Asian countries not only to their past experience with SARS but also to their more solidaristic approach, in which "each individual's self interest is best taken care of by contributing to the welfare of the community as a whole." Many Western countries not only were divided but also failed to deal well with the pandemic because of their "complacency, hubris even," in believing that they could easily manage the threat. This crisis might mark an inflection point in global history, Tan suggests: "Up until now, much of the West saw itself and was often seen by others—consciously or not—as more advanced, superior to the rest of the world and deserving of its lecturing of others. Its handling of the pandemic has put paid to much of that."[73]

Conclusion

We can illuminate the full ramifications of global issues such as the novel coronavirus and climate change only if we acknowledge their kaleidoscopic complexity. Every turn of the kaleidoscope lets the pieces shift and reveals a new pattern. By refracting these multifaceted issues through different narrative lenses, we can see how different narratives make sense of what these issues mean with respect to their core concerns. Such complex integrative thinking is helpful in identifying different potential policy options around which new alliances might coalesce.

CHAPTER 14

Potential Alliances

The traditional lines of political battle are fracturing. Old divisions between left and right are giving way to multiple vectors of political disagreement, with long-standing alliances unraveling and new ones coalescing kaleidoscopically. In some Western countries, working-class voters have defected to the right, transforming the old left-of-center parties into coalitions of educated professionals and ethnic minorities and the old right-of-center ones into coalitions of the business rich and working class. French economist Thomas Piketty describes this new cleavage as being between the "Brahmin Left" and the "Merchant Right."[1] Others see divides between advocates of open and closed societies, globalists and patriots, or Somewheres and Anywheres.[2]

Politicians have taken different approaches to these new divides. Some have tried to deepen and accentuate them, tying their political fortunes to their ability to mobilize their own supporters rather than to win over converts from other camps. In championing a particular perspective, these types of politicians come to embody a single narrative. Other politicians try to bridge the divides by assembling coalitions of actors with diverse perspectives. As we note in Chapter 1, the Biden administration's trade and national security policies exemplify the latter approach, as he tempers the establishment view that trade always drives prosperity with countervailing concerns about the welfare of US workers, the power of corporations, China's economic practices, and the need to tackle climate change.[3]

As the political landscape in the West is reconfigured, we need to identify the potential for these sorts of alliances in various policy areas. The narratives that we analyze in this book can be an important tool in that endeavor. In this chapter, we overlay different narratives to identify areas in which they intersect, thereby opening opportunities for new coalitions, but also to show where they diverge, potentially creating new divisions. We explore these possibilities by examining three current controversies: the role of work and workers in society, the future of international economic interdependence, and policy responses to climate change.

The narrative alignment that we chart does not allow us to predict which alliances will in fact materialize. Even to attempt such predictions would require us to assess too many political and economic factors that are outside the scope of the book. What our analysis *can* do is highlight areas in which alliances *should* be possible based on what various actors are saying. If these alliances do not come about, the disconnect between rhetoric and reality may indicate that commitments are held weakly or even hypocritically, or may provide a starting point for examining the obstacles that prevent actors in different camps from working together.

The Role of Work and Workers in Society

The establishment narrative is squarely focused on growing the overall economic pie and demonstrates little direct concern for individual workers. It is proudly indifferent as to who does what where. If offshoring, automating production, or opening borders to imports and immigrants boost productivity and thereby help to grow the pie, the establishment narrative is all in. After all, any individual losers can always be compensated with pieces of the now-bigger pie.

The focus on economic efficiency shapes the establishment narrative's view on how much people should be paid and what types of work are valuable. After the 2008 global financial crisis, many criticized the exorbitant wages and bonuses paid to investment bankers. "I often hear references to higher compensation at Goldman," the CEO of Goldman Sachs noted in 2011. "What people fail to mention is that net income generated per head is a multiple of our peer average. The people of Goldman Sachs are among the most productive in the world."[4] In an efficient market, pay is linked to productivity, so higher pay—the assumption goes—must be evidence of higher productivity.

The flip side of this logic is that low wages reflect low productivity. Cooks, cleaners, nannies, and janitors do not get paid much because they are not highly productive. In the establishment narrative's telling, there is no reason for policy interventions to ensure that service workers at the bottom of the income distribution are paid a living wage; the laws of supply and demand will suffice. "People will get paid on how valuable they are to the enterprise," former US treasury secretary John Snow has explained.[5]

The establishment narrative also features a built-in bias in favor of remunerated work that contributes to a country's GDP: it implicitly values the work of a lawyer or bond trader more highly than that of volunteers at a food bank or those who stay home to care for their children or for an elderly relative. A childcare worker gets paid, while a stay-at-home parent does not. Activities that do not grow the economic pie, as measured by the standard metric, are rendered invisible, however valuable they may be by other criteria.

At least three of the other narratives push back against this indifference to individual workers and the value of their work. The left-wing populist narrative points to what it sees as the glaring unfairness of the conditions that low-wage workers must endure, especially in the service sector. The right-wing populist narrative focuses on how communities unravel when the blue-collar jobs that sustain them disappear. And the resilience narrative argues not only that hyperspecialization and offshoring can leave societies vulnerable but also that our perspective on the types of work that are valuable can change radically in life-threatening emergencies such as pandemics. Although these three narratives differ in emphasis, we see three broad areas of overlap that could form the basis of new alliances (Figure 14.1).

Solidarity with Essential Workers

Proponents of the left-wing populist narrative have long argued that the wages and benefits of service sector workers must be understood as the product of political power relations, such as employers' ability to undermine unions and politicians' unwillingness to raise the minimum wage. Proponents of this narrative assert that workers deserve better—that anyone who works full-time should be paid a living wage, and that the low wages and poor working conditions associated with these jobs do not reflect the workers' contribution to society. Their work is not unskilled, just underpaid. Their current working conditions reflect a bargain-basement economy paradigm in which workers are treated as "costs to be minimized rather than assets to be maximized."[6]

The resilience narrative, which gained salience after the onset of the coronavirus pandemic, has added wind to the sails of some of these demands. The pandemic prompted a sudden recognition of the extent to which we rely on "essential" workers for our very survival—not only doc-

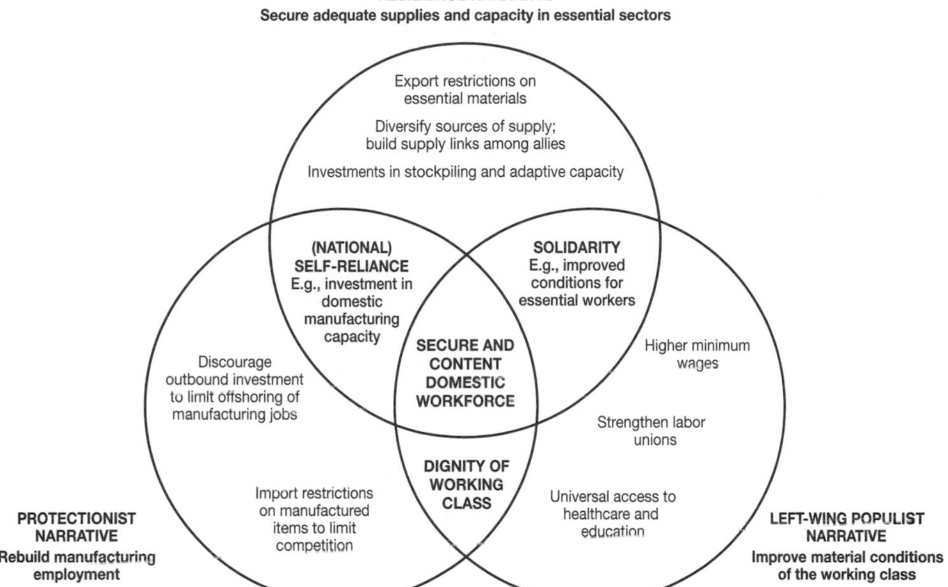

Fig. 14.1: Rethinking the Role of Work and Workers in Society
Note: This diagram shows areas of overlap—highlighted in bold—between the resilience, protectionist, and left-wing populist narratives in relation to the role of work and workers in society. These areas of overlap could potentially provide the basis for alliances between the proponents of these narratives.
Credit: © Anthea Roberts and Nicolas Lamp

tors and nurses but also truckers, care workers, hospital cleaners, meatpackers, farmworkers, and grocery store clerks. The essential role of these workers in keeping our societies functional—sometimes putting their lives at risk in the process—is jarringly at odds with the rewards that Western societies have bestowed upon them. As the *Financial Times* journalist Sarah O'Connor has put it, the pandemic "has exposed an uncomfortable truth: the people we need the most are often the ones we value the least."[7]

The left-wing populist and resilience narratives thus converged around calls for greater solidarity with essential workers. Public displays of gratitude to essential workers in many countries during the pandemic, such as clapping at certain hours of the day, suggested that this sense of a need to better recognize and reward the role of essential workers was shared widely. According to Gene Sperling, national economic advisor to Presidents Clinton and Obama, the key question for the future is whether "our overdue recognition of the contributions of so many workers" will lead to more than "temporary applause and pats on the back" and instead "move us toward a true social compact ensuring economic dignity for all."[8]

For philosopher Michael Sandel, a new social compact would require that we "reconfigure our economy and society to accord such workers the compensation and recognition that reflects the true value of their contributions—not only in an emergency but in our everyday lives." O'Connor is more concrete, arguing that "these jobs need to be made better. Insecure contracts and loopholes should be replaced with permanent jobs, better wages and more training and accreditation." Some governments have moved cautiously in that direction. The German government agreed with care providers that caregivers would be paid a bonus of €1,500 in July 2020, a move that kick-started a national conversation about raising wages for essential workers on a permanent basis. In Ontario, the right-wing populist government of Doug Ford announced that it would raise the wages of 350,000 frontline workers by CAD 4 per hour for four months and would pay an additional CAD 250 monthly bonus to any essential worker who put in more than 100 hours per month. And Biden campaigned on a promise to enact "premium pay" for frontline workers who were putting themselves at risk.[9]

It remains to be seen whether the emerging alliance between proponents of the left-wing populist and resilience narratives persists after the shock of the pandemic wears off. However, the pandemic has at least temporarily raised the political profile of questions that left-wing populists have long asked, namely, what types of work create real value for society, and how such work should be recognized and rewarded. Moreover, the central role of governments, parliaments, and the public in searching for answers has—again, at least temporarily—undermined the idea that "markets can decide these questions on their own."[10] The new prominence of the question of how we value and reward work may portend a larger shift in state-market relations when it comes to the role of work in society.

The Dignity of the Working Class

Proponents of the protectionist strand of the right-wing populist narrative take issue with the establishment narrative's indifference to the fate of individual workers for a different reason: in their view, the elite's original sin was to tolerate and even encourage the decline of manufacturing employment in Western countries. Protectionists associate that decline and the concomitant rise of the service sector, especially the high-tech and high-finance industries, with consumerism and national decadence. According to writer J. D. Vance, the coronavirus pandemic revealed a US economy "built on consumption, debt, financialization, and sloth," which is reflected in the vastly unequal fortunes of different locations and classes. "Production, where it still exists in our country, clusters in mega-cities, where 'knowledge economy' workers live uptown from the low-wage servants (disproportionately immigrants) who clean their laundry, care for their children, and serve their food," Vance observes. "Perhaps we shouldn't build our cities like that. Perhaps we should make things in America."[11]

Oren Cass likewise argues that society's definition of prosperity should "emphasize the ability to produce rather than the ability to consume," but he adopts a broader conception of production than Vance does. According to Cass, "Most of the activities and achievements that give life purpose and meaning are, whether in the economic sphere or not, fundamentally acts of production." Cass argues that "accomplishments like fulfilling traditional obligations, building strong personal relationships, succeeding at work, supporting a family, and raising children capable of doing all these things themselves are far more important to life satisfaction" than simple material gains. From this perspective, the decline of productive opportunities, especially for men, has had deleterious effects on many individuals and the broader social fabric. Cass argues that "without work—the quintessential productive activity—self-esteem declines and helplessness increases." He traces many of America's social problems, such as declining marriage rates, rising deaths of despair, and decaying communities, to the damage that the loss of employment opportunities in the manufacturing sector has done to working-class livelihoods: "Cheap goods and plentiful transfer payments ensured that nearly all Americans could afford cable television and air conditioning but not that they could build fulfilling lives around productive work, strong families, and healthy communities."[12]

The importance of a sense of dignity and respect for the working class is also emphasized by Chris Arnade in his reporting from "back row America." Despite being "stigmatized, ignored, and made fun of," most of the poor and working-class people he spoke with—whether black, white, Hispanic, rural, or urban—were "fighting to maintain dignity" in the face of "feeling disrespected."[13] This chimes with Tamara Draut's reporting on the new working class in her book *Sleeping Giant:* workers fighting for a $15 minimum wage were not just trying to improve their material conditions but also seeking recognition for the "dignity and value" of their work. In dozens of conversations across the United States, from the Bible Belt to the East Coast, her interviewees described their work as "meaningful and embedded with purpose," yet also spoke about the "disrespect they get on the job from their bosses and in society from politicians."[14]

Is there any common ground here among the right-wing and left-wing populists? Despite their focus on the manufacturing and service sectors, respectively, the two narratives share an appreciation for the dignity of work and a willingness to prioritize that dignity over considerations of overall economic efficiency. As Cass puts it, "Departing from the market's default outcome will always appear expensive if the 'efficient' default *is defined as the overriding social goal.*" Neither proponents of the right-wing populist narrative nor those advocating the left-wing populist narrative accept that economic efficiency should be the overriding social goal.[15]

Although proponents of the right-wing and left-wing populist narratives share the common objective of restoring dignity and respect for the working class, their policy proposals for achieving this goal often differ. Proponents of the left-wing populist narrative advocate raising the minimum wage, restoring the power of organized labor, and ensuring job security with humane schedules and decent benefits. This approach is evident in, for example, the Biden-Sanders Unity Task Force recommendations.[16] Proponents of the right-wing populist narrative tend to favor other strategies. Cass has proposed a wage subsidy whereby the government would top up the pay of low-wage workers, which would make hiring them more attractive for employers while ensuring that the workers take home decent pay. During the coronavirus pandemic, this proposal was picked up by US senator Mitt Romney, who proposed that essential workers should receive "patriot pay," a temporary bonus of up to $12 an hour, three-quarters of which would be covered by the government. While Romney's proposal failed to gain traction in the gridlocked US Senate, and it remains to be seen whether Biden's plans for premium pay can avoid a similar fate, the fact that proposals in this vein are coming from both sides of the political spectrum suggests that, as

Sperling puts it, there has "never been a more fitting time to legislate the principle that if there is dignity in all work, there must be a dignified wage for all workers."[17]

National Self-Reliance

Cass's and Romney's advocacy for a wage subsidy notwithstanding, the primary weapon in the protectionists' arsenal has long been another one: imposing barriers on imports to make domestic manufacturers more competitive and increase manufacturing employment. As countries scrambled to procure ventilators, personal protective equipment, and vaccines during the coronavirus pandemic, some proponents of the resilience narrative also embraced the reshoring of supply chains and bolstering of national manufacturing capacities, an objective that created an area of convergence between the two narratives. Still, even though proponents of the right-wing populist and resilience narratives find common ground in advocating for greater self-reliance, their reasons differ.

Proponents of the right-wing populist narrative focus on the manufacturing sector as a source of employment that can sustain families and communities and as an activity that promotes national pride and self-sufficiency. For them, a society that does not produce anything is deficient, almost decadent. Proponents of the resilience narrative, by contrast, are not concerned about the beneficial effects of the *activity* of manufacturing on workers, their communities, and the national psyche; rather, they seek control over manufacturing *outputs*. During the pandemic, even ardent advocates of economic globalization, such as Angela Merkel and Emmanuel Macron, acutely felt the loss of control resulting from outsourced production of key goods and began to call for greater self-reliance in essential industries. The Biden administration has likewise emphasized the need to make critical supply chains more resilient in the face of "global shocks" such as the coronavirus pandemic or the disruptions caused by climate change.[18]

These different rationales for national self-reliance limit the overlap between the two narratives and hence also circumscribe the scope for potential alliances between their proponents in support of specific policies. Whereas right-wing populists advocate for import barriers across the board, proponents of the resilience narrative are likely to favor more targeted interventions focused on ensuring adequate manufacturing capacity for essential goods. It is in the use of such targeted tools that proponents of these narratives are most likely to find common ground; they include the use of industrial policy, which encompasses investments in research and development, in addition to subsidies to companies that build up or maintain manufacturing capacity especially for essential goods (e.g., "Make It in America") as well as preferential government procurement (e.g., "Buy American").[19]

A More Secure Domestic Workforce

Taken together, these three narratives converge in calling for a more secure domestic workforce. All the narratives advocate that we move away from fixating on GDP growth and pay closer attention to the fate of individual workers, be it to ensure that we reward them fairly for their contribution to society, secure sufficient decently paid job opportunities to allow them to sustain a family, or ensure that we have a capable and adaptive workforce in case of emergencies. The narratives also concur on another point that departs from the establishment narrative: all advocate a greater role for the state as compared to the market in shaping the conditions of work.

These broad points of convergence do not imply that it will be easy to form alliances. Proponents of the protectionist strand of the right-wing populist narrative will continue to favor much broader trade restrictions and a more radical retreat from economic globalization than the potential allies would countenance. Proponents of the left-wing populist narrative remain highly skeptical of corporations and would prefer to make corporations pay a living wage rather than to see the government top up low earnings with a subsidy. Yet a focus on work-related measures appears to be the most promising area of convergence: right-wing populists tend to reject benefits that are not tied to work, such as a universal basic income, on the basis that they foster a culture of welfare dependency and may benefit people who are "undeserving"; advocates of economic globalization tend to reject retrenchment unless it serves to build national capacity for an emergency; and gratitude to essential workers can be harnessed most effectively to improve their working conditions—a big step toward acknowledging the dignity of their work—rather than to achieve other left-wing populist priorities.[20]

Rethinking International Economic Interdependence

Some of the potential alliances around the role of work also have implications for international economic interdependence. In advocating increased national self-reliance, backers of the protectionist and resilience narratives can count on support from people concerned with geoeconomics, many of whom favor repatriating some industries to decrease their country's vulnerability to strategic competitors. This potential alliance is notably apparent in the United States, where politicians such as Senator Marco Rubio and commentators such as Vance have been actively trying to bring together proponents of all three camps.

Rubio has argued for a more active industrial policy in protectionist terms, as a way of ensuring resilience, and on the grounds of national security. He laments the fate of "hard-working Americans who felt helpless as they watched jobs disappear and their communities crumble because businesses and lawmakers prioritized maximizing short-term gains over the long-term security of America, its communities and its people." He notes that the coronavirus pandemic left America "scrambling because we by and large lack the ability to make things." And he calls for the "re-shoring of supply chains integral to our national interest" on everything from "basic medicines and equipment to vital rare earth minerals and technologies of the future."[21]

Although investment in domestic manufacturing capacity is a shared objective of all three narratives, they differ in emphasis. Depending on which combination of narratives gains the upper hand, we could see either a greater weight placed on the diversification of international supply chains to increase resilience or heightened concern about interstate competition (Figure 14.2).

Diversification of Supply Chains

The resilience and geoeconomic narratives share an apprehension about the fragility of international supply chains: proponents of both narratives fear that dependence on foreign suppliers will leave their country vulnerable in a crisis. For proponents of the geoeconomic narrative, that fear is directed primarily against a strategic competitor: some Western governments are increasingly unwilling to rely on China for key inputs because they worry that China could use such dependence as leverage. For proponents of the resilience narrative, however, the fear is more generalized: they do not worry so much about intentional weaponization by a foe as about the inability to rely on any other countries, whether friend or foe, at a time of crisis.

To those primarily concerned with resilience and geoeconomics, national self-reliance is not the only option for addressing these supply chain

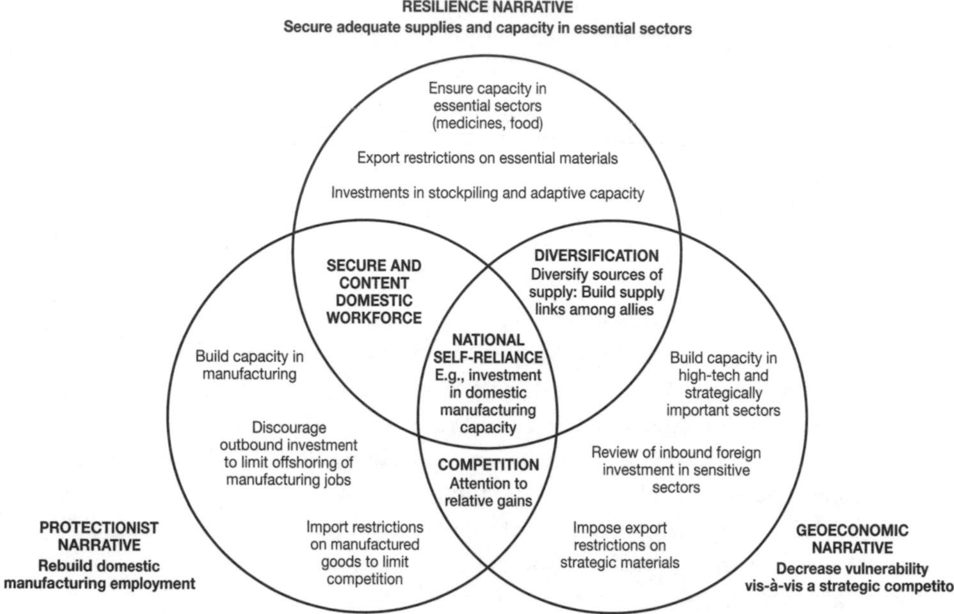

Fig. 14.2: Rethinking Approaches to the Risks and Benefits of International Economic Interdependence

Note: This diagram shows areas of overlap—highlighted in bold—between the resilience, protectionist, and geoeconomic narratives in relation to international economic interdependence. These areas of overlap could potentially provide the basis for alliances between the proponents of these narratives.

Credit: © Anthea Roberts and Nicolas Lamp

concerns: diversifying sources of supply (preferably among allied countries) and stockpiling are alternatives. Biden's policy proposals during the election stressed the importance of resilient supply chains, not fully reshored ones; the goal is "not pure self-sufficiency, but broad-based resilience." Biden's stated aim was to ensure that the United States never again faced a shortage of vital goods, and he planned to achieve that goal through a combination of increased domestic production, strategic stockpiles, enhanced surge capacity, and close coordination with allies. Similarly, the EU's trade commissioner has explained that "strategic autonomy does not mean that we should aim for self-sufficiency. Given the complexity of supply chains, this would be an unattainable goal." Instead, the aim is to build resilient supply chains, based on diversification and stockpiling, while working together at the European level.[22]

To proponents of the protectionist variant of the right-wing populist narrative, by contrast, diversifying international supply chains or working with trusted allies to develop secure international supplies does not achieve the goal of bringing manufacturing jobs back home. Trump and key members of his administration, such as Commerce Secretary Wilbur Ross, viewed imports from Mexico and the European Union with only slightly less hostility than imports from China. Nor is stockpiling the answer to their concerns: they want manufacturing to return to the United States so that people can make things and support their families. Continuing to buy products from international suppliers and stockpiling them for use in the event of a crisis does not achieve that objective.

Competition or Cooperation between Countries?

There is another fault line in debates about international economic independence, which pits the resilience narrative against the right-wing populist and geoeconomic narratives. In the former, resilient supply chains do not necessarily come at the expense of other countries' economic security. As far as this narrative is concerned, if all countries have access to sufficient supplies of essential materials, such as medications and personal protective equipment, the world will be the better for it. Proponents of this narrative are concerned about protecting themselves against absolute losses, not about ensuring relative gains vis-à-vis other countries.

The matter is different in the geoeconomic and right-wing populist narratives, which stress relative gains. The geoeconomic narrative emphasizes that technological supremacy is essential for both economic and security reasons, whereas protectionists tend to conceptualize international trade as a zero-sum competition over jobs, particularly in manufacturing. For both, the sense of competition is heightened by the perception that other countries—primarily China, from the US perspective—are not playing fair because they are using their tax regimes, subsidies, and undervalued currencies to give their companies an edge. A key feature of both narratives is hence a focus on interstate competition rather than cooperation.

Evolving Climate Change Policies

In this section, we explore four policy approaches that have gained traction with proponents of different narratives as ways of addressing climate change: green growth, degrowth, a Green New Deal, and environmental nationalism (Figure 14.3).[23] These proposals are closely aligned with the

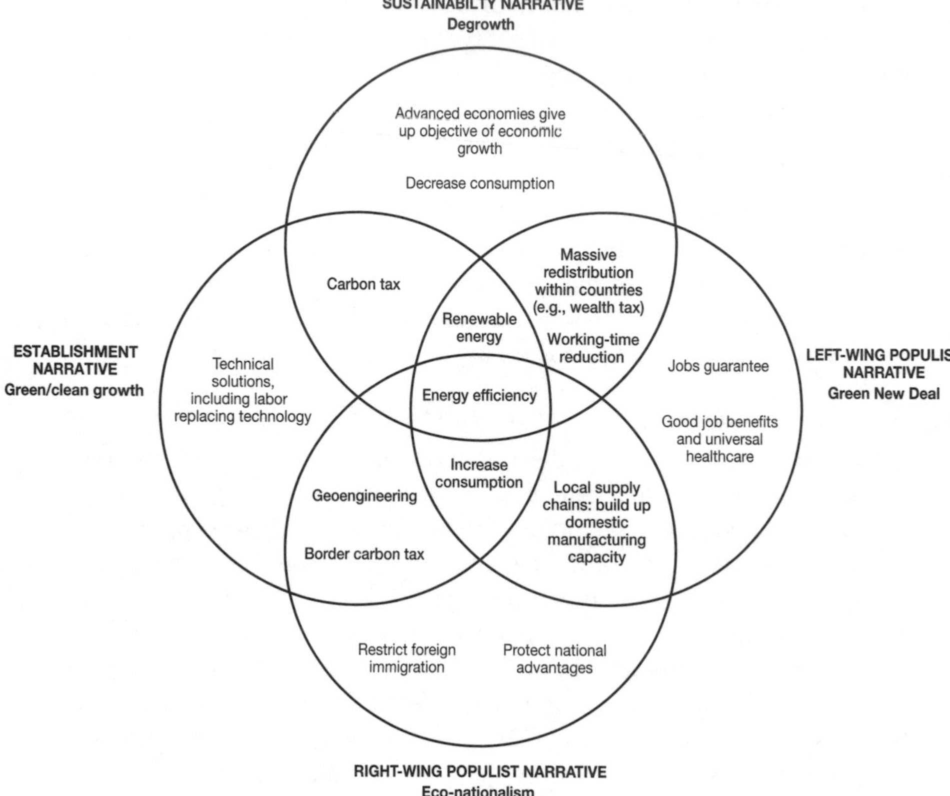

Fig. 14.3: Different Climate Change Policies Mapped onto Four Narratives
Note: This diagram shows areas of overlap—highlighted in bold—between the sustainability, left-wing populist, establishment, and right-wing populist narratives in their approaches to climate change policies. These areas of overlap could potentially provide the basis for alliances between the proponents of these narratives.
Source: The diagram is an adapted and extended version of a diagram in Daniel W. O'Neill, "Beyond Green Growth," Nature Sustainability *3 (2020): 260, figure 1.*
Credit: © Anthea Roberts and Nicolas Lamp

establishment, sustainability, left-wing populist, and right-wing populist narratives, respectively.

Narratives and Proposals

The green growth approach is based on the techno-optimist outlook of the establishment narrative. Instead of treating the ecological limits of the earth as fixed and preaching the necessity of living within our planet's means, the green growth proposal views the best way forward as pursuing wizardly technological developments that would allow us to simultaneously improve our standard of living and green our energy consumption.[24] To achieve these goals, this approach recommends a combination of market incentives—such as cap-and-trade schemes, carbon taxes, and border tax adjustments—with subsidies for renewable energy and innovation. It aims to delink carbon emissions and economic growth by scaling up the use of renewable energy and investing in energy efficiency. Proponents of this approach hold out hope that if we succeed in reducing the carbon intensity of economic growth, we can continue to produce and consume while safeguarding the planet.[25]

The degrowth approach takes the opposite view; it is more techno-pessimist in orientation and most consonant with the sustainability narrative. Its proponents view the earth's ecological limits as largely fixed; they forecast disaster if countries do not impose significant cuts in consumption, particularly on the rich. Advocates of degrowth strategies doubt that all ecological problems can be overcome by human ingenuity and that market-based solutions, such as carbon taxes and subsidies, can deliver the radical change in our patterns of production and consumption that is required to avert catastrophe. The burden of these adjustments would need to be borne primarily by rich people and rich countries, whose wealth (and carbon emissions) would be redistributed to the poor to allow them to attain an adequate standard of living.[26]

The Green New Deal proposed by left-wing populists in the United States seeks to rapidly decarbonize the American economy (in line with the sustainability narrative) while redressing systemic injustices (in line with the left-wing populist narrative). The plan centers on a series of industrial projects—upgrading buildings, decarbonizing the electricity grid, and electrifying transportation—that would reduce carbon emissions and provide plentiful jobs with decent pay and good benefits. Rather than relying primarily on stimulating innovation, the proposal emphasizes the role of the state in investing in infrastructure and creating demand for green products. It also envisages the revitalization of blue-collar work in a manner reminiscent of the New Deal and the mobilization for World War II.[27]

Finally, some proponents of right-wing populism reject the climate crisis as a liberal hoax; these denialists are not captured by the Venn diagram in Figure 14.3. Others, depicted here, accept that climate change is happening but argue for nationalist or nativist responses, in line with the protectionist and anti-immigration elements of the right-wing populist narrative. Some of these policies, such as a carbon border tax, building up domestic manufacturing capacity, and reshoring supply chains, overlap with the other narratives. Others are unique to the narrative, such as severely limiting immigration. In line with the philosophy of humans over nature, this narrative also includes those who share the green growth advocates' openness to geoengineering.[28]

The relative prominence of these climate policies has varied over time. A study of the economic ideas that have influenced climate policy advice by major international organizations such as the OECD and the World Bank identifies a distinct shift in policy preferences around the turn of the century. In the 1990s, consideration of how to redress climate change was largely limited to debates within the establishment narrative, revolving around market solutions such as carbon taxes and cap-and-trade schemes. Since the 2000s, the dominant market-based paradigm has been displaced by more diverse policy debates that put much more emphasis on green industrial policy in the form of government investment in technological innovation and infrastructure. Other policies, including degrowth, have received less attention from international organizations but have gained prominence in recent years as the public has become ever more conscious of the severity of the climate crisis.[29]

Overlaps and Divisions

Given the magnitude and all-encompassing nature of the challenge posed by the climate crisis, it is not surprising that the public discourse about climate policies is marked by diversity and disagreement. Layering the narrative faces of globalization and the policy recommendations that are most commonly associated with them on top of each other provides us a glimpse of the main vectors of disagreement, but also reveals potential for alliances.

Two proposals being considered by the two largest economies in the West—Biden's Climate Plan and the European Green Deal—hew closely to the green growth framing favored by the establishment narrative. Both adopt the goal of achieving carbon neutrality by 2050, but seek to do so mainly through massive investments in everything from clean energy research and development to greening infrastructure that will wean the economy off fossil fuels while spurring economic growth at the same time.

The idea, in the language of the European Green Deal, is to build an economy where "growth is decoupled from resource use."[30]

Both proposals also pick up concerns articulated by the other narratives. While Biden's plan does not openly embrace the massive redistribution advocated by proponents of degrowth and left-wing populists, taxpayer-funded investment on the scale envisaged by Biden (financed in part by rolling back the Trump tax cuts that disproportionately favored corporations and the wealthy) is expected to spread the benefits of the green transition far and wide. The European Green Deal even more explicitly confronts distributive concerns through a "just transition mechanism" that is designed to ensure that no one is left behind. Both plans also address the competitiveness concerns that animate proponents of the right-wing populist narrative. The European Union is designing a "carbon border adjustment mechanism" to reduce the risk that imports from countries with less ambitious climate policies will outcompete European companies during the transition to a low-carbon economy. And Biden is planning to use the procurement power of the US government to ensure that American workers play a key role in the electrification of America's transport system.[31]

By appealing to proponents of various other narratives, both the Biden plan and the European Green Deal follow the approach of marrying ecological and economic concerns that was pioneered by advocates of the Green New Deal in the United States. Some have criticized that approach as counterproductive, because it ties together multiple difficult issues. Others view it as a bold and innovative attempt to mix and match support from actors with different priorities to create a new and broader coalition. As the *Economist* explains, "Any plan to free an industrialised economy from fossil-fuel dependence will create losers. To succeed politically, it must mobilise groups of winners more powerful and passionate than those losers." By combining ecological benefits with economic reform, proponents of the Green New Deal are trying to "gather a winning political coalition."[32]

While the Biden administration and the European Union attempt to appear as inclusive as possible, the left-wing populist proponents of the Green New Deal have been more explicit in setting limits on how broadly they are willing to spread their tent. The conscious effort to police the boundaries of their coalition is evident in the language of the deal's proponents. On the inclusive side, Kate Aronoff and her colleagues emphasize that fossil fuel industry workers and frontline communities must be ensured a just transition and a "dignified quality of life" as the industries they depend on are dismantled. The message is one of care and concern. On the exclusive side, they insist that "our enemies" must be named, and call for fossil fuel executives to be "tried for crimes against humanity." The climate fight has "clear villains," they declare: it is "long past time to drag their reputations through the mud." "We have met the enemy and he is a few hundred fabulously wealthy executives."[33]

In drawing these lines in the sand, proponents of the Green New Deal take clear aim at the cultural and security bases of the right-wing populist and geoeconomic narratives. "Right-wing populists promise to protect labor from competition with lower wage workers in the Global South and to restrict immigration. But nativism is a tool to paper over domestic class conflict." The problem is not China, the Green New Deal's proponents declare, it is corporate power. "Workers share interests across national boundaries, and dividing the working class only weakens its bargaining position against globe-trotting capital."[34] This approach takes seriously the economic anxieties informing the right-wing populist narrative but not the cultural ones. Nor does it give credence to the security concerns animating the geoeconomic narrative.

Whereas the Green New Deal represents a largely left-leaning coalition, very different alliances are also possible. In 2020, conservative and Green Party organizations formed governments in Austria and Ireland. Such "Greencon" coalitions typically combine conservative policies on immigration with aggressive climate action.[35] Greencon coalitions can exploit the areas of overlap among the establishment and sustainability narratives that we illustrate in Figure 14.3, which include tools such as carbon taxes as well as investments in renewable energy and energy efficiency. Conservatives are increasingly comfortable with ambitious carbon reduction targets, as long as they are achieved without the broader interventions in the economy envisaged by advocates of a US-style Green New Deal. Moreover, Greencon coalitions can draw on a common interest of conservative and green voters in conservation; they trust that voters see no contradiction in "vaunting the nation at the same time as valuing the Earth."[36] As the old left-wing electorate splinters—with many blue-collar workers moving into the right-wing populist camp and professionals increasingly mobilizing around the climate crisis—these sort of diverse coalitions may become more common.

Conclusion

When it comes to complex issues such as economic globalization, climate change, and the coronavirus pandemic, there is no single valid perspective and no single solution to the problem. The issues look different when viewed from different angles and through different narrative lenses. No one narrative is likely to prevail when it comes to developing policy responses to these problems; instead, coalitions are likely to splinter and recoalesce kaleidoscopically. By layering multiple narratives and policy proposals on top of one another, it is possible to map out the potential alliances and divisions that may shape future political battles.

CHAPTER 15

Globalization for Foxes

In this book, we have used the shape of elephants, the color of swans, and the vision of dragonflies to illuminate the problems of global inequality, the importance of perspectives from outside the West, and the skill of integrating multiple lenses to create a more three-dimensional view of reality. At this juncture, as we sum up our exploration of narratives about economic globalization, we would like to add a final pair of animals to our menagerie: the fox and the hedgehog.

Isaiah Berlin understood the well-known saying that "the fox knows many things, but the hedgehog knows one big thing" as a metaphor for two styles of thinking. Hedgehogs "relate everything to a single central vision, one system, less or more coherent or articulate, in terms of which they understand, think and feel—a single, universal, organising principle." Foxes, on the other hand, "pursue many ends, often unrelated and even contradictory"; their thinking is "scattered or diffused, moving on many levels, seizing upon the essence of a vast variety of experiences and objects for what they are in themselves, without, consciously or unconsciously, seeking to fit them into, or exclude them from, any one unchanging, all-embracing, . . . at times fanatical, unitary inner vision."[1]

Debates about economic globalization have been dominated by hedgehogs—actors who interpret and evaluate the dynamics and consequences of globalization through a single lens. The perspectives brought to light by these hedgehogs are invaluable. Some of them harness the empirical and theoretical tools of their academic disciplines to build our knowledge of the global economy, polity, and environment. Others articulate a particular value system and spell out its ethical ramifications for organizing the global flow of goods, people, capital, data, and ideas. Each of these perspectives expresses a different viewpoint and sheds light on a specific piece of the puzzle.

We need these experts and advocates for the depth of their knowledge and the strength of their convictions. And it is not surprising that these hedgehogs have dominated debates about economic globalization, since our societies reward hedgehogs over foxes in manifold ways. The media favors succinct sound bites and forceful predictions, rather than "on the one hand, on the other hand" nuance. At the same time, politics in some countries is at its most polarized in decades, with some parties drifting toward ideological extremes and becoming more internally homogeneous, making it harder for flexible pragmatists to reach and retain positions of power. Academic training is becoming ever more specialized, as universities reward depth over breadth and publications in academic journals increasingly address narrow groups of peers.[2]

Yet a debate dominated by hedgehogs may be unhelpful in moving us forward, especially at a time when so much about economic globalization is in question. Hedgehogs roll up into a ball of spikes when they are threatened. Many proponents of the establishment narrative reacted in a similar fashion to the challenges posed by other narratives. President Trump's election and the Brexit vote were met with a mixture of alarm and ridicule by the establishment, which proceeded to marshal studies and data to underscore the success of its original approach, often without engaging in a deeper reassessment of the assumptions underlying its economic models. For their part, proponents of the insurgent narratives have drawn much of their energy from their ability to present a radically different perspective on the world, which has sometimes come at the cost of nuance and a willingness to compromise.

What results is a public debate that oscillates between two extremes: on some issues, the proponents of the different narratives seem to inhabit different worlds, with little or no interaction, while on others, the advocates of rival approaches clash forcefully, but the sides are so deeply entrenched in their own worldviews and echo chambers that genuine dialogue seems impossible. Neither extreme gives hope that we can find enough common ground to move forward.

Although our book provides a compilation of six perspectives generated by the hedgehogs of the public debate about economic globalization, our central aim is to offer a framework for a more fox-like approach. We believe that an approach that works against specialization and polarization by presenting an empathetic account of diverse perspectives within an overarching framework gives us a better sense of the effects of economic globalization and all their ramifications and lays the groundwork for developing policy responses that are responsive to the concerns of diverse and sometimes competing parties.

At the analytical level, the benefits of adopting a fox-like approach that holds many different perspectives in tension are well known. As Philip Tetlock explains in his book *Expert Political Judgment*, *what* experts think matters far less than *how* they think. When it comes to understanding complex phenomena, Tetlock finds that hedgehog-like thinkers who know one big thing often (over)extend the explanatory reach of their expertise into new domains, display brisk impatience with those who "do not get it," and express considerable confidence that they are proficient forecasters, at least in the long term. Yet they are typically far less accurate in their predictions than fox-like thinkers who know many small things, are skeptical of parsimonious answers and logical deductions, see explanations as exercises in flexible "ad hocery" that require stitching together diverse sources of information, and are diffident about their own forecasting prowess.[3]

At the normative level, a fox-like approach to economic globalization can help to overcome some of the mutual incomprehension among entrenched actors and thinkers that plagues current debates and can potentially even furnish the basis for compromise and convergence. A fox-like approach encourages us to step into the shoes of the proponents of narratives with which we disagree. It does not require us to adopt their narrative as our own—we may still contest some of the narrative's empirical claims, value judgments, and policy prescriptions. But if we make a genuine attempt to see economic globalization through the lens of another narrative, we will gain a better understanding of that narrative's focus, internal logic, and appeal, and a clearer vision of the blind spots and biases of our own preferred narratives. At least, that was the experience we had in writing this book: the more deeply we delved into the individual narratives, the more we saw merit in each of them. Each narrative seemed to us to capture a part of the reality of economic globalization that the other narratives missed. No narrative contained the whole truth, but there was truth in each.

What we have learned has convinced us that the best chance of reaching a new consensus on economic globalization lies in integrating insights from across a range of narratives, rather than attempting to shore up the dominant establishment view with a few superficial changes or to replace it with a single new narrative. With this in mind, we draw four broad lessons from our work, which we discuss in turn. These lessons are both procedural—relating to the importance of integrative thinking and diverse teams—and substantive—relating to the importance of distributive questions and value pluralism. We end with a final caveat regarding the future of economic globalization: we raise the possibility that another issue, such as geopolitical competition or climate change, might displace economic globalization as the zeitgeist of our time and become the focal point around which competing narratives coalesce. In that case, the narratives we discuss in this book will likely reorient themselves toward a new frame of reference and be refracted through the lens of a new meta-narrative.

Integrative Thinking

Universities have typically organized their research and teaching largely along disciplinary lines, encouraging depth, specialization, and mastery over breadth, connectivity, and creativity. Policymakers often also work in a relatively siloed fashion as different departments take principal carriage of a problem and keep a tight hold of the drafting pen. Yet the wicked problems that we discuss in this book result from kaleidoscopic collisions of a multitude of intersecting and interdependent issues that do not fall neatly within the disciplinary and subject-matter lines along which much of our knowledge production and policymaking are organized. It follows that we can only hope to understand the complex interdependencies and unpredictable system-level effects that define our most challenging policy dilemmas if we develop more integrative approaches to knowledge production and policy development.

Nobel Prize–winning physicist Murray Gell-Mann—who cofounded the renowned interdisciplinary Sante Fe Institute, which is dedicated to the study of complex systems—once said: "In the twenty-first century, the most important kind of mind will be the synthesizing mind."[4] The distinctive feature of the synthesizing mind is that it takes in and evaluates information from disparate sources and puts that information together in ways that make sense to the synthesizer and others. It is a quintessentially foxy approach. The developmental psychologist Howard Gardner has observed that the ability to "knit together information from disparate sources into a coherent whole is vital today," particularly given the explosion of information and the complexity of the problems societies are facing. Traversing across fields and disciplines and attempting to cross-apply lessons or find integrative solutions also provides fertile ground for producing creative breakthroughs.[5]

The importance of broad-ranging synthesis and integrative thinking is also stressed by former Rotman School of Management dean Roger Martin. When Martin interviewed exceptional business leaders, he found that the common denominator in their thought processes was their ability to engage in integrative thinking, which he defined as the ability to hold (at least) two diametrically opposed ideas in one's head and then, instead of simply picking one or the other, producing a synthesis that is superior to either opposing idea. He and his coauthors have variously described this sort of thinking as resulting from an *opposable mind* (in analogy to opposable thumbs) and *diaminds* (referring to the ability to understand reality through a variety of opposing plans and models and still to be able to act by producing dialectical and dialogical solutions to complex problems). Such minds combine informational breadth with logical depth. They embrace difference, ambiguity, conflict, and tension instead of seeking to reduce the world's complexity into simple, one-right-way approaches to seeing, thinking, and feeling.[6]

The challenge that we confront is that, although our universities have developed sophisticated ways to teach disciplinary thinking, we have few guidelines about how to develop broad-ranging syntheses or how to assess the merits of different attempts.[7] University training often also encourages academics to examine narrow questions in which they attempt to hold "all other things equal," as though complex problems could be reduced into constituent parts that could be analyzed independently and treated separately. In doing so, academia frequently privileges simple models and parsimonious explanations over an effort to understand complex interdependencies, unpredictable outcomes, multifaceted and multidirectional causality, and nonlinear system-level effects, such as tipping points. We favor Ockham's razor—the assumption that the simplest explanation is usually the right one—over "Ockham's quilt"—the acceptance that most events occur as a result of a patchwork of causes. And we often study parts of systems, rather than systems themselves as integrated wholes.[8]

Consciously adopting multiple perspectives on a problem, as we have tried to do in this book, leads us to ask a wide range of questions and helps us to develop frameworks and syntheses that draw on and integrate diverse perspectives instead of endorsing one at the expense of the others.[9] It encourages us to engage in "both/and" thinking rather than "either/or" thinking, stitching together different perspectives and diverse insights rather than focusing on one and ignoring or refuting the others. This sort of integrative thinking is important because the challenge that policymakers confront is not how to address inequality *or* security *or* great power competition *or* climate change in isolation; it is how to grapple with all of these problems simultaneously while taking account of their complex interdependencies and unpredictable interactions. Is it possible to curb the power of Big Tech to encourage greater domestic competition *and* compete effectively with other countries in the economic and technological realm *and* cooperate among friends and foes alike on climate change, or does action in one arena undermine goals in another?

If policymakers concentrate on perfecting one face of the Rubik's cube while ignoring the others, we might end up with a cube with one coherent face and the rest an incoherent mess. We need to be conscious of how a move with respect to one face of the cube may have implications with respect to the cube's other faces. Recognition of the need for this sort of integrative approach is evident in recent government policy statements. For instance, as US trade representative Katherine Tai explained at her confirmation hearing: "China is simultaneously a rival, a trade partner, and an outsized player whose cooperation we'll also need to address certain global challenges. We must remember how to walk, chew gum, and play chess at the same time." And, we would add, play the Chinese game of Weiqi (or Go) as well, incorporating perspectives from outside the West. This sort of integrative thinking recognizes the complex interdependencies of different issues. For instance, it might be easier for governments to curb the power of Big Tech (as per the corporate power narrative) if they have already decided that they are heading toward more separated technology ecosystems (as per the geoeconomic narrative)—something that might help to explain the moves against Big Tech in 2020 and 2021 in both the United States and China.[10]

Our integrative approach chimes with the methods advocated by scholars and practitioners who examine how to engage in effective leadership in complex and dynamic environments. For instance, developmental coach Jennifer Garvey Berger explores the way in which people's craving for a simple world often misleads them in an increasingly complex and unpredictable world. When people are trapped by simple stories, a feeling of rightness, and a desire to find agreement with others, they often fail to notice how the stories they tell shape the data they look for in the first place, how their sense of rightness undermines their curiosity about what they do not know, and how their desire for agreement leads them to avoid conflict rather than productively harnessing it.[11] She emphasizes the importance of considering many stories and being open to different perspectives, even ones that make us feel uncomfortable or which strike us as wrong. As Berger concludes: "Complex situations have so many pieces and perspectives that each one of us might see a slightly different set of possibilities. And even those with bewilderingly different (and seemingly wrong) perspectives are giving voice to something in the complex system that we probably need to pay attention to. Only in this way can we escape from the trap of simple agreement and use conflict and disagreement as a way to deepen our relationships and expand our possibilities."[12]

Diverse Teams

Integrative, fox-like thinking is not just a skill that individuals can acquire; it can also be built into teams and institutions. The key to achieving this objective is to bring together people with diverse backgrounds, perspectives, and cognitive approaches. Complexity theorists such as Scott Page emphasize that having teams made up of people who are cognitively diverse—that is, who differ in how they identify, interpret, and solve problems—presents tangible benefits when it comes to understanding and responding to complex problems. In the words of historian Arnold Toynbee: "No tool is omnicompetent. There is no such thing as a master-key that will unlock all doors." The best toolkit for building a house is one that includes a variety of tools, not just the ten best hammers. Moreover, differences in education, life experiences, and identity can all contribute to cognitive diversity, helping to produce what Page calls the "diversity bonus."[13]

Modern societies, however, often take us in the opposite direction. In our social groups, neighborhoods, professions, and disciplines we are frequently surrounded by others who have relatively similar backgrounds, experiences, viewpoints, and ways of thinking. This sort of siloing tends to reinforce the impression of group members that their perspective is natural or correct, while increasing the group's chance of acquiring a form of collective blindness to other experiences and perspectives. As the journalist Matthew Syed observes in *Rebel Ideas: The Power of Diverse Thinking,* it is common for people to enjoy being around those like themselves. This tendency, known as homophily, means that people often choose to work with and befriend others who look and think like them. The members of such groups enjoy engaging with one another, basking in the glow of their mutual agreement. In doing so, their way of thinking often becomes more extreme as they reinforce each other's perspectives, assumptions, and beliefs, and persuade themselves of the correctness of their views. But groups of people who are individually intelligent may be "collectively, well, stupid," in Syed's words, because the group members compound each other's blind spots (Figure 15.1). When two individuals think in very similar ways, putting two heads together is not really better than one, and may sometimes be worse.[14]

Wise groups are composed of diverse actors and perspectives so that they integrate varied insights and ways of thinking. Each person contributes both information and errors. But in diverse teams, the information is more likely to end up being confirmed by multiple sources, whereas the errors are more likely to point in different directions, which results in them canceling each other out. That is why a growing body of work emphasizes the need for cognitive diversity—different ways of thinking—in reaching good judgments, as well as the link between cognitive and other types of diversity, such as race, gender, and socioeconomic status. The benefits of relying on the wisdom of the many have been explored in areas ranging from collective intelligence to deliberative democracy.[15] Participating in diverse teams can be uncomfortable because of the difficulties of communicating across different backgrounds and perspectives, but that very diversity helps guard against groupthink and tunnel vision, which is particularly important when tackling complex problems.[16]

Lack of diversity can cause problems within disciplines. The economics profession is, for instance, notoriously homogeneous and hierarchical. Of all the social science fields, it tends to be the most white, male, and Anglo-American, and it has established a clear hierarchy of the best journals and graduate schools. As the self-proclaimed queen of the social sciences, economics also boasts a track record of citation by many other fields, but economists rarely engage in interdisciplinary citation themselves, which leaves the discipline relatively impervious to insights from other areas such as political science, sociology, and anthropology. This lack of diversity makes it harder to integrate nondominant perspectives into the core of economic thinking. The field's position within the social sciences is best described as dominant but insular.[17]

Lack of diversity also has a socioeconomic dimension. In the United States, for example, limited upward mobility and increased residential segregation mean that most of the educated professional class have parents in the professional class and are surrounded by friends and colleagues

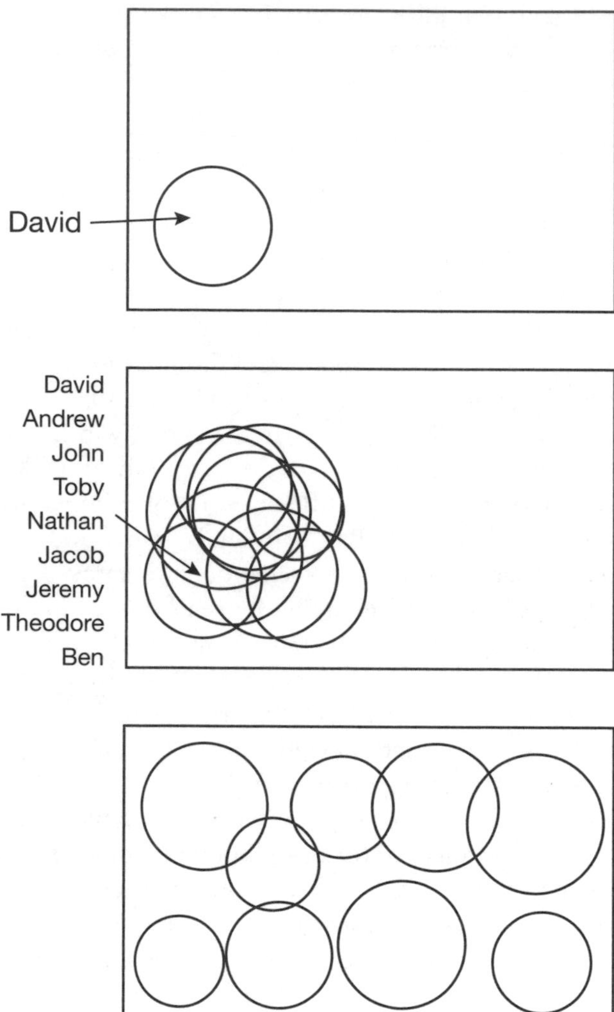

Fig. 15.1: Lots of Intelligent People Can Make an Unintelligent Team if They Lack Diversity

Note: Matthew Syed's diagrams juxtapose a team of "clones" who resemble each other in outlook and expertise with a team of "rebels" who have different backgrounds and perspectives; the team of rebels has broader "coverage" and is more intelligent (collectively) than the team of clones. A group of intelligent individuals may produce an unintelligent team if they are not diverse.

Source: Matthew Syed, Rebel Ideas: The Power of Diverse Thinking *(London: John Murray, 2019), 46–47. © 2019 Matthew Syed. Reproduced by permission of John Murray Publishers, an imprint of Hodder and Stoughton Limited.*

in the professional class. Members of this class often hold important positions in the media, the government, and elsewhere, and they are able to spread their ideas despite having little or no experience growing up with or being friends or coworkers with people from different socioeconomic classes or rural backgrounds. Arguably, one of the reasons that the establishment narrative was so dominant—and why disruptions of it, such as Trump's election and Brexit, came as such a surprise—was the narrow composition of the economics profession and elite media, business, and policy circles.

In addition, geography and cultural complacency can have an isolating (and asymmetrical) effect. Elite Chinese actors often have a much better understanding of Western debates than vice versa because they are more likely to speak English and to have studied or worked in the West than Westerners are to know Chinese or to have studied or worked in China. Yet it would behoove any Western actors wanting to understand how to approach issues of competition and cooperation between China and the United States to avoid tunnel vision by familiarizing themselves with the narratives that make up Chinese discourses. Our effort to introduce some narratives from outside the West speaks to this concern about blind spots and biases. Yet, again, real-world developments often take us in the opposite direction: As China's power increases and Sino-American rivalry intensifies, the number of students from Western countries traveling to live and study in China is dropping.[18]

Formulating good policies about economic globalization depends not just on how we understand and evaluate data but also on what data we look for in the first place. One of the problems posed by a lack of diversity, and by its attendant problem of perspective blindness, is not so much that the data is analyzed poorly but that many questions are not asked in the first place. The wicked policy challenges our societies face will require input from diverse communities and perspectives, including across disciplinary boundaries and fields of expertise. This may require changes not only in our university curricula and educational offerings but also in our governmental structures. Along these lines, the Biden administration's *Interim National Security Strategic Guidance* reflects a recognition of the need to break down existing walls and bring more perspectives into policy formation. It concludes:

> Because traditional distinctions between foreign and domestic policy—and among national security, economic security, health security, and environmental security—are less meaningful than

> ever before, we will reform and rethink our agencies, departments, interagency processes, and White House organization to reflect this new reality. We will ensure that individuals with expertise in science, technology, engineering, and mathematics, economics and finance, and critical languages and regions are fully integrated into our decision-making. Because the federal government does not, and never will, have a monopoly on expertise, we will develop new processes and partnerships to ensure that state, municipal, tribal, civil society, non-profit, diaspora, faith-based, and private sector actors are better integrated into policy deliberations. And we will develop new mechanisms to coordinate policy and implementation across this diverse set of stakeholders.[19]

By developing diverse teams and encouraging individuals to think in more diverse ways, we can work to overcome perspective blindness. At both individual and group levels, adopting dragonfly eyes will enable us to see, appreciate, and evaluate complex and contested questions from multiple perspectives.

Where will more integrative thinking about economic globalization lead us? Although we do not have a definite answer to this question, our survey of competing narratives about economic globalization suggests that the debate's center of gravity is shifting in at least two respects. The first is the increasing centrality of questions of distribution—both within countries and between countries—which anyone defending a vision of economic globalization will have to address. The second relates to the increasing weight being given to non-economic values, if necessary at the cost of efficiency and economic growth. The latter goals, long championed by the establishment narrative, appear to be somewhat in retreat on multiple fronts.

Distribution

Advocates of the establishment narrative endorsed a two-step approach to international economic integration. The first imperative was to maximize the size of the pie by opening up markets to international trade and investment. Distributional questions about how the pie was divided were left to the domestic level. Economic thinking in this mold focused on increasing efficiency so as to promote economic growth for the country as a whole. By mathematical implication, a growing economy meant that the winners could compensate the losers and still be better off. Whether the winners actually compensated the losers, and if so, how, was a matter for messy distributive politics rather than elegant economic models. "Of the tendencies that are harmful to sound economics, the most seductive, and in my opinion the most poisonous, is to focus on questions of distribution," the Nobel Prize–winning Chicago economist Robert Lucas once warned. "The potential for improving the lives of poor people by finding different ways of distributing current production is *nothing* compared to the apparently limitless potential of increasing production."[20]

Contrary to this approach, a common theme that emerges when we look at economic globalization from the perspective of other narratives is that distribution is highly significant, along multiple axes. The left-wing populist narrative zeroes in on the distribution of wealth and opportunity among socioeconomic classes within a particular country. It is animated by concerns that the top 1 percent or 20 percent are pulling away, and doing so in ways that hollow out the middle class and put further downward pressure on the working class and poor. For proponents of the left-wing populist narrative, growth is pointless if it is not broadly shared. The right-wing populist narrative argues that distribution also matters horizontally, in geographic space. It contrasts dynamic cities that move ahead and communities in smaller towns that decay when factories close. This realization directs attention to the plight of the periphery and highlights how spatial economic distribution reflects and reinforces differences in sociopolitical attitudes.

Distributive effects across countries also figure prominently in the narratives. Whereas the establishment narrative celebrates the fact that economic globalization has lifted millions out of poverty in developing countries, the geoeconomic narrative draws attention to the challenges that can arise from economic convergence among countries, such as geopolitical competition between great powers. Although China and the United States have both gained from economic globalization in absolute terms, China's success in closing the gap in relative terms has sharpened the sense of economic and security competition between the two. The loss of relative status by formerly dominant groups is a common thread among the geoeconomic and right-wing populist narratives. People and countries acutely feel the loss of economic preeminence and its attendant benefits.[21] This sensitivity does not mean we should not seek greater equality, but it could help explain some of the social and political volatility that we are currently witnessing and might be relevant to determining how political change should be handled in order to defuse rather than inflame antagonism.

Distributive concerns are also central to the corporate power narrative, which unearths the rules and dynamics that allow multinational corporations to garner a disproportionate share of the gains from international trade and investment. The narrative traces how economic globalization strengthens capital owners and weakens the hand of labor, and how it has enabled mobile capital to push countries into tax and regulatory competition with each other, resulting in declining corporate tax rates and watered down standards. Distributive questions also play a crucial role in narratives that assert that everyone will ultimately lose. Although all countries and people are threatened in one way or another by climate change and the coronavirus pandemic, the effects of these crises vary greatly across countries and socioeconomic groups within those countries.

The message of all these narratives is that it is not enough to increase the size of the pie; the way the pie is sliced is just as important, and sometimes more so. At the same time, the narratives differ in which distributive effects of economic globalization they regard as politically salient and normatively problematic. These differences in perspective reflect not only varied vantage points, but also different values.

Value Pluralism

The establishment narrative assumed that our overall "welfare" could be represented in economic metrics that could then be maximized. This view either ignored non-monetary values or treated them as reducible to economic measures. Critics of the establishment narrative take issue with this approach to non-economic values; they contend that sometimes these other values are not commensurable with and may be more important than economic goals. We believe that any new consensus on economic globalization will need to give weight to a plurality of values and find ways of incorporating them into policymaking.[22]

Chris Arnade was a Wall Street banker who came to question the narrowness of the establishment's goals when he left banking and spent time talking to and photographing people in towns and city neighborhoods that his friends and colleagues warned him were too poor and too dangerous. "We have implemented policies that focus narrowly on one value of meaning: the material. We emphasize GDP and efficiency, those things that we can measure, leaving behind the value of those things that are harder to quantify—like community, happiness, friendship, pride, and integration." He concludes that "we all need to listen to each other more. . . . We need everyone—those in the back row, those in the front row—to listen to one another and try to understand one another and understand what they value and try to be less judgmental."[23]

The idea that values other than wealth maximization matter is an essential element of the sustainability narrative that forms part of the global threats discourse. Environmentalists and their allies ask us to recast economic growth as a means to an end rather than an end in itself. They insist that policies focus on how we survive and thrive within the limits of our planet. And they remind us that not all economic growth actually contributes to human well-being, especially when it is pursued without respect for planetary boundaries. Human well-being and ecological safety become the paramount goals, displacing economic growth as the raison d'être of government policy. Many who pursue this approach also value nature for its intrinsic worth, not just for its instrumental value to humans.

Non-economic values also animate other narratives. The right-wing populist narrative prizes the ties that bind families, communities, and nations, and it values tradition, stability, loyalty, and hierarchy. Its advocates see work as important not just for providing an income but also for conferring a sense of identity, self-worth, and dignity, which in turn helps in building stable families and communities. Even if trade encourages greater efficiency and cheaper production, it can damage the fabric that holds societies together, particularly when change is rapid and highly concentrated in particular regions or sectors. It can also cause security concerns, proponents of the geoeconomic narrative urge, by developing deep interdependencies across borders and undermining a state's capacity to be self-sufficient in times of crisis.

Failure to recognize the significance of non-economic values sometimes leads proponents of the establishment narrative to dismiss proponents of other narratives as either ill-informed ("they do not understand the concept of comparative advantage") or disingenuous ("they are just appealing to conservative notions like family, community, and national security in order to hoodwink voters"). But seeking to understand other narratives prompts us to consider whether, in people's lived experience, a dollar is simply a dollar regardless of whether it comes from earning a wage as a worker or from saving money as a consumer. It focuses attention on how the source of the dollar matters; earning a living wage can feel very different from receiving welfare, even if the amount is the same. And it raises the question of which things money can buy or recompense, and which it cannot.

Two themes emerge from this discussion. The first is that other values matter, whether they be human well-being, environmental protection, community cohesion, or national security. Sometimes economic growth is helpful in achieving these goals; sometimes it stands in tension with achieving these goals. Taking a more explicit and plural approach to values allows for a more open discussion about which values individuals or societies should be pursuing and how best to achieve them. Such recognition has meaningful implications for economic and social policies. The establishment narrative, for instance, says little about the importance of local communities, focusing instead on economic growth for the country as a whole. But the right-wing populist narrative stresses that communities are consequential because they offer their members a sense of identity and belonging. This mindset markedly affects policy because people who value staying in their community are not very mobile. "Since they cannot move to work where growth occurs, they need economic growth in their own community," economist Raghuram Rajan concludes. "If we care about the community, we need to care about the geographic distribution of growth."[24]

The second theme is that some of these other values are not reducible to money, so attempts to price them, to provide compensation for their loss, or to suggest economic responses to them may strike holders of these values as tone-deaf or even offensive. Such reactions occur particularly when the holders of these other values treat them as akin to sacred values. According to cultural anthropologist Scott Atran and political scientist Robert Axelrod, many people across the world believe that devotion to essential or core values—such as the welfare of their family, community, or country or their religious values—is, or ought to be, absolute and inviolable. These sorts of sacred values are often bound up with people's identities in ways that trump other interests, especially economic ones. Not only will people seek to protect these sacred values even when it goes against their material interests, but often they will view offers of compensation in exchange for giving up a sacred value as an insult.[25]

According to social psychologist Jonathan Haidt, those on the left and right in America share values of caring and fairness, but the right is much more likely to value other traits as well, such as in-group loyalty, obedience to authority, and purity. Moreover, not only do people's moral foundations differ, but many individuals struggle to recognize the moral foundations underlying beliefs with which they disagree. Certain non-economic values that underlie the right-wing populist and geoeconomic narratives reflect the desire to protect the family, community, and country. Assuming that someone's interests are only economic, so that any decision to vote a different way is irrational, misses the devotion of many people to non-economic values.[26] When sociologist Arlie Russell Hochschild spent time in the American "heartland," what struck her was that people were not voting against their economic self-interest but voting in favor of their emotional self-interest—their interest in not feeling like a stranger within their own land.[27]

One of the deficiencies of a liberal democratic system is the insistence on liberal neutrality, which seeks to avoid judgments about moral and cultural issues. As philosopher Michael Sandel explains: "Liberal neutrality flattens questions of meaning, identity, and purpose into questions of fairness. It therefore misses the anger and resentment that animate the populist revolt; it lacks the moral and rhetorical and sympathetic resources to understand the cultural estrangement, even humiliation, that many working class and middle class voters feel; and it ignores the meritocratic hubris of elites."[28] We use market mechanisms to look for evidence of what people value and how much they are prepared to pay. But many of the values underlying the different narratives are not captured (at all or well) by these market mechanisms.

If both economic values and non-economic values matter, and if different actors with different experiences and interests are likely to embrace different values, we need to encourage public discourse and policy frameworks that will allow these values to be more openly articulated and the trade-offs between them to be more forthrightly discussed. This approach requires difficult discussions, such as how to weigh tradition against economic progress, the wealth of the nation against the well-being of particular areas or groups, and the importance of nationality against the value of global and cosmopolitan identities. There is no single correct answer to these questions. As Sandel argues: "To reinvigorate democratic politics, we need to find our way to a morally more robust public discourse, one that honors pluralism by *engaging* with our moral disagreements, rather than *avoiding* them."[29]

A Changing Zeitgeist?

The dominance of the establishment narrative over the past three decades has been reflected not only in its wide acceptance by government officials and intellectual elites around the world but also in its use as the primary point of reference for competing narratives, which defined themselves against it. That position allowed the establishment narrative to frame the terms of public debate and ensured that economic globalization—a project that the narrative promoted and championed—would occupy a central place within that debate. Economic globalization did not constitute just one story that we could tell about the world; rather, it served as the dominant stage for many stories about the economic fortunes of people in contemporary societies.

In 2020, people all over the world got a taste of what it feels like when that positioning changes. The coronavirus pandemic became, at least temporarily, the dominant force in public life, and public health imperatives took precedence over almost all other considerations. From the perspective of this book, what was striking about the crisis was that *all* the narratives that we discussed in this book suddenly became narratives *about* the coronavirus pandemic. One hopes that the pandemic will dominate public discourse for only a few years, rather than decades. But other, more enduring meta-narratives could surface as the "all-encompassing setting" in which the contestation among other narratives plays out.[30]

The first of these potential new settings is shaped by the forces that are pulling China and the West apart in an increasingly deep and comprehensive fashion. The concerns that pervaded the debate about this relationship in the era of economic globalization—trade deficits, exchange rates, subsidies—are increasingly overshadowed by more fundamental anxieties about national security, ideological conflict, technological competition, and the prospect of decoupling. The question of which posture the West and China should adopt vis-à-vis each other is starting to touch on virtually all areas of policy, from education and cultural exchange to business and scientific collaboration. More and more, liberal democracies are being urged to band together to form a counterweight to China and other authoritarian powers. If this sort of division and competition becomes all-encompassing, each narrative will confront the question of how great power rivalry will impact our ability to pursue other objectives.[31]

A second candidate for a new meta-narrative centers around climate change. As the climate crisis "colonizes and darkens our lives and our world," David Wallace-Wells suggests, it "may come to be regarded . . . as the only truly serious subject."[32] US president Biden concurs; he has said of climate change that "if we don't get this right, nothing else will matter."[33] The increasing centrality of climate change in public life may force the participants in public discourse to recast their narratives through the lens of the climate crisis. Proponents of the establishment narrative who seek to maximize economic growth would have to show how we can do this while avoiding a climate catastrophe. Right-wing populists who seek to protect communities from the loss of manufacturing jobs would have to explain how they will shield them from floods and droughts as well. Left-wing populists might become just as attuned to the inequities created by geography and weather conditions as they are to the unfairness produced by income inequality and a rigged economy. Critics of corporate power would need to grapple with the ambiguous role of corporations as both climate villains and indispensable allies in transforming our economies. Similarly, proponents of the geoeconomic narrative would need to balance their mistrust and hostility toward China with its essential role in efforts to bend the emissions curve.

These two potential meta-narratives share a much darker outlook than the establishment narrative's. The establishment narrative was (and remains) progressive at its core: ultimately, proponents of the narrative believed that GDP would rise, trade would become freer, and societies would grow more politically open and democratic. We would continue to travel up the hockey stick of prosperity. Our children would be better off than we are. The potential new meta-narratives partake of no such optimism. If the West finds itself in an ongoing technological, economic, and political rivalry with the world's most populous nation and soon-to-be largest economy, there is no guarantee that future generations will be able to live as peacefully, communicate as openly, and travel as freely as was possible in the past three decades. And as climate change blights everyday life with ever more overlapping disasters—flooding, heatwaves, wildfires, and crop failures—future generations will be poorer and live more precariously all over the world.

What will happen to the narratives we have reviewed in this book if geopolitical competition, climate change, some blend of the two, or some other narrative (such as increased inequality and rising corporate power in an age of automation) comes to be seen as the dominant reality of our age? In this case, we believe that gradually, and more or less reluctantly, the proponents of the narratives will have to refract their concerns through the lens of such a new zeitgeist or meta-narrative. This prospect does not mean that the champions of the different narratives will be any less divided than they are now. But economic globalization may no longer be the primary subject that they are divided about.

NOTES

Ch. 1: Unscrambling Globalization Narratives

1. Martin Wolf, *Why Globalization Works* (New Haven: Yale University Press, 2004); Francis Fukuyama, *The End of History and the Last Man* (New York: Free Press, 1992). In the final part of his book, Fukuyama anticipated some of the potential challenges to the liberal democratic settlement of the post–Cold War era—passages that appear prophetic in hindsight.

2. Branko Milanovic, "The Two Faces of Globalization: Against Globalization as We Know It," *World Development* 31, no. 4 (2003): 667–683, 667.

3. For the Brexit slogan, see Macer Hall, "Boris Johnson Urges Brits to Vote Brexit to 'Take Back Control,'" *Express*, June 20, 2016; for Trump's rhetoric, see Donald J. Trump, "Inaugural Address," January 20, 2017, https://trumpwhitehouse.archives.gov/briefings-statements/the-inaugural-address/.

4. On the idea of critical junctures, see Ruth Berins Collier and David Collier, *Shaping the Political Arena: Critical Junctures, the Labor Movement, and Regime Dynamics in Latin America* (Notre Dame, IN: University of Notre Dame Press, 2002), 27–39; Giovanni Capoccia and R. Daniel Kelemen, "The Study of Critical Junctures: Theory, Narrative, and Counterfactuals in Historical Institutionalism," *World Politics* 59, no. 3 (2007): 341–369.

5. On the distinction between left-wing and right-wing populism, see Cas Mudde, "The Populist Zeitgeist," *Government and Opposition* 39, no. 3 (2004): 543, 549; Cas Mudde, "Populism: An Ideational Approach," in *The Oxford Handbook of Populism*, edited by Cristóbal Rovira Kaltwasser, Paul Taggart, Paulina Ochoa Espejo, and Pierre Ostiguy (Oxford: Oxford University Press, 2017), 29–30, 32; Barry Eichengreen, "The Two Faces of Populism," CEPR, October 29, 2019, https://voxeu.org/article/two-faces-populism; Barry Eichengreen, *The Populist Temptation: Economic Grievance and Political Reaction in the Modern Era* (New York: Oxford University Press, 2018). We adopt the ideational approach to populism identified by writers such as Mudde, viewing it as a thin ideology that pits "the people" against "the elite" in a way that can be combined with other normative agendas, such as socialism on the left and nationalism or nativism on the right.

6. On the possibility of left-wing populism, see Chantal Mouffe, *For a Left Populism* (New York: Verso, 2018), 50–51; John B. Judis, *The Populist Explosion: How the Great Recession Transformed American and European Politics* (New York: Columbia Global Reports, 2016), 14–16; Ernesto Laclau, *On Populist Reason* (London: Verso, 2005),

4; Mudde, "The Populist Zeitgeist," 549; Joseph Lowndes, "Populism in the United States," in *The Oxford Handbook of Populism,* 233. The focus on immigration has led many to characterize western European populism as right-wing, though both left- and right-wing forms exist in western Europe. Paul Taggart, "Populism in Western Europe," in *The Oxford Handbook of Populism,* 248, 252, 260.

7. This form of populism is often also called national populism. Roger Eatwell and Matthew Goodwin, *National Populism: The Revolt against Liberal Democracy* (London: Pelican, 2018); John B. Judis, *The Nationalist Revival: Trade, Immigration, and the Revolt against Globalization* (New York: Columbia Global Reports, 2018).

8. Pippa Norris and Ronald Inglehart, *Cultural Backlash* (New York: Cambridge University Press, 2019), 7; Judis, *The Populist Explosion,* 15; Lowndes, "Populism in the United States," 233; Mouffe, *For a Left Populism,* 50–51; Cas Mudde, *The Far Right Today* (Cambridge, UK: Polity Press, 2019), 7–8; Mudde, "The Populist Zeitgeist," 543; Mudde, "Populism: An Ideational Approach," 32–33.

9. Chloe Farand, "Marine Le Pen Launches Presidential Campaign with Hardline Speech," *Independent,* February 5, 2017; David Goodhart and Helen Armstrong, *The Road to Somewhere: The Populist Revolt and the Future of Politics* (London: Hurst, 2017); Mudde, "Populism: An Ideational Approach," 33; Jonathan Haidt, "When and Why Nationalism Beats Globalism," *Politico,* July 7, 2016.

10. Robert M. Cover, "The Supreme Court, 1982 Term—Foreword: Nomos and Narrative," *Harvard Law Review* 97, no. 1 (1983): 4–5.

11. Molly Patterson and Kristen Renwick Monroe, "Narrative in Political Science," *Annual Review of Political Science* 1, no. 1 (1998): 315–331; Emery M. Roe, *Narrative Policy Analysis: Theory and Practice* (Durham, NC: Duke University Press, 1994); Amrita Narlikar, *Poverty Narratives and Power Paradoxes in International Trade Negotiations and Beyond* (Cambridge, UK: Cambridge University Press, 2020).

12. Robert J. Shiller, *Narrative Economics* (Princeton, NJ: Princeton University Press, 2019), viii; Robert J. Shiller, "Narrative Economics," presidential address delivered at the 129th Annual Meeting of the American Economic Association, Chicago, January 7, 2017, https://cowles.yale.edu/sites/default/files/files/pub/d20/d2069.pdf.

13. John Kay and Mervyn King, *Radical Uncertainty: Decision-Making for an Unknowable Future* (London: Bridge Street Press), 314–316, 410–411.

14. Dani Rodrik, "Populism and the Economics of Globalization," *Journal of International Business Policy* 1, nos. 1–2 (2018): 12–33.

15. Milanovic, "The Two Faces of Globalization," 668; for an early example of applying narrative analysis to issues of high uncertainty and polarization, see Janne Hukkinen, Emery Roe, and Gene I. Rochlin, "A Salt on the Land: A Narrative Analysis of the Controversy over Irrigation-Related Salinity and Toxicity in California's San Joaquin Valley," *Policy Sciences* 23 (1990): 307–329. For a recent example applying multiple frames to understand how climate change is presented, see Mike Hulme, *Why We Disagree about Climate Change* (Cambridge, UK: Cambridge University Press, 2009), 225–230; Mike Hulme, "You've Been Framed: Six New Ways to Understand Climate Change," *The Conversation,* July 4, 2011.

16. On polarization, Shanto Iyengar and Sean J. Westwood, "Fear and Loathing across Party Lines: New Evidence on Group Polarization," *American Journal of Political Science*

59, no. 3 (2015): 690–707; Jonathan Haidt and Sam Abrams, "The Top 10 Reasons American Politics Are So Broken," *Washington Post,* January 7, 2015; Ezra Klein, *Why We're Polarized* (New York: Simon and Schuster, 2020), 1–17. On geographical sorting, see Ryan D. Enos, *The Space between Us: Social Geography and Politics* (Cambridge, UK: Cambridge University Press, 2017); Bill Bishop and Robert G. Cushing, *The Big Sort: Why the Clustering of Like-Minded America Is Tearing Us Apart* (Boston: Houghton Mifflin Harcourt, 2008). On contempt, Arthur C. Brooks, "Our Culture of Contempt," *New York Times,* March 2, 2019; Arthur C. Brooks, *Love Your Enemies: How Decent People Can Save America from the Culture of Contempt* (New York: Broadside Books, 2019).

17. Jonathan Haidt, *The Righteous Mind: Why Good People Are Divided by Politics and Religion* (New York: Pantheon Books, 2012), 49.

18. On the importance of encouraging empathy in today's fractured world, see Jamil Zaki, *The War for Kindness: Building Empathy in a Fractured World* (New York: Broadway Books, 2019).

19. Philip Tetlock, *Superforecasting: The Art and Science of Prediction* (New York: Crown, 2015), 121–127, 191–192.

20. Karen Guttieri, Michael D. Wallace, and Peter Suedfeld, "The Integrative Complexity of American Decision Makers in the Cuban Missile Crisis," *Journal of Conflict Resolution* 39, no. 4 (1995): 595–621; Peter Suedfeld and Philip Tetlock, "Integrative Complexity of Communications in International Crises," *Journal of Conflict Resolution* 21, no. 1 (1977): 169–184; Peter Suedfeld, Philip Tetlock, and Carmenza Ramirez, "War, Peace, and Integrative Complexity: UN Speeches on the Middle East Problem, 1947–1976," *Journal of Conflict Resolution* 21, no. 3 (1977): 427–442.

21. Definitions of "the West" are inevitably controversial; we use the term here to refer to the countries that make up the "Western Europe and other States" group at the United Nations. This grouping includes countries from western Europe (such as Belgium, France, Germany, Greece, the Netherlands, and Spain) and from Anglo-America (Australia, Canada, New Zealand, the United Kingdom, and the United States). Although debate abounds about whether the West should also include countries such as Japan and those in Latin America, we focus on this narrower group, over which there is no debate. See "United Nations Regional Groups of Member States," United Nations Department for General Assembly and Conference Management, https://www.un.org/dgacm/en/content/regional-groups.

Ch. 2: Why Narratives Matter

1. Branko Milanovic, *Global Inequality: A New Approach for the Age of Globalization* (Cambridge, MA: Harvard University Press, 2016).

2. For proponents of this interpretation of the Elephant Graph, see, e.g., Paul Krugman, "Recent History in One Chart," *New York Times,* January 1, 2015; Matt O'Brien, "This May Be the Most Important Chart for Understanding Politics Today," *Washington Post,* January 13, 2016; Luke Kawa, "Get Ready to See This Globalization 'Elephant Chart' over and over Again," Bloomberg, June 27, 2016 (quoting Toby Nangle). For critiques of the graph and of this interpretation, see, e.g., Adam Corlett, *Examining an Elephant,* Resolution Foundation Report, September 2016, https://www.resolutionfoundation.org/app/uploads/2016/09/Examining-an-elephant.pdf; Caroline Freund, "Deconstructing Branko Milanovic's 'Elephant Chart': Does It Show What Everyone Thinks?," Peterson Institute for International Economics, November 30, 2016, https://www.piie.com/blogs

/realtime-economic-issues-watch/deconstructing-branko-milanovics-elephant-chart-does-it-show. For a response, see Christopher Lakner and Branko Milanovic, "Response to Adam Corlett's 'Examining an Elephant: Globalisation and the Lower Middle Class of the Rich World,'" City University of New York, September 2016, https://www.gc.cuny.edu/CUNY_GC/media/CUNY-Graduate-Center/LIS%20Center/elephant_debate-4,-reformatted.pdf?mod=article_inline.

3. Jeremy Diamond, "Trump: 'We Can't Continue to Allow China to Rape Our Country,'" CNN, May 2, 2016; Dan Primack, "Is Donald Trump Right that Mexico Is 'Killing Us' on Trade?," *Fortune,* August 10, 2015; "President Trump's Inauguration Speech, Annotated," *Vox,* January 20, 2017, https://www.vox.com/a/president-trump-inauguration-speech-transcript-annotations.

4. Bernie Sanders, "Democrats Need to Wake Up," *New York Times,* June 28, 2016.

5. Our conception of narratives builds on the Narrative Policy Framework. See Elizabeth A. Shanahan, Michael D. Jones, Mark K. McBeth, and Claudio M. Radaelli, "The Narrative Policy Framework," in *Theories of the Policy Process,* 4th ed., edited by Christopher M. Weible and Paul A. Sabatier (New York: Routledge, 2018), 173–213; see also Deborah A. Stone, "Causal Stories and the Formation of Policy Agendas," *Political Science Quarterly* 104, no. 2 (1989): 281–300.

6. Carol Bacchi, *Analysing Policy: What's the Problem Represented to Be?* (Sydney: Pearson Education Australia, 2009).

7. Erving Goffman, *Frame Analysis: An Essay on the Organization of Experience* (Boston: Northeastern University Press, 1974).

8. Gareth Morgan, *Images of Organization* (Beverly Hills, CA: Sage Publications, 1986), 5.

9. Dani Rodrik, *Economics Rules* (New York: W. W. Norton, 2015), 44.

10. On the importance and role of ideas, see the symposium "Ideas, Political Power, and Public Policy," *Journal of European Public Policy* 23, no. 3 (2016); Mark Blyth, "Powering, Puzzling, or Persuading? The Mechanisms of Building Institutional Orders," *International Studies Quarterly* 51, no. 4 (2007): 761–777; Kathleen R. McNamara, *The Currency of Ideas: Monetary Politics in the European Union* (Ithaca, NY: Cornell University Press, 1998); Mark Blyth, "Structures Do Not Come with an Instruction Sheet: Interests, Ideas, and Progress in Political Science," *Perspectives on Politics* 1, no. 4 (2003): 695–706; Deirdre McCloskey, *The Rhetoric of Economics,* 2nd ed. (Madison: University of Wisconsin Press, 1998); Martin B. Carstensen and Vivien A. Schmidt, "Power through, over and in Ideas: Conceptualizing Ideational Power in Discursive Institutionalism," *Journal of European Public Policy* 23, no. 3 (2016): 318–337; Vivien A. Schmidt, "Discursive Institutionalism: The Explanatory Power of Ideas and Discourse," *Annual Review of Political Science* 11 (2008): 303–326; Wesley Widmaier, "The Power of Economic Ideas—through, over and in—Political Time: The Construction, Conversion and Crisis of the Neoliberal Order in the US and UK," *Journal of European Public Policy* 23, no. 3 (2016): 338–356.

11. Mark Blyth, *Great Transformations: Economic Ideas and Institutional Change in the Twentieth Century* (New York: Cambridge University Press, 2002), 38–39.

12. On the role of crises, see, e.g., Wesley W. Widmaier, Mark Blyth, and Leonard Seabrooke, "Exogenous Shocks or Endogenous Constructions? The Meanings of Wars and Crises," *International Studies Quarterly* 51, no. 4 (2007): 747–759; Blyth, "Powering, Puz-

zling, or Persuading?"; Wesley W. Widmaier, "Constructing Foreign Policy Crises: Interpretive Leadership in the Cold War and War on Terrorism," *International Studies Quarterly* 51, no. 4 (2007): 779–794; Leonard Seabrooke, "The Everyday Social Sources of Economic Crises: From 'Great Frustrations' to 'Great Revelations' in Interwar Britain," *International Studies Quarterly* 51, no. 4 (2007): 795–810.

13. Robert Gilpin, "The Political Economy of the Multinational Corporation: Three Contrasting Perspectives," *American Political Science Review* 70, no. 1 (1976): 184–191.

14. David Corn, "Secret Video: Romney Tells Millionaire Donors What He Really Thinks of Obama Voters," *Mother Jones,* September 17, 2012.

15. Katie Reilly, "Read Hillary Clinton's 'Basket of Deplorables' Remarks about Donald Trump Supporters," *Time,* September 10, 2016.

16. On contempt in marital relations, see John M. Gottman, *Why Marriages Succeed or Fail* (New York: Simon and Schuster, 1994). On contempt and political polarization, see Arthur C. Brooks, "Our Culture of Contempt," *New York Times,* March 2, 2019; Arthur C. Brooks, *Love Your Enemies: How Decent People Can Save America from the Culture of Contempt* (New York: Harper Collins, 2019).

17. Mayhill Fowler, "Obama: No Surprise That Hard-Pressed Pennsylvanians Turn Bitter," *Huffington Post,* November 17, 2008.

18. Thomas Frank, *What's the Matter with Kansas?* (New York: Henry Holt, 2004), 7.

19. Dani Rodrik, "Populism and the Economics of Globalization," *Journal of International Business Policy* 1 (2018): 12–33.

20. See, e.g., Barry Eichengreen, "The Two Faces of Populism," CEPR, October 29, 2019, https://voxeu.org/article/two-faces-populism; Guido Tabellini, "The Rise of Populism," CEPR, October 29, 2019, https://voxeu.org/article/rise-populism; Italo Colantone and Piero Stanig, "Heterogeneous Drivers of Heterogeneous Populism," CEPR, October 10, 2019, https://voxeu.org/article/heterogeneous-drivers-heterogeneous-populism; John Sides, Michael Tesler, and Lynn Vavreck, "The 2016 U.S. Election: How Trump Lost and Won," *Journal of Democracy* 28, no. 2 (2017): 34–44; Pippa Norris and Ronald Inglehart, *Cultural Backlash: Trump, Brexit, and Authoritarian Populism* (Cambridge, UK: Cambridge University Press, 2019), 87–174; Cas Mudde, *The Far Right Today* (Cambridge, UK: Polity Press, 2019), 100–101; Noam Gidron and Peter A. Hall, "The Politics of Social Status: Economic and Cultural Roots of the Populist Right," *British Journal of Sociology* 68 (2017): S57–S84; David Goodhart and Helen Armstrong, *The Road to Somewhere: The Populist Revolt and the Future of Politics* (London: Hurst, 2017); Luigi Guiso, Helios Herrera, Massimo Morelli, and Tommaso Sonno, "Demand and Supply of Populism," working paper, Einaudi Institute for Economics and Finance, October 1, 2017, https://populism.wcfia.harvard.edu/files/global-populism/files/newghms300917_withfigure.pdf; Italo Colantone and Piero Stanig, "The Trade Origins of Economic Nationalism: Import Competition and Voting Behaviour in Western Europe," *American Journal of Political Science* 62, no. 4 (October 2018): 936–953; Italo Colantone and Piero Stanig, "The Economic Determinants of the 'Cultural Backlash': Globalization and Attitudes in Western Europe," working paper, Università Bocconi, October 2018, https://papers.ssrn.com/sol3/papers.cfm?abstract_id=3267139; Eric Kaufmann, *Whiteshift: Populism, Immigration, and the Future of White Majorities* (New York: Abrams, 2019).

21. Working-class people, defined as those who are not college-educated, and professional-class people inhabit different cultural worlds. The kinds of values that need to

be inculcated into children to succeed in working-class jobs, including conformity and obedience, are often very different from those needed to succeed at professional jobs, which include self-direction and independence. Melvin Kohn, *Class and Conformity* (Homewood, IL: Dorsey Press, 1969); Michele Gelfand, *Rule Makers, Rule Breakers: How Tight and Loose Cultures Wire Our World* (New York: Scribner, 2019), 112–138.

22. Tabellini, "The Rise of Populism"; Will Wilkinson, "The Density Divide: Urbanization, Polarization, and Populist Backlash," research paper, Niskanen Center, June 2019, https://www.niskanencenter.org/wp-content/uploads/2019/09/Wilkinson-Density-Divide-Final.pdf.

23. Gelfand, *Rule Makers,* 69–72, 107–111; Mudde, *The Far Right Today,* 100–101 (explaining the complementary relationship between the economic and cultural explanations).

24. See, e.g., Jason Le Miere, "Russia Election Hacking: Countries Where the Kremlin Has Allegedly Sought to Sway Votes," *Newsweek,* May 9, 2017; Hunt Allcott and Matthew Gentzkow, "Social Media and Fake News in the 2016 Election," *Journal of Economic Perspectives* 31, no. 2 (2017): 211–236; Andrew Weisburd, Clint Watts, and Jim Berger, "Trolling for Trump: How Russia Is Trying to Destroy Our Democracy," War on the Rocks, November 6, 2016, https://warontherocks.com/2016/11/trolling-for-trump-how-russia-is-trying-to-destroy-our-democracy/; Jessikka Aro, "The Cyberspace War: Propaganda and Trolling as Warfare Tools," *European View* 15 (2016): 121–132.

25. Naomi Oreskes and Erik M. Conway, *Merchants of Doubt: How a Handful of Scientists Obscured the Truth on Issues from Tobacco Smoke to Global Warming* (London: Bloomsbury Press, 2010); Naomi Oreskes and Erik M. Conway, "Defeating the Merchants of Doubt," *Nature* 465 (2010): 686–687.

26. For instance, psychologist Michele Gelfand explains how when politicians stoke fears of immigration threats, this has the effect of tightening the culture in that country so that voters are more likely to elect conservative or authoritarian leaders who embrace nationalism over globalism. Gelfand, *Rule Makers,* 222–226.

27. For a critique of the way in which we analyze narratives in this book, see Bernhard Hoekman and Douglas Nelson, "How Should We Think about the Winners and Losers from Globalization? A Reply to Nicolas Lamp," *European Journal of International Law* 30, no. 4 (2019): 1399–1408; for a response to this critique, see Nicolas Lamp, "How We Stop Talking Past Each Other: A Rejoinder to Hoekman and Nelson's Reply to My Article on Narratives about Winners and Losers from Globalization," *EJIL:Talk!* (blog), April 24, 2020.

28. Our project of creating an overarching framework for analyzing different narratives is also consistent with the approach advocated by some theorists of deliberative democracy who seek to resolve tensions between the goals of pluralism and consensus by developing a meta-consensus on different points. This can take the form of a meta-normative consensus, where actors agree on the relevant values to be considered even if they disagree on how they should be prioritized, and a meta-cognitive consensus, where actors agree that different forms of knowledge and pieces of evidence are relevant despite ongoing uncertainty or disagreement over the true state of affairs. See John S. Dryzek and Simon Niemeyer, "Reconciling Pluralism and Consensus as Political Ideals," *American Journal of Political Science* 50, no. 3 (2006): 634–649.

29. Robert H. Bates et al., *Analytic Narratives* (Princeton, NJ: Princeton University Press, 1998), 10–18.

Ch. 3: The Establishment Narrative

1. See Steven Rattner, "Trump Is Wrong about the General Motors Bailout," *New York Times*, November 28, 2018 ("For some Americans, it's too late for retraining or relocation. They deserve a stronger social safety net, including programs to reduce the tendency to turn to alcohol and opioids").

2. Likening international trade to a "production technique" is a common conceptual device used by economists to explain the benefits of free trade; see, for example, Paul Krugman, "What Should Trade Negotiators Negotiate About?," *Journal of Economic Literature* 35, no. 1 (1997): 115; on "magic," see Kimberly Clausing, *Open: The Progressive Case for Free Trade, Immigration, and Global Capital* (Cambridge, MA: Harvard University Press, 2019), 53; Binder is quoted in David Wessel and Bob Davis, "Pain from Free Trade Spurs Second Thoughts," *Wall Street Journal*, March 28, 2007; for Mankiw, see N. Gregory Mankiw and Phillip Swagel, "The Politics and Economics of Offshore Outsourcing," *Journal of Monetary Economics* 53, no. 5 (2006): 1031.

3. David Ricardo, *On the Principles of Political Economy and Taxation* (London: John Murray, 1817).

4. Thomas Thwaites, "The Toaster Project," http://www.thomasthwaites.com/the-toaster-project/; Kim Willsher, "Monsieur Made-in-France Eschews Foreign Goods in Name of Patriotism," *Guardian*, September 29, 2013; Clausing, *Open*, 9.

5. See Richard Baldwin, *The Great Convergence* (Cambridge, MA: Harvard University Press, 2016), 120–124.

6. Benjamin N. Dennis and Talan B. İşcan, "Engel versus Baumol: Accounting for Structural Change Using Two Centuries of U.S. Data," *Explorations in Economic History* 46, no. 2 (2009): 186–202, 186; see also Berthold Herrendorf, Richard Rogerson, and Ákos Valentinyi, "Growth and Structural Transformation," in *Handbook of Economic Growth*, Vol. 2B, edited by Philippe Aghion and Steven Durlauf (Amsterdam: Elsevier, 2013), 855–941.

7. Clausing, *Open*, 66.

8. Paul Krugman, "Enemies of the WTO," *Slate*, November 24, 1999.

9. Martin Wolf, *Why Globalization Works* (New Haven: Yale University Press, 2004), xvii.

10. See Krugman, "Trade Negotiators," 113 ("If economists ruled the world, there would be no need for a World Trade Organization").

11. Cordell Hull, *The Memoirs of Cordell Hull* (New York: Macmillan, 1948), 84.

12. Arthur W. Schatz, "The Anglo-American Trade Agreement and Cordell Hull's Search for Peace 1936–1938," *Journal of American History* 57, no. 1 (1970): 85–103.

13. United Nations Economic and Social Council, "Second Session of the Preparatory Committee of the United Nations Conference on Trade and Employment: Verbatim Report," E/PC/T/A/PV/22 (July 1, 1947), 17, as corrected by E/PC/T/A/PV/22.Corr.4, 4.

14. General Agreement on Tariffs and Trade, Contracting Parties, Special Session, "Summary Record of the First Meeting," 4SS/SR/1, 14 (September 30, 1985).

15. Statement by Olivier Long, director-general of General Agreement on Tariffs and Trade, to Ad Hoc Committee on Restructuring of the Economic and Social Sectors of the United Nations System, L/4306, United Nations, New York, February 12, 1976, 2.

16. World Trade Organization, "10 Benefits of the World Trading System," July 2007, https://apeda.gov.in/apedawebsite/about_apeda/10%20benefits.pdf.

17. World Trade Organization, *10 Things the WTO Can Do* (Geneva: WTO, 2012), https://www.wto.org/english/res_e/publications_e/wtocan_e.pdf.

18. Pascal Lamy, "Multilateral Trading System and the Threat of Protectionism in Times of Economic Crisis," speech at the Round Table Centre for Public Studies, Santiago, Chile, April 15, 2010, https://www.wto.org/english/news_e/sppl_e/sppl153_e.htm.

19. Robert Schuman, "Schuman Declaration," May 9, 1950, https://europa.eu/european-union/about-eu/symbols/europe-day/schuman-declaration_en.

20. "European Union (EU)—Facts," Nobel Media, April 21, 2020, https://www.nobelprize.org/prizes/peace/2012/eu/facts/; The Nobel Prize, "The Nobel Peace Prize for 2012" (Nobel Media AB 2021, February 8, 2021), https://www.nobelprize.org/prizes/peace/2012/press-release/.

21. Caroline Mortimer, "EU Referendum: Second World War Veterans Come Out against Brexit," *Independent,* May 9, 2016; Jo Swinson and Ed Davey, "Brexiteers Take European Peace for Granted," *New Statesman,* May 8, 2019.

22. Erich Weede, *Balance of Power, Globalization and the Capitalist Peace* (Berlin: Liberal Verlag, 2005), 28–41.

23. Immanuel Kant, *Perpetual Peace,* trans. Louis White Beck (Indianapolis, IN: Bobbs-Merrill, 1957), 24.

24. Baron de Montesquieu, *The Spirit of Laws,* trans. Thomas Nugent (New York: Collier Press, 1900), 316.

25. Norman Angell, *The Great Illusion: A Study of the Relation of Military Power to National Advantage,* 4th ed. (London: G. P. Putnam's Sons, 1913).

26. Thomas L. Friedman, *The Lexus and the Olive Tree* (New York: Farrar, Straus and Giroux, 2000), 240.

27. Thomas L. Friedman, *The World Is Flat* (New York: Farrar, Straus and Giroux), 587.

28. George L. Ridgeway, *Merchants of Peace: The History of the International Chamber of Commerce,* 2nd ed. (Boston: Little, Brown, 1959).

29. Richard Baldwin, *The Globotics Upheaval: Globalization, Robotics and the Future of Work* (New York: Oxford University Press, 2019), 11, 271.

30. WTO, *World Trade Report 2017: Trade, Technology and Jobs* (Geneva: WTO, 2017), https://www.wto.org/english/res_e/booksp_e/world_trade_report17_e.pdf.

31. WTO, "10 Things," 16.

32. Tony Blair, "Tony Blair on Globalization," *The Globalist,* October 5, 2005, https://www.theglobalist.com/tony-blair-on-globalization/.

33. Stacey Vanek Smith and Cardiff Garcia, "Economists on Screen, Episode 3: Aaron Sorkin," *Planet Money,* NPR, January 3, 2019, https://www.npr.org/sections/money/2019/01/03/681795728/economists-on-screen-episode-3-aaron-sorkin.

34. In the 1960s, a group of experts in the GATT debated what they called the "concept of non-differentiation as to the cause of dislocation in providing adjustment assistance."

GATT, "Secretariat Note on the Meeting of Experts on Adjustment Assistance Measures," COM.TD/H/2, June 29–30, 1965.

35. Donald J. Boudreaux, "Trade Has No Losers," American Institute for Economics Research, December 24, 2018, https://www.aier.org/article/trade-has-no-losers/.

36. This section draws heavily on Edward Alden, *Failure to Adjust: How Americans Got Left behind in the Global Economy* (Lanham, MD: Rowman and Littlefield, 2016), 117, 121; the GATT Group of Experts considered the view of experts from the ILO who had argued that differentiation "could lead to injustice for the worker." See GATT, "Secretariat Note on Adjustment Assistance Measures." See also Ronald Reagan, "Address before a Joint Session of the Congress on the Program for Economic Recovery," February 18, 1981, in *Public Papers of the Presidents of the United States* (Washington, DC: US Government Printing Office, 1982), 111 ("We wind up paying greater benefits to those who lose their jobs because of foreign competition than we do to their friends and neighbors who are laid off due to domestic competition. Anyone must agree that this is unfair"). For "perpetuates the myth," see Sallie James, "Maladjusted: The Misguided Policy of 'Trade Adjustment Assistance,'" Trade Briefing Paper, CATO Institute, November 8, 2017, https://www.cato.org/sites/cato.org/files/pubs/pdf/tbp-026.pdf; for "has the effect of demonizing," see Simon Lester, "Saving the Trading System," *International Economic Law and Policy Blog,* December 1, 2017, https://ielp.worldtradelaw.net/2017/12/saving-the-trading-system.html; for the idea that nobody loses from trade per se, see Boudreaux, "Trade Has No Losers"; for the interpretation of the backlash against globalization as an expression of illegitimate anti-foreigner bias, see Charles Kenny, "The Bogus Backlash to Globalization," *Foreign Affairs,* November 9, 2018, https://www.foreignaffairs.com/articles/united-states/2018-11-09/bogus-backlash-globalization.

37. Alden, *Failure to Adjust,* 116–117; Baldwin, *The Globotics Upheaval,* 11; Timothy Meyer, "Saving the Political Consensus in Favor of Free Trade," *Vanderbilt Law Journal* 70, no. 3 (2017): 985–1026.

38. Alden, *Failure to Adjust,* 112, 117; the original source for the "unemployment caused" quotation is Commission on Foreign Economic Policy, *Report to the President and the Congress* (Washington, DC: U.S. Government Printing Office, 1954), 55.

39. David H. Autor, David Dorn, and Gordon H. Hanson, "The China Shock: Learning from Labor-Market Adjustment to Large Changes in Trade," *Annual Review of Economics* 8 (2016): 205–240; David H. Autor, "When Work Disappears: Manufacturing Decline and the Falling Marriage Market Value of Young Men," *American Economic Review: Insights* 1, no. 2 (2019): 161–178; Daron Acemoglu, David Autor, David Dorn, Gordon H. Hanson, and Brendan Price, "Import Competition and the Great US Employment Sag of the 2000s," *Journal of Labor Economics* 34, no. S1 (2016): 141–198; Anne Case and Angus Deaton, "Mortality and Morbidity in the 21st Century," Brookings Papers on Economic Activity, spring 2017, https://www.brookings.edu/wp-content/uploads/2017/08/casetextsp17bpea.pdf; Philip Levy, "Was Letting China into the WTO a Mistake?," *Foreign Affairs,* April 2, 2018, https://www.foreignaffairs.com/articles/china/2018-04-02/was-letting-china-wto-mistake.

40. Daniel R. Pearson, "Is Manufacturing Employment the Only Thing That Counts?," Morning Consult, March 2, 2017; Martin Neil Baily and Barry P. Bosworth, "US Manufacturing: Understanding Its Past and Its Potential Future," *Journal of Economic Perspectives* 28, no. 1 (2014): 3–26.

41. Pearson, "Manufacturing Employment"; Colin Grabow, "Sometimes Factories Move Abroad. That's OK," *Cato at Liberty* (blog), April 30, 2018, https://www.cato.org/blog/sometimes-factories-move-abroad-thats-ok; George J. Borjas, Richard B. Freeman, and Lawrence F. Katz, "How Much Do Immigration and Trade Affect Labor Market Outcome?," Brookings Papers on Economic Activity, 1997, https://www.brookings.edu/wp-content/uploads/1997/01/1997a_bpea_borjas_freeman_katz_dinardo_abowd.pdf; Michael J. Hicks, "Donald, Hillary, and Bernie Are Lying to Us about Those Lost Manufacturing Jobs," *Market Watch,* May 14, 2016.

42. WTO, *World Trade Report 2017,* 14 ("There is no question that technology is the dominant force," 3).

43. Lorenzo Caliendo et al., "Trade and Labor Market Dynamics: General Equilibrium Analysis of the China Trade Shock," *Econometrica* 87, no. 3 (May 2019): 741–835; Pearson, "Manufacturing Employment"; Cohn is quoted in Bob Woodward, *Fear: Trump in the White House* (New York: Simon and Schuster, 2018), 138.

44. See Timothy Taylor, "The Smile Curve: The Distribution of Benefits from Global Value Chains," *The Conversable Economist* (blog), August 25, 2017; Richard Baldwin, Tadashi Ito, and Hitoshi Sato, "The Smile Curve: Evolving Sources of Value Added in Manufacturing," March 2014, www.uniba.it/ricerca/dipartimenti/dse/e.g.i/egi2014-papers/ito; Ming Ye, Bo Meng, and Shang-Jin Wei, "Measuring Smile Curves in Global Value Chains," *IDE Discussion Paper* No. 530, August 27, 2015.

45. Scott Lincicome, "A Failure to Adjust," Bulwark, January 15, 2019, https://thebulwark.com/a-failure-to-adjust/; for further discussion of the "smile curve," see the literature on "neurofacturing," e.g., Teresa C. Fort, Justin R. Pierce, and Peter K. Schott, "New Perspectives on the Decline of US Manufacturing Employment," *Journal of Economic Perspectives* 32, no. 2 (2018): 47–72; John D. Stoll, "Tesla Should Pull an Apple: Leave 'Production Hell' to Other People," *Wall Street Journal,* January 25, 2019; Grabow, "Sometimes Factories Move Abroad."

46. The study on the benefits of Chinese imports is cited by Lincicome, "Failure"; the quote is from Clausing, *Open,* 92.

47. Clausing, *Open,* 7.

48. G20 Leaders' Communiqué: Hangzhou Summit, September 4–5, 2016, http://www.g20.utoronto.ca/2016/160905-communique.html; World Bank, IMF, and WTO, "Making Trade an Engine of Growth for All: The Case for Trade and for Policies to Facilitate Adjustment," for discussion at the meeting of G20 Sherpas, Frankfurt, Germany, March 23–24, 2017, 21, https://www.imf.org/en/Publications/Policy-Papers/Issues/2017/04/08/making-trade-an-engine-of-growth-for-all.

49. For "blaming foreigners," see Clausing, *Open,* 4–6; the OECD quote is from OECD, *Making Trade Work for All* (Paris: OECD, May 2017), 7; the calculations of the cost of US tire tariffs are from Gary Clyde Hufbauer and Sean Lowry, "US Tire Tariffs: Saving Few Jobs at High Cost," Policy Brief No. PB 12-9, Peterson Institute for International Economics, April 2012, 11–13, https://www.piie.com/publications/pb/pb12-9.pdf; "Australia's Automotive Manufacturing Industry," Australian Government Productivity Commission, Inquiry Report No. 70, March 31, 2014, https://www.pc.gov.au/inquiries/completed/automotive/report/automotive.pdf; Michael McGowan, "Angry Scott Morrison Accuses GM of Letting Holden 'Wither Away' after Taking $2b in Subsidies," *Guardian,* February 16, 2020, https://www.theguardian.com/business/2020/feb

/17/holden-brand-to-be-axed-after-general-motors-announces-it-will-exit-australian-market.

50. Meyer, "Saving the Political Consensus," 997.

51. "G20 Leaders' Communiqué."

52. World Bank, IMF, and WTO, "Making Trade an Engine of Growth," 4, 27.

53. Friedman, *The World Is Flat,* 434.

Ch. 4: The Left-Wing Populist Narrative

1. John B. Judis, *The Populist Explosion* (New York: Columbia Global Reports, 2016).

2. On the concept of "pre-distribution," see Jacob S. Hacker, "The Institutional Foundations of Middle-Class Democracy," *Policy Network* 6 (2011): 33–37; Steven K. Vogel, "Elizabeth Warren Wants to Stop Inequality before It Starts," *New York Times,* January 3, 2019.

3. Sarah Anderson and Sam Pizzigati, "No CEO Should Earn 1,000 Times More than a Regular Employee," *Guardian,* March 18, 2018; Elizabeth Warren and Amelia Warren Tyagi, *The Two-Income Trap: Why Middle-Class Parents Are Going Broke* (New York: Basic Books, 2004); Eileen Applebaum and Rosemary Batt, *Private Equity at Work: When Wall Street Manages Main Street* (New York: Russell Sage Foundation, 2014); Jerome Roos, *Why Not Default? The Political Economy of Sovereign Debt* (Princeton, NJ: Princeton University Press, 2019).

4. The concept of a "rigged" economy is central to the left-wing populist narrative. See, e.g., Dean Baker, *Rigged: How Globalization and the Rules of the Modern Economy Were Structured to Make the Rich Richer* (Washington, DC: Center for Economic and Policy Research, 2016); Steven Greenhouse, "Yes, America Is Rigged against Workers," *New York Times,* August 3, 2019; Anand Giridharadas, *Winners Take All: The Elite Charade of Changing the World* (New York: Alfred A. Knopf, 2018), 4 ("many millions of Americans, on the left and right, feel one thing in common: that the game is rigged against people like them"). On the related sense that inequality is undermining another fundamental value—a sense of fair play—see Joseph Stiglitz, *The Price of Inequality* (New York: W. W. Norton, 2012), xlvii.

5. Baker, *Rigged,* 153–155, 211–212.

6. We note that the graph only represents compensation for "production/nonsupervisory workers in the private sector" and therefore does not capture the extraordinary rise in elite labor income. Proponents of the left-wing populist narrative refer to the group that has not benefited from productivity growth in recent decades in various ways: Thomas Frank describes them as "the lower 90 percent of the population, a group we might call 'the American people,'" whereas Giridharadas simply refers to the "bottom half of Americans" or "117 million Americans"; Thomas Frank, *Listen, Liberal, or: What Ever Happened to the Party of the People?* (New York: Picador, 2016), 2, and Giridharadas, *Winners Take All,* 4.

7. See Marcus Leroux, "It's Plain Sailing for One Manufacturing Industry," *Sunday Times,* September 25, 2013, reporting the following statement by then UK Labour leader Ed Miliband: "They used to say a rising tide lifted all boats. Now the rising tide just seems

to lift the yachts." See also Alice H. Amsden, *Escape from Empire: The Developing World's Journey through Heaven and Hell* (Cambridge, MA: MIT Press, 2007), 1.

8. C. Wright Mills, *The Power Elite,* new ed. (New York: Oxford University Press, 2000), 148.

9. Stewart Lansley, "The Hourglass Society," *L.A. Review of Books,* May 28, 2013.

10. Anton Korinek and Ding Xuan Ng, "The Macroeconomics of Superstars," November 2017, https://www.imf.org/-/media/Files/Conferences/2017-stats-forum/session-3-korinek.ashx; Enrico Moretti, *The New Geography of Jobs* (Boston, MA: Houghton Mifflin Harcourt, 2012).

11. Bernie Sanders, "The War on the Middle Class," *Boston Globe,* June 12, 2015; for "chipped, squeezed and hammered," see Elizabeth Warren, "Elizabeth Warren DNC Speech," ABC News video posted September 5, 2012, at 3:50, https://www.youtube.com/watch?v=YBtij5dR3dA; Jeremy Corbyn (@jeremycorbyn), Twitter, December 30, 2019, 6:49 a.m., https://twitter.com/jeremycorbyn/status/1211615351831699458; Peter Temin, *The Vanishing Middle Class: Prejudice and Power in a Dual Economy* (Cambridge, MA: MIT Press, 2017).

12. Occupy Wall Street, "About," http://occupywallst.org/about/.

13. Heather Gautney, "What Is Occupy Wall Street? The History of Leaderless Movements," *Washington Post,* October 10, 2011.

14. Emmanuel Saez and Gabriel Zucman, *The Triumph of Injustice: How the Rich Dodge Taxes and How to Make Them Pay* (New York: W. W. Norton, 2019), 6.

15. David Brooks, "Dems, Please Don't Drive Me Away," *New York Times,* June 27, 2019; Stephen Rose, *The Growing Size and Incomes of the Upper Middle Class* (Washington, DC: Urban Institute, June 2016), https://www.urban.org/research/publication/growing-size-and-incomes-upper-middle-class; Richard Reeves, *Dream Hoarders: How the American Upper Middle Class Is Leaving Everyone Else in the Dust, Why That Is a Problem, and What to Do about It* (Washington, DC: Brookings Institution Press, 2017).

16. Daniel Markovits, *The Meritocracy Trap* (New York: Penguin Press, 2019), 5.

17. Michael Lind, *The New Class War: Saving Democracy from the Managerial Elite* (New York: Portfolio Press, 2020), 9.

18. Roos, *Why Not Default?,* 239, 263.

19. Roos, *Why Not Default?,* 267–268.

20. Alexis Tsipras, "End Austerity before Fear Kills Greek Democracy," *Financial Times,* January 20, 2015; the second Tsipras quote is from David Adler, "The Three Mistakes behind Syriza's Demise in Greece," *Guardian,* July 8, 2019; see also "Greece PM Urges 'No' Vote to 'Live with Dignity in Europe,'" *EU Business,* July 3, 2015.

21. Roos, *Why Not Default?,* 226, 280, 285–287.

22. Yanis Varoufakis, *Adults in the Room: My Battle with the European and American Deep Establishment* (New York: Farrar, Straus and Giroux, 2017), 312.

23. *Podemos and the New Political Cycle: Left-Wing Populism and Anti-Establishment Politics,* edited by Óscar García Agustín and Marco Briziarelli (London: Palgrave Macmillan, 2017), 4.

24. Jorge Sola and César Rendueles, "Podemos, the Upheaval of Spanish Politics and the Challenge of Populism," *Journal of Contemporary European Studies* 26, no. 1 (2018): 99–116.

25. John Carlin, "What Does Podemos Want?," *El País,* February 3, 2015.

26. Elizabeth Warren, "End Wall Street's Stranglehold on Our Economy," *Medium,* July 18, 2019.

27. Rana Foroohar, *Makers and Takers: The Rise of Finance and the Fall of American Business* (New York: Crown, 2016); Mariana Mazzucato, *The Value of Everything* (New York: Public Affairs, 2018).

28. Warren, "End Wall Street's Stranglehold."

29. Jesse Barron, "How America's Oldest Gun Maker Went Bankrupt: A Financial Engineering Mystery," *New York Times,* May 1, 2019; Alex Shephard, "The Real Retail Killer," *New Republic,* March 28, 2018.

30. Warren, "End Wall Street's Stranglehold"; Rosemary Batt and Eileen Appelbaum, "Private Equity Pillage: Grocery Stores and Workers at Risk," *American Prospect,* October 26, 2018.

31. "Die Namen der 'Heuschrecken,'" *Stern,* April 28, 2005, https://www.stern.de/politik/deutschland/kapitalismusdebatte-die-namen-der--heuschrecken--5351566.html.

32. Michael C. Jensen, "Agency Costs of Free Cash Flow, Corporate Finance, and Takeovers," *American Economic Review* 76, no. 2 (1986): 323–329; Michael C. Jensen and Kevin J. Murphy, "Performance Pay and Top Management Incentives," *Journal of Political Economy* 98, no. 2 (1990): 225–264.

33. See generally Greta R. Krippner, *Capitalizing on Crisis: The Political Origins of the Rise of Finance* (Cambridge, MA: Harvard University Press, 2011); Natascha van der Zwan, "Making Sense of Financialization," *Socio-economic Review* 12, no. 1 (2014): 99–129.

34. Foroohar, *Makers and Takers,* 11.

35. William H. Lazonick, "From Innovation to Financialization: How Shareholder Value Ideology Is Destroying the US Economy," in *The Handbook of the Political Economy of Financial Crises,* edited by Martin H. Wolfson and Gerald A. Epstein (New York: Oxford University Press, 2013), 491–511.

36. Anna Ratcliff, "Just 8 Men Own Same Wealth as Half the World," Oxfam, January 16, 2017.

37. Baker, *Rigged,* 134–139; "total compensation paid to the top five executives at public companies amounted to $350 billion over the 10-year period from 1993 to 2003" (137).

38. Erin Duffin, "Ratio between CEO and Average Worker Pay in 2018, by Country," Statista, March 20, 2020.

39. Carmin Chappell, "Alexandria Ocasio-Cortez: A System That Allows Billionaires to Exist Alongside Extreme Poverty Is Immoral," CNBC, January 22, 2019.

40. Maggie Astor, "Should Billionaires Exist? Sanders, Warren and Steyer Debate It," *New York Times,* October 15, 2019.

41. Ollie Williams, "The U.K. Election Campaign Will Be a Battle over Billionaires," *Forbes,* November 7, 2019.

42. Saskia Sassen, *The Global City* (Princeton, NJ: Princeton University Press, 2001).

43. Katharina Pistor, *The Code of Capital* (Princeton, NJ: Princeton University Press, 2019).

44. David Leonhardt, "The Rich Really Do Pay Lower Taxes than You," *New York Times,* October 6, 2019; Chris Isidore, "Buffett Says He's Still Paying Lower Tax Rate than His Secretary," CNN Money, March 4, 2013, https://money.cnn.com/2013/03/04/news/economy/buffett-secretary-taxes/index.html; Angie Drobnic Holan, "Does a Secretary Pay Higher Taxes than a Millionaire?," PolitiFact, September 21, 2011; Warren E. Buffett, "Stop Coddling the Super-Rich," *New York Times,* August 14, 2011; "Warren Buffett's Tax Rate Is Lower than His Secretary's," video posted October 29, 2007, at 1:55, https://www.youtube.com/watch?v=Cu5B-2LoC4s.

45. Saez and Zucman, *The Triumph,* viii, xi.

46. Pistor, *The Code.*

47. For the quote from Jean-Luc Mélenchon, see Jean-Luc Mélenchon (@JLMélenchon), Twitter, December 11, 2016, 6:44 a.m., https://twitter.com/JLMelenchon/status/807913908975652865; see also Jean-Luc Mélenchon (@JLMélenchon), Twitter, November 1, 2015, 11:40 a.m., https://twitter.com/jlmelenchon/status/660859047671898112; and Jean-Luc Mélenchon (@JLMélenchon), Twitter, October 11, 2016, 12:56 p.m., https://twitter.com/jlmelenchon/status/785886689298292737; for the quote from Pablo Iglesias, see PODEMOS (@PODEMOS), Twitter, October 2, 2019, 5:44 a.m., https://twitter.com/PODEMOS/status/1179331311368069121; for the quote from Irene Montero, see PODEMOS (@PODEMOS), Twitter, April 13, 2019, 6:11 p.m., https://twitter.com/PODEMOS/status/1117188650171863040; for Syriza, see Tsipras, "End Austerity."

48. Warren, "DNC Speech" at 5:20.

49. Bernie Sanders, "Bernie Brief: Income Equality | Ep. 1," video posted September 14, 2015, at 3:29, https://www.youtube.com/watch?time_continue=232&v=VePpQBCbKBw&feature=emb_logo.

50. Matthew Goodwin and Roger Eatwell, *National Populism: The Revolt against Liberal Democracy* (London: Random House, 2018), 209.

51. Steven Greenhouse, *Beaten Down, Worked Up: The Past, Present, and Future of American Labor* (New York: Knopf, 2019), 13.

52. Zephyr Teachout, "The Upheaval in the American Workplace," *New York Times,* October 3, 2019.

53. For "Labor unions are weaker," see Greenhouse, "Yes, America"; for "studies," see Henry S. Farber et al., *Unions and Inequality over the Twentieth Century: New Evidence from Survey Data,* National Bureau of Economic Research, Working Paper No. 24587, May 2018, 24–34; Bruce Western and Jake Rosenfield, "Unions, Norms, and the Rise in U.S. Wage Inequality," *American Sociological Review* 76, no. 4 (2011): 533; for "one study," see Center for Responsive Politics, "Business-Labor-Ideology Split in PAC & Individual Donations to Candidates, Parties, Super PACs and Outside Spending Groups," Open Secrets, https://www.opensecrets.org/overview/blio.php?cycle=2016; the Draut quote is from

Tamara Draut, *Sleeping Giant: The Untapped Economic and Political Power of America's New Working Class* (New York: Anchor Books, 2018), 12–13.

54. Draut, *Sleeping Giant*, 6–7, 40–48.

55. Bernie Sanders, "The Minimum Wage," video posted June 26, 2013, at 1:22, https://www.youtube.com/watch?v=zMZbNIAkc5A&t=214s.

56. Greenhouse, "Yes, America."

57. Greenhouse, *Beaten Down*, 13.

58. Draut, *Sleeping Giant*, 41.

59. Sanders, "Minimum Wage," at 1:40.

60. Gregory Krieg, "Bernie Sanders Confronts Walmart Leaders at Annual Shareholders Meeting," CNN, June 5, 2019, https:www.cnn.com/2019/06/05/politics/bernie-sanders-walmart-meeting/index.html.

61. Bernie Sanders, "Introducing the Stop Bad Employers by Zeroing Out Subsidies (BEZOS) Act," Facebook, video posted September 5, 2018, at 15:33, https://www.facebook.com/senatorsanders/videos/2276207615741918/.

62. Draut, *Sleeping Giant*, 9–10, 47–48.

63. Warren and Tyagi, *Two-Income Trap*.

64. James Manyika et al., "The Social Contract in the 21st Century," McKinsey Global Institute, February 2020; see also Annie Lowrey, "The Great Affordability Crisis Breaking America," *The Atlantic*, February 7, 2020.

65. Reeves, *Dream Hoarders*, 102–106. On artificial housing scarcity created by land-use regulation, see also Brink Lindsey and Steven M. Teles, *The Captured Economy: How the Powerful Become Richer, Slow Down Growth, and Increase Inequality* (New York: Oxford University Press, 2017).

66. Benjamin Hennig and Danny Dorling, "The Hollowing Out of London: How Poverty Patterns Are Changing," *New Statesman*, March 13, 2015.

67. Jeremy Corbyn (@JeremyCorbyn), Twitter, October 4, 2019, 3:49 a.m., https://twitter.com/jeremycorbyn/status/1180027077409591296.

68. Jagmeet Singh (@theJagmeetSingh), Twitter, November 5, 2019, 12:55 p.m., https://twitter.com/thejagmeetsingh/status/1191776165108879360?lang=en; Jean-Luc Mélenchon (@JLMélenchon), Twitter, March 4, 2020, 4:45 a.m., https://twitter.com/JLMelenchon/status/1235139236577366016; for an analysis of similar developments in the United States in general and in New York in particular, see Derek Thompson, "Why Manhattan's Skyscrapers Are Empty," *Atlantic*, January 16, 2020; Binyamin Appelbaum, "America's Cities Could House Everyone If They Chose To," *New York Times*, May 15, 2020.

69. Karl Lauterbach, *Der Zweiklassenstaat: Wie die Privilegierten Deutschland ruinieren* (Berlin: Rowohlt Berlin Verlag, 2007).

70. Goodwin and Eatwell, *National Populism*, 217.

71. UN Human Rights Office of High Commissioner, "'American Dream Is Rapidly Becoming American Illusion,' Warns UN Rights Expert on Poverty," December 15, 2017, https://www.ohchr.org/EN/NewsEvents/Pages/DisplayNews.aspx?NewsID=22546&LangID=E.

Ch. 5: The Right-Wing Populist Narrative

1. The decline of Flint was memorialized in Michael Moore's first documentary, *Roger & Me* (1989; New York: Dog Eat Dog Films). Bruce Springsteen wrote a tribute to Youngstown in 1995; Bruce Springsteen, composer and vocalist, "Youngstown," recorded April–June 1995, track 4 on *The Ghost of Tom Joad,* Columbia. Janesville's struggles with the effects of deindustrialization are chronicled in Amy Goldstein's award-winning 2017 book *Janesville: An American Story* (New York: Simon and Schuster, 2017).

2. Donald J. Trump, "Inaugural Address," Washington, DC: January 20, 2017, https://trumpwhitehouse.archives.gov/briefings-statements/the-inaugural-address/.

3. On the importance of immigration and Euro-skepticism in right-wing populist movements in Europe, see Paul Taggart, "Populism in Western Europe," in *The Oxford Handbook of Populism,* edited by Cristóbal Rovira Kaltwasser et al. (Oxford: Oxford University Press, 2017), 181–185.

4. Pippa Norris and Ronald Inglehart, *Cultural Backlash* (New York: Cambridge University Press, 2019), 7; John B. Judis, *The Populist Explosion* (New York: Columbia Global Reports, 2016), 15; Chantal Mouffe, *For a Left Populism* (New York: Verso, 2018), 50–51; Cas Mudde, *The Far Right Today* (Cambridge, UK: Polity Press, 2019), 7–8; Cas Mudde, "Populism: An Ideational Approach," 32–33; Joseph Lowndes, "Populism in the United States," in *The Oxford Handbook of Populism,* 233.

5. Trump, "Inaugural Address."

6. 78 *Cong. Rec.,* 5663 (1934) (statement of Rep. Martin).

7. Protectionists had always had a strong voice in US trade policy even before the passage of the Reciprocal Trade Agreements Act introduced something new: it allowed the US president to use the dismantling of trade protection as a bargaining chip to gain access to foreign markets. Martin was objecting precisely to this mechanism.

8. Statement of Rep. Martin, 5663.

9. Enrico Moretti, *The New Geography of Jobs* (New York: Houghton Mifflin Harcourt, 2012).

10. Jeff Ferry, "Manufacturing Jobs and Income Decline," Coalition for a Prosperous America Working Paper, August 15, 2019, https://www.prosperousamerica.org/working_paper_manufacturing_jobs_and_income_decline.

11. Scott Horsley, "Peter Navarro: A 'Bricklayer' of Trump's Protectionist Wall," NPR, May 3, 2017.

12. See the discussion of the "smile curve" in Chapter 3.

13. Ferry, "Manufacturing Jobs."

14. Moretti, *New Geography,* 24; Horsley, "Peter Navarro"; Anne Case and Angus Deaton, *Deaths of Despair and the Future of Capitalism* (Princeton, NJ: Princeton University Press, 2020); Chris Arnade, *Dignity: Seeking Respect in Back Row America* (New York: Sentinel Press, 2019), 17.

15. Moretti, *New Geography,* 60.

16. For "three Americas," see Moretti, *New Geography,* 13–14; for "hubs and heartlands," see Michael Lind, *The New Class War* (New York: Portfolio Press, 2020), 14–27.

17. Christophe Guilluy, *Twilight of the Elites: Prosperity, Periphery and the Future of France* (New Haven: Yale University Press, 2019); Jon Henley, "Twilight of the Elites by Christophe Guilluy Review—France and a New Class Conflict," *Guardian,* January 17, 2019.

18. Arnade, *Dignity,* 150–154.

19. Latoya Ruby Frazier and Dan Kaufman, "The End of the Line," *New York Times,* May 1, 2019.

20. Frazier and Kaufman, "End of the Line."

21. Joan Williams, *White Working Class* (Cambridge, MA: Harvard Business Review Press, 2017), 32, 36, 41.

22. Theresa May, "Theresa May's Conference Speech in Full," *Financial Times,* October 5, 2016.

23. Chloe Farand, "Marine Le Pen Launches Presidential Campaign with Hardline Speech," *Independent,* February 5, 2017.

24. Frazier and Kaufman, "End of the Line."

25. Eunice Yoon, "Trump Rails against China Stealing US Jobs, But China Has Concerns about the Reverse," *CNBC,* April 5, 2017; Michael J. Sandel, "Populism, Trump, and the Future of Democracy," Open Democracy, May 9, 2018, https://www.opendemocracy.net/en/populism-trump-and-future-of-democracy/.

26. For Unifor, see Unifor Canada, "GM Leaves Canadians Out in the Cold," video posted January 21, 2019, at 0:28, https://www.youtube.com/watch?v=QEAAz3fr2EU; for the practice of companies asking the soon-to-be-laid-off workers to train their foreign replacements, see Joshua Holland, "Romney's Bain Capital Is Sending Many Jobs to China the Day before the Election," Truthout, October 17, 2012; Jerry Treharn, founder of J. L. Treharn and Company, speaking about a colleague in *Death by China,* directed by Peter Navarro (New York: Virgil Films & Entertainment, 2013), at 6:29, https://www.youtube.com/watch?v=mMlmjXtnIXI; *Inside a Steel Plant Facing Layoffs,* directed by Brent McDonald, Jonah M. Kessel, and John Woo (New York: Times Documentaries, 2017), https://www.nytimes.com/video/us/100000005007829/layoffs-steel-plant-rexnord-mexico.html; for the final quote, see Representative Tim Ryan of Ohio, speaking in *Death by China,* at 6:18.

27. David Goodhart, *The Road to Somewhere: The Populist Revolt and the Future of Politics* (London: Hurst, 2017), 3–7.

28. J. D. Vance, "Why I'm Moving Home," *New York Times,* March 16, 2017.

29. Wilkinson, "Density Divide"; Joe Cortright, "Cities and Brexit," City Observatory, June 27, 2016; Gregor Aisch et al., "How France Voted," *New York Times,* May 7, 2017; Christian Franz, Marcel Fratzscher, and Alexander S. Kritikos, "German Right-Wing Party AfD Finds More Support in Rural Areas with Aging Populations," *DIW Weekly Report* 7–8 (February 2017), https://www.diw.de/documents/publikationen/73/diw_01.c.578785.de/dwr-18-07-1.pdf; Jonathan Rodden, "The Urban-Rural Divide," *Stanford Magazine,* May 2018.

30. Williams, *White Working Class,* 36.

31. Sabrina Tavernise, "With His Job Gone, an Autoworker Wonders: What Am I as a Man?," *New York Times,* May 27, 2019.

32. "The Long-Term Decline in Prime-Age Male Labor Force Participation," Executive Office of the President of the United States, 2016, https://obamawhitehouse.archives.gov/sites/default/files/page/files/20160620_cea_primeage_male_lfp.pdf. The decline is most pronounced with respect to Black men, but that point is less emphasized by proponents of this narrative.

33. Williams, *White Working Class*, 91–92.

34. David Autor, David Dorn, and Gordon Hanson, "When Work Disappears: Manufacturing Decline and the Falling Marriage-Market Value of Young Men," NBER Working Paper 23173, January 2018; Anne Case and Angus Deaton, "Mortality and Morbidity in the 21st Century," Brookings Paper on Economic Activity, spring 2017, http://www.ledevoir.com/documents/pdf/18-09-casetextsp17bpea.pdf.

35. Oren Cass, *The Once and Future Worker: A Vision for the Renewal of Work in America* (n.p.: Encounter Books, 2018), 47–49. See also Claudia Geist, "Marriage Formation in Context: Four Decades in Comparative Perspective," *Social Sciences* 6, no. 1 (2017): 9.

36. Tucker Carlson, "Mitt Romney Supports the Status Quo, but for Everyone Else It's Infuriating," Fox News, January 3, 2019, https://www.foxnews.com/opinion/tucker-carlson-mitt-romney-supports-the-status-quo-but-for-everyone-else-its-infuriating.

37. Donald J. Trump, remarks at Make America Great Again Rally, Murphysboro, IL, October 27, 2018, https://www.presidency.ucsb.edu/documents/remarks-make-america-great-again-rally-murphresboro-illinois; Donald Trump, "Trump Speaks on Jobs in the Valley: 'Don't Sell Your House,'" video posted July 25, 2017, at 0:32, https://www.youtube.com/watch?v=7qpk52Mz164; Tavernise, "With His Job Gone."

38. Trump, remarks at rally in Murphysboro, IL.

39. Martin Sandbu has explained Trump, Navarro, and Lighthizer's infatuation with manufacturing jobs as flowing from their "factory worker machismo." Martin Sandbu, "Donald Trump's Love of Manufacturing Is Misguided," *Financial Times,* February 14, 2017. We are grateful to Jennifer Hillman for drawing our attention to Trump's lack of consideration for the textile industry and the high proportion of women employed in that industry.

40. Lind, *New Class War,* 59.

41. Julia Preston, "Pink Slips at Disney. But First, Training Foreign Replacements," *New York Times,* June 3, 2015.

42. For Germany, see "AfD-Parteitag: Interview mit Georg Pazderski und Björn Höcke vom 30.06.2018" [interview of Georg Pazderski and Björn Höcke by Claudius Crönert], *On Scene,* Phoenix [German public broadcast service], video posted June 30, 2018, at 10:03, https://www.youtube.com/watch?v=xaE04tyx1H0; Guilluy, *Twilight,* 43–44; see also 52.

43. "'Bimbos,' 'Parasiten,' 'widerliches Gewürm,'" *Südddeutsche Zeitung,* September 20, 2016, https://www.sueddeutsche.de/politik/wahl-in-berlin-afd-abgeordneter-schmaeht-fluechtlinge-als-widerliches-gewuerm-1.3170025-2.

44. "AfD-Parteitag: Interview mit Georg Pazderski und Björn Höcke," at 6:39. The quote is our translation. Unless otherwise noted, all translations from German sources are our own.

45. Melissa Eddy, "Reports of Attack on Women in Germany Heighten Tension over Migrants," *New York Times*, January 5, 2016; Georg Mascolo and Britta von der Heide, "1200 Frauen wurden Opfer von Silvester-Gewalt," *Süddeutsche Zeitung,* July 10, 2016.

46. For the idea that resistance to immigration can seem necessary to defend "a liberal and open society" and to resist "imported antisemitism and homophobic and misogynistic attitudes," see Herfried Münkler and Marina Münkler, *Die neuen Deutschen: Ein Land vor seiner Zukunft* (Berlin: Rowohlt, 2016), 70; for "importation of criminality," see "Nürnberger Parteitag mit Riesen-Applaus für Rede von Gauland," Alternative für Deutschland, June 10, 2018, https://www.afdbayern.de/nuernberger-parteitag-mit-riesen-applaus-fuer-rede-von-gauland/.

47. Hans-Thomas Tillschneider, "Die Kernfrage," 2017, https://hans-thomas-tillschneider.de/die-kernfrage/.

48. Tania Kambouri, *Deutschland im Blaulicht: Notruf einer Polizistin* (Munich: Piper, 2015).

49. For "strangers," see "+++ *Das muss jeder zum UN-Migrationspakt wissen!* +++," AfD TV video posted December 6, 2018, at 1:08, https://www.youtube.com/watch?v=YMcReYJrPe4; for "Germans who live," see "AfD-Hochburg Usedom: Was war da los?," *Der Spiegel* video posted September 12, 2016, at 2:40, https://www.youtube.com/watch?v=Tbnb7LsXbMI; for "a similar phenomenon," see Nick Clegg, "Why Did Ebbw Vale in Wales Vote Brexit?," *Newsnight*, BBC video posted March 28, 2017, at 8:45, https://www.youtube.com/watch?v=V-WEDoXx910; for "older, less educated," see Goodhart, *Road to Somewhere*, 2–3; for the Le Pen quote, see James Chessell, "'This Election Is a Choice of Civilisation': In France, Le Pen Plays High Stakes Game," *Australian Financial Review*, February 10, 2017; for "Weltvertrauen," see Münkler and Münkler, *Die neuen Deutschen*, 72.

50. Norris and Inglehart, *Cultural Backlash*, 4.

51. Arlie Russell Hochschild, *Strangers in Their Own Land: Anger and Mourning on the American Right* (New York: The New Press, 2016), 22–23, 225, 228.

52. "Boris Johnson: EU Exit 'Win-Win for Us All,'" BBC News, March 11, 2016.

53. Donald J. Trump (@realDonaldTrump), Twitter, June 24, 2016, 11:21 a.m., https://twitter.com/realdonaldtrump/status/746272130992644096?lang=en.

54. Quinn Slobodian, *Globalists: The End of Empire and the Birth of Neoliberalism* (Cambridge, MA: Harvard University Press, 2018), chap. 3.

55. Vox (@vox_es), Twitter, November 9, 2016, 2:18 a.m., https://twitter.com/vox_es/status/796250599507525638; Vox (@vox_es), Twitter, November 4, 2019, 6:33 p.m., https://twitter.com/vox_es/status/1191498734376488960; Matteo Salvini (@mattteosalvinimi), Twitter, October 18, 2019, 2:23 a.m., https://twitter.com/matteosalvinimi/status/1185078876680212480; Pauline Hanson, "Pauline Hanson's 2016 Maiden Speech to the Senate," transcript, ABC News, September 14, 2016.

56. Nigel Farage (@Nigel_Farage), Twitter, April 29, 2015, 4:06 a.m., https://twitter.com/Nigel_Farage/status/593325461163347969.

57. The only other "old" EU member states that opened their labor markets to workers from the new eastern European members immediately after the accession in 2004 were Sweden and Ireland. All other EU member states invoked their right under the accession agreements to adopt "transitional measures," which limited freedom of movement for eastern European workers in those countries for up to seven years. Natalie Shimmel, "Welcome to Europe, but Please Stay Out," *Berkeley Journal of International Law* 24, no. 3 (2006): 777–783.

58. Glenn Campbell, "What Are the Party Leaders Saying on Europe?," BBC, February 2, 2016.

59. Nick Clegg, "Why Did Ebbw Vale?" ("It isn't that they have been left behind, it's their feeling about what they have left behind"); as an example of the establishment narrative's diagnosis that the losers from economic globalization have been "left behind," see the headline on the cover of the October 21, 2017, edition of the *Economist* ("Left Behind: How to Help Places Hurt by Globalisation"), https://www.economist.com/weeklyedition/2017-10-21.

60. For "human dignity and self-worth," see Steve Bannon, "Full Address and Q&A at the Oxford Union," video posted November 16, 2018, at 7:04, https://www.youtube.com/watch?v=8AtOw-xyMo8; for "Here's the bottom line," see Channel 4 News, "Steve Bannon Extended Interview on Europe's Far-Right and Cambridge Analytica," video posted May 29, 2018, at 13:17, https://www.youtube.com/watch?v=pold15c8H70.

Ch. 6: The Corporate Power Narrative

1. Edmund G. Brown Jr., "Free Trade Is Not Free," in *The Case against Free Trade: GATT, NAFTA, and the Globalization of Corporate Power* (Berkeley: North Atlantic Press, 1993), 65–69.

2. Some have called this form of power "structural power," as it emanates from the structure of a liberalized global economy. Stephen R. Gill and David Law, "Global Hegemony and the Structural Power of Capital," *International Studies Quarterly* 33, no. 4 (1989): 475–499; Milan Babic, Jan Fichtner, and Eelke M. Heemskerk, "States versus Corporations: Rethinking the Power of Business in International Politics," *International Spectator* 52, no. 4 (2017): 20–43. For an analysis of the structural power of corporations in the domestic context, see Kevin A. Young, Tarun Banerjee, and Michael Schwartz, "Capital Strikes as a Corporate Political Strategy: The Structural Power of Business in the Obama Era," *Politics and Society* 46, no. 1 (2018): 3–28.

3. On the "mega-regulation" attempted by recent trade agreements, such as the TPP, see *Megaregulation Contested: Global Economic Ordering,* edited by Benedict Kingsbury, David M. Malone, Paul Mertenskötter, Richard B. Stewart, Thomas Streinz, and Atsushi Sunami (Oxford: Oxford University Press, 2019).

4. On the economic dynamics that favor the creation of superstars, see Sherwin Rosen, "The Economics of Superstars," *American Economic Review* 71, no. 5 (1981): 845–858.

5. Ralph Nader, "Introduction: Free Trade and the Decline of Democracy," in *The Case against Free Trade,* 1–12.

6. Nader, "Introduction," 6. For a review about the debate on whether globalization leads to a race to the bottom, see Daniel W. Drezner, "Globalization and Policy Convergence," *International Studies Review* 3, no. 1 (2001): 53–78.

7. Nader, "Introduction," 8–11. See also Lori Wallach, "Hidden Dangers of GATT and NAFTA," in *The Case against Free Trade,* 23–64.

8. Tim Wu, *The Curse of Bigness* (New York: Columbia Global Reports, 2018); Rana Foroohar, *Don't Be Evil: The Case against Big Tech* (New York: Penguin Random House LLC, 2019), xxi.

9. These threefold losses—to workers, consumers, and citizens—are captured in the AFL-CIO's summary of the "harm" of globalization, which runs "from lost jobs and lower wages to unsafe imports and reduced freedom to make domestic economic policy choices." AFL-CIO, "Making NAFTA Work for Working People," June 2017, https://aflcio.org/sites/default/files/2017-06/NAFTA%20Negotiating%20Recommendations%20from%20AFL-CIO%20%28Witness%3DTLee%29%20Jun2017%20%28PDF%29_0.pdf.

10. Michael Keen and Kai A. Konrad, "The Theory of International Tax Competition and Coordination," ch. 5 in *Handbook of Public Economics,* edited by Alan J. Auerbach et al. (Amsterdam: North Holland, 2013).

11. Joseph Stiglitz, "How Can We Tax Footloose Multinationals?," Project Syndicate, February 13, 2019.

12. Thomas Tørsløv, Ludvig Wier, and Gabriel Zucman, "The Missing Profit of Nations," National Bureau of Economic Research Working Paper No. 24701, June 2018 (non-oil US multinationals), https://gabriel-zucman.eu/files/TWZ2018.pdf.

13. Thomas Wright and Gabriel Zucman, "The Exorbitant Tax Advantage," National Bureau of Economic Research Working Paper No. 24983, September 2018 (non-oil US multinationals), https://gabriel-zucman.eu/files/WrightZucman2018.pdf.

14. Gabriel Zucman, *The Hidden Wealth of Nations* (Chicago: University of Chicago Press, 2015), 2, 4.

15. Jannick Damgaard, Thomas Elkjaer, and Niels Johannesen, "What Is Real and What Is Not in the Global FDI Network?," Working Paper No. 19/274, International Monetary Fund, December 2019, https://www.imf.org/en/Publications/WP/Issues/2019/12/11/what-is-real-and-what-is-not-in-the-global-fdi-network.

16. Harriet Taylor, "How Apple Managed to Pay a 0.005 Percent Tax Rate in 2014," CNBC, August 30, 2016; Joseph Stiglitz, Todd N. Tucker, and Gabriel Zucman, "The Starving State," *Foreign Affairs,* December 10, 2019; AFL-CIO, "Making NAFTA Work," 25–28.

17. Taylor, "How Apple Managed to Pay a 0.005 Percent Tax Rate in 2014."

18. Tax Justice Network, "Tax and Corporate Responsibility," https://www.taxjustice.net/topics/corporate-tax/tax-corporate-responsibility/; Stiglitz, "Tax Footloose Multinationals."

19. Eduardo Porter, "Nafta May Have Saved Many Autoworkers' Jobs," *New York Times,* March 29, 2016 ("In the final analysis, Nafta might have saved hundreds of thousands of jobs. By offering a low-wage platform, Mexican plants increased the scale of production in North America, allowing domestic and foreign automakers to amortize their large fixed costs"). See also "Two Women Joined GM More Than a Decade Ago. Their Futures Couldn't Be More Different," Bloomberg, October 25, 2019 ("General Motors is betting its future on an army of engineers who can build cars by code, leaving little room for the assembly line workers"); for the concept of the smile curve, see our discussion in Chapter 3.

20. Jerry Dias, "NAFTA Took Good Canadian Jobs and Made Them Bad Ones in Mexico," *Huffington Post,* August 30, 2017.

21. AFL-CIO, "Making NAFTA Work," 2, 32.

22. AFL-CIO, "Making NAFTA Work," 33.

23. Testimony of Jeffrey S. Vogt before the Senate Finance Committee, Hearing on U.S. Preference Programs: Options for Reform, March 9, 2010, https://www.finance.senate.gov/imo/media/doc/030910jvtest.pdf.

24. Dani Rodrik, *Straight Talk on Trade: Ideas for a Sane World Economy* (Princeton, NJ: Princeton University, 2018), xi–xii.

25. AFL-CIO, "Making NAFTA Work," 2.

26. Testimony of Vogt, 1.

27. William Greider, "The Global Marketplace: A Closet Dictator," in *The Case against Free Trade,* 196, 198.

28. Greider, "Global Marketplace," 197.

29. Kevin P. Gallagher and Lyuba Zarsky, *The Enclave Economy. Foreign Investment and Sustainable Development in Mexico's Silicon Valley* (Cambridge, MA: MIT Press, 2007), 9. See also Harley Shaiken, "The Nafta Paradox," *Berkeley Review of Latin American Studies,* Spring 2014: 38 ("only 3 percent of border plant exports are sourced domestically, and a mere 0.4 percent of gross domestic product [GDP] is invested in research and development").

30. Nader, "Introduction," 8.

31. AFL-CIO, "Making NAFTA Work," 33.

32. Unifor Canada, "Jerry Dias Speaks at Mexican Labour Rally," video posted September 26, 2017, at 2:07, https://www.youtube.com/watch?v=BA6BAeHNVR8; Joe Warmington, "GM Relying on 'Slave Labour' in Mexico," *Toronto Sun,* January 9, 2019; Shaiken, "The Nafta Paradox," 39 ("Mexican manufacturing productivity rose by almost 80 percent under Nafta between 1994 and 2010, while real hourly compensation—wages and benefits—slid by nearly 20 percent. In fact, this data understates the productivity/wage disconnect. Wages in 1994, the base year, were already 30 percent below their 1980 level despite significant increases in productivity during this period. Although they are producing more, millions of Mexican workers are earning less than they did three decades ago").

33. Shaiken, "The Nafta Paradox," 39.

34. Unifor Canada, "Jerry Dias Speaks at Mexican Labour Rally," at 1:11.

35. Statement of Lori Wallach, director of Public Citizen's Global Trade Watch, "Public Citizen Denounces Bush Administration Attack on European Food Safety Policy at WTO; European Consumers and their Democratically Elected Governments Should Decide, Not WTO," May 13, 2013, https://www.citizen.org/news/public-citizen-denounces-bush-administration-attack-on-european-food-safety-policy-at-wto-european-consumers-and-their-democratically-elected-governments-should-decide-not-wto/; Public Citizen, "The GMO Trade War (Friends of the Earth Europe)," https://www.citizen.org/article/the-gmo-trade-war-friends-of-the-earth-europe/.

36. Rodrik, *Straight Talk on Trade,* 34–35.

37. Thilo Bode, *Die Freihandelslüge: Warum TTIP nur den Konzernen nützt - und uns allen schadet* (Munich: DVA Dt.Verlags-Anstalt, 2015), 135, 139.

38. Bode, *Die Freihandelslüge,* 158; Attac, "Das Regulierungsabkommen EU-USA—Konzerne Profiteren, Menschen Verlieren!," https://www.attac.de/kampagnen/freihandelsfalle-ttip/hintergrund/.

39. Michael Lind, *The New Class War: Saving Democracy from the Managerial Elite* (New York: Portfolio, 2020), 54.

40. Lind, *New Class War,* 53–54.

41. Wallach is quoted in "'A Corporate Trojan Horse': Obama Pushes Secretive TPP Trade Pact, Would Rewrite Swath of U.S. Laws," *Democracy Now!,* October 4, 2013; for Krugman's assessment, see Paul Krugman, "This Is Not a Trade Agreement," *The Conscience of a Liberal* (blog), *New York Times,* April 26, 2015, https://krugman.blogs.nytimes.com/2015/04/26/this-is-not-a-trade-agreement/; the concept of a "generalized freedom to operate" was introduced by Dan Ciuriak, "Generalized Freedom to Operate," *NYU IILJ Megareg Forum Paper* 2016/3 (2016), and is expanded on in Benedict Kingsbury, Paul Mertenskötter, Richard B. Stewart, and Thomas Streinz, "The Trans-Pacific Partnership as Megaregulation," in *Megaregulation Contested,* 36.

42. Dani Rodrik, "What Do Trade Agreements Actually Do?," *Journal of Economic Perspectives* 32, no. 2 (2018): 73–76.

43. Chad P. Bown, "The Truth about Trade Agreements and Why We Need Them," Peterson Institute for International Economics, November 26, 2016; Robert Staiger and Guido Tabellini, "Discretionary Trade Policy and Excessive Protection," *American Economic Review* 77, no. 5 (1987): 823–837; Giovanni Maggi and Andres Rodriguez-Clare, "The Value of Trade Agreements in the Presence of Political Pressures," *Journal of Political Economy* 106, no. 3 (1998): 574–601.

44. Rodrik, "Trade Agreements," 75–76.

45. See Susan K. Sell, *Private Power, Public Law* (Cambridge: Cambridge University Press, 2003), for a history of lobbying that led to the incorporation of the TRIPS Agreement into the World Trade Organization.

46. On the transition from the industrial economy to the knowledge-based economy, see Dan Ciuriak, "Economic Rents and the Contours of Conflict in the Data-Driven Economy," *CIGI Papers* No. 245, July 2020; Doctors Without Borders, more commonly known by its French name Médecins Sans Frontières, established its Access Campaign in 1999. See Médecins Sans Frontières Access Campaign, "1999–2019: 20 Years of Advocacy in Action," https://20years.msfaccess.org/.

47. The Canadian Press, "Canada-EU Drug Patent Demand in Trade Talks Costs Almost $2B," CBC News, October 15, 2012; Janyce McGregor, "Canada-EU Trade Deal: Costs for New Drugs May Rise, but Not for Years," CBC News, December 1, 2016; Canada House of Commons, Standing Committee on International Trade, "Evidence," CIIT 48, 42nd Parliament, November 29, 2016, https://www.ourcommons.ca/Content/Committee/421/CIIT/Evidence/EV8654468/CIITEV48-E.PDF.

48. Dan Ciuriak, "A New Name for Modern Trade Deals: Asset Value Protection Agreements," Centre for International Governance Innovation, April 11, 2017, https://www.cigionline.org/articles/new-name-modern-trade-deals-asset-value-protection-agreements.

49. Lee Drutman, "How Big Pharma (and Others) Began Lobbying on the Trans-Pacific Partnership before You Ever Heard of It," Sunlight Foundation, March 13, 2014, https://sunlightfoundation.com/2014/03/13/tpp-lobby; Klas Rönnbäck, "Interest-Group Lobbying for Free Trade: An Empirical Case Study of International Trade Policy Formation," *Journal of International Trade and Economic Development* 24, no. 2 (2015): 281–293.

50. Thomas Streinz, "Digital Megaregulation Uncontested? TPP's Model for the Global Digital Economy," in *Megaregulation Contested,* 312–342.

51. Michael Nienaber, "Tens of Thousands Protest in Europe against Atlantic Free Trade Deals," Reuters, September 17, 2016; Alexsia T. Chan and Beverly K. Crawford, "The Puzzle of Public Opposition to TTIP in Germany," *Business and Politics* 19, no. 4 (2017): 683–708.

52. Paul Ames, "ISDS: The Most Toxic Acronym in Europe," Politico, September 17, 2015; Treaty between the Federal Republic of Germany and Pakistan for the Promotion and Protection of Investments, November 25, 1959, 457 U.N.T.S. 23.

53. Maude Barlow, "Fighting TTIP, CETA, and ISDS: Lessons from Canada," Council of Canadians, April 2016, https://canadians.org/sites/default/files/publications/report-ceta-ttip-isds-1015.pdf.

54. Bode, *Die Freihandelslüge,* 107; Ames, "ISDS."

55. "Germany to Pay Nuclear Operators 2.6 bln Euros for Plant Closures," Reuters, March 5, 2021.

56. Joseph Stiglitz, "The Secret Corporate Takeover of Trade Agreements," *Guardian,* May 13, 2015; Eric Crosbie and George Thomson, "Regulatory Chills: Tobacco Industry Legal Threats and the Politics of Tobacco Standardised Packaging in New Zealand," *New Zealand Medical Journal* 131 (2018): 25–41.

57. Bernie Sanders, "The TPP Must Be Defeated," *Huffington Post,* May 21, 2019; Elizabeth Warren, "The Trans-Pacific Partnership Clause Everyone Should Oppose," *Washington Post,* February 25, 2015; for a claim by a fossil-fuel company against climate measures taken by a government, see "Coal Company Sues Netherlands for €1.4 Billion for Coal Phase Out," Friends of the Earth Europe Press Release, February 4, 2021.

58. Tim Wu, *The Curse of Bigness* (New York: Columbia Global Reports, 2018), 20–21.

59. Foroohar, *Don't Be Evil,* xii.

60. Team Warren, "Here's How We Can Break up Big Tech," *Medium,* March 8, 2019.

61. Patrick Barwise and Leo Watkins, "The Evolution of Digital Dominance: How and Why We Got to GAFA," in *Digital Dominance: The Power of Google, Amazon, Facebook, and Apple,* edited by Martin Moore and Damian Tambini (Oxford: Oxford University Press), 21–49; see also Nick Srnicek, *Platform Capitalism* (Cambridge: Polity Press, 2017).

62. Robert H. Bork, *The Antitrust Paradox* (New York: Free Press, 1978), 66, 97.

63. United Nations Conference on Trade and Development, "Competition Issues in Digital Economy," TD/B/C.I/CLP/54, May 1, 2019.

64. Wu, *The Curse of Bigness,* 123; Tim Wu and Stuart A. Thompson, "The Roots of Big Tech Run Disturbingly Deep," *New York Times,* June 7, 2019.

65. Thomas Philippon, *The Great Reversal: How America Gave Up on Free Markets* (Cambridge, MA: Belknap Press, 2019), 111–123; for a discussion of the book, see David Leonhardt, "Big Business Is Overcharging You $5,000 a Year," *New York Times,* November 10, 2019.

66. On innovation, see Jonathan B. Baker, "Beyond Schumpeter vs. Arrow: How Antitrust Fosters Innovation," *Antitrust Law Journal* 74 (2007): 575–602; Kenneth J. Arrow, "Economic Welfare and the Allocation of Resources to Invention," in *The Rate and Direction of Inventive Activity: Economic and Social Factors* (Nat'l Bureau of Econ. Research ed., 1962): 609, 620; for the quote, see Tim Wu, "Don't Fall for Facebook's China Argument," *New York Times,* December 10, 2018.

67. On the rise of superstar firms and their lower-than-average labor share of income, see David Autor, David Dorn, Lawrence F. Katz, Christina Patterson, and John Van Reenen, "The Fall of the Labor Share and the Rise of Superstar Firms," *Quarterly Journal of Economics* 135, no. 2 (2020): 645–709.

68. José Azar, Ioana Marinescu, and Marshall I. Steinbaum, "Labor Market Concentration," National Bureau of Economic Research, Working Paper No. 24147, 2019; Efraim Benmelech, Nittai Bergman, and Hyunseob Kim, "Strong Employers and Weak Employees: How Does Employer Concentration Affect Wages?," National Bureau of Economic Research, Working Paper No. 24307, 2018; Alan Krueger & Eric Posner, "Corporate America Is Suppressing Wages for Many Workers," *New York Times,* February 28, 2018; Bryce Covert, "When Companies Supersize, Paychecks Shrink," *New York Times,* May 13, 2018.

69. Lina M. Khan, "Sources of Tech Platform Power," *Georgetown Law Technology Review* 2 (2018): 325–334; Shaoul Susman, "Amazon's Latest Supplier Purge Is a Classic Indicator of Price Predation," *Pro Market Blog,* March 14, 2019, https://promarket.org/amazons-latest-supplier-purge-is-a-classic-indicator-of-price-predation/.

70. Ciuriak, "Economic Rents and the Contours of Conflict."

71. Wu, *Curse of Bigness,* 14–15.

72. Jim Balsillie, "Data Is Not the New Oil—It's the New Plutonium," *Financial Post,* May 28, 2019.

73. Margrethe Vestager, Competition in a Digital Age, European Internet Forum, March 17, 2021, https://ec.europa.eu/commission/commissioners/2019-2024/vestager/announcements/competition-digital-age_en.

Ch. 7: The Geoeconomic Narrative

1. Robert Spalding, *Stealth War: How China Took over While America's Elite Slept* (New York: Penguin, 2019), x–xii.

2. Spalding, *Stealth War,* xii, xvi–xvii.

3. On the distinction between relative and absolute gains, see Joseph Grieco, Robert Powell, and Duncan Snidal, "The Relative-Gains Problem for International Cooperation," *American Political Science Review* 87, no. 3 (1993): 729–743; Michael Wesley, "Australia and the Rise of Geoeconomics," *Centre of Gravity* 29, no. 1 (2016): 4.

4. For a discussion of the relationship between economics and security in the context of the Cold War, see Kal J. Holsti, "Politics in Command: Foreign Trade as National Security Policy," *International Organization* 40, no. 3 (1986): 643–671.

5. Antony J. Blinken, "A Foreign Policy for the American People," March 3, 2021, https://au.usembassy.gov/secretary-blinken-speech-a-foreign-policy-for-the-american-people/.

6. Edward Luttwak, "From Geopolitics to Geo-Economics: Logic of Conflict, Grammar of Commerce," *National Interest* 20 (1990): 17–19.

7. Robert D. Blackwill and Jennifer M. Harris, *War by Other Means: Geoeconomics and Statecraft* (Cambridge, MA: Harvard University Press, 2016), 9.

8. Anthea Roberts, Henrique Choer Moraes, and Victor Ferguson, "Toward a Geoeconomic Order," *Journal of International Economic Law* 22, no. 4 (2019): 655–676.

9. Robert Lighthizer, "The Era of Offshoring U.S. Jobs Is Over," *New York Times,* May 11, 2020.

10. On the "pivot to Asia," see Kenneth Lieberthal, "The American Pivot to Asia," *Foreign Policy,* December 21, 2011; on the "future of politics," see Hillary Clinton, "America's Pacific Century," *Foreign Policy,* October 11, 2011; on the need for "economic statecraft," see Hillary Clinton, "Speech on Economic Statecraft," Economic Club of New York, October 14, 2011, https://2009-2017.state.gov/secretary/20092013clinton/rm/2011/10/175552.htm; on "write the rules," see Barack Obama, "Remarks by the President on Trade," May 8, 2015, https://obamawhitehouse.archives.gov/the-press-office/2015/05/08/remarks-president-trade; on "aircraft carrier," see Ash Carter, "Remarks on the Next Phase of the U.S. Rebalance to the Asia-Pacific," McCain Institute of Arizona State University, Washington, DC, April 6, 2015, https://www.defense.gov/Newsroom/Speeches/Speech/Article/606660/remarks-on-the-next-phase-of-the-us-rebalance-to-the-asia-pacific-mccain-instit/; on the "geoeconomics game," see Robert D. Blackwill, "America Must Play the Geoeconomics Game," *The National Interest,* June 20, 2016, https://nationalinterest.org/feature/america-must-play-the-geoeconomics-game-16658.

11. "National Security Strategy of the United States of America," December 2017, https://trumpwhitehouse.archives.gov/wp-content/uploads/2017/12/NSS-Final-12-18-2017-0905-2.pdf.

12. "Summary of the 2018 National Defense Strategy of the United States of America: Sharpening the American Military's Competitive Edge," US Department of Defense, 2018, https://dod.defense.gov/Portals/1/Documents/pubs/2018-National-Defense-Strategy-Summary.pdf.

13. Mike Pence, "Vice President Mike Pence's Remarks on the Administration's Policy towards China," Hudson Institute, Washington, DC, October 4, 2018, https://www.hudson.org/events/1610-vice-president-mike-pence-s-remarks-on-the-administration-s-policy-towards-china102018.

14. Joe Biden, "Why America Must Lead Again," *Foreign Affairs* 99, no. 2 (2020): 64–76; Hal Brands and Jake Sullivan, "China Has Two Paths to Global Domination," *Foreign Policy,* May 22, 2020; Kurt M. Campbell and Jake Sullivan, "Competition without Catastrophe: How American Can Both Challenge and Coexist with China," *Foreign Affairs* 98, no. 5 (2019): 96–110.

15. Blinken, "A Foreign Policy for the American People."

16. Christopher Wray, "Responding Effectively to the Chinese Economic Espionage Threat," Department of Justice China Initiative Conference, Center for Strategic and International Studies, Washington, DC, February 6, 2020, https://www.fbi.gov/news/speeches/responding-effectively-to-the-chinese-economic-espionage-threat.

17. Many of these concerns are laid out in the Section 301 report prepared by the US Trade Representative, "Findings of the Investigation into China's Acts, Policies, and Prac-

tices Related to Technology Transfer, Intellectual Property, and Innovation under Section 301 of the Trade Act of 1974," Office of the U.S. Trade Representative, Executive Office of the President, March 22, 2018, https://www.hsdl.org/?abstract&did=809992.

18. We are grateful to Timothy Stratford for the inspiration for the football analogy. Ross Chainey, "Don't Understand the US-China Trade War? This Metaphor Could Help," *World Economic Forum*, September 18, 2018 (quoting Timothy P. Stratford).

19. On the argument that China and the United States represent different varieties of capitalism, see, for example, Christopher McNally, "Sino-Capitalism: China's Reemergence and the International Political Economy," *World Politics* 64, no. 4 (2012): 741–776; Tobias ten Brink, "Paradoxes of Prosperity in China's New Capitalism," *Journal of Current Chinese Affairs* 42, no. 4 (2013): 17–44. On the argument that the two approaches are different in kind rather than degree, see, for example, Mark Wu, "The 'China, Inc.' Challenge to Global Trade Governance," *Harvard International Law Journal* 57, no. 2 (2016): 269–270.

20. See Philip Levy, "Was Letting China into the WTO a Mistake?," *Foreign Affairs*, April 2, 2018, https://www.foreignaffairs.com/articles/china/2018-04-02/was-letting-china-wto-mistake; Kurt Campbell and Ely Ratner, "The China Reckoning: How Beijing Defied American Expectations," *Foreign Affairs* 97, no. 2 (2018): 60–70.

21. On weapons and firepower, Peter Navarro, *Death by China* (Upper Saddle River, NJ: Prentice Hall), 2, 50; on arsenal of democracy, Peter Navarro, "Why Economic Security Is National Security," *RealClear Politics*, December 9, 2018, https://www.realclearpolitics.com/articles/2018/12/09/why_economic_security_is_national_security_138875.html; on declaration of war, Theo Sommer, *China First: Die Welt auf dem Weg ins Chinesische Jahrhundert* (Munich: C. H. Beck, 2018), 13.

22. James Rodgers et al., "Breaking the China Supply Chain: How the 'Five Eyes' Can Decouple from Strategic Dependency," Henry Jackson Society, London, May 2020, https://henryjacksonsociety.org/publications/breaking-the-china-supply-chain-how-the-five-eyes-can-decouple-from-strategic-dependency/.

23. "Assessing and Strengthening the Manufacturing and Defense Industrial Base and Supply Chain Resiliency of the United States," Department of Defense, September 2018, https://media.defense.gov/2018/Oct/05/2002048904/-1/-1/1/ASSESSING-AND-STRENGTHENING-THE-MANUFACTURING-AND%20DEFENSE-INDUSTRIAL-BASE-AND-SUPPLY-CHAIN-RESILIENCY.PDF.

24. Donald J. Trump, "We Cannot Have National Security without Economic Security," CNBC video posted September 29, 2017, 4:12, https://www.cnbc.com/video/2017/09/29/trump-we-cannot-have-national-security-without-economic-security.html.

25. The White House, *Interim National Security Strategic Guidance* (March 2021).

26. Navarro, "Why Economic Security Is National Security"; concerns that neoliberal globalization would undermine the United States' defense industrial base were articulated as early as 1990; see Theodore H. Moran, "The Globalization of America's Defense Industries: Managing the Threat of Foreign Dependence," *International Security* 15, no. 1 (1990): 57–99.

27. Campbell and Sullivan, "Competition without Catastrophe"; Lorand Laskai and Samm Sacks, "The Right Way to Protect America's Innovation Advantage," *Foreign Affairs*, October 23, 2018, https://www.foreignaffairs.com/articles/2018-10-23/right-way-protect-americas-innovation-advantage.

28. Henry Farrell and Abraham Newman, "Weaponized Interdependence," *International Security* 44, no. 1 (2019): 42–79; Mark Leonard, ed., *Connectivity Wars* (London: European Council on Foreign Relations Press, 2016).

29. Jonathan Kirshner, "Political Economy in Security Studies after the Cold War," *Review of International Political Economy* 5, no. 1 (1998): 64.

30. Thomas J. Wright, *All Measures Short of War: The Contest for the 21st Century and the Future of American Power* (New Haven: Yale University Press, 2017), xii.

31. Mark Leonard, "Weaponising Interdependence," in *Connectivity Wars.*

32. Sommer, *China First,* 28.

33. Frank Sieren, *Zukunft? China! Wie die neue Supermacht unser Leben, unsere Politik, unsere Wirtschaft verändert* (Munich: Penguin, 2018), 25–30; Liz Alderman, "Under Chinese, a Greek Port Thrives," *New York Times,* October 10, 2012.

34. Michael Abramowitz and Michael Chertoff, "The Global Threat of China's Digital Authoritarianism," *Washington Post,* November 1, 2018.

35. Sommer, *China First,* 27.

36. Simeon Gilding, "5G Choices: A Pivotal Moment in World Affairs," *The Strategist* (Australian Strategic Policy Institute), January 29, 2020, https://www.aspistrategist.org.au/5g-choices-a-pivotal-moment-in-world-affairs/; see also Cassell Bryan-Low et al., "Special Report: Hobbling Huawei: Inside the U.S. War on China's Tech Giant," *Reuters,* May 21, 2019, https://www.reuters.com/article/huawei-usa-5g/rpt-special-report-hobbling-huawei-inside-the-u-s-war-on-chinas-tech-giant-idUSL4N22Y02S.

37. Cecilia Kang, "Huawei Ban Threatens Wireless Service in Rural Areas," *New York Times,* May 25, 2019.

38. James Kynge and Nic Fildes, "Huawei: The Indispensable Telecoms Company," *Financial Times,* January 31, 2020.

39. Michael Hirsch, "How America's Top Tech Companies Created the Surveillance State," *National Journal,* July 26, 2013, http://www.nextgov.com/ciobriefing/2013/07/analysis-how-americas-top-tech-companies-created-surveillance-state/67490/.

40. On the US government's weaponization of the semiconductor supply chain, see Chad Bown, "How the United States Marched the Semiconductor Industry into its Trade War with China," Peterson Institute for International Economics Working Paper 20-16, December 2020; the exchange between European telecommunications operators and a US official is reported in Bryan-Low et al., "Special Report."

41. Christopher Ashley Ford, "Huawei and Its Siblings, the Chinese Tech Giants: National Security and Foreign Policy Implications," Multilateral Action on Sensitive Technologies Conference, Washington, DC, September 11, 2019, https://2017-2021.state.gov/huawei-and-its-siblings-the-chinese-tech-giants-national-security-and-foreign-policy-implications//index.html.

42. See Sarah Bauerle Danzman and Geoffrey Gertz, "Why Is the U.S. Forcing a Chinese Company to Sell the Gay Dating App Grindr?," *Washington Post,* April 3, 2019; Zen Soo, "iCarbonX Could Be the Latest Chinese Company Forced to Sell Stake in US Firm over National Security Concerns," *South China Morning Post,* April 6, 2019.

43. "A New Kind of Cold War," *The Economist,* May 16, 2019.

44. Andrew B. Kennedy and Darren J. Lim, "The Innovation Imperative: Technology and US–China Rivalry in the Twenty-First Century," *International Affairs* 94, no. 3 (2018): 553–572.

45. Christopher Ashley Ford, "Coalitions of Caution: Building a Global Coalition against Chinese Technology-Transfer Threats," FBI–Department of Commerce Conference on Counter-Intelligence and Export Control, Indianapolis, IN, September 13, 2018, https://2017-2021.state.gov/remarks-and-releases-bureau-of-international-security-and-nonproliferation/coalitions-of-caution-building-a-global-coalition-against-chinese-technology-transfer-threats//index.html.

46. Hugo Meijer, *Trading with the Enemy: The Making of US Export Control Policy toward the People's Republic of China* (Oxford: Oxford University Press, 2016).

47. Roberts, Moraes, and Ferguson, "Toward a Geoeconomic Order."

48. Zachary Evans, "Senator Tom Cotton Suggests Denying Visas for Chinese Students to Study Science in U.S.," Yahoo, April 27, 2020.

49. Elsa Kania, "America Must Invest in Expertise and Skills to Compete with China," *The Hill,* July 26, 2019; Remco Zwetsloot and Dahlia Peterson, "The US-China Tech Wars: China's Immigration Disadvantage," *The Diplomat,* December 31, 2019; Sigal Samuel, "Trump Wants Better AI. He Also Wants Less Immigration. He Can't Have Both," *Vox,* February 19, 2019.

50. Sommer, *China First,* 157.

51. Jean-Claude Juncker, "State of the Union Address," Brussels, September 13, 2017, https://ec.europa.eu/commission/presscorner/detail/en/SPEECH_17_3165.

52. Ian Rogers and Arne Delfs, "Germany Steps Up Efforts to Rebuff China's Swoop for Assets," Bloomberg, July 27, 2018; Federal Office for the Protection of the Constitution (BfV), "Infrastruktur, Energie und Hightech—Chinesische Einflussnahme auf die deutsche Wirtschaft durch Direktinvestitionen und Übernahmen," *BfV-Newsletter* 3/2018, October 2018 (on file with authors).

53. Alan Rappeport, "Chinese Money in the U.S. Dries up as Trade War Drags On," *New York Times,* July 21, 2019; "Chinese Investment in Europe and North America Hits 9-Year Low; Signs of Recovery for 2020," Baker McKenzie Newsroom, January 8, 2020, https://www.bakermckenzie.com/en/newsroom/2020/01/chinese-investment-in-europe-na.

54. Ashley Feng and Lorand Laskai, "Welcome to the New Phase of US-China Tech Competition," Defense One, September 3, 2019, https://www.defenseone.com/ideas/2019/09/welcome-new-phase-us-china-tech-competition/159598/.

55. Lee Hsien Loong, "In Full: PM Lee Hsien Loong's Speech at the 2019 Shangri-La Dialogue," Channel News Asia, June 1, 2019, 12:06 a.m., https://www.channelnewsasia.com/news/singapore/lee-hsien-loong-speech-2019-shangri-la-dialogue-11585954.

56. "Brussels Forum 2019: Victoria Espinel, Dennis Shea, Sabine Weyand" (Main Session no. 4: Trade Disrupted), German Marshall Fund video posted June 28, 2018, 1:00:47, https://www.gmfus.org/videos/brussels-forum-2019-victoria-espinel-dennis-shea-sabine-weyand.

57. Mark Leonard et al., "Redefining Europe's Economic Sovereignty," Bruegel, Brussels, June 25, 2019, https://www.bruegel.org/wp-content/uploads/2019/06/PC-09_2019_final-1.pdf.

58. Lili Bayer, "Meet von der Leyen's 'Geopolitical Commission,'" Politico, December 9, 2019, https://www.politico.eu/article/meet-ursula-von-der-leyen-geopolitical-commission/; Jana Puglierin and Kiklas Helwig, "Europe's Geo-Economic Commission," *Berlin Policy Journal,* October 7, 2019, https://berlinpolicyjournal.com/europes-geo-economic-commission/.

59. European Commission and High Representative of the Union for Foreign Affairs and Security Policy, "Joint Communication to the European Parliament, the European Council, and the Council: EU-China—A Strategic Outlook," March 12, 2019, https://eur-lex.europa.eu/legal-content/EN/TXT/PDF/?uri=CELEX:52019JC0005&from=EN.

60. For the *Handelsblatt* quote, see Sommer, *China First,* 158; for "Europe is open," see "Europe's Sinatra Doctrine on China," *Economist,* June 11, 2020.

61. Sommer, *China First,* 28.

62. Tobias Gehrke, "What Could a Geoeconomic EU Look like in 2020?," Egmont Security Policy Brief 123, Egmont—The Royal Institute for International Relations, Brussels, February 2020, http://www.egmontinstitute.be/what-could-a-geoeconomic-eu-look-like-in-2020/; Carsten Jäkel and Helko Borchert, "The European Way: How to Advance Europe's Strategic Autonomy by Pairing Liquidity with Data to Make Supply Chains More Transparent, Resilient and Sustainable," Ernst & Young, 2020, https://borchert.ch/content/en/cmsfiles/publications/2006_Jaekel_Borchert_Supply_Chain.pdf.

63. "Transcript: Europe Is No Longer at the Centre of World Events," interview of Angela Merkel by Lionel Barber, *Financial Times,* January 16, 2020.

64. Reinhard Bütikofer, "TAI Conversations: You Can't Be Systemic Rivals on Monday and Then Go Back to Partnering for the Rest of the Week," *The American Interest,* May 28, 2020, https://www.the-american-interest.com/2020/05/28/you-cant-be-systemic-rivals-on-monday-and-then-go-back-to-partnering-for-the-rest-of-the-week/

65. European Commission, European Political Strategy Centre, *Rethinking Strategic Autonomy in the Digital Age,* EPSC Strategic Notes Issue 30 (Luxembourg: Publications Office of the European Union, July 2019), https://op.europa.eu/en/publication-detail/-/publication/889dd7b7-0cde-11ea-8c1f-01aa75ed71a1/language-en/format-PDF/source-118121846; Matthias Bauer and Fredrik Erixon, *Europe's Quest for Technology Sovereignty: Opportunities and Pitfalls* (Brussels: European Centre for International Political Economy, 2020), https://ecipe.org/publications/europes-technology-sovereignty/.

66. "Joint Communication from the European Commission to the European Parliament, the European Council and the Council: A New EU-US Agenda for Global Change," JOIN (2020) 22 final, December 2, 2020, available at https://ec.europa.eu/info/sites/info/files/joint-communication-eu-us-agenda_en.pdf.

67. "Cynicism Explains a Flawed New EU-China Commercial Pact," *The Economist,* January 9, 2021.

Ch. 8: The Global Threats Narratives

1. Chip Le Grand, "The Sky Turned Black. The Beast Had Arrived in Mallacoota," *The Age,* December 31, 2019, https://www.theage.com.au/national/victoria/the-sky-turned-black-the-beast-had-arrived-in-mallacoota-20191231-p53nyq.html.

2. Helen Davidson, "Mallacoota Fire: Images of 'Mayhem' and 'Armageddon' as Bushfires Rage," *Guardian,* December 31, 2019.

3. Jessie Yeung, Isaac Yee, and Sheena McKenzie, "Thousands of Australian Residents Had to Take Refuge on a Beach as Wildfires Raged," CNN, December 31, 2019.

4. Lily Kuo, "Coronavirus: Wuhan Doctor Speaks out against Authorities," *Guardian,* March 11, 2020.

5. Anne-Marie Slaughter, "Redefining National Security for the Post Pandemic World," Project Syndicate, June 3, 2020, https://www.project-syndicate.org/commentary/redefining-national-security-for-world-after-covid19-by-anne-marie-slaughter-2020-06?barrier=accesspaylog. For an earlier argument about the need to reframe climate change as a global "hyperthreat," see Elizabeth Boulton, "Climate Change as a Hyperthreat," *Australian Contributions to Strategic and Military Geography* 69 (2018).

6. Commission for the Human Future, "Surviving and Thriving in the 21st Century," Discussion and Call to Action on Global Catastrophic Risks, Expert Round Table, March 2020, http://humansforsurvival.org/sites/default/files/CHF_Roundtable_Report_March_2020.pdf.

7. António Guterres, "UN Secretary: Recovery from the Coronavirus Crisis Must Lead to a Better World," *Guardian,* April 2, 2020.

8. Michelle Bachelet and Filippo Grandi, "The Coronavirus Outbreak Is a Test of Our Systems, Values and Humanity," *Telegraph,* March 10, 2020.

9. Roger L. Martin, *When More Is Not Better: Overcoming America's Obsession with Economic Efficiency* (Boston: Harvard Business Review Press, 2020), 15.

10. United Nations, *2009 UNISDR Terminology on Disaster Risk Reduction* (Geneva: United Nations Office for Disaster Risk Reduction, 2009), 24. On different definitions of resilience, see Bernard Manyena, Fortunate Machingura, and Phil O'Keefe, "Disaster Resilience Integrated Framework for Transformation (DRIFT): A New Approach to Theorising and Operationalising Resilience," *World Development* 123, no. 1 (2019).

11. Ian Goldin and Mike Mariathasan, *The Butterfly Defect: How Globalization Creates Systemic Risks, and What to Do about It* (Princeton, NJ: Princeton University Press, 2014), 30.

12. OECD, *Emerging Systemic Risks in the 21st Century: An Agenda for Action* (Paris: OECD, 2003), https://www.oecd.org/governance/risk/37944611.pdf.

13. Yossi Sheffi, *The Power of Resilience* (Cambridge, MA: MIT Press, 2015), 32–33.

14. Anne-Marie Slaughter, *The Chessboard and the Web: Strategies of Connection in a Networked World* (New Haven: Yale University Press, 2017), 88.

15. Ezra Klein, "The Most Predictable Disaster in the History of the Human Race," *Vox,* May 27, 2015.

16. "Air Transport, Passenger Carried," World Bank, https://data.worldbank.org/indicator/IS.AIR.PSGR.

17. "Outbreak Readiness and Business Impact Protecting Lives and Livelihoods across the Global Economy," World Economic Forum White Paper, January 2019, http://www3.weforum.org/docs/WEF%20HGHI_Outbreak_Readiness_Business_Impact.pdf.

18. Klein, "The Most Predictable Disaster."

19. Guterres, "Recovery from the Coronavirus Crisis."

20. While producers of medical supplies were allowed to continue operations even as other parts of the economy were shut down, the indirect effects of shutdowns had the potential to disrupt international supply chains. For example, Malaysian manufacturers of medical gloves feared that they would run out of cartons to ship the gloves due to the restrictions imposed on "non-essential" industries. Liz Lee and Krishna N. Das, "Virus Fight at Risk as World's Medical Glove Capital Struggles with Lockdown," Reuters, March 25, 2020.

21. Rym Momtaz, "Macron Urges Massive Increase in Local Production of Medical Equipment," Politico, March 31, 2020.

22. Statement by Angela Merkel, "Coronavirus in Deutschland," April 6, 2020, https://www.bundesregierung.de/breg-de/themen/coronavirus/statement-by-federal-chancellor-merkel-1739724.

23. Doug Ford (@fordnation), Twitter, April 3, 2020, 5:26 p.m., https://twitter.com/fordnation/status/1246187361819598849.

24. David McKay, "How to Make Canada a More Self-Reliant Country in the Aftermath of the Coronavirus Pandemic," *Globe and Mail,* April 5, 2020.

25. Julian Borger, "Trump Privately Appeals to Asia and Europe for Medical Help to Fight Coronavirus," *Guardian,* March 24, 2020.

26. Uri Friedman, "China Hawks Are Calling the Coronavirus a 'Wake-Up Call,'" *The Atlantic,* March 11, 2020.

27. Goldin and Mariathasan, *The Butterfly Defect,* 54–56.

28. Alexandra Stevenson, "China Stopped Its Economy to Tackle Coronavirus. Now the World Suffers," *New York Times,* March 2, 2020.

29. Richard Baldwin and Beatrice Weder di Mauro, "Introduction," in *Economics in the Time of COVID-19,* edited by Richard Baldwin and Beatrice Weder di Mauro (London: Centre for Economic Policy Research Press, 2020), 1–2; Richard Baldwin and Eiichi Tomiura, "Thinking Ahead about the Trade Impact of COVID-19," in *Economics in the Time of COVID-19,* 59–72.

30. Michael Heath, "The World's Most China-Reliant Economy Reels from Virus Shockwaves," Bloomberg, February 26, 2020; Marguerite Dennis, "How Will Higher Education Have Changed After COVID-19?," *University World News,* March 28, 2020. See also Salvatore Babones, "The China Student Boom and the Risks It Poses to Australian Universities," Centre for Independent Studies Analysis Paper 5, August 2019, https://www.cis.org.au/app/uploads/2019/08/ap5.pdf.

31. "The Changes Covid-19 Is Forcing on to Business," *The Economist,* April 11, 2020.

32. Peter S. Goodman, "A Global Outbreak Is Fueling the Backlash to Globalization," *New York Times,* March 5, 2020; Martin Sandbu, "Globalisation and National Resilience Can Coexist Despite Covid-19," *Financial Times,* April 1, 2020; Mark Carney, "A Chance to Reboot Globalisation," *Financial Times,* March 19, 2021.

33. Goldin and Mariathasan, *The Butterfly Defect,* 78.

34. Geoffrey Gertz, "The Coronavirus Will Reveal Hidden Vulnerabilities in Complex Global Supply Chains," Brookings Institution, March 5, 2020.

35. Kate Andrews, "Will Coronavirus Push Globalisation into Reverse?," *The Spectator,* March 7, 2020; Andrew Edgecliffe-Johnson, "US Supply Chains and Ports under Strain from Coronavirus," *Financial Times,* March 2, 2020; Peng He and Zili Huang, "This Industry Was Crippled by the Coronavirus—Here's How It's Fighting Back," *World Economic Forum,* February 25, 2020; Ben Foldy, "Coronavirus Fallout Threatens Auto Industry's Supply Chain," *Wall Street Journal,* February 7, 2020.

36. Chris Cook, "The NHS at Capacity," Tortoise Media, March 30, 2020, https://members.tortoisemedia.com/2020/03/30/chris-cook-coronavirus-nhs-at-capacity/content.html.

37. Cook, "The NHS at Capacity."

38. Shawn Donnan, "The Pandemic Protectionism Is Spreading," Bloomberg, April 6, 2020. Switzerland provides an example of extensive stockpiling, see Sam Jones, "Swiss Keep Calm and Rest on Their Months of Stockpiles," *Financial Times,* March 27, 2020; John Miller and John Revill, "Swiss Tap Pharmaceutical Reserves as Coronavirus Deaths Rise," Reuters, March 27, 2020.

39. Shannon K. O'Neil, "How to Pandemic-Proof Globalization," *Foreign Affairs,* April 1, 2020.

40. Nassim Taleb, *Anti-Fragile: Things That Gain from Disorder* (New York: Random House, 2012), 44–45.

41. David Marler, "'This Is Coal': Scott Morrison's 'Coalaphobia' Speech," video posted February 9, 2017, https://www.youtube.com/watch?v=3KoMeJB_ywY.

42. Nathaniel Rich, "Losing Earth: The Decade We Almost Stopped Climate Change," *New York Times Magazine,* August 1, 2018.

43. The link between globalization and rising emissions is made most explicitly by Naomi Klein in *This Changes Everything: Capitalism vs. the Climate* (New York: Simon and Schuster, 2014), connecting the West's sense of triumphalism at the end of the Cold War with the failure to take action on climate change (73–75).

44. David Wallace-Wells, *The Uninhabitable Earth* (New York: Duggan Books, 2019), 4, 53; see also 54: "To a large degree what could be called the humanitarian growth of the developing world's middle class since the end of the Cold War has been paid for by fossil-fuel-driven industrialization—an investment in the well-being of the global south made by mortgaging the ecological future of the planet."

45. Klein, *This Changes Everything,* 75, 80, 82.

46. Wallace-Wells, *The Uninhabitable Earth,* 54.

47. Julia Conley, "Coronavirus a 'Clear Warning Shot' From Nature to Humanity, Top Scientists Say," *Common Dreams,* March 25, 2020.

48. David Bryce Yaden et al., "The Overview Effect: Awe and Self-Transcendent Experience in Space Flight," *Psychology of Consciousness: Theory, Research, and Practice* 3, no. 1 (2016): 1, 3, 5.

49. Archibald MacLeish, "A Reflection: Riders on Earth Together, Brothers in Eternal Cold," *New York Times,* December 25, 1968.

50. John S. Dryzek, *The Politics of the Earth: Environmental Discourses,* 2nd ed. (Oxford: Oxford University Press, 2015), 42.

51. Kenneth E. Boulding, "The Economics of the Coming Spaceship Earth," in *Environmental Quality in a Growing Economy,* edited by H. Jarrett (Baltimore, MD: Resources for the Future/Johns Hopkins Press, 1966), 3–14. This notion links to Daly's foundational idea for ecological economics that, instead of the world being "empty" with no tension existing between economic growth and use of environmental resources, the world is increasingly "full," so economic growth has to be pursued in light of the earth's ecological limits. See Herman Daly, "Economics for a Full World," Great Transition Initiative, June 2015, https://greattransition.org/publication/economics-for-a-full-world.

52. Jem Bendell, "Doom and Boom: Adapting to Collapse," in *This Is Not a Drill: An Extinction Rebellion Handbook,* edited by Clare Farrell et al. (London: Penguin, 2019), 77.

53. Vandana Shiva, "Foreword," in *This Is Not a Drill,* 5.

54. Greta Thunberg, *No One Is Too Small to Make a Difference* (London: Penguin, 2019), 19, 24.

55. Climate Central, "Top 10 Warmest Years on Record," January 15, 2020, https://www.climatecentral.org/gallery/graphics/top-10-warmest-years-on-record.

56. Paul J. Crutzen and Eugene F. Stoermer, "The 'Anthropocene,'" *Global Change Newsletter,* May 2000, 17–18; see also Stephen Daniels and Georgina H. Endfield, "Narratives of Climate Change: Introduction," *Journal of Historical Geography* 35, no. 2 (2009): 215, 217.

57. Ben Purvis, Yong Mao, and Darren Robinson, "Three Pillars of Sustainability: In Search of Conceptual Origins," *Sustainability Science* 14 (2019): 681–695; Lynley Tulloch, "On Science, Ecology and Environmentalism," *Policy Futures in Education* 11, no. 1 (2013): 100–114; Dryzek, *The Politics of the Earth,* 16, 147–164.

58. Wallace-Wells, *The Uninhabitable Earth,* 3, 20, 23, 32–33, 36; on the "Anthropocene" terminology, see 153.

59. Extinction Rebellion, "The Truth," https://rebellion.earth/the-truth; "floods, fires, extreme weather," Extinction Rebellion, "Act Now," https://rebellion.earth/act-now/.

60. Klein, *This Changes Everything,* 15 ("clear and present danger," citing Lonnie G. Thompson, "Climate Change: The Evidence and Our Options," *The Behavior Analyst* 33 [2010]: 153), 21 ("war"), 22 ("battle").

61. Kate Raworth, *Doughnut Economics: Seven Ways to Think Like a 21st-Century Economist* (White River Junction, VT: Chelsea Green Publishing, 2017); Kate Raworth, "A Safe and Just Space for Humanity," Oxfam Discussion Paper, February 2012, https://www-cdn.oxfam.org/s3fs-public/file_attachments/dp-a-safe-and-just-space-for-humanity-130212-en_5.pdf; Herman E. Daly, *From Uneconomic Growth to a Steady-State Economy* (Cheltenham, UK: Edward Elgar, 2014); Jason Hickel, "Time for Degrowth: To Save the Planet, We Must Shrink the Economy," The Conversation, August 23, 2016.

62. Kate Raworth, "A New Economics," in *This Is Not a Drill,* 149–151.

63. Raworth, "A New Economics," 146.

64. Anthony McMichael, *Climate Change and the Health of Nations: Famines, Fevers, and the Fate of Populations* (New York: Oxford University Press, 2017), 14.

65. Sharon Friel, *Climate Change and the People's Health* (New York: Oxford University Press, 2019), 57.

66. Raworth, "A New Economics," 149.

67. Kate Raworth, "What on Earth Is the Doughnut? . . . ," https://www.kateraworth.com/doughnut/.

68. Thunberg, *No One Is Too Small to Make a Difference,* 64–65.

69. Academics such as Richard Wilkinson and Kate Pickett have called on governments to "shift attention from material standards and economic growth to ways of improving the psychological and social wellbeing of whole societies." Richard Wilkinson and Kate Pickett, *The Spirit Level: Why More Equal Societies Almost Always Do Better* (London: Allen Lane, 2009), 4.

70. "The Wellbeing Budget," Government of New Zealand Treasury, May 30, 2019, https://treasury.govt.nz/sites/default/files/2019-06/b19-wellbeing-budget.pdf.

71. Klein, *This Changes Everything,* 75–80.

72. Michael Jakob and Robert Marschinski, "Interpreting Trade-Related CO_2 Emission Transfers," *Nature Climate Change* 3 (2013): 19–23.

73. Klein, *This Changes Everything,* 80–82.

74. Klein, *This Changes Everything,* 79.

75. Greta Thunberg, "Fridays for a Future: Greta Thunberg's Climate Strike," Climate Denial Crocks of the Week, September 28, 2018, https://climatecrocks.com/2018/09/28/fridays-for-a-future-greta-thunbergs-climate-strike/.

76. Lucas Chancel, *Unsustainable Inequalities: Social Justice and the Environment* (Cambridge, MA: Harvard University Press, 2020), 3.

77. "Extreme Carbon Inequality," Oxfam Media Briefing, December 2, 2015, https://www-cdn.oxfam.org/s3fs-public/file_attachments/mb-extreme-carbon-inequality-021215-en.pdf.

78. Henry Shue, *Climate Justice: Vulnerability and Protection* (Oxford: Oxford University Press, 2014), 44, 46.

79. Jason Hickel, "Why Growth Can't Be Green," *Foreign Policy,* September 12, 2018.

80. Jason Hickel, "Is It Possible to Achieve a Good Life for All within Planetary Boundaries?," *Third World Quarterly* 40, no. 1 (2018): 28–30.

81. Thunberg, "Fridays for a Future."

Ch. 9: Switching Narratives

1. For Zuckerberg's notes, see Jordan Novet, "Mark Zuckerberg's Notes for His Senate Hearing, Revealed," CNBC, April 10, 2018; for Facebook's China Argument, see Tim Wu, "Don't Fall for Facebook's China Argument," *New York Times,* December 10, 2018.

See also Kurt Wagner, "Mark Zuckerberg Says Breaking up Facebook Would Pave the Way for China's Tech Companies to Dominate," *Vox,* July 18, 2018.

2. Sheelah, *New Yorker,* June 14, 2019.

3. Kolhatkar, "Can Elizabeth Warren Win It All?"

4. Carol Bacchi, *Analysing Policy: What's the Problem Represented to Be?* (Sydney: Pearson Education Australia, 2009).

5. David Freedlander (@freelander), Twitter, March 16, 2019, 4:21 P.M., https://twitter.com/freedlander/status/1107014149819846657.

6. Tilo Jung, "Gysi & ein Bürger, der nicht für andere verantwortlich sein möchte . . . ," video posted September 3, 2015, at 4:44, https://www.youtube.com/watch?v=bMoAIh3buig.

7. Matthew C. Klein and Michael Pettis, *Trade Wars Are Class Wars: How Rising Inequality Distorts the Global Economy and Threatens International Peace* (New Haven: Yale University Press, 2020), 2.

8. Lina M. Khan, "Amazon's Antitrust Paradox," *Yale Law Journal* 126 (2017): 710–805.

9. Team Warren, "Here's How We Can Break Up Big Tech," *Medium,* March 8, 2019; Tim Wu, *The Curse of Bigness* (New York: Columbia Global Reports, 2018); Chris Hughes, "It's Time to Break up Facebook," *New York Times,* May 9, 2019.

10. Robert D. Atkinson and Michael Lind, "National Developmentalism: From Forgotten Tradition to New Consensus," *American Affairs* 3, no. 2 (2019).

11. Gilad Edelman, "Biden Is Assembling a Big Tech Antitrust All-Star Team," *Wired,* March 9, 2021.

12. European Commission, "Mergers: Commission Prohibits Siemens' Proposed Acquisition of Alstom," IP/19/881, press release, February 6, 2019; Rochelle Toplensky and Alex Barker, "The Franco-German Deal That Could Derail Europe's Competition Police," *Financial Times,* June 14, 2018.

13. For swift geoeconomic reactions, see European Commission: European Political Strategy Centre, "EU Industrial Policy After Siemens-Alstom," March 18, 2019, https://op.europa.eu/en/publication-detail/-/publication/03fb102b-10e2-11ea-8c1f-01aa75ed71a1#; for the response of French and German governments, see German Ministry for Economy and Energy and French Ministry for Economy and Finances, "A Franco-German Manifesto for a European Industrial Policy Fit for the 21st Century," February 19, 2019, https://www.bmwi.de/Redaktion/DE/Downloads/F/franco-german-manifesto-for-a-european-industrial-policy.pdf?__blob=publicationFile&v=2.

14. Shoshana Zuboff, *The Age of Surveillance Capitalism* (New York: Public Affairs, 2019), 9.

15. Zuboff, *The Age of Surveillance Capitalism,* 11.

16. Zuboff, *The Age of Surveillance Capitalism,* 24, 388–394.

17. For the first subplot, see Tarun Chhabra, "The China Challenge, Democracy, and U.S. Grand Strategy," Brookings Institution Policy Brief, February 15, 2019; Christina Larson, "Who Needs Democracy When You Have Data," *MIT Technology Review,*

August 20, 2018; for the second, see Executive Office of the President, Securing the Information and Communications Technology and Services Supply Chain, Executive Order No. 13873, 84 Fed. Reg. 22689, May 15, 2019; Jim Finkle and Christopher Bing, "China's Hacking against U.S. on the Rise: U.S. Intelligence Official," Reuters, December 11, 2018; for the third, see Louis Lucas and Richard Waters, "China and US Compete to Dominate Big Data," *Financial Times,* May 1, 2018; Elsa B. Kania, "Artificial Intelligence and Chinese Power," *Foreign Affairs,* December 5, 2017; Ana Swanson, "As Trade Talks Continue, China Is Unlikely to Yield on Control of Data," *New York Times,* April 30, 2019; for the fourth, see Adam Segal, "When China Rules the Web," *Foreign Affairs,* August 13, 2018; Samm Sacks, "Beijing Wants to Rewrite the Rules of the Internet," *The Atlantic,* June 18, 2018; for the fifth, see Jon Porter, "The NYT Investigates China's Surveillance-State Exports," *Verge,* April 29, 2019; Michael Abramowitz and Michael Chertoff, "The Global Threat of China's Digital Authoritarianism," *Washington Post,* November 1, 2018; Bennett Murray, "Vietnam Doesn't Trust Huawei an Inch," *Foreign Policy,* May 9, 2019.

18. For "when studies find," see Sarah Logan, Brendan Molloy, and Graeme Smith, "Chinese Tech Abroad: Baidu in Thailand," Internet Policy Observatory at the Annenberg School, University of Pennsylvania, 2018, https://papers.ssrn.com/sol3/papers.cfm?abstract_id=3810369; for "censorship at home," see Freedom House, "Freedom on the Net 2018: The Rise of Digital Authoritarianism," press release, October 31, 2018; Samuel Woodhams, "How China Exports Repression to Africa," *The Diplomat,* February 23, 2019; for "triple helix," see Anthea Roberts, Henrique Choer Moraes, and Victor Ferguson, "Toward a Geoeconomic World Order," *Journal of International Economic Law* 22 (2019): 655–676; for "national team," see Meng Jing and Sarah Dai, "China Recruits Baidu, Alibaba and Tencent to AI 'National Team,'" *South China Morning Post,* November 21, 2017.

19. Mark Wu, "The 'China, Inc.' Challenge to Global Trade Governance," *Harvard International Law Journal* 57 (2016): 261–324.

20. Yasmin Tadjdeh, "Dunford Knocks Tech Companies That Work with China, Not Pentagon," *National Defense,* May 13, 2019.

21. Nicholas Thompson and Ian Bremmer, "The AI Cold War That Threatens Us All," *Wired,* October 23, 2018.

22. Rana Foroohar, "Patriotic Capitalism," *Financial Times,* October 8, 2018.

23. Vice President Mike Pence, "Speech on the Administration's Policy Toward China," Hudson Institute, Washington, DC, October 4, 2018, https://trumpwhitehouse.archives.gov/briefings-statements/remarks-vice-president-pence-administrations-policy-toward-china/.

24. Peter Navarro, *Death by China* (Upper Saddle River, NJ: Prentice Hall), 77–78.

25. See, e.g., Michelle Fox, "Sen. Mark Warner Warns That Breaking up Tech Giants Could Open the Door to Chinese Firms," CNBC, April 9, 2019.

26. Wu, "The 'China, Inc.' Challenge."

27. Jeffrey Sachs, "China Is Not the Source of Our Economic Problems," CNN, May 27, 2019.

28. Cody Cain, "No, Mr. President: China Didn't Steal Our Jobs. Corporate America Gave Them Away," *Salon,* May 27, 2019.

29. Benjamin Shobert, *Blaming China: It Might Feel Good but It Won't Fix America's Economy* (Lincoln, NE: Potomac Books, 2018), ix–x, 77–81.

30. See Lois Weis, "Identity Formation and the Processes of 'Othering,'" *Educational Foundations* 9 (1995): 17–33, and Shogo Suzuki, "The Importance of 'Othering' in China's National Identity: Sino-Japanese Relations as a Stage of Identity Conflicts," *Pacific Review* 20, no. 1 (2007): 23–47.

31. Jeff D. Colgan and Robert O. Keohane, "The Liberal Order Is Rigged," *Foreign Affairs,* April 17, 2017.

32. Tim Weiner, "China Syndrome; Seeing Beyond Spies Is the Hard Part," *New York Times,* March 14, 1999.

33. Stephen Wertheim, "Is It Too Late to Stop a New Cold War with China?," *New York Times,* June 8, 2019.

34. Stephen Pampinella, "The Internationalist Disposition and US Grand Strategy," *The Disorder of Things,* January 23, 2019, https://thedisorderofthings.com/2019/01/23/the-internationalist-disposition-and-us-grand-strategy/.

35. Jimmy Carter, "How to Repair the U.S.-China Relationship—and Prevent a Modern Cold War," *Washington Post,* December 31, 2018.

36. Michael T. Klare, "The United States Is Already at War with China," *The Nation,* February 18, 2019.

37. Xi Jinping, speech at opening ceremony of Paris Climate Summit, December 1, 2015, https://www.chinadaily.com.cn/world/XiattendsParisclimateconference/2015-12/01/content_22592469.htm.

38. "'Zero-Sum Game' Mindset Destructive to China-U.S. Ties, Says Chinese Ambassador," Xinhua, February 9, 2019.

39. Joseph R. Biden Jr., "Why America Must Lead Again: Rescuing U.S. Foreign Policy after Trump," *Foreign Affairs,* March/April 2020; Kurt M. Campbell and Jake Sullivan, "Competition without Catastrophe: How American Can Both Challenge and Coexist with China," *Foreign Affairs,* September/October 2019; "Biden Foreign Policy Advisor Antony Blinken on Top Global Challenges," CBS News, September 25, 2020, https://www.cbsnews.com/news/biden-foreign-policy-adviser-antony-blinken-on-top-global-challenges/.

40. Alex Joske, "Picking Flowers, Making Honey," Australia Strategic Policy Institution, Report No. 10/2018, October 31, 2018, https://www.aspi.org.au/report/picking-flowers-making-honey.

41. Nadia Schadlow, "Consider the Possibility That Trump Is Right about China," *The Atlantic,* April 5, 2020.

42. Samantha Power, "How the COVID-19 Era Will Change National Security Forever," *Time,* April 14, 2020.

43. Bill Gates, "The First Modern Pandemic," *Gates Notes,* April 23, 2020, https://www.gatesnotes.com/Health/Pandemic-Innovation.

44. Matt Apuzo and David D. Kirkpatrick, "Covid-19 Changed How the World Does Science, Together," *New York Times,* April 1, 2020; see also Xin Xu, "The Hunt for a Coronavirus Cure Is Showing How Science Can Change for the Better," *The Conversation,* February 24, 2020; Bob Davis and Lingling Wei, "U.S., China Trade Blame for Coronavirus," *Wall Street Journal,* March 27, 2020.

Ch. 10: Overlaps among Narratives

1. Cass R. Sunstein, "Incompletely Theorized Agreements," *Harvard Law Review* 108 (1995): 1733–1772.

2. In accordance with the establishment narrative: "Findings of the Investigation into China's Acts, Policies, and Practices Related to Technology Transfer, Intellectual Property, and Innovation under Section 301 of the Trade Act of 1974," Office of the U.S. Trade Representative, Executive Office of the President, March 22, 2018, https://www.hsdl.org/?abstract&did=809992. In accordance with the geoeconomic narrative: Peter Navarro, "Why Economic Security Is National Security," Real Clear Politics, December 9, 2018; Henry Farrell and Abraham L. Newman, "Weaponized Interdependence: How Global Economic Networks Shape State Coercion," *International Security* 44, no. 1 (2019): 42–79. In accordance with the protectionist narrative: Donald Trump (@realDonaldTrump), Twitter, June 1, 2019, 6:20 p.m., https://www.thetrumparchive.com/.

3. Ana Swanson and Brad Plumer, "Trump Slaps Steep Tariffs on Foreign Washing Machines and Solar Products," *New York Times,* January 22, 2018; Keith Bradsher and Sui-Lee Wee, "U.S. Tariffs, Aimed at China and South Korea, to Hit Targets Worldwide," *New York Times,* January 23, 2018.

4. "Section 201 Cases: Imported Large Residential Washing Machines and Imported Solar Cells and Modules," Office of the U.S. Trade Representative, Fact Sheet, https://ustr.gov/sites/default/files/files/Press/fs/201%20FactSheet.pdf.

5. Safeguards differ in this respect from other so-called trade remedies, such as anti-dumping and countervailing duties. The purpose of anti-dumping and countervailing duties is to level the playing field between domestic producers and their foreign competitors by providing a remedy for "unfair" practices, such as dumping and subsidization. In the case of safeguards, there is no need to show that the exporter of the product has engaged in or benefited from "unfair" practices; instead, serious injury to domestic producers caused by imports is the key fact that has to be shown.

6. All that was at issue was whether the proper legal procedures for the imposition of the safeguards had been followed and whether the tariffs were substantively warranted by the injury to US industry, among other legal criteria. The legality of the safeguard measures was challenged by South Korea and China at the WTO: "United States—Safeguard Measures on Imports of Large Residential Washers," Request for the Establishment of a Panel by the Republic of Korea, WT/DS546/4, August 8, 2018; "United States—Safeguard Measure on Imports of Crystalline Silicon Photovoltaic Products," Request for the Establishment of a Panel by China, WT/DS562/8, December 7, 2019; "United States—Safeguard Measure on Imports of Crystalline Silicon Photovoltaic Products," Request for Consultations by the Republic of Korea, WT/DS545/7, August 16, 2018.

7. While the US administration ultimately decided not to pursue the WTO case, China made some changes to its intellectual property legislation, which were later locked in by the "Phase 1" agreement reached between the administration and China in December 2019. The WTO dispute is "China—Certain Measures Concerning the Protection of Intellectual Property Rights," Request for the Establishment of a Panel by the United States, WT/DS/542/8 (October 19, 2018); the efforts by the United States to work with the European Union and Japan are recorded in "Joint Statement of the Trilateral Meeting of the Trade Ministers of Japan, the United States and the European Union," January 14, 2020, and "Joint Statement of the Trilateral Meeting of the Trade Ministers of the United States, European Union, and Japan," May 23, 2019.

8. In its 2018 Annual Report to Congress, the U.S.-China Economic and Security Review Commission advocated bringing a comprehensive case against China at the WTO, working together with US allies. See "2018 Report to Congress of the U.S.-China Economic and Security Review Commission," U.S.-China Economic and Security Review Commission, 115th Congress, 2nd Session, November 2018, https://www.uscc.gov/sites/default/files/2019-09/2018%20Annual%20Report%20to%20Congress.pdf. While the US case fell well short of that ambition, the European Union brought a related case on its own: "China—Certain Measures on the Transfer of Technology," Request to Consultations by the European Union, WT/DS/549/1, June 6, 2018.

9. Executive Office of the President, Securing the Information and Communications Technology and Services Supply Chain, Executive Order No. 13,873, 84 Fed. Reg. 22689 (May 15, 2019).

10. We say "typically" because it is possible to accept the diagnosis underlying a particular narrative but disagree on how best to fix the problem. However, certain narratives are often associated with, or tend to lend themselves to, some solutions more than others.

11. "Findings of the Investigation into China's Acts."

12. Ana Swanson, "Trump's Tariffs, Once Seen as Leverage, May Be Here to Stay," *New York Times,* May 14, 2019; Shawn Donnan, "Tariffs Are Starting to Look Like the Goal, Not a Tool, for Trump," Bloomberg, May 14, 2019.

13. Eric Martin, "Biden Trade Pick Tai Pledges to Ensure China Tariffs Appropriate," Bloomberg, March 1, 2021.

14. "The Effect of Imports of Steel on the National Security: An Investigation Conducted under Section 232 of the Trade Expansion Act of 1962, as Amended," U.S. Department of Commerce, Bureau of Industry and Security, Office of Technology Evaluation, January 11, 2018; "The Effects of Imports of Aluminum on the National Security: An Investigation Conducted under Section 232 of the Trade Expansion Act of 1962, as Amended," U.S. Department of Commerce, Bureau of Industry and Security, Office of Technology Evaluation, January 17, 2018.

15. For an overview of other countries' reactions to the US measures, see Geraldo Vidigal, "Westphalia Strikes Back: The 2018 Trade Wars and Threat to the WTO Regime," Amsterdam Law School Legal Studies Research Paper, No. 2018-31, October 2, 2018, https://bit.ly/2LMHKIH; Kathleen Claussen, "Arguing about Trade Law in the Interstices," unpublished manuscript (on file with authors).

16. Senator Chuck Grassley prominently linked Senate consideration of the revised NAFTA to the rescission of the steel and aluminum tariffs on Canada and Mexico, eventually leading the US administration to fold. Adrian Morrow and Stephanie Nolen, "How Canada and Mexico Ironed Out an End to the U.S. Tariff War," *Globe and Mail,* May 22, 2019.

17. Sherisse Pham and Abby Phillip, "Trump Suggests Using Huawei as a Bargaining Chip in US-China Trade Deal," CNN, May 24, 2019; Jacob Lew, "America Is Surrendering the Moral High Ground over Huawei," *Financial Times,* June 6, 2019.

18. Yuan Yang, "US Tech Backlash Forces China to Be More Self-Sufficient," *Financial Times,* January 15, 2020.

19. Darren Lim and Victor Ferguson, "Huawei and the Decoupling Dilemma," *Lowy Institute: The Interpreter,* May 28, 2019; Darren J. Lim and Victor Ferguson, "Conscious

Decoupling: The Technology Security Dilemma," in *China Dreams*, edited by Jane Golley, Linda Jaivin, Ben Hillman, and Sharon Strange (Acton: Australian National University Press, 2020).

20. Geoffrey Gertz, "Trump Can't Decide What He Wants from China," *Foreign Policy*, September 11, 2019.

21. Patrick Gillespie, "Trump Hammers America's 'Worst Trade Deal,'" CNN, September 27, 2016.

22. In Canada the agreement is referred to as the Canada-US-Mexico Agreement (CUSMA) and in Mexico as the Tratado entre México, Estados Unidos y Canadá (T-MEC). For ease of reference, we will use USMCA in the text.

23. "Address by Canadian Foreign Affairs Minister on the Modernization of the North American Free Trade Agreement (NAFTA)," Ottawa, August 14, 2017, https://www.canada.ca/en/global-affairs/news/2017/08/address_by_foreignaffairsministeronthemodernizationofthenorthame.html.

24. Statement of the U.S. Chamber of Commerce to Office of the U.S. Trade Representative and the Trade Policy Staff Committee, "Negotiating Objectives Regarding Modernization of the North American Free Trade Agreement with Canada and Mexico," August 25, 2006, https://www.uschamber.com/sites/default/files/us_chamber_priorities_for_nafta_modernization.pdf, 3, 11.

25. "Opening Statement of USTR Robert Lighthizer at the First Round of NAFTA Renegotiations," Office of U.S. Trade Representative, Executive Office of the President, August 17, 2017, https://ustr.gov/about-us/policy-offices/press-office/press-releases/2017/august/opening-statement-ustr-robert-0.

26. Jenny Leonard, "USTR Set to Demand 50 Percent U.S. Content in NAFTA Auto Rules of Origin," *Inside U.S. Trade*, October 13, 2017.

27. "In His Own Words: Lighthizer Lets Loose on Business, Hill Opposition to ISDS, Sunset Clause," *World Trade Online*, October 19, 2017.

28. AFL-CIO, "Making NAFTA Work for Working People," June 2017, https://aflcio.org/sites/default/files/2017-06/NAFTA%20Negotiating%20Recommendations%20from%20AFL-CIO%20%28Witness%3DTLee%29%20Jun2017%20%28PDF%29_0.pdf.

29. "In the Matter of Guatemala—Issues Relating to the Obligations Under Article 16.2.1(a) of the CAFTA-DR," Final Report of the Arbitral Panel, June 14, 2017.

30. Kelsey Johnson, "U.S. Auto Content Demand Meant to Scare Canada and Mexico: Auto Industry," *iPolitics*, January 24, 2018.

31. Alexander Panetta and Joanna Smith, "Wages in Mexico Key to NAFTA Auto Talks," *The Record*, March 28, 2018; "NAFTA Auto Talks Center on 'Focused Value' Approach; Lighthizer Sticks to Wage Component," *World Trade Online Daily News*, April 6, 2018 (reporting that the proposal was designed to achieve the "same objective" as the original US proposal and would "de facto shift production to the U.S by ensuring that important stuff [is] made by high-wage people").

32. Kathleen Claussen, "A First Look at the New Labor Provisions in the USMCA Protocol of Amendment," *International Economic Law and Policy Blog*, December 12,

2019. The revised agreement also strengthened the environmental protections of the agreement, though not sufficiently to win the support of environmental groups. Sierra Club, LCV, and NDRC, "Joint NAFTA Environmental Letter," December 9, 2019, https://www.sierraclub.org/sites/www.sierraclub.org/files/uploads-wysiwig/Joint%20NAFTA%20Enviro%20Letter%2012-9-19.pdf.

33. AFL-CIO, "AFL-CIO Endorses USMCA After Successfully Negotiating Improvements," press release, December 10, 2019, https://aflcio.org/pressreleases/afl-cio-endorses-usmca-after-successfully-negotiating-improvements.

34. Megan Cassella, "'We Ate Their Lunch': How Pelosi Got to 'Yes' on Trump's Trade Deal," *Politico,* December 10, 2019.

35. "Opening Statement of Ambassador-Designate Katherine Tai before the Senate Finance Committee," February 24, 2021.

36. Ana Swanson, "In Washington, 'Free Trade' Is No Longer Gospel," *New York Times,* March 17, 2021; Ana Swanson, "Biden's Pick for Trade Representative Promises Break with Past Policy," *New York Times,* February 25, 2021.

Ch. 11: Trade-offs among Narratives

1. Rebecca Klar, "Cuomo: It's Not the Economy or Public Health, It's Both," *The Hill,* March 24, 2020.

2. Maggie Haberman and David E. Sanger, "Trump Says Coronavirus Cure Cannot 'Be Worse than the Problem Itself,'" *New York Times,* March 23, 2020.

3. Eduardo Porter, *The Price of Everything: The True Cost of Living* (London: Windwill Books, 2012); on the trade-offs that governments have faced in the context of the coronavirus pandemic, see "Covid-19 Presents Stark Choices between Life, Death and the Economy," *The Economist,* April 2, 2020; "The Hard Choices Covid Policymakers Face," *The Economist,* April 4, 2020.

4. Zachary Liscow, "The Dilemma of Moral Commitments in Addressing Inequality," unpublished manuscript, November 2018, https://ntanet.org/wp-content/uploads/2019/03/Session1194_Paper2013_FullPaper_1.pdf. Oren Cass calls the establishment narrative's approach "economic piety." See Oren Cass, *The Once and Future Worker: A Vision for the Renewal of Work in America* (New York: Encounter Books, 2018), 15–28.

5. Donald Trump, speech in Monessen, PA, June 28, 2016, *Time,* http://time.com/4386335/donald-trump-trade-speech-transcript/; Donald Trump, rally in Murphysboro, IL, October 27, 2018, https://factba.se/transcript/donald-trump-speech-maga-rally-murphysboro-il-october-27-2018. For a sense of what it means to lose a job that one has held for decades, see *Inside a Steel Plant Facing Layoffs,* directed by Brent McDonald, Jonah M. Kessel, and John Woo (New York: Times Documentaries, 2017), https://www.nytimes.com/video/us/100000005007829/layoffs-steel-plant-rexnord-mexico.html.

6. Of course, this right is limited by the government's right to expropriate under certain circumstances, which typically include an obligation to pay compensation. Some have argued that private property rights should be loosened to improve 'allocative efficiency' by forcing property owners to sell at a price that reflects the value of the property to them; see Eric Posner and E. Glen Weyl, "Property Is Only Another Name for Monopoly," *Journal of Legal Analysis* 9 (2017): 51–123.

7. For the Trump quote, see Chris Isidore, "The U.S. Auto Industry Doesn't Need Donald Trump's Help," *CNN Money,* August 24, 2015, https://money.cnn.com/2015/08/24/news/companies/donald-trump-mexico-cars/index.html; on the concept of "sacred values," see Scott Atran and Robert Axelrod, "Reframing Sacred Values," *Negotiation Journal* 24, no. 3 (2008): 221–246.

8. J. D. Vance, "End the Globalization Gravy Train," *American Mind,* April 21, 2020, https://americanmind.org/essays/end-the-globalization-gravy-train/.

9. Tucker Carlson, "Mitt Romney Supports the Status Quo: But for Everyone Else, It's Infuriating," Fox News, January 3, 2019.

10. Richard H. Thaler, "Anomalies. Saving, Fungibility, and Mental Accounts," *Journal of Economic Perspectives* 4, no. 1 (1990): 193–205.

11. Megan McArdle, "How Free-Traders Blew It," *Washington Post,* June 27, 2018.

12. Cass, *The Once and Future Worker,* 29.

13. Cass, *The Once and Future Worker,* 6.

14. Organisation for Economic Co-operation and Development, *Multifunctionality in Agriculture: Evaluating the Degree of Jointness, Policy Implications* (Paris: OECD, 2008).

15. National Farmers Union, "Letter to Prime Minister Urging Canada Not to Sign New NAFTA Agreement in Its Present Form," November 29, 2018, https://www.nfu.ca/letter-to-prime-minister-urging-canada-not-to-sign-new-nafta-agreement-in-its-present-form/.

16. "Opening Statement of Ambassador-Designate Katherine Tai before the Senate Finance Committee," February 24, 2021.

17. The foundational book is Arthur M. Okun, *Equality and Efficiency: The Big Tradeoff* (Washington, DC: Brookings Institution Press, 2015).

18. Heather Boushey, *Unbound: How Inequality Constricts Our Economy and What We Can Do about It* (Cambridge, MA: Harvard University Press, 2019); Rana Foroohar, *Makers and Takers: How Wall Street Destroyed Main Street* (New York: Crown, 2016).

19. Dani Rodrik, "What Do Trade Agreements Really Do?," *Journal of Economic Perspectives* 32, no. 2 (2018): 75, 89.

20. Bernie Sanders, "21st Century Economic Bill of Rights," https://berniesanders.com/21st-century-economic-bill-of-rights/.

21. John S. Odell and Susan K. Sell, "Reframing the Issue: The WTO Coalition on Intellectual Property and Public Health, 2001," in *Negotiating Trade: Developing Countries in the WTO and NAFTA,* edited by John S. Odell (Cambridge: Cambridge University Press, 2006), 85–114; Jean-Frédéric Morin and E. Richard Gold, "Consensus-Seeking, Distrust and Rhetorical Entrapment: The WTO Decision on Access to Medicines," *European Journal of International Relations* 16, no. 4 (2010): 563–587; on the "commodification" of public policies in trade negotiations generally, see Nicolas Lamp, "Value and Exchange in Multilateral Trade Lawmaking," *London Review of International Law* 4, no. 1 (2016): 7–55.

22. Dani Rodrik, "Globalisation after Covid-19: My Plan for a Rewired Planet," *Prospect Magazine,* May 4, 2020; see also Dani Rodrik, *The Globalization Paradox: Democracy and the Future of the World Economy* (New York: W. W. Norton, 2011), 200–201.

23. Tyler Cowen, "Welcome (?) to the New World Economic Order," *Business Standard,* December 17, 2019.

24. Robert Gilpin, *War and Change in World Politics* (Cambridge: Cambridge University Press, 1981), 7.

25. Robert Powell, "Guns, Butter, and Anarchy," *American Political Science Review* 87 (1993): 115–132.

26. "EU Coordinated Risk Assessment of the Cybersecurity of 5G Networks," NIS Cooperation Group Report, October 9, 2019; Department of the Treasury, Office of Investment Security, "Guidance Concerning the National Security Review Conducted by the Committee on Foreign Investment in the United States," https://www.treasury.gov/resource-center/international/foreign-investment/Documents/CFIUSGuidance.pdf#page=3; Remarks by Treasury Deputy Assistant Secretary for Investment Security Aimen Mir, Council on Foreign Relations, Washington, DC, April 1, 2016, https://www.treasury.gov/press-center/press-releases/Pages/jl0401.aspx.

27. David Singh Grewal, *Network Power: The Social Dynamics of Globalization* (New Haven, CT: Yale University Press, 2008), 235–237.

28. Anthea Roberts, Henrique Choer Moraes, and Victor Ferguson, "Toward a Geoeconomic Order," *Journal of International Economic Law* 22, no. 4 (2019): 655–676.

29. Jonathan B. Tucker, "Partners and Rivals: A Model of International Collaboration in Advanced Technology," *International Organization* 45, no. 1 (1991): 83–120.

30. Robert O. Keohane and Joseph S. Nye, *Power and Interdependence,* 4th ed. (Boston: Longman, 2012), 9–10.

31. Eurasia Group, "The Geopolitics of 5G," Eurasia Group White Paper, November 15, 2018, https://www.eurasiagroup.net/siteFiles/Media/files/1811-14%205G%20special%20report%20public(1).pdf.

32. The phrase "tail risk" refers to risks that are very unlikely, often three or more standard deviations away from the most likely outcome, which appear on the tail ends of probability curves as they tail off to zero.

33. Nassim Nicholas Taleb, *The Black Swan: The Impact of the Highly Improbable* (New York: Random House, 2007), 77.

34. Taleb, *The Black Swan.*

35. On fat-tail risks in complex systems, see Jessica Flack and Melanie Mitchell, "Complex Systems Science Allows Us to See New Paths Forward," *Aeon,* August 23, 2020; on the significance of superspreader events in the pandemic, see Zeynep Tufekci, "K: The Overlooked Variable That's Driving the Pandemic," *The Atlantic,* September 30, 2020.

36. Joëlle Gergis, "We Are Seeing the Very Worst of Our Scientific Predictions Come to Pass in These Bushfires," *Guardian,* January 2, 2020.

37. Intergovernmental Panel on Climate Change, "Chapter Outline of the Working Group I Contribution to the IPCC Sixth Assessment Report (Ar6)," September 6–10, 2017, https://www.ipcc.ch/site/assets/uploads/2018/09/AR6_WGI_outlines_P46.pdf.

38. Intergovernmental Panel on Climate Change, *Managing the Risks of Extreme Events and Disasters to Advance Climate Change Adaptation: Special Report of the Intergovernmental Panel on Climate Change* (Cambridge: Cambridge University Press, 2018), 452.

39. Nicholas Stern, "The Structure of Economic Modeling of the Potential Impacts of Climate Change: Grafting Gross Underestimation of Risk onto Already Narrow Science Models," *Journal of Economic Literature* 51 (2013): 838–859; see also Nicholas Stern, "Current Climate Models Are Grossly Misleading," *Nature,* February 25, 2016; Martin L. Weitzman, "On Modeling and Interpreting the Economics of Catastrophic Climate Change," *Review of Economics and Statistics* 91 (2009): 1–19.

40. Ruth DeFries et al., "The Missing Economic Risks in Assessments of Climate Change Impacts," Grantham Research Institute on Climate Change and the Environment, London School of Economics and Political Science, September 2019, http://www.lse.ac.uk/GranthamInstitute/wp-content/uploads/2019/09/The-missing-economic-risks-in-assessments-of-climate-change-impacts-2.pdf.

41. Thomas Stoerk, Gernot Wagner, and Robert E. T. Ward, "Policy Brief—Recommendations for Improving the Treatment of Risk and Uncertainty in Economic Estimates of Climate Impacts in the Sixth Intergovernmental Panel on Climate Change Assessment Report," *Review of Environmental Economics and Policy* 12 (2018): 371–376.

42. Richard McGregor, "Australia Can Teach the UK a Lesson in Chinese Wrath," *Financial Times,* March 20, 2021; Jeffrey Wilson, *Adapting Australia to an Era of Geoeconomic Competition,* January 2021.

43. Leslie Hook, "Threat from Extreme Mega-Fires Forces Rethink on Fighting Blaze," *Financial Times,* January 17, 2020.

44. On fire risks, see Carrie Fellner and Pallavi Singhal, "Fighters Brace for 'Long Night' Ahead after Sydney Swelters through Hottest Ever Day," *Sydney Morning Herald,* January 4, 2020. On insurance risks, see Mark Carney, "Breaking the Tragedy of the Horizon—Climate Change and Financial Stability—Speech by Mark Carney," video posted October 1, 2015, https://www.youtube.com/watch?v=V5c-eqNxeSQ.

Ch. 12: Blind Spots and Biases

1. Aurora Milroy, "Black Swans Make Better Policy," The Power to Persuade, October 31, 2019, http://www.powertopersuade.org.au/blog/black-swans-make-better-policy/30/10/2019.

2. Kishore Mahbubani, *Has the West Lost It? A Provocation* (London: Penguin, 2018), 28; Parag Khanna, *The Future Is Asian: Global Order in the Twenty-First Century* (London: Weidenfeld & Nicolson, 2019), 17–18.

3. Kristen Hopewell, *Breaking the WTO: How Emerging Powers Disrupted the Neoliberal Project* (Stanford: Stanford University Press, 2016); Gregory Shaffer, *Emerging Powers and the World Trading System: The Past and Future of International Economic Law* (Cambridge: Cambridge University Press, 2021, forthcoming).

4. Xi Jinping, "Jointly Shoulder Responsibility of Our Times, Promote Global Growth," speech at the opening session of the World Economic Forum annual meeting, Davos, Switzerland, January 17, 2017, http://www.china.org.cn/node_7247529/content_40569136.htm.

5. Jude Blanchette, *China's New Red Guards: The Return of Radicalism and the Rebirth of Mao Zedong* (New York: Oxford University Press, 2019), 66.

6. Aseema Sinha, *Globalizing India: How Global Rules and Markets Are Shaping India's Rise to Power* (Cambridge: Cambridge University Press, 2016); Rahul Mukherji,

Globalization and Deregulation: Ideas, Interests and Institutional Change in India (New Delhi: Oxford University Press, 2014); Balakrishnan Rajagopal, *International Law from Below: Development, Social Movements and Third World Resistance* (Cambridge: Cambridge University Press, 2003).

7. Christophe Jaffrelot and Louise Tillin, "Populism in India," in *The Oxford Handbook of Populism,* edited by Cristóbal Rovira Kaltwasser et al. (Oxford: Oxford University Press, 2017), 184.

8. UN Economic and Social Council, Second Session of the Preparatory Committee of the United Nations Conference on Trade and Employment, Verbatim Report, Twenty-Second Meeting of Commission A, E/PC/T/A/PV/22, ¶ 44, July 1, 1947, https://docs.wto.org/gattdocs/q/UN/EPCT/APV-22.PDF. For further examples, see Nicolas Lamp, "The 'Development' Discourse in Multilateral Trade Lawmaking," *World Trade Review* 16, no. 3 (2017): 475–500.

9. UN Department of Economic Affairs, "The Economic Development of Latin America and Its Principal Problems," E/CN.12/89/Rev.l, April 27, 1950, https://repositorio.cepal.org/bitstream/handle/11362/29973/002_en.pdf?sequence=1&isAllowed=y; H. W. Singer, "The Distribution of Gains between Investing and Borrowing Countries," *American Economic Review* 40, no. 2 (1950): 473–485; Theotonio Dos Santos, "The Structure of Dependence," *American Economic Review* 60, no. 2 (1970): 231–236; Fernando Henrique Cardoso and Enzo Faletto, *Dependency and Development in Latin America* (Berkeley: University of California Press, 1979).

10. Chakravarthi Raghavan, *Recolonization: GATT, the Uruguay Round and the Third World* (London: Zed Books, 1990), 178–188; Roberto da Oliveira Campos et al., *Trends in International Trade: A Report by a Panel of Experts* (Geneva: World Trade Organization, 1958), https://www.wto.org/english/res_e/booksp_e/gatt_trends_in_international_trade.pdf.

11. Timothy E. Josling, Stefan Tangermann, and T. K. Warley, *Agriculture in the GATT* (London: Palgrave Macmillan, 1996); General Agreement on Tariffs and Trade, "Avoidance of Market Disruption: Statement by the Representative of the United States on 3 May 1960," W.16/14, June 7, 1960, https://docs.wto.org/gattdocs/q/GG/W/16-14.PDF; Martin Wolf, "Managed Trade in Practice: Implications of the Textile Arrangements," in *Trade Policy in the 1980s,* edited by William R. Cline (Washington, DC: Institute of International Economics, 1983), 455–482.

12. Fatoumata Jawara and Aileen Kwa, *Behind the Scenes at the WTO: The Real World of International Trade Negotiations* (London: Zed Books, 2004); "rich men's club," see Hugo Paemen and Alexandra Bensch, *From the GATT to the WTO: The European Community in the Uruguay Round* (Philadelphia: Coronet Books, 1995), 253; "the leading countries," see Robert E. Hudec, *The GATT Legal System and World Trade Diplomacy* (New York: Praeger, 1975), 51.

13. See Multilateral Trade Negotiations Uruguay Round, Negotiating Group on Trade-Related Aspects of Intellectual Property Rights, Including Trade in Counterfeit Goods, Standards and Principles Concerning the Availability, Scope, and Use of Trade-Related Intellectual Property Rights, Communication from India, MTN.GNG/NG11/W/37, ¶ 2, July 10, 1989, https://www.wto.org/gatt_docs/English/SULPDF/92070115.pdf.

14. For an overall account, see Nicolas Lamp, "The Club Approach to Multilateral Trade Lawmaking," *Vanderbilt Journal of Transnational Law* 49, no. 1 (2016): 165–181;

Robert Hudec, "GATT and Developing Countries," *Columbia Business Law Review* 1992, no. 1 (1992): 76; for objections by developing countries, see Chakravarthi Raghavan, "G77 Assail 'Single Undertaking' and MTO Efforts in Round," SUNS Online, March 18, 1991, http://www.sunsonline.org/trade/process/during/uruguay/mto/03180091.htm; on the "contract of adhesion," see Daniel K. Tarullo, "The Hidden Costs of International Dispute Settlement: WTO Review of Domestic Anti-Dumping Decisions," *Law and Policy in International Business* 34, no. 1 (2002): 170, 176.

15. On "rebalance," see Kristen Hopewell, "Different Paths to Power: The Rise of Brazil, India and China at the World Trade Organization," *Review of International Political Economy* 22, no. 2 (2015): 331; Hopewell, *Breaking the WTO*, 77–104, 176–207; on the failure of the Doha Round, see also Paul Blustein, *Misadventures of the Most Favored Nations: Clashing Egos, Inflated Ambitions, and the Great Shambles of the World Trade System* (New York: Public Affairs, 2009).

16. Sundhya Pahuja, "From Permanent Sovereignty to Investor Protection," in *Decolonising International Law: Development, Economic Growth and the Politics of Universality* (Cambridge: Cambridge University Press, 2011).

17. Muthucumaraswamy Sornarajah, *The International Law of Foreign Investment*, 2nd ed. (Cambridge: Cambridge University Press, 2004), 22, 41–42.

18. Andrew Guzman, "Why LDCs Sign Treaties That Hurt Them: Explaining the Popularity of Bilateral Investment Treaties," *Virginia Journal of International Law* 38, no. 4 (1998): 639–688; Zachary Elkins, Andrew Guzman, and Beth A. Simmons, "Competing for Capital: The Diffusion of Bilateral Investment Treaties, 1960–2000," *International Organization* 60, no. 4 (2006): 811–846.

19. See, for example, B. S. Chimni, "Capitalism, Imperialism and International Law in the Twenty-First Century," *Oregon Review of International Law* 14, no. 1 (2012): 17–46; Rajagopal, *International Law from Below*; Sornarajah, *The International Law of Foreign Investment*, 2, 4.

20. For structural adjustment programs, see Kato Gogo Kingston, "The Impacts of the World Bank and IMF Structural Adjustment Programmes on Africa: The Case Study of Cote d'Ivoire, Senegal, Uganda, and Zimbabwe," *Sacha Journal of Policy and Strategic Studies* 1, no. 2 (2011): 110–130; Nana Yaw Oppong, "Failure of Structural Adjustment Programmes in Sub-Saharan Africa: Policy Design or Policy Implementation?," *Journal of Empirical Economics* 3, no. 5 (2014): 321–331. For "essence of neo-colonialism," see Kwame Nkrumah, *Neo-Colonialism: The Last Stage of Imperialism* (London: Thomas Nelson & Sons, Ltd., 1965), ix. See also Kwame Akonor, *Africa and IMF Conditionality: The Unevenness of Compliance, 1983–2000* (New York: Routledge, 2006); Kwame A. Ninsin, "Introduction: Globalization and Africa—A Subjective View," in *Globalized Africa: Political, Social and Economic Impact*, ed. Kwame A. Ninsin (Accra: Napasvil Ventures, 2012), 25.

21. For the elite in developing countries, see Yves Dezalay and Bryant G. Garth, *The Internationalization of Palace Wars: Lawyers, Economists, and the Contest to Transform Latin American States* (Chicago: University of Chicago Press, 2002), 9, 44–47; Bruce G. Carruthers and Terence C. Halliday, "Negotiating Globalization: Global Scripts and Intermediation in the Construction of Asian Insolvency Regimes," *Law and Social Inquiry* 31, no. 3 (2006): 546–548. For the Chicago Boys, see Juan Gabriel Valdés, *Pinochet's Economists: The Chicago School in Chile* (Cambridge: Cambridge University Press, 1995); Dezalay and Garth, *The Internationalization of Palace Wars*, 44–47; Glen Biglaiser, "The Internationalization of Chicago's Economics in Latin America," *Economic Development and*

Cultural Change 50, no. 2 (2002): 269–286. For the Vanderbilt Boys, see Carlos Eduardo Suprinyak and Ramón García Fernández, "The 'Vanderbilt Boys' and the Modernization of Brazilian Economics," Working Paper No. 2018.1, Center for Latin American Studies, University of Chicago, February 2018, https://clas.uchicago.edu/sites/clas.uchicago.edu/files/uploads/Suprinyak%20%26%20Ferna%CC%81ndez%2C%20The%20Vanderbilt%20Boys%20and%20the%20Modernization%20of%20Brazilian%20Economics_FINAL.pdf. For the Berkeley Mafia, see Howard Dick et al., *The Emergence of a National Economy: An Economic History of Indonesia 1800–2000* (Honolulu: University of Hawaii Press, 2002); David Ransom, "The Berkeley Mafia and the Indonesian Massacre," *Ramparts,* October 1970.

22. Nancy M. Birdsall et al., *The East Asian Miracle: Economic Growth and Public Policy* (New York: Oxford University Press, 1993), v.

23. Alice H. Amsden, *Escape from Empire: The Developing World's Journey through Heaven and Hell* (Cambridge, MA: MIT Press, 2007), 14–15.

24. Pranab Bardhan, *Awakening Giants: Feet of Clay* (Princeton, NJ: Princeton University Press, 2010), 2.

25. Xi, "Jointly Shoulder Responsibility of Our Times."

26. Jagdish Bhagwati, *In Defense of Globalization* (New York: Oxford University Press, 2004), 63.

27. Montek S. Ahluwalia, "India's 1991 Reforms: A Retrospective Overview," in *India Transformed: 25 Years of Economic Reforms,* ed. Rakesh Mohan (Washington, DC: Brookings Institution Press, 2017), 47; Montek S. Ahluwalia, "Economic Reforms in India Since 1991: Has Gradualism Worked?," *Journal of Economic Perspectives* 16, no. 3 (2002): 67–88; Arvind Virmani, "India's External Reforms: Modest Globalisation, Significant Gains," *Economic and Political Weekly* 38, no. 32 (2003): 3373–3390; Dani Rodrik and Arvind Subramanian, "From 'Hindu Growth' to Productivity Surge: The Mystery of the Indian Growth Transition," National Bureau of Economic Research, Working Paper No. 10376, March 2004, https://www.nber.org/papers/w10376.

28. Some commentators question whether these changes were due solely or mainly to economic reforms and opening up to the world market; see Bardhan, *Awakening Giants,* 90–103.

29. Kenneth Pomeranz, *The Great Divergence: China, Europe, and the Making of the Modern World Economy* (Princeton, NJ: Princeton University Press, 2000).

30. Kishore Mahbubani, "The Chinese Century," *American Review,* May–October 2010.

31. For the Asian Century, see Yiping Huang and Bijun Wang, "From the Asian Miracle to an Asian Century? Economic Transformation in the 2000s and Prospects for the 2010s," in *The Australian Economy in the 2000s,* edited by Hugo Gerard and Jonathan Kearns (Sydney: Reserve Bank of Australia, 2011), 7–8; for "the future is Asian," see Parag Khanna, "The Future Is Asian: Commerce, Conflict, and Culture in the 21st Century," https://www.paragkhanna.com/home/ourasianfuture. For the Indian prime minister's quote, see Valentina Romei and John Reed, "The Asian Century Is Set to Begin," *Financial Times,* June 21, 2019; for the final quote, see Wang Huiyao, "At the Center of Global Gravity," *China Daily,* June 21, 2019, http://www.chinadaily.com.cn/global/2019-06/21/content_37483205.htm.

32. Khanna, *The Future Is Asian,* 158–163.

33. Facundo Alvaredo et al., "The Elephant Curve of Global Inequality and Growth," *American Economic Association Papers and Proceedings* 108 (2018): 103–108; Filip Novokmet, Thomas Piketty, and Gabriel Zucman, "From Soviets to Oligarchs: Inequality and Property in Russia 1905–2016," National Bureau of Economic Research, Working Paper No. 23712, August 2017, https://www.nber.org/papers/w23712.pdf.

34. Joseph E. Stiglitz, *Globalization and its Discontents Revisited: Anti-Globalization in the Era of Trump* (New York: W. W. Norton, 2018), 157. Branko Milanovic has highlighted the importance of distinguishing between the process of macroeconomic stabilization (the so-called Big Bang), on the one hand, and the "hurried and inequitable privatizations" that started at the same time, on the other hand. Milanovic argues that the former process was "both inevitable and successful," and that Western advisors played "a very positive role" in that process. It was the second process that has created long-lasting negative consequences for Russia—consequences that other post-communist economies, such as Poland, managed to avoid. See Branko Milanovic, "Distinguishing Post-Communist Privatizations from the Big Bang," *globalinequality* (blog), March 4, 2021, http://glineq.blogspot.com/2021/03/distinguishing-post-communist.html.

35. Branko Milanovic, *Global Inequality: A New Approach for the Age of Globalization* (Cambridge, MA: Harvard University Press, 2016), 137–139.

36. For Vladimir Putin's account, see "Transcript: 'All This Fuss about Spies . . . It Is Not Worth Serious Interstate Relations,'" interview of Vladimir Putin by Lionel Barber, *Financial Times,* June 26, 2019; Lev Gudkov, "Resources of Putin's Conservatism," in *Putin's Russia: How It Rose, How It Is Maintained, and How It Might End,* ed. Leon Aron (Washington, DC: American Enterprise Institute, 2015), 54. See also Ivan Krastev and Stephen Holmes, *The Light That Failed: A Reckoning* (London: Penguin Books, 2019), 83.

37. Putin is quoted in Associated Press, "Putin: Soviet Collapse a 'Genuine Tragedy,'" NBC News, April 25, 2005; see also Shaun Walker, "The Humiliation That Pushed Putin to Try and Recapture Russian Glory," History, March 26, 2019, https://www.history.com/news/vladimir-putin-russia-power; Oleg Shchedrov, "Putin Restored Russia's Pride, at a Price," Reuters, April 25, 2005; Michele A. Berdy, "Catastrophes, Geopolitical and Otherwise," *Moscow Times,* January 11, 2019, https://www.themoscowtimes.com/2019/01/11/catastrophes-geopolitical-and-otherwise-a64118; for "harrowing loss," see Krastev and Holmes, *The Light That Failed,* 87.

38. Stephen Kotkin, "The Resistible Rise of Vladimir Putin: Russia's Nightmare Dressed like a Daydream," *Foreign Affairs,* March/April 2015.

39. For Putin's quote, see Anders Åslund, *Russia's Crony Capitalism* (New Haven: Yale University Press, 2019), 239; see also Lilia Shevtsova, *Putin's Russia* (Washington, DC: Carnegie Endowment for International Peace, 2005).

40. Shevtsova, *Putin's Russia,* 16, 347. Shevtsova cites a poll in which 71 percent of respondents answered the question of what Russia needed with "a strong leader," whereas only 13 percent named "democratic institutions"; see Shevtsova, *Putin's Russia,* 73. See also Anne Garrels, *Putin Country: A Journey into the Real Russia* (New York: Farrar, Straus and Giroux, 2016).

41. "Transcript: 'All This Fuss about Spies.'"

42. Vladimir Putin, "Address by President of the Russian Federation," Moscow, March 18, 2014, http://en.kremlin.ru/events/president/news/20603.

43. Vladimir Putin, speech at Plenary Session of St. Petersburg International Economic Forum, St. Petersburg, June 7, 2019, http://en.kremlin.ru/events/president/news/60707.

44. Sergei Karaganov and Dmitry V. Suslov, "A New World Order: A View from Russia," *Russia in Global Affairs,* April 10, 2018, https://eng.globalaffairs.ru/articles/a-new-world-order-a-view-from-russia.

45. Zhou Xin and Sarah Zheng, "Xi Jinping Rallies China for Decades-Long 'Struggle' to Rise in Global Order, amid Escalating US Trade War," *South China Morning Post,* September 5, 2019.

46. Xi Jinping, "Secure a Decisive Victory in Building a Moderately Prosperous Society in All Respects and Strive for the Great Success of Socialism with Chinese Characteristics for a New Era," speech at the 19th National Congress of the Communist Party of China, Beijing, October 18, 2017, http://www.xinhuanet.com/english/download/Xi_Jinping's_report_at_19th_CPC_National_Congress.pdf. See also Xi Jinping, speech at the Reception in Celebration of the 70th Anniversary of the Founding of the People's Republic of China, Beijing, September 30, 2019, https://www.fmprc.gov.cn/mfa_eng/wjdt_665385/zyjh_665391/t1704400.shtml.

47. For commentators on the "China threat theory," see Xiang Yi, "US Should Take a Long, Hard Look in the Mirror Rather than Blaming China," *People's Daily,* May 28, 2019, http://en.people.cn/n3/2019/0528/c90000-9582218.html; 刘卫东 [Liu Weidong], "新一轮'中国威胁论'意欲何为?" [What is the intention behind the new round of "China threat theory"?], *QS Theory,* August 11, 2018, http://www.qstheory.cn/dukan/hqwg/2018-08/11/c_1123251001.htm; 释清仁 [Shi Qingren], "从容淡定应对'中国威胁论'" [Calmly responding to the "China threat theory"], *China Youth Daily,* April 6, 2012, http://zqb.cyol.com/html/2012-04/06/nw.D110000zgqnb_20120406_1-09.htm; 鲁世巍 [Lu Shiwei], "新一轮'中国威胁论': 解析与应对" [A new round of "China threat theory": analysis and response], *Aisixiang,* August 10, 2013, http://www.aisixiang.com/data/66591.html; 胡泽熙 [Hu Zexi], "'中国威胁论'为何成美心魔? 相对实力下降系根源" [Why the "China threat theory" became Washington's "demon"? The Decline in Relative Strength is the Root Cause], *Sina,* March 1, 2018; 徐进 [Xu Jin], "新一轮'中国威胁论'具有三大特点" [The new "China threat theory" has three characteristics], *Beijing Daily News,* February 18, 2019; 俞邃 [Yu Sui], "我看'中国威胁论'" [My view of the "China threat theory"], *Global Times,* April 2, 2018, https://opinion.huanqiu.com/article/9CaKrnK7i8b.

48. On big security, Julian Gewirtz, "The Chinese Reassessment of Interdependence," *China Leadership Monitor,* June 1, 2020, https://www.prcleader.org/gewirtz; Weixing Hu, "Xi Jinping's 'Big Power Diplomacy' and China's Central National Security Commission (CNSC)," *Journal of Contemporary China* 25, no. 98 (2016): 163–177; "十四, 坚决维护国家主权'安全'发展利益(习近平新时代中国特色 社会主义思想学习纲要" [Resolutely safeguard national sovereignty, security, and development interests (Xi Jinping's study outline of socialism with Chinese characteristics for a new era)], *People's Daily,* August 9, 2019, http://politics.people.com.cn/n1/2019/0809/c1001-31284589.html. On self-reliance and mastering core technologies, Orange Wang and Zhou Xin, "Xi Jinping Says Trade War Pushes China to Rely on Itself and 'That's Not a Bad Thing,'" *South China Morning Post,* September 26, 2018; "Core Technology Depends on One's Own Efforts: President Xi," *People's Daily* (CRI Online), April 19, 2018, 8:25, http://en.people.cn/n3/2018/0419/c90000-9451186.html. On reducing reliance on Western technology, Chris Buckley and Paul Mozur, "What Keeps Xi

Jinping Awake at Night," *New York Times,* May 11, 2018; Julian Baird Gewirtz, "China's Long March to Technological Supremacy," *Foreign Affairs,* August 27, 2019.

49. See, for example, 姚洋 [Yao Yang], "警惕中美脱钩论中的利益企图" [Be alert to the interests behind China-U.S. decoupling], Peking University, August 13, 2019, http://nsd.pku.edu.cn/sylm/gd/495979.htm; Zeng Peiyan, "US-China Trade and Economic Relations: What Now, What Next," speech at the CCIEE-Brookings-LKYSPP International Symposium on US and China: Forging a Common Cause for the Development of Asia and the World, Singapore, October 30–31, 2019; Gewirtz, "The Chinese Reassessment of Interdependence."

50. For Xi's quote, see "Xi's article on China's science, innovation development to be published," *Xinhua,* March 15, 2021, http://www.xinhuanet.com/english/2021-03/15/c_139812141.htm; for discussion of China's 14th five-year plan, see Lauren Dudley, "China's Quest for Self-Reliance in the Fourteenth Five-Year Plan," *Council on Foreign Relations,* March 8, 2021, https://www.cfr.org/blog/chinas-quest-self-reliance-fourteenth-five-year-plan; for China's movements with respect to core technologies, such as semiconductors, see Elizabeth Chen, "Semiconductor Scandal a Concerning Backdrop to Xi's Pursuit of 'Core Technologies,'" *Jamestown Foundation,* March 26, 2021, https://jamestown.org/program/semiconductor-scandal-a-concerning-backdrop-to-xis-pursuit-of-core-technologies/.

51. On Africa being left behind, see Angus Deaton, *The Great Escape: Health, Wealth, and the Origins of Inequality* (Princeton, NJ: Princeton University Press, 2013), 5, 218–219; for the effects of globalization on Africa, see Antony Njau Ntuli, "Is Globalisation Good for Sub-Saharan Africa? Threats and Opportunities," Transformation, Integration and Globalization Economic Research Working Paper No. 66, October 2004, https://www.econstor.eu/bitstream/10419/140718/1/394318943.pdf; Ninsin, "Introduction: Globalization and Africa—A Subjective View," 9–10.

52. See Walter Rodney, *How Europe Underdeveloped Africa* (Baltimore, MD: Black Classic Press, 2011); Branko Milanovic, "The Two Faces of Globalization: Against Globalization as We Know It," *World Development* 31, no. 4 (2003): 667–683.

53. Dani Rodrik, "Premature Deindustrialization," National Bureau of Economic Research, Working Paper No. 20935, February 2015, https://www.nber.org/papers/w20935.pdf; Ian Taylor, "Dependency Redux: Why Africa Is Not Rising," *Review of African Political Economy* 43, no. 147 (2016): 8–25.

54. Alhaji Ahmadu Ibrahim, "The Impact of Globalization on Africa," *International Journal of Humanities and Social Sciences* 3, no. 15 (2013): 88.

55. Republic of Mozambique–International Monetary Fund "Africa Rising" Conference, Maputo, Mozambique, May 29–30, 2014; Christine Lagarde, "Africa Rising—Building to the Future," speech at the "Africa Rising" Conference, May 29, 2014, https://www.imf.org/en/News/Articles/2015/09/28/04/53/sp052914; Noah Smith, "The Future Is in Africa, and China Knows It," Bloomberg, September 20, 2018; Noah Smith, "Africa's Only Hope Is Industrialization," Bloomberg, April 23, 2019.

56. "Africa is on the move: Barack Obama," *Free Press Journal,* July 26, 2015, https://www.freepressjournal.in/world/africa-is-on-the-move-barack-obama.

57. For the Flying Geese paradigm of development, see Kaname Akamatsu, "A Historical Pattern of Economic Growth in Developing Countries," *The Developing Economies*

1, no. S1 (1962): 3–25; for the final quote, see Justin Yifu Lin, "China and the Global Economy," *China Economic Journal* 4, no., 1 (2011): 1–14. See also Irene Yuan Sun, *The Next Factory of the World: How Chinese Investment Is Reshaping Africa* (Cambridge, MA: Harvard Business Review Press, 2017).

58. Xi Jinping, "Work Together for Common Development and a Shared Future," 2018 Beijing Summit of the Forum On China–Africa Cooperation (speech, Beijing, China, September 3, 2018), http://www.xinhuanet.com/english/2018-09/03/c_129946189.htm.

59. Taylor, "Dependency Redux," 15–16; Rodney, *How Europe Underdeveloped Africa.*

60. Pádraig Carmody, *The New Scramble for Africa,* 2nd ed. (Cambridge: Polity Press, 2016); Pádraig Carmody, *The Rise of the BRICS in Africa: The Geopolitics of South-South Relations* (London: Zed Books, 2013); Charles Mangwiro, "BRICS Won't Colonise Africa," *Southern Times,* April 14, 2013, http://panafricannews.blogspot.com/2013/04/won-colonize-africa.html.

61. Andrew Brooks, "Was Africa Rising? Narratives of Development Success and Failure among the Mozambican Middle Class," *Territory, Politics, Governance* 6, no. 4 (2018): 447–467; Henning Melber, ed., *The Rise of Africa's Middle Class: Myths, Realities and Critical Engagements* (London: Zed Books, 2016); Oluyele Akinkugbe and Karl Wohlmuth, "Africa's Middle Class, Africa's Entrepreneurs and the 'Missing Middle,'" in *The Rise of Africa's Middle Class,* ed. Henning Melber (London: Zed Books, 2016), 69–94; "A Majority of Africans Say National Economic Conditions Are Bad," Afrobarometer, October 1, 2013, https://afrobarometer.org/sites/default/files/press-release/round-5-releases/ab_r5_pr_economic_conditions.pdf; Thandika Mkandawire, "Can Africa Turn from Recovery to Development?," *Current History,* May 2014, 171–177.

62. Paul Collier, *The Bottom Billion: Why the Poorest Countries Are Failing and What Can Be Done about It* (New York: Oxford University Press, 2007), 5–8.

Part IV

1. Corinne Purtill, "It Took the Inventor of the Rubik's Cube a Month to Solve His Own Puzzle," *Quartz,* March 19, 2017, https://qz.com/935952/it-took-the-inventor-of-the-rubiks-cube-a-month-to-solve-his-own-puzzle/.

2. See, for example, Cars Hommes, "Behavioral and Experimental Macroeconomics and Policy Analysis: A Complex Systems Approach," *Journal of Economic Literature* 59, no. 1 (2021): 149–219; Amandine Orsini et al., "Forum: Complex Systems and International Governance," *International Studies Review* 22, no. 4 (2020): 1008–1038; Fariborz Zelli, Lasse Gerrits, and Ina Möller, "Global Governance in Complex Times: Exploring New Concepts and Theories on Institutional Complexity," *Complexity, Governance and Networks* 6, no. 1 (2020): 1–13; Thomas Oatley, "Toward a Political Economy of Complex Interdependence," *European Journal of International Relations* 25, no. 4 (2019): 957–978; Andrew G. Haldane and Arthur E. Turrell, "An Interdisciplinary Model for Macroeconomics," *Oxford Review Economic Policy* 34 (2018): 219–251; Stefano Battiston et al., "Complexity Theory and Financial Regulation: Economic Policy Needs Interdisciplinary Network Analysis and Behavioral Modeling," *Science* 351 (2016): 818–819; W. Brian Arthur, "Complexity Economics: A Different Framework for Economic Thought," ch. 1 in W. Brian Arthur, *Complexity and the Economy* (Oxford: Oxford University Press, 2015); Joost Pauwelyn, "At the Edge of Chaos? Foreign Investment Law

as a Complex Adaptive System, How It Emerged and How It Can Be Reformed," *ICSID Review* 29 (2014): 372–418.

Ch. 13: Kaleidoscopic Complexity

1. Mike Hulme, "Why We Disagree about Climate Change," *The Carbon Yearbook,* https://www.mikehulme.org/wp-content/uploads/2009/10/Hulme-Carbon-Yearbook.pdf; David Wallace-Wells, *The Uninhabitable Earth: Life after Warming* (New York: Tim Duggan Books, 2019), 143. During the early days of the pandemic, we wrote about the kaleidoscopic complexity of the coronavirus; Anthea Roberts and Nicolas Lamp, "Is the Virus Killing Globalization? There's No One Answer," *Barron's,* March 15, 2020, https://www.barrons.com/articles/is-the-virus-killing-globalization-theres-no-one-answer-51584209741.

2. Paul Wilmott and David Orrell, *The Money Formula: Dodgy Finance, Pseudo Science, and How Mathematicians Took Over the Markets* (Chichester: John Wiley & Sons Ltd., 2017), 150.

3. Mike Hulme, *Why We Disagree about Climate Change* (Cambridge: Cambridge University Press, 2009), 325.

4. For the description of the uneven impact of climate change as one of the "historical ironies of climate change that would better be called cruelties," see Wallace-Wells, *The Uninhabitable Earth,* 24; for "suffer worst and first," see Bradley C. Parks and J. Timmons Roberts, "Globalization, Vulnerability to Climate Change, and Perceived Injustice," *Society and Natural Resource* 19, no. 4 (2006): 341.

5. The People's Republic of China State Council, "China's Policies and Actions for Addressing Climate Change," white paper, November 22, 2011, http://english.www.gov.cn/archive/white_paper/2014/09/09/content_281474986284685.htm.

6. "Dead or Comatose?," *The Globalist,* July 12, 2001, https://www.theglobalist.com/dead-or-comatose/.

7. On historical per capita emissions: Zhong Li Ding et al., "Control of Atmospheric CO_2 Concentrations by 2050: A Calculation on the Emission Rights of Different Countries," *Science in China Series D: Earth Sciences* 52, no. 10 (2009): 1447–1469; Fei Teng et al., "Metric of Carbon Equity: Carbon Gini Index Based on Historical Cumulative Emission per Capita," *Advances in Climate Change Research* 2, no. 3 (2001): 134–140. On carbon equity: 何建坤 [He Jiankun], 刘滨 [Liu Bin], and 陈文颖 [Chen Wenying], "有关全球气候变化问题上的公平性分析" (Analysis on the equity of global climate change issues), 中国人口资源与环境 [*China Population Resources and Environment*] 14, no. 6 (2004): 12–15; 潘家华 [Pan Jiahua], "满足基本需求的碳预算及其国际公平与可持续含义" [Carbon budget for basic needs satisfaction: implications for international equity and sustainability), 国际政治与经济 [*World Economics and Politics*] 1 (2008): 35–42; 潘家华 [Pan Jiahua] and 郑艳 [Zheng Yan], "基于人际公平的碳排放概念及其理论含义" (Responsibility and individual equity for carbon emissions rights), 国际政治与经济 [*World Economics and Politics*] 10 (2009): 6–16.

8. Jill Lawler, "Children's Vulnerability to Climate Change and Disaster Impacts in East Asia and the Pacific," UNICEF Technical Paper, 2011, https://www.unicef.org/media/files/Climate_Change_Regional_Report_14_Nov_final.pdf; Donovan Burton, Johanna Mustelin, and Peter Urich, "Climate Change Impacts on Children in the Pacific: A Focus on Kiribati and Vanuatu," UNICEF Technical Report, 2011, https://reliefweb.int/sites/reliefweb.int/files/resources/Children_and_Climate_Change_.pdf.

9. Nobuo Mimura, "Vulnerability of Island Countries in the South Pacific to Sea Level Rise and Climate Change," *Climate Research* 12 (1999): 137–143; Anita Augustin, "Globalization Challenges for Small Island Developing States," unpublished thesis, University of Trier, 2007, https://www.academia.edu/1889824/GLOBALIZATION_CHALLENGES_FOR_SMALL_ISLAND_DEVELOPING_STATES; Adele Thomas et al., "Climate Change and Small Island Developing States," *Annual Review of Environment and Resources* 45, no. 1 (2020), 1–27.

10. Anote Tong, "While My Island Nation Sinks, Australia Is Doing Nothing to Solve Climate Change," *Guardian,* October 10, 2018.

11. Pacific Islands Forum Secretariat, "Forty-Fourth Pacific Islands Forum Communiqué," September 5, 2013, 10, http://www.unohrlls.org/UserFiles/2013_Forum_Communique1(2).pdf; see also Pacific Islands Forum Secretariat, "Forty-Ninth Pacific Islands Forum Communiqué," September 6, 2018, 4, https://www.un.org/humansecurity/wp-content/uploads/2018/09/49th-Pacific-Islands-Forum-Communiqu%C3%A9.pdf.

12. Pacific Islands Forum Secretariat, "Pacific Islands Forum Statement: Blue Pacific's Call for Urgent Global Climate Change Action," May 15, 2019, https://www.forumsec.org/pacific-islands-forum-statement-blue-pacifics-call-for-urgent-global-climate-change-action/.

13. Pacific Islands Forum Secretariat, "Call for Urgent Action."

14. Shyam Saran, "Paris Climate Talks: Developed Countries Must Do More than Reduce Emissions," *Guardian,* November 23, 2015.

15. The People's Republic of China State Council, "China's Policies and Actions"; Zhang Chun, "What Is China's Position at Paris Climate Talks?," *China Dialogue,* November 30, 2015, https://www.chinadialogue.net/article/show/single/en/8356-What-is-China-s-position-at-Paris-climate-talks-.

16. Sunita Narain et al., "Climate Change: Perspectives from India," United Nations Development Programme, Lasting Solutions for Development Challenges, November 2009, 33, https://www.undp.org/content/dam/india/docs/undp_climate_change.pdf.

17. Pacific Islands Forum Secretariat, "Call for Urgent Action," Pacific Islands Forum, May 15, 2019, https://www.forumsec.org/2019/05/15/pacific-islands-forum-statement-blue-pacifics-call-for-urgent-global-climate-change-action/ (emphasis added).

18. Marian L. Tupy, "How the Profit Motive Can Help Fight Climate Change," CATO Institute, August 3, 2018, https://www.cato.org/publications/commentary/how-profit-motive-can-help-fight-climate-change.

19. Jason Hickel, "Time for Degrowth: To Save the Planet, We Must Shrink the Economy," *The Conversation,* August 23, 2016; Jonathan Watts, "Vaclav Smil: 'Growth Must End. Our Economist Friends Don't Seem to Realise That,'" *Guardian,* September 21, 2019.

20. Noah Smith (@Noahpinion), Twitter, February 14, 2020, 2:54 a.m., https://twitter.com/Noahpinion/status/1228225976804335616 ("I can't find it now, but someone wrote that degrowth is 'the abstinence education of climate policy,' and that's exactly correct").

21. For example, the Canadian government has negotiated a Pan-Canadian Framework on Clean Growth and Climate Change that aims to "address climate change and grow the economy." See Environment and Climate Change Canada, *Pan-Canadian Framework*

on Clean Growth and Climate Change: Canada's Plan to Address Climate Change and Grow the Economy (Gatineau, Canada: Environment and Climate Change Canada, 2016), 4, http://publications.gc.ca/collections/collection_2017/eccc/En4-294-2016-eng.pdf. The International Energy Agency has also released data tracking the decoupling of global emissions and economic growth. See "Decoupling of Global Emissions and Economic Growth Confirmed," International Energy Agency, March 16, 2016.

22. Yamiche Alcindor, "In Sweltering South, Climate Change Is Now a Workplace Hazard," *New York Times,* August 3, 2017.

23. Tim Arango, "'Turn off the Sunshine': Why Shade Is a Mark of Privilege in Los Angeles," *New York Times,* December 1, 2019.

24. Sam Bloch, "Shade," *Places Journal,* April 2019; "UN Expert Condemns Failure to Address Impact of Climate Change on Poverty," Office of the High Commissioner for Human Rights, United Nations, June 25, 2019, https://www.ohchr.org/EN/NewsEvents/Pages/DisplayNews.aspx?NewsID=24735&LangID=E; Wallace-Wells, *The Uninhabitable Earth,* 24.

25. Mitch Smith and John Schwartz, "In Flood-Hit Midwest, Mayors See Climate Change as a Subject Best Avoided," *New York Times,* May 15, 2019.

26. Patrick Chamorel, "Macron versus the Yellow Vests," *Journal of Democracy* 30, no. 4 (2019): 51.

27. Jonas Anshelm and Martin Hultman, "A Green Fatwa? Climate Change as a Threat to Masculinity of Industrial Modernity," *International Journal for Masculinity Studies* 9 (2013): 84–96; Paul Pulé and Martin Hultman, "Industrial/Breadwinner Masculinities and Climate Change: Understanding the 'White Male Effect' of Climate Change Denial," in *Climate Hazards, Disasters and Gender Ramifications,* ed. Catarina Kinvall and Helle Rydstrom (London: Routledge, 2019).

28. Hettie O'Brien, "Climate Denialism Is Rooted in a Reactionary Form of Masculinity," *New Statesman,* September 18, 2019, https://www.newstatesman.com/politics/environment/2019/09/climate-denialism-rooted-reactionary-form-masculinity. See also Aaron M. McCright and Riley E. Dunlap, "Cool Dudes: The Denial of Climate Change among Conservative White Males in the United States," *Global Environmental Change* 21 (2011): 1163–1172; Olve Krange, Bjørn P. Kaltenborn, and Martin Hultman, "Cool Dudes in Norway: Climate Change Denial among Conservative Norwegian Men," *Environmental Sociology* 5 (2018): 1–11.

29. Orlando Crowcroft, "#FridaysForHubraum: German Car Lovers Mock Greta's Climate Movement with New Hashtag," *Euro News,* September 27, 2019, https://www.euronews.com/2019/09/27/fridaysforhubraum-german-car-lovers-mock-greta-s-climate-movement-with-new-hashtag.

30. Cas Mudde, *The Far Right Today* (Cambridge: Polity Press, 2019), 172–173.

31. Megan MacKenzie, "Is Fragile Masculinity the Biggest Obstacle to Climate Action?," ABC (Australia), December 14, 2019.

32. O'Brien, "Climate Denialism"; Martin Gelin, "The Misogyny of Climate Deniers," *New Republic,* August 28, 2019, https://newrepublic.com/article/154879/misogyny-climate-deniers; Vivian Kane, "A Lot of Grown-Ass Men Sure Do Seem to Feel Threatened by Teen Climate Activist Greta Thunberg," *Mary Sue,* August 16, 2019, https://www.themarysue.com/greta-thunberg-harassment-online/; Amanda Marcotte, "Why They're Scared of Greta: Youth Climate Activist Has the Trolls in Retreat," *Salon,* September 24, 2019,

https://www.salon.com/2019/09/24/why-theyre-scared-of-greta-youth-climate-activist-has-the-trolls-in-retreat/.

33. Shannon Proudfoot, "Why Would Anyone Hate Catherine McKenna?," *Maclean's,* November 4, 2019.

34. Gelin, "The Misogyny of Climate Deniers."

35. Joshua Conrad Jackson et al., "Ecological and Cultural Factors Underlying the Global Distribution of Prejudice," *PloS One* 14, no. 9 (2019): e0221953; Joshua Conrad Jackson and Michele Gelfand, "Could Climate Change Fuel the Rise of Right-Wing Nationalism?," *The Conversation,* September 25, 2019, https://theconversation.com/could-climate-change-fuel-the-rise-of-right-wing-nationalism-123503; Kate Aronoff, "The European Far Right's Environmental Turn," *Dissent,* May 31, 2019, https://www.dissentmagazine.org/online_articles/the-european-far-rights-environmental-turn; Naomi Klein, "Only a Green New Deal Can Douse the Fires of Eco-Fascism," *The Intercept,* September 16, 2019, https://theintercept.com/2019/09/16/climate-change-immigration-mass-shootings/?comments=1; Naomi Klein, *On Fire* (New York: Simon & Schuster, 2019), 45; Sarah Manavis, "Eco-fascism: The Ideology Marrying Environmentalism and White Supremacy Thriving Online," *New Statesman,* September 21, 2018, https://www.newstatesman.com/science-tech/social-media/2018/09/eco-fascism-ideology-marrying-environmentalism-and-white-supremacy.

36. Mark Musser, "Inside the Christchurch Killer's Mind," *American Thinker,* March 31, 2019. The El Paso shooter represents another example. See Natasha Lennard, "The El Paso Shooter Embraced Eco-Fascism. We Can't Let the Far Right Co-Opt the Environmental Struggle," *The Intercept,* August 5, 2019, https://theintercept.com/2019/08/05/el-paso-shooting-eco-fascism-migration/.

37. Alvin Cheung-Miaw and Max Elbaum, "Climate Change. War. Poverty. How the U.S.-China Relationship Will Shape Humanity's Path," *In These Times,* March 21, 2019, http://inthesetimes.com/article/21799/china-united-states-trump-war-poverty-imperialism-climate-change-diplomacy.

38. John Helveston and Jonas Nahm, "China's Key Role in Scaling Low-Carbon Energy Technologies," *Science* 366, no. 6467 (2019): 794–796.

39. Daniel R. Coats, Director of National Intelligence, for the Senate Select Committee on Intelligence, "Worldwide Threat Assessment of the US Intelligence Community," January 29, 2019, 21–23, https://www.dni.gov/files/ODNI/documents/2019-ATA-SFR--SSCI.pdf; U.S. Department of Defense, "Quadrennial Defense Review 2014," vi, 8, 25, https://dod.defense.gov/Portals/1/Documents/pubs/2014_Quadrennial_Defense_Review.pdf; see also U.S. Department of Defense, "Quadrennial Defense Review 2010," 84–85, https://history.defense.gov/Portals/70/Documents/quadrennial/QDR2010.pdf?ver=2014-08-24-144223-573; CNA Military Advisory Board, "National Security and the Accelerating Risks of Climate Change," 2014, 2, 7, https://www.cna.org/cna_files/pdf/MAB_5-8-14.pdf; Melissa Clarke, "Defence Chief's Speech: Climate Change 'May Stretch Our Capability,'" ABC (Australia), audio, 3:40, September 25, 2019, https://www.abc.net.au/radio/programs/am/climate-change-may-stretch-our-capability/11545162.

40. Kathy Mulvey et al., "The Climate Deception Dossiers: Internal Fossil Fuel Industry Memos Reveal Decades of Corporate Disinformation," Union of Concerned Scientists, June 29, 2015, 9, https://www.ucsusa.org/sites/default/files/attach/2015/07/The-Climate-Deception-Dossiers.pdf; Geoffrey Supran and Naomi Oreskes, "Assessing Exxon-

Mobil's Climate Change Communications (1977–2014)," *Environmental Research Letters* 12, no. 8 (2017): 1–18.

41. "The Carbon Majors Database: CDP Carbon Majors Report," CDP, 2017, 8.

42. "The Carbon Majors Database." See also B. Ekwurzel et al., "The Rise in Global Atmospheric CO_2, Surface Temperature, and Sea Level from Emissions Traced to Major Carbon Producers," *Climatic Change* 144 (2017): 579–590.

43. "Big Oil's Real Agenda on Climate Change," Influence Map, March 2019, https://influencemap.org/report/How-Big-Oil-Continues-to-Oppose-the-Paris-Agreement-38212275958aa21196dae3b76220bddc; Sandra Laville, "Top Oil Firms Spending Millions Lobbying to Block Climate Change Policies, Says Report," *Guardian,* March 22, 2019; Peter C. Frumhoff and Naomi Oreskes, "Fossil Fuel Firms Are Still Bankrolling Climate Denial Lobby Groups," *Guardian,* March 25, 2015; Robert J. Brulle, "The Climate Lobby: A Sectoral Analysis of Lobbying Spending on Climate Change in the USA, 2000 to 2016," *Climatic Change* 149 (2018): 289–303.

44. Roberts and Lamp, "Is the Virus Killing Globalization?"

45. Thomas J. Bollyky and Chad P. Bown, "The Tragedy of Vaccine Nationalism," *Foreign Affairs,* July 27, 2020.

46. Chad P. Bown, "Trump's Trade Policy Is Hampering the US Fight against COVID-19," Peterson Institute for International Economics, March 13, 2020, https://www.piie.com/blogs/trade-and-investment-policy-watch/trumps-trade-policy-hampering-us-fight-against-covid-19.

47. Simon J. Everett, "Tackling Coronavirus: The Trade Policy Dimension," Global Trade Alert, March 11, 2020, https://www.globaltradealert.org/reports/50; "New Trade Barriers Could Hamper the Supply of Masks and Medicines," *Economist,* March 11, 2020; Shawn Donnan, "The Pandemic Protectionism Is Spreading," Bloomberg, April 6, 2020, https://www.bloomberg.com/news/articles/2020-04-06/supply-chains-latest-the-pandemic-protectionists-are-winning; World Trade Organization, "COVID-19 and Beyond: Trade and Health: Communication from Australia, Brazil, Canada, Chile, the European Union, Japan, Kenya, Republic of Korea, Mexico, New Zealand, Norway, Singapore and Switzerland," WT/GC/223, November 24, 2020.

48. Mark Trumbull, "Why COVID-19 Is Likely to Change Globalization, Not Reverse It," *Christian Science Monitor,* March 9, 2020; Ed Conway, "Coronavirus Can Trigger a New Industrial Revolution," *Times* (London), March 5, 2020.

49. Carmen Paun, "Populists Seize on Coronavirus to Stoke Immigration Fear," Politico, February 18, 2020, https://www.politico.eu/article/populists-cite-coronavirus-outbreak-to-advance-anti-immigration-agenda/.

50. Lorenzo Quadri is quoted in Matina Stevis-Gridneff, "Coronavirus Nightmare Could Be the End for Europe's Borderless Dream," *New York Times,* February 26, 2020; for Trump's tweets, see Maanvi Singh, "'We Need the Wall!': Trump Twists Coronavirus Fears to Push His Own Agenda," *Guardian,* March 11, 2020; Donald J. Trump (@realDonaldTrump), Twitter, March 23, 2020, 10:16 a.m., https://www.thetrumparchive.com/.

51. Luke McGee, "Self-Isolate or Get Paid? That's the Choice for Gig Workers in a Virus Outbreak, and It's a Big Problem for the Rest of Us," CNN, March 8, 2020.

52. Steve Neale, "'Inequality Is a Comorbidity': AOC Backs Coronavirus Relief 'With a Lens of Reparations,'" *Washington Examiner,* April 3, 2020, https://www.washington examiner.com/news/inequality-is-a-comorbidity-aoc-backs-coronavirus-relief-with-a-lens -of-reparations (emphasis added).

53. Stephen Burgen and Sam Jones, "Poor and Vulnerable Hardest Hit by Pandemic in Spain," *Guardian,* April 1, 2020.

54. "The Companies Putting Profits Ahead of Public Health," editorial, *New York Times,* March 14, 2020.

55. Seth McLaughlin, "America 'Only as Safe as the Least Insured Person,' Sanders Says Regarding Coronavirus Emergency," *Washington Times,* March 13, 2020, https://www .washingtontimes.com/news/2020/mar/13/coronavirus-only-safe-least-insured-bernie -sanders/.

56. Bernie Sanders, "Coronavirus Speech Transcript," March 12, 2020, https://www .rev.com/blog/transcripts/bernie-sanders-coronavirus-speech-transcript-march-12-2020.

57. Laurie McGinley and Carolyn Y. Johnson, "Coronavirus Raises Fears of U.S. Drug Supply Disruptions," *Washington Post,* February 26, 2020; Christine Crudo Blackburn et al., "The Silent Threat of the Coronavirus: America's Dependence on Chinese Pharmaceuticals," *The Conversation,* February 11, 2020, https://theconversation.com/the-silent -threat-of-the-coronavirus-americas-dependence-on-chinese-pharmaceuticals-130670; Nathan Picarsic and Emily de La Bruyère, "The Reach of China's Military-Civil Fusion: Coronavirus and Supply Chain Crises," *Real Clear Defense,* March 4, 2020, https://www .realcleardefense.com/articles/2020/03/04/the_reach_of_chinas_military-civil_fusion _coronavirus_and_supply_chain_crises_115092.html; Yanzhong Huang, "U.S. Dependence on Pharmaceutical Products from China," Council on Foreign Relations, August, 14, 2019, https://www.cfr.org/blog/us-dependence-pharmaceutical-products-china?mod=article _inline.

58. For controlling supplies, see Rosemary Gibson, "Time to Act: Author Warns of U.S. Dependence on China Drugs," *American Association for Physician Leadership,* August 12, 2019, https://www.physicianleaders.org/news/dependence-on-china-drugs; for the potential for drug supplies to be weaponized, see Hearing Exploring the Growing U.S. Reliance on China's Biotech and Pharmaceutical Products, Before the U.S.-China Economic and Security Review Commission, 116th Congress, 1st Session (July 31, 2019). See also Rosemary Gibson and Janardan Prasad Singh, *China Rx: Exposing the Risks of America's Dependence on China for Medicine* (Amherst, NY: Prometheus Books, 2018).

59. Nathan Vanderklippe and Ivan Semeniuk, "CanSino Blames Chinese Officials for Abandonment of Joint Vaccine Program with Canada," *Globe and Mail,* August 25, 2020; Sam Cooper, "China Blamed for Canada's Multimillion-Dollar Coronavirus Vaccine Deal Collapse," *Global News,* August 27, 2020.

60. Donald J. Trump, "Remarks by President Trump and Members of the Coronavirus Force in Meeting with Pharmaceutical Companies," March 2, 2020, https:// trumpwhitehouse.archives.gov/briefings-statements/remarks-president-trump-members -coronavirus-task-force-meeting-pharmaceutical-companies/; Ana Swanson, "Coronavirus Spurs U.S. Efforts to End China's Chokehold on Drugs," *New York Times,* March 11, 2020.

61. "Coronavirus: Trump Stands by China Lab Origin Theory," BBC, May 1, 2020; Chris Buckley and Steven Lee Myers, "From 'Respect' to 'Sick and Twisted': How Corona-

virus Hit U.S.-China Ties," *New York Times,* May 15, 2020; Colum Lynch and Robbie Gramer, "U.S. and China Turn Coronavirus into a Geopolitical Football," *Foreign Policy,* March 11, 2020; Hua Chunying, "Foreign Ministry Spokesperson Hua Chunying's Regular Press Conference," Ministry of Foreign Affairs of the People's Republic of China, April 2, 2020, https://www.fmprc.gov.cn/mfa_eng/xwfw_665399/s2510_665401/2511_665403/t1765251.shtml; Jin Canrong, "West's Arrogance Key Obstacle to Solidarity in Global Pandemic Fight," *Global Times,* April 7, 2020, https://www.globaltimes.cn/content/1184885.shtml.

62. Elena Collinson and Thomas Pantle, "Australia-PRC Trade and Investment Developments: a Timeline," Australia-China Relations Institute, last updated on March 2, 2021, https://www.australiachinarelations.org/content/australia-prc-trade-and-investment-developments-timeline; Jeffrey Wilson, "Adapting Australia to an Era of Geoeconomic Competition," video posted February 16, 2021, https://perthusasia.edu.au/our-work/adapting-australia-to-an-era-of-geoeconomic-compet.

63. Elizabeth Dwoskin, "Tech Giants Are Profiting—and Getting More Powerful—Even as the Global Economy Tanks," *Washington Post,* April 27, 2020.

64. Matt Phillips, "Investors Bet Giant Companies Will Dominate after Crisis," *New York Times,* April 28, 2020.

65. Ian Mosby and Sarah Rotz, "As Meat Plants Shut Down, COVID-19 Reveals the Extreme Concentration of Our Food Supply," *Globe and Mail,* April 29, 2020; Sophie Kevany, "Millions of Farm Animals Culled as US Food Supply Chain Chokes Up," *Guardian,* April 29, 2020; Executive Office of the President, Delegating Authority Under the Defence Production Act With Respect to Food Supply Chain Resources during the National Emergency Caused by the Outbreak of COVID-19, Executive Order No. 13 917, 85 Fed. Reg. 26313, May 1, 2020.

66. "COVID-19 Reduces Economic Activity, Which Reduces Pollution, Which Saves Lives," G-Feed (Global Food, Environment and Economic Dynamics), March 8, 2020, http://www.g-feed.com/2020/03/covid-19-reduces-economic-activity.html.

67. Dr. Genevieve Guenther (@DoctorVive), "In the past 3 weeks 2,800 people in China have died from #COVID19. In three regular weeks, fossil-fuel air pollution kills over SIX TIMES that number of people," Twitter, March 1, 2020, 8:08 a.m., https://twitter.com/DoctorVive/status/1234103259679395841?s=20.

68. Abiy Ahmed, "If Covid-19 Is Not Beaten in Africa It Will Return to Haunt Us All," *Financial Times,* March 25, 2020; David Pilling et al., "Threat of Catastrophe Stalks Developing World," *Financial Times,* April 3, 2020. See generally David Finnan, "Lack of Covid-19 Treatment and Critical Care Could Be Catastrophic for Africa," RFI, March 4, 2020, http://www.rfi.fr/en/africa/20200403-lack-of-covid-19-treatment-and-critical-care-could-be-catastrophic-for-africa; Robert Malley and Richard Malley, "When the Pandemic Hits the Most Vulnerable: Developing Countries Are Hurtling towards Coronavirus Catastrophe," *Foreign Affairs,* March 31, 2020; Kelsey Piper, "The Devastating Consequences of Coronavirus Lockdowns in Poor Countries," *Vox,* April 18, 2020, https://www.vox.com/future-perfect/2020/4/18/21212688/coronavirus-lockdowns-developing-world.

69. Ahmed, "If Covid-19 Is Not Beaten"; Pilling, "Threat of Catastrophe Stalks Developing World"; Alexandre Dayant, "Aid Links: Coronavirus and the Developing World," *Lowy Institute: The Interpreter,* March 25, 2020, https://www.lowyinstitute.org/the-interpreter/aid-links-coronavirus-and-developing-world.

70. Piper, "The Devastating Consequences of Coronavirus Lockdowns"; Adam Vaughan, "Coronavirus Will Play Out Very Differently in World's Poorest Nations," *New Scientist,* April 3, 2020; Amanda Glassman, Kalipso Chalkidou, and Richard Sullivan, "Does One Size Fit All? Realistic Alternatives for COVID-19 Response in Low-Income Countries," Centre for Global Development, April 2, 2020, https://www.cgdev.org/blog/does-one-size-fit-all-realistic-alternatives-covid-19-response-low-income-countries. On what appeared at the time to be the surprisingly low death toll in South Asia and sub-Saharan Africa, see Siddhartha Mukherjee, "Why Does the Pandemic Seem to Be Hitting Some Countries Harder Than Others?," *New Yorker,* March 1, 2021.

71. Ahmed, "If Covid-19 Is Not Beaten."

72. Javier C. Hernández, "China Spins Coronavirus Crisis, Hailing Itself as a Global Leader," *New York Times,* February 28, 2020; Haifeng Huang, "China Is Also Relying on Propaganda to Tackle the Covid-19 Crisis," *Washington Post,* March 11, 2020.

73. Tan Tarn How, "Why the West's Coronavirus Response Shows It Isn't Better than the Rest of Us," *South China Morning Post,* April 6, 2020, https://www.scmp.com/week-asia/opinion/article/3078618/why-wests-coronavirus-response-shows-it-isnt-better-rest-us.

Ch. 14: Potential Alliances

1. Thomas Piketty, *Capital and Ideology* (Cambridge, MA: Harvard University Press, 2020), 719–965.

2. Chloe Farand, "Marine Le Pen Launches Presidential Campaign with Hardline Speech," *Independent,* February 5, 2017, https://www.independent.co.uk/news/world/europe/marine-le-pen-front-national-speech-campaign-launch-islamic-fundamentalism-french-elections-a7564051.html; Jonathan Haidt, "When and Why Nationalism Beats Globalism," *The American Interest,* July 10, 2016, https://www.the-american-interest.com/2016/07/10/when-and-why-nationalism-beats-globalism/; Christopher D. Johnston, Christopher M. Federico, and Howard Lavine, *Open versus Closed: Personality, Identity, and the Politics of Redistribution* (Cambridge: Cambridge University Press, 2017); David Goodhart, *The Road to Somewhere: The Populist Revolt and the Future of Politics* (London: Hurst, 2017).

3. The White House, *Interim National Security Strategic Guidance* (March 2021), 15–16, 20.

4. Greg Farrell, "Goldman Chief Defends Employees' Pay," *Financial Times,* November 10, 2009.

5. John Snow is quoted in "The Jobs We Need," editorial, *New York Times,* June 24, 2020.

6. Tamara Draut, *Sleeping Giant: How the New Working Class Will Transform America* (New York: Doubleday, 2016), 48, and see also 43–44; Thomas B. Edsall, "Why Do We Pay So Many People So Little Money?," *New York Times,* June 24, 2020.

7. Sarah O'Connor, "It Is Time to Make Amends to the Low-Paid Essential Worker," *Financial Times,* April 1, 2020.

8. Gene B. Sperling, "Martin Luther King Jr. Predicted This Moment," *New York Times,* April 24, 2020.

9. Michael J. Sandel, "Are We All in This Together? The Pandemic Has Helpfully Scrambled How We Value Everyone's Economic and Social Roles," *New York Times,* April 13, 2020; O'Connor, "It Is Time to Make Amends"; "Pflegekräfte sollen 1500 Euro Corona-Prämie erhalten" ["Nursing Staff Should Receive a Corona Bonus of 1500 Euros"], *Spiegel,* April 6, 2020; Frank Gunn, "Ford Calls Out 'Reckless' Protesters while Announcing Plan to Raise Pay of Front-Line Workers by $4 an Hour," *Globe and Mail,* April 25, 2020; "Joe Biden's 4-Point Plan for Our Essential Workers," Biden for President: Official Campaign Website, September 17, 2020, https://joebiden.com/joe-bidens-4-point-plan-for-our-essential-workers/.

10. Sandel, "Are We All in This Together?"

11. J. D. Vance, "End the Globalization Gravy Train," *American Mind,* April 21, 2020, https://americanmind.org/essays/end-the-globalization-gravy-train/.

12. Oren Cass, *The Once and Future Worker: A Vision for the Renewal of Work in America* (New York: Encounter Books, 2018), 19, 30–31.

13. Chris Arnade, *Dignity: Seeking Respect in Back Row America* (New York: Sentinel Press, 2019), 17.

14. Draut, *Sleeping Giant,* 3.

15. Cass, *The Once and Future Worker,* 6.

16. "Biden-Sanders Unity Task Force Recommendations," press release, Biden for President, July 8, 2020, https://joebiden.com/wp-content/uploads/2020/08/UNITY-TASK-FORCE-RECOMMENDATIONS.pdf.

17. "Romney 'Patriot Pay' Plan Would Support America's Frontline Workers," Mitt Romney, U.S. Senator for Utah, May 1, 2020, https://www.romney.senate.gov/romney-patriot-pay-plan-would-support-americas-frontline-workers; Sperling, "Martin Luther King Jr. Predicted This Moment."

18. *Interim National Security Strategic Guidance,* 16.

19. "The Biden-Harris Plan to Fight for Workers by Delivering on Buy America and Make It in America," Biden for President: Official Campaign Website, https://joebiden.com/the-biden-harris-plan-to-fight-for-workers-by-delivering-on-buy-america-and-make-it-in-america/.

20. See only Cass's view on a universal basic income: "We have reached a point where the rich think paying everyone else to go away represents compassionate thinking." Cass, *The Once and Future Worker,* 27.

21. Marco Rubio, "We Need a More Resilient American Economy," op-ed, *New York Times,* April 20, 2020.

22. "The Biden Plan to Rebuild U.S. Supply Chains and Ensure the U.S. Does Not Face Future Shortages of Critical Equipment," Biden for President: Official Campaign Website, https://joebiden.com/supplychains/; Phil Hogan, "Introductory Statement by Commissioner Phil Hogan at Informal Meeting of EU Trade Ministers," April 16, 2020, https://ec.europa.eu/commission/commissioners/2019-2024/hogan/announcements/introductory-statement-commissioner-phil-hogan-informal-meeting-eu-trade-ministers_en.

23. Simone D'Alessandro et al., "Feasible Alternatives to Green Growth," *Nature Sustainability* 3 (2020): 329–335; Daniel W. O'Neill, "Beyond Green Growth," *Nature*

Sustainability 3 (2020): 260–261. Along with some other modifications, we have added eco-nationalist policies to O'Neill's Venn diagram to capture some of the policies favored by green-conservative coalitions.

24. See Charles Mann's discussion of "wizards," who believe in technological solutions to problems such as climate change, compared to "prophets," who warn of doom and gloom and preach about the need to pare back. See Charles C. Mann, *The Wizard and the Prophet: Two Remarkable Scientists and Their Dueling Visions to Shape Tomorrow's World* (New York: Vintage Books, 2018).

25. Daron Acemoglu et al., "The Environment and Directed Technical Change," *American Economic Review* 102, no. 1 (2012): 131–166; Daron Acemoglu et al., "Transition to Clean Technology," *Journal of Political Economy* 124, no. 1 (2016): 52–104.

26. Jason Hickel, *Less Is More: How Degrowth Will Save the World* (Penguin Random House, 2020); Thomas Wiedmann, Manfred Lenzen, Lorenz T. Keyßler, and Julia K. Steinberger, "Scientists' Warning on Affluence," *Nature Communications* 11 (2020): 3107; Jag Bhalla, "What's Your 'Fair Share' of Carbon Emissions? You're Probably Blowing Way Past It," *Vox*, February 24, 2021; for early precursors of this approach, see Donella H. Meadows et al., *The Limits to Growth: A Report for the Club of Rome's Project on the Predicament of Mankind* (New York: Universe Books, 1972); Herman E. Daly, "The World Dynamics of Economic Growth: The Economics of the Steady State," *American Economic Review* 64, no. 2 (1974): 15–21.

27. Edward B. Barbier, *A Global Green New Deal: Rethinking the Economic Recovery* (New York: Cambridge University Press, 2010); Alex Bowen and Nicolas Stern, "Environmental Policy and the Economic Downturn," *Oxford Review of Economic Policy* 26, no. 2 (2010): 137–163.

28. For example, the argument that protectionism is better for the environment has been advanced by the Coalition for a Prosperous America; see Kenneth Rapoza, "Transoceanic Shipping: Navigating 'Global Pollution Chains,'" *Coalition for a Prosperous America*, February 4, 2021, https://prosperousamerica.org/transoceanic-shipping-navigating-global-pollution-chains/.

29. See Jonas Meckling and Bentley B. Allan, "The Evolution of Ideas in Global Climate Policy," *Nature Climate Change* 10, no. 5 (2020): 434–438.

30. Communication from the Commission to the European Parliament, the European Council, the Council, the European Economic and Social Committee, and the Committee of the Regions, "The European Green Deal," COM/2019/640 final, December 11, 2019, 2, https://eur-lex.europa.eu/legal-content/EN/TXT/?uri=COM:2019:640:FIN; "The Biden Plan to Build a Modern, Sustainable Infrastructure and an Equitable Clean Energy Future," Biden for President: Official Campaign Website, https://joebiden.com/clean-energy/.

31. "The European Green Deal"; "The Biden Plan to Build a Modern, Sustainable Infrastructure"; Jim Tankersley, "Biden Team Prepares $3 Trillion in New Spending for the Economy," *New York Times*, March 22, 2021.

32. "A Bold New Plan to Tackle Climate Change Ignores Economic Orthodoxy," *Economist*, February 7, 2019.

33. Kate Aronoff et al., *A Planet to Win: Why We Need a Green New Deal* (New York: Verso, 2019), 39, 60–65.

34. Aronoff et al., *A Planet to Win,* 162.

35. "A Political Experiment Unfolds on the Danube," editorial, *Financial Times,* January 7, 2020; "'Greencons' Are a New Political Alliance for an Uncertain Age," *Economist,* June 28, 2020; "A New Right-Wing-Green Coalition Takes Office in Austria," *Economist,* January 9, 2020.

36. "'Greencons' Are a New Political Alliance for an Uncertain Age."

Ch. 15: Globalization for Foxes

1. Isaiah Berlin, *The Hedgehog and the Fox: An Essay on Tolstoy's View of History* (Princeton, NJ: Princeton University Press, 2nd ed., 2013), 1–2.

2. Daniel W. Drezner, *The Ideas Industry: How Pessimists, Partisans, and Plutocrats Are Transforming the Marketplace of Ideas* (Oxford: Oxford University Press, 2017); David Epstein, *Range* (New York: Macmillan, 2019); Ezra Klein, *Why We're Polarized* (New York: Avid Reader Press, 2020).

3. Philip E. Tetlock, *Expert Political Judgment: How Good Is It? How Can We Know?* (Princeton, NJ: Princeton University Press, new ed., 2017), 72–75.

4. Quoted in Howard Gardner, *A Synthesizing Mind: A Memoir from the Creator of Multiple Intelligences Theory* (Cambridge, MA: The MIT Press, 2020), 216.

5. Howard Gardner, *Five Minds for the Future* (Boston: Harvard Business Review Press, 2008), 3, 46–76.

6. Roger Martin, *The Opposable Mind: How Successful Leaders Win through Integrative Thinking* (Boston: Harvard Business Review Press, 2007), 5–10; Mihnea Moldoveanu and Roger Martin, *Diaminds: Decoding the Mental Habits of Successful Thinkers* (Toronto: Rotman-University of Toronto Press Publishing, 2010), 3–8.

7. Howard Gardner, *A Synthesizing Mind,* xii–xv, 212–235.

8. For an explanation of how we can use complexity theory to shed light on these issues, see Jessica Flack and Melanie Mitchell, "Complex Systems Science Allows Us to See New Paths Forward," *Aeon,* August 23, 2020. For "Ockham's quilt," see Siddhartha Mukherjee, "Why Does the Pandemic Seem to Be Hitting Some Countries Harder Than Others?," *New Yorker,* February 22, 2021.

9. Martin, *The Opposable Mind,* 107–138.

10. For Tai's quote, see "Opening Statement of Ambassador-Designate Katherine Tai before the Senate Finance Committee," February 24, 2021. On the importance of Western actors understanding Weiqi for the purposes of strategy, including how it differs from chess, see Scott A. Boorman, *The Protracted Game: A Wei-ch'i Interpretation of Maoist Revolutionary Strategy* (New York: Oxford University Press, 1969); David Lai, *Learning from the Stones: A Go Approach to Mastering China's Strategic Concept,* Shi (May 2004), https://fas.org/man/eprint/lai.pdf. On moves against Big Tech in China, see Josh Freedman, "Why Beijing Is Bringing Big Tech to Heel: China Appreciates Monopolies It Can Control," *Foreign Affairs,* February 4, 2021; Marietje Schaake, "China's Move on Ant Makes the Fight on Big Tech Global," *Financial Times,* December 2, 2020.

11. Jennifer Garvey Berger, *Unlocking Leadership Mindtraps: How to Thrive in Complexity* (Stanford: Stanford University Press, 2019).

12. Berger, *Unlocking Leadership Mindtraps,* 73.

13. Scott E. Page, *The Diversity Bonus: How Great Teams Pay Off in the Knowledge Economy* (Princeton, NJ: Princeton University Press, 2017); Arnold J. Toynbee, *A Study of History* (London: Oxford University Press, 1961), vol. XII, 42.

14. Matthew Syed, *Rebel Ideas: The Power of Diverse Thinking* (London: John Murray, 2019), 41–67, for collectively stupid, 47.

15. On group intelligence, see Howard Rheingold, *Smart Mobs: The Next Social Revolution* (New York: Basic Books, 2003); James Surowiecki, *The Wisdom of Crowds: Why the Many Are Smarter than the Few and How Collective Wisdom Shapes Business, Economies, Societies and Nations* (New York: Anchor Books, 2005). On epistemic democracy, see Hélène E. Landemore, "Why the Many Are Smarter than the Few and Why It Matters," *Journal of Public Deliberation* 8, no.1 (2012): article 7; Hélène E. Landemore, *Democratic Reason: Politics, Collective Intelligence, and the Rule of the Many* (Princeton, NJ: Princeton University Press, 2012); Melissa Schwartzberg, "Epistemic Democracy and Its Challenges," *Annual Review of Political Science* 18 (2015): 187–203.

16. On the importance of diversity, see Scott E. Page, *The Difference: How the Power of Diversity Creates Better Groups, Firms, Schools, and Societies* (Princeton, NJ: Princeton University Press, 2007); Lu Hong and Scott E. Page, "Groups of Diverse Problem Solvers Can Outperform Groups of High-Ability Problem Solvers," *Proceedings of the National Academy of Sciences* 101, no. 46 (2004): 16385–16389; Scott E. Page, "Where Diversity Comes from and Why It Matters," *European Journal of Social Psychology* 44, no. 4 (2014): 267–279.

17. Marion Fourcade, Etienne Ollion, and Yann Algan, "The Superiority of Economists," *Journal of Economic Perspectives* 29, no. 1 (2015): 89–114; Marion Fourcade, "The Construction of a Global Profession: The Transnationalization of Economics," *American Journal of Sociology* 112, no. 1 (July 2006): 145–194.

18. "As China's Power Waxes, the West's Study of It Is Waning," *The Economist,* November 28, 2020.

19. The White House, *Interim National Security Strategic Guidance* (March 2021).

20. Robert E. Lucas, "The Industrial Revolution: Past and Future," Federal Reserve Bank of Minneapolis, 2003 Annual Report Essay, May 1, 2004, https://www.minneapolisfed.org/article/2004/the-industrial-revolution-past-and-future.

21. On loss aversion generally, see Daniel Kahneman and Amos Tversky, "Prospect Theory: An Analysis of Decision under Risk," *Econometrica* 47, no. 2 (1979): 263–292. On the sense of loss in the white working class, see Joan Williams, *White Working Class: Overcoming Class Cluelessness in America* (Cambridge, MA: Harvard Business Review Press, 2017), 67–70; on the importance of relative deprivation, see, e.g., Roger Eatwell and Matthew Goodwin, *National Populism: The Revolt against Liberal Democracy* (London: Pelican Books, 2018), 212–222.

22. For a debate about the commensurability of different values and the merits of integrating them into a single "welfare" metric, see Bernhard Hoekman and Douglas Nelson, "How Should We Think about the Winners and Losers from Globalization? A Reply to Nicolas Lamp," *European Journal of International Law* 30, no. 4 (2019): 1399–1408, and Nicolas Lamp, "How We Stop Talking past Each Other: A Rejoinder to Hoekman and Nelson's Reply to My Article on Narratives about Winners and Losers from Globalization," *EJIL:Talk!* (blog), April 24, 2020.

23. Chris Arnade, *Dignity: Seeking Respect in Back Row America* (New York: Sentinel Press, 2019), 282–284.

24. Raghuram Rajan, *The Third Pillar: How Markets and the State Leave the Community Behind* (New York: Penguin, 2019), xvii.

25. Scott Atran and Robert Axelrod, "Reframing Sacred Values," *Negotiation Journal* 24, no. 3 (2008): 221–246.

26. On different moral foundations, see Jonathan Haidt, *The Righteous Mind* (New York: Pantheon Books, 2012), 112–186; Jesse Graham, Jonathan Haidt, and Brian A. Nosek, "Liberals and Conservatives Rely on Different Sets of Moral Foundations," *Journal of Personality and Social Psychology* 96, no. 5 (2009): 1029–1046. On the difficulty of recognizing the moral foundations of those with whom you disagree, see Jonathan Haidt and Jesse Graham, "When Morality Opposes Justice: Conservatives Have Moral Intuitions That Liberals May Not Recognize," *Social Justice Research* 20, no. 1 (March 2007): 98–116.

27. Arlie Russell Hochschild, *Strangers in Their Own Land: Anger and Mourning on the American Right* (New York: New Press, 2016), 228.

28. Michael J. Sandel, "Populism, Trump, and the Future of Democracy," Open Democracy, May 9, 2018, https://www.opendemocracy.net/en/populism-trump-and-future-of-democracy/.

29. Sandel, "Populism, Trump, and the Future of Democracy."

30. This concept is adapted from David Wallace-Wells, *The Uninhabitable Earth* (New York: Duggan Books, 2019), 145.

31. On a new alliances of democracies, see Walter Russel Mead, "Transcript: Dialogues on American Foreign Policy and World Affairs: A Conversation with Former Deputy Secretary of State Antony Blinken," Hudson Institute, July 9, 2020; Sam Fleming, Jim Brunsden, and Michael Peel, "EU Proposes Fresh Alliance with US in Face of China Challenge," *Financial Times,* November 29, 2020, https://www.ft.com/content/e8e5cf90-7448-459e-8b9f-6f34f03ab77a.

32. Wallace-Wells, *The Uninhabitable Earth,* for meta-narrative, see 146; for quotes, see 145.

33. Joseph R. Biden, Jr., "Why America Must Lead Again Rescuing U.S. Foreign Policy After Trump," *Foreign Affairs,* March/April 2020.

ACKNOWLEDGMENTS

The origins of this book go back to the twin shocks of 2016: the Brexit vote in the United Kingdom and the presidential election in the United States. Like many others, we were struck by how deeply fundamental critiques of economic globalization appeared to resonate among voters in these two countries. We were also concerned about the dismissive reactions of many establishment figures toward the competing narratives. Some seemed to view the logic of economic globalization as beyond question and focused their energies on discrediting the critiques put forward by populist politicians as economically illiterate and xenophobic.

Our instincts told us there was more to the story. Although some of the populist arguments were clearly based on fabrications or half-truths, we also saw something else in the new narratives: a genuine challenge to the normative assumptions underlying the establishment's support for globalization coming from people with different experiences, perspectives, and preferences. We wanted to understand the experiences that inspired the groundswell of popular support for these narratives. What did their proponents see that we had missed? And what did those insights mean for the future of economic globalization?

In early 2017, we each began independently to identify and analyze key features of the competing narratives. For Anthea, the work of Branko Milanovic, and especially his Elephant Graph, provided a framework for thinking through different narratives. She initially focused on the left-wing and right-wing populist narratives, taking Bernie Sanders and Donald Trump as representatives of the two views. Anthea published a first take as an *EJIL:Talk!* blog post, entitled "Being Charged by an Elephant: A Story of Globalization and Inequality," in April 2017. She then began working on how changing the levels and units of analysis in examining complex issues changes what is seen and what stories are told.

For Nicolas, conversations with Dan Ciuriak about his work on asset value protection agreements at a workshop at New York University in November 2016 served as a catalyst for developing a similar framework, which he expanded into a short paper in March 2017. That paper featured the establishment, protectionist, and corporate power narratives. Nicolas remembers reading Anthea's blog post and being struck by the parallels. He subsequently incorporated the idea of mapping the different narratives onto the Elephant Graph into his paper, which was eventually published by the *European Journal of International Law*.

In 2018, Anthea focused on a new geoeconomic narrative she saw emerging based on increasing hostility and security concerns in the US-China relationship, which she, Henrique Choer Moraes, and Victor Ferguson described in a series of *Lawfare* blog posts and a follow-up article in the *Journal of International Economic Law*. At this point, we owe a debt of gratitude to our mutual friend Wolfgang Alschner, who sensed something similar in what we were doing and encouraged us to work together. In late 2018, we traded drafts and began to consider whether we could develop an overall framework for understanding these narratives—which ones were motivated by absolute or relative gains, for instance, and which resulted in horizontal or vertical hostility. We also wondered how other developments might fit in, like growing concerns about climate change.

We lived on opposite sides of the world, so our discussions took place over WhatsApp calls. Luckily, Anthea is an early bird, whereas Nicolas is a night owl. Many of these discussions therefore took place while Anthea took early morning walks or jogs in Australia and Nicolas burned the midnight oil in Canada. We explored ideas, swapped reading recommendations, and started sketching structures for showing how different narratives related to one another. (We are both strong believers in the importance of visuals and metaphors in communicating concepts.) During the course of these discussions, the first five narratives and their relationships began to take shape in a pyramid structure. On a beach walk over the Christmas break, the sustainability narrative crystallized, along with the diamond-shaped win-win, win-lose, and lose-lose structure of the narratives. The Rubik's cube as an explanatory device followed shortly afterward.

Still, we had never really met. We had an idea that excited us, but no experience writing together and no idea what sort of venue might work for publication. In February, Anthea headed off to London and, on arrival, received a message from a friend saying that Branko had posted on Twitter that he too had just arrived in London. Embracing the serendipity, the two met for dinner, leading to wide-ranging discussions, including about their current projects. Branko seemed intrigued about the narratives and framework and offered to put Anthea in touch with his editor at Harvard University Press, Ian Malcolm. That night, Anthea posted a photo of the two of them on Twitter with the message: "You know you are in a @SaskiaSassen global city when two friends from different continents realise through Twitter that they both landed in London today and can meet up for dinner. Enjoyed talking about #WinnersLosers and #geoeconomics with @BrankoMilan."

Branko emailed Ian about the project, explaining that it was "multidisciplinary in the best meaning of the term" and a "very global perspective," but "not very easy to classify . . . because it combines international relations, economics, international law etc." When Ian googled Anthea, the first thing that popped up was the tweet—another serendipitous coincidence, as he had also edited Saskia Sassen's *Global Cities*. A few days later, the two met for coffee. Fortuitously, it turned out that Ian had also edited many of the books that had shaped our thinking—from Milanovic's *Global Inequality* to Richard Baldwin's *The Great Convergence* to Thomas Piketty's *Capital in the Twenty-First Century*. Ian's books are often effectively signed over coffee, and so it transpired with this one. It seemed that the book should be out right then, Ian commented;

was it close to ready for submission? No, Anthea replied, they'd only been drafting for about eleven days at that point. So that began the whirlwind process of writing a book that sought to explore a large, complex, and fast-changing field and that encouraged us to read and think more broadly, and to question our assumptions more deeply, than we had done previously. The process was exhilarating, though often exhausting, and has taught us a lot.

It was not all smooth sailing. In addition to the usual curveballs that attend life, we directly experienced some of the developments we were writing about. Anthea was caught in the Australian bushfires and redrafted the sustainability narrative after being evacuated from the coast and while the air in Canberra was thick with smoke, making it the most polluted capital in the world. Nicolas and Anthea were both planning to travel to the United States for workshops on the draft book in March and April 2020, only to have all the sessions canceled or moved online owing to the outbreak of the novel coronavirus. This development also led to the crystallization of the resilience narrative and the decision to group both climate change and pandemics as part of a global threats narrative.

But we made it. Locked down and home-schooling young children, we finished the first draft at the end of March 2020. That we completed the draft was due in no small part to a myriad of conversations with a large number of colleagues. We are particularly grateful to the participants in our three online workshops on the first draft in April 2020: Harlan Cohen, Dan Ciuriak, Kathleen Claussen, Jeff Ferry, Miles Kahler, Jesse Kreier, Thea Lee, Simon Lester, Josh Meltzer, Tim Meyer, Mona Pinchis-Paulsen, Shubha Prasad, Bill Reinsch, Greg Shaffer, Alexandra Stark, and Marty Weiss. We are indebted to Inu Manak and Huan Zhu for their help in organizing the workshops.

We also benefited from comments on drafts and presentations, as well as materials relating to different narratives, provided to us by many others at various stages of the project, including Julian Arato, Aditya Balasubramanian, Sam Bide, Heiko Borchert, Liz Boulton, Val Braithwaite, Rachel Brewster, Colin Brown, Jesse Clarke, Deb Cleland, Christian Downie, Robin Effron, Frank Garcia, Jane Golley, Victor Ferguson, Miranda Forsyth, Tobias Gehrke, Ben Heath, Paul Hubbard, Neha Jain, Alyssa King, Francisco-José Quintana, Sebastian Lamp, Werner Lamp, Darren Lim, Sarah Logan, Katherine Mansted, Daniel Markovits, Paul Mertenskötter, Tim Meyer, Henrique Choer Moraes, Tom Moylan, Sam Moyn, Delphine Nougayrède, Mark Pollack, Sergio Puig, Prabhash Ranjan, Nina Reiners, Stefan Robel, Sabine von Schorlemer, Ashley Schram, Taylor St. John, Thomas Streinz, Michael Trebilcock, Marina Trunk-Fedorova, Sabine Tsuruda, Justina Uriburu, Tony VanDuzer, Ingo Venzke, Ken Yang, and Margaret Young.

Moreover, we owe an immense debt to some colleagues who read the entire draft, or large parts of it, and offered extensive comments: Wolfgang Alschner, Nikhil Kalyanpur, Andrew Lang, Jensen Sass, Bill Reinsch, Greg Shaffer, and Robert Wolfe. Miles Kahler pointed us toward Philip Tetlock's work, while Chris Davies helped us to realize that this book represents a "how-to guide" to thinking about complex issues more generally.

We are grateful for research assistance by James Brooymans-Quinn, Tayler Farrell, Raymond Gao, Michael Glanzel, Isabelle Guevara, Larry Hong, Towheedul

Islam, Sienna Liu, and John Nyanje. Larry deserves special mention for his exceptional engagement with the content of the book. For help with many aspects of organizing this book, we thank Susan McLean. For editing the full first draft, we thank Anna Ascher, who edited Anthea's first article with the *American Journal of International Law* and many of her other pieces since. We also owe tremendous thanks to Kay Dancey, Karina Pelling, and Jenny Sheehan from CartoGIS at the Australian National University for helping to prepare our graphics.

For his initial inspiration for this book through his work on global inequality, and for his recommendation to Ian at Harvard University Press, we are very grateful to Branko. Ian proved to be a remarkable editor for us, offering everything from cutting-edge reading recommendations to suggestions on restructuring and streamlining. Ian edits at both macro and micro levels, and offers guidance on so much more in between. We could not have wished for a better guide. We would also like to thank the two anonymous reviewers for Harvard University Press for their helpful feedback.

We are grateful to the Australian National University (ANU), whose Futures Scheme funding supported us in writing this book. University funding is often tied to specific, well-defined projects that are clearly within a scholar's existing expertise and which can be clearly mapped out in advance. This project was none of those things. We are indebted to the ANU for taking the opposite approach. In a world that often favors narrow, disciplinary contributions, this flexible funding gave us the freedom to expand our areas of expertise and to complete this broad, interdisciplinary, integrative project. We also benefited from a Social Sciences and Humanities Research Council Institutional Grant awarded by Queen's University.

Every effort has been made to identify copyright holders and obtain their permission for the use of copyright material. Notification of any additions or corrections that should be incorporated in future reprints or editions of this book would be greatly appreciated.

Finally, we would like to thank our families and our partners. We recognize that writing a book takes a toll not only on the writers but often also on their families. We further recognize that we are the product of our families, both immediate and extended. In this vein, we offer the following dedications for this book.

From Anthea: I would like to dedicate this book to my husband, Jesse; my daughters, Ashley and Freya; and my parents, Alan and Helen. Jesse and I have been following each other around the globe since our early twenties, enjoying many of the benefits of economic globalization, from study to work to tourism. In 2015, we left the bright lights of New York and London to relocate back to Australia. We love the opportunities of the wide-open world but treasure the peace, beauty, and sense of place we experience from being in our Australian home. We are Anywheres who have returned to our Somewhere. I will always be grateful for Jesse's encouragement and support in pursuing whatever path I find interesting, and for my daughters' exercise of forbearance over me reading yet "another boring book about China." Finally, I'm greatly indebted to my parents for instilling in me a lifelong love of learning and for offering suggestions and critique on everything from my school projects to this book.

From Nicolas: I would like to dedicate this book to the memory of my grandparents: Ursel and Hans-Joachim Held, and Luise and Carl Lamp. They saw the world fall apart in ways much more profound than those we are witnessing today. When Carl was seven, his father died on a hunger strike in prison, in the course of his fight for a socialist republic in post–World War I Germany. During World War II, Luise, who had been prevented from becoming a doctor, trained to become a nurse and joined her wounded husband in a field hospital. Hans-Joachim was injured as a teenager while digging anti-tank trenches in France; he learned about Nazi Germany's crimes from a Dutch forced laborer while recovering in a hospital. Ursel was an enthusiastic member of the Hitler Youth as a teenager; as a deeply disillusioned refugee in West Germany, she became an ardent advocate for socialism. I received much of my political education from listening to their stories of loss and newfound hope. I do not know whether they would have agreed with the conciliatory approach that we advocate in this book, but I know they would have loved to hold it in their hands.

INDEX

The letter *t* following a page number denotes a table; the letter *f* denotes a figure.

Abascal, Santiago, 96
Abiy Ahmed, 259, 260
Achey, Jonathan, Jr., 85, 87
acquisitions, foreign, 138–140
adjustment, 7, 44–47, 53, 77, 82, 83, 85–86. *See also* job loss; manufacturing jobs; offshoring; policy/policymaking; workers
advantage, comparative, 38, 110, 210
advocacy, 27
AFL- CIO (American Federation of Labor and Congress of Industrial Organizations), 104–105, 106, 107, 196, 201
Africa, 225–226; coronavirus and, 259–260; in left behind narratives, 236–239; poverty in, 236, 237*f*, 239
Africa-rising narrative, 237–239
agreements, incompletely theorized, 184, 187, 198. *See also* narratives, overlapping
agriculture, 206–207, 223, 224
AI (artificial intelligence), 119. *See also* innovation; technology; technology industry
Akamatsu, Kaname, 237
alcohol abuse, 84, 89, 232
Alden, Edward, 47
alliances. *See* consensus; narratives, overlapping; perspectives, multiple; policy/policymaking
Alston, Philip, 76, 251
Amazon, 117, 119, 120. *See also* Big Tech
American Federation of Labor and Congress of Industrial Organizations (AFL- CIO), 104–105, 106, 107, 196, 201
Andersen, Inger, 154
Angell, Norman, 43–44
Anthropocene, 156, 219
Anti-Fragile (Taleb), 151
antitrust policy/enforcement, 19, 99, 116, 118–119, 173–175. *See also* Big Tech; corporate power narrative
Apple, 103, 117. *See also* Big Tech
Argentinian debt crisis (2001), 4, 225
Arnade, Chris, 83, 85, 267, 292–293
Aronoff, Kate, 277
artificial intelligence (AI), 119. *See also* innovation; technology; technology industry
Asian Century, 228, 229*f*
Asian financial crisis (1998), 4
Asia-rising narratives, 18, 226–230, 260–261
asset value protection, 113
Atkinson, Robert, 173
Atran, Scott, 294
austerity, 4, 63–64
Australia: China and, 129, 133–134, 150, 218, 257–258; concerns about loss of control in, 96; fires in, 5, 143, 218–219; inequality in, 59*f*, 75; Philip Morris case in, 115–116; subsidies to automotive sector in, 53

Australian Signals Directorate, 133
Austria, 278
authoritarianism, digital, 133
automation, 48, 78. *See also* job loss; productivity
autonomy, 95–96, 100, 101, 208, 209–210. *See also* Brexit; immigration; nativism
Autor, David, 47
autoworkers, 85–87. *See also* manufacturing jobs; North American Free Trade Agreement (NAFTA)
awakening-giants narrative, 227–228
Axelrod, Robert, 294

bailouts, 62, 65. *See also* global financial crisis (2008)
bait-and-switch, 30–31
Baker, Dean, 67
Baldwin, Richard, 45, 149, 255
Balsillie, Jim, 120
bankers, 9. *See also* elites; financial institutions
bankruptcy, 73, 76
banks. *See* financial institutions
Bannon, Steve, 97
bargaining power, 99, 100, 101–108. *See also* corporate power narrative
Beigneux, Aurélia, 255
belittling, 30
Bendell, Jem, 154
Berger, Jennifer Garvey, 285–286
Berlin, Isaiah, 280
Bhagwati, Jagdish, 221, 228
Bhutan, 158
biases. *See* narratives, non-Western; perspectives, non-Western
Biden, Joe: antitrust enforcement and, 174; China and, 19, 127; climate change and, 276–277, 296; combining of narratives by, 182; election of, 4; on security, 130, 262, 289–290; on supply chains, 272; trade policies, 19, 188, 262; workers and, 266
Big Tech, 118–119, 120, 173–174, 175, 177–178, 258. *See also* antitrust policy/enforcement
billionaires, 9; left-wing populist narrative on, 66–68; tax rates of, 68–70. *See also* elites
Binder, Alan, 37
biologics (drugs), 193, 197, 201
Blackwill, Robert, 124, 126
Blair, Tony, 96
Blaming China (Shobert), 180
blind spots. *See* narratives, non-Western; perspectives, non-Western
Blinken, Antony, 123
Blyth, Mark, 28
Bode, Thilo, 109, 115
Bolsonaro, Jair, 221
Bork, Robert, 118, 174
Boudreaux, Donald, 46
Boulding, Kenneth, 154
Bown, Chad, 255
Brazil, 221
Breaking the China Supply Chain (report), 129–130
Brewster, David, 242
Brexit, 10, 47; autonomy and, 95, 96; debates on, 43; immigration and, 4, 10, 79, 91; reaction to, 281, 289; Somewheres vs. Anywheres in, 87–88. *See also* European Union (EU); United Kingdom (UK)
Britain. *See* Brexit; United Kingdom (UK)
Brooks, David, 61
Brown, Jerry, 98
buffers, 150–151
Buffett, Warren, 68
Bütikofer, Reinhard, 142
buybacks, 66

Cain, Cody, 180
campaigns, 22, 29–31. *See also* Biden, Joe; Sanders, Bernie; Trump, Donald J.; Warren, Elizabeth
Canada: agriculture in, 207; CETA and, 112; coronavirus and, 257; dependence on China, 129, 257; ISDS and, 114–115; NAFTA, 99, 104–105, 106, 107, 114–115, 191–202; supply failures during corona-

virus pandemic in, 148; USMCA, 191, 201; workers in, 266
capitalism: in China, 234; climate change and, 156; patriotic, 178; Russia's transition to, 230–233
capitalism, surveillance, 175–176
carbon emissions. *See* emissions
Carle, Benjamin, 38
Carlson, Tucker, 89, 205
Carney, Mark, 150, 219
Carter, Ashton, 126, 177
Carter, Jimmy, 181
Case, Anne, 48
Cass, Oren, 89, 206, 267, 268
Centre for International Governance Innovation, 120
centrism, 4, 5
CEOs (chief executive officers), 9, 66–68. *See also* elites
CETA (Comprehensive Economic and Trade Agreement), 112, 113–115
CFIUS (Committee on Foreign Investment in the United States), 138
Chancel, Lucas, 161
change: after Cold War, 3; openness to, 88
characters, 25
Charlesworth, Anita, 151
chief executive officers (CEOs), 9, 66–68. *See also* elites
childcare, cost of, 73
China, 10; awakening-giants narrative, 227–228; Belt and Road Initiative, 132, 174, 238; Biden and, 19, 127; changing relationships with, 296; climate change and, 160, 247, 248, 253; economic rise of, 124–129; efficiency vs. security and, 210–212; establishment narrative and, 47–53, 142; 5G technology and, 133–136, 214, 215 (*see also* Huawei); GDP of, 126*f*; innovation imperative for, 137; integrative approach to, 285; interdependence with US, 131, 132*f*; investment in US/Europe, 138–140; Made in China 2025 policy, 129, 235; narratives in, 221, 234–235; purchases of technology companies, 138; rare earth market and, 130, 211; regulatory approach to internet, 133; relationship with West, 210; rivalry with US, 10–11, 122–123, 136 (*see also* geoeconomic narrative; technology); share of world economy, 229*f*; state-capitalist orientation, 234; stealth war by, 122; in surveillance capitalism analysis, 176; as threat, 10–11, 136 (*see also* geoeconomic narrative; security); Trump and, 126–127, 180, 186–188, 190–191, 234, 255; as "villain," 176–178; Western corporations and, 122 (*see also* geoeconomic narrative; security); Western oppression of, 234; WTO and, 48, 234. *See also* Asia-rising narratives; coronavirus; supply chains
China Shock, 47–53
Chinese Communist Party (CCP), 122, 135–136
cities, 83–85, 88, 256, 267
citizenship, 86, 87, 101
Ciuriak, Dan, 112–113, 118
class, socioeconomic: climate change and, 278; coronavirus and, 256–257; divisions between, 31; educational attainment and, 62; morals and, 69; social mobility, 62, 76–77, 287. *See also* bankers; billionaires; chief executive officers (CEOs); elites; middle class; poor; professional class; workers; working class
Clausing, Kimberly, 38, 52
climate change, 5, 143–144, 152–163; coronavirus and, 254; corporate power narrative and, 253–254, 278, 297; developing countries and, 246–248; distribution and, 161–163, 292; economic modeling of effects of, 217–218; establishment narrative and, 249, 274–278, 297; geoeconomic narrative and, 252–253, 278, 297; increasing centrality of, 296–297; kaleidoscope method and, 246–254; left-wing populist narrative and, 249–251,

climate change (*continued*)
274–278, 297; perspectives on, 18, 246–254; policymaking and, 251, 273–278; regulations and, 160; responsibility for, 160, 161, 162*f*, 246–247; right-wing populist narrative and, 251–252, 274–278, 297; risk assessment in, 217–219; as security threat, 248; sustainability narrative and, 246–248, 252–253, 258, 274–278; switching narratives and, 181–182; as threat multiplier, 253. *See also* emissions; global threats narratives; sustainability narrative
climate change denial, 32, 251, 275
climate modeling, 217
Clinton, Bill, 29, 192
Clinton, Hillary, 29, 125–126
coalitions, 169, 187–188. *See also* narratives, overlapping; policy/policymaking
Cohn, Gary, 49
Cold War, 3, 125, 131, 232–233. *See also* Soviet Union
Colgan, Jeff, 180
collective goods, protection of, 209–210. *See also* autonomy; democracy
Collier, Paul, 239
colonialism, 224, 236. *See also* neocolonial narrative
Commission for the Human Future, 144
Committee on Foreign Investment in the United States (CFIUS), 138
communism, 230, 232. *See also* Soviet Union
community, 256. *See also* place
comparative advantage, 38, 110, 210
competition: vs. cooperation, 273; effects of, 78; elites' protection from, 56; lack of, 119 (*see also* antitrust policy/enforcement; concentration); trade restrictions and, 41 (*see also* protectionism; tariffs; trade agreements); US-Chinese, 10–11, 122–123, 136 (*see also* China; geoeconomic narrative; technology)
complex integrative thinking, 16–17, 261
complexity, 241–243
Comprehensive and Progressive Agreement on Trans-Pacific Partnership (CPTPP), 113
Comprehensive Economic and Trade Agreement (CETA), 112, 113–115
concentration, 116–120, 149–150, 258. *See also* antitrust policy/enforcement; Big Tech
concepts of globalization narratives, 166–168*t*
conflict, 41, 122, 184, 188–189, 212, 214. *See also* peace; security
connectivity, 131–133, 146–147. *See also* 5G technology
consensus, 169, 282. *See also* narratives, overlapping; perspectives, multiple; policy/policymaking
consolidation. *See* antitrust policy/enforcement; concentration
conspiracy theories, 32
construction work, 50
consumers, 100–101, 205–206
consumption, 153, 160–161, 204–207, 267, 275. *See also* climate change; growth, economic
contagion, 146–147. *See also* coronavirus; global financial crisis (2008)
contempt, 30
control. *See* autonomy
Cook, Chris, 151
cooperation, 182–183, 255, 273
Corbyn, Jeremy, 60, 68, 76
coronavirus, 5, 296; Africa and, 259–260; climate change and, 254; concentration and, 149–150; connectivity and, 146–147; corporate power narrative and, 258; decoupling and, 254; developing countries and, 259–260; distribution and, 292; establishment narrative and, 255; framing of, 183; geoeconomic narrative and, 254, 257–258; immigration and, 256; interdependence and, 144, 150, 214, 254, 257, 269, 271; left-wing populist narrative and, 254, 256–257, 266; need for redundancy

and, 151; non-Western narratives and, 260–261; outbreak of, 143–144; pandemic protectionism, 255; perspectives on, 254–261; right-wing populist narrative and, 254, 255–256; supply chains and, 144, 150, 254, 257, 271; sustainability narrative and, 258; trade-offs and, 203; values and, 208–209; viewing through multiple lenses, 18; workers and, 264–266. *See also* service sector
Corporate Europe Observatory, 115
corporate power narrative: analytical structure of, 167*t*; antitrust enforcement and, 174; bargaining power in, 99, 100, 101–108; climate change and, 253–254, 278, 297; consumers and, 100–101; coronavirus and, 258; described, 9; distributive concerns in, 292; "good" jobs and, 103–104; intellectual property rights and, 111–113; ISDS and, 113–116, 225; legal entitlements in, 99, 100, 108–116; market power in, 99, 100, 116–120; Nader and, 99–100; NAFTA and, 192–193, 195–197, 200–202; normative commitments of, 33–34; offshoring in, 104–108; race to bottom in, 99, 100, 101, 102*f*, 107; rights and, 209; risk and, 216; schematic representation of, 13*f*; standards and, 108–110; trade agreements in, 111; US trade policy and, 202; values and, 208; "villains" in, 175, 179; virtues vs. vices in, 178; wages and, 100, 103–108; winners in, 9, 104–106; working conditions and, 100, 106–108. *See also* narratives, globalization
corporations: influence of, 100; perspectives on, 29; right to sue governments, 114 (*see also* investor-state dispute settlement [ISDS]); sources of power, 98–99, 100–101 (*see also* corporate power narrative); taxes and, 68, 71, 101–103. *See also* Big Tech; chief executive officers (CEOs); corporate power narrative; elites
Cotton, Tom, 134, 138
Cowen, Tyler, 210
CPTPP (Comprehensive and Progressive Agreement on Trans-Pacific Partnership), 113
creative jobs, 82–83
crime, anti-immigrant sentiment and, 92
Crimea, 233
crises, 254. *See also* climate change; coronavirus; financial crises
crocodile curve, 105
Cuba, 223
Cui Tiankai, 182
cultural differences, 31. *See also* educational attainment; values
Cuomo, Andrew, 203, 208

Daly, Herman, 153
data, 113, 117, 118, 119, 136, 211. *See also* geoeconomic narrative; technology; technology industry
deaths of despair, 83, 84*f*, 232, 267
Deaton, Angus, 48
debt, 65–66, 73. *See also* financial crises
decoupling, 190–191, 235, 254
defense, 130. *See also* security
degrees. *See* educational attainment
degrowth, 34, 249, 258, 273–276
deindustrialization, 35, 78, 82–85, 236. *See also* automation; job loss; manufacturing jobs; offshoring
Dell Theory, 43
democracy, 122, 208, 209
Democrats, renegotiation of NAFTA and, 195–196, 197, 200–201, 202
density divide, 88
dependency theory, 223
developing countries: climate change and, 246–248; coronavirus and, 259–260; elites in, 226; international financial institutions and, 225. *See also* narratives, non-Western
development. *See* globalization
Dias, Jerry, 104, 107–108
differentiation (analytical step), 16

digital markets, 117. *See also* Big Tech; technology; technology industry
disagreement, constructive, 16
dislocation. *See* job loss
distribution, 8, 55, 56, 69, 119, 161–163, 166–168*t*, 290–292. *See also* income; income inequality; inequality; poverty; wages
diversification, need for, 149–150
diversity. *See* perspectives, multiple
division of labor, 38. *See also* specialization; trade
divorce, 89
Doctors Without Borders, 112
Doha Round, 224
Donnan, Shawn, 187
dragonfly approach, 17
Draut, Tamara, 71, 72, 268
dream hoarding, 61, 75
drug abuse, 83, 84*f*, 89, 232
Duncan, Sherria, 85–86
Dunford, Joseph F., Jr., 177

Earth, 154. *See also* climate change
Earthrise (image), 154, 155*f*
East Asian miracle narrative, 226–227
Eberhardt, Pia, 115
ECB (European Central Bank), 63, 64
ecological crisis, 152. *See also* climate change
Economic Benefits of US Trade, The, 52
economic divisions, 31. *See also* class, socioeconomic
economic globalization. *See* globalization
economic liberalization. *See* free trade; globalization; liberalization, economic; neoliberalism; trade agreements
economic policy, securitization of, 123. *See also* geoeconomic narrative
economics: vs. environmental risks, 217–219; security and, 124, 129–131, 215–216, 217*f*
economics, doughnut, 157, 158, 159*f*
Economist, The, 15*f*, 173
economists, 287
economy: financialization of, 66; steady-state, 157
education: cost of, 55, 73, 75–76; right to, 208, 209
educational attainment, 61; cultural differences and, 31; income and, 71; job loss and, 48; socioeconomic class and, 62. *See also* cultural differences; values
efficiency, 219; emphasis on, 125, 145, 263–264; vs. equality, rights, and democracy, 208–210; vs. redundancy, 150–151; vs. security, 210–214. *See also* supply chains
Elephant Graph, 20–21, 23*f*, 24*f*, 238*f*, 239
elites: cloistered communities of, 92, 287, 289; in developing countries, 226; distrust of, 79, 94 (*see also* left-wing populist narrative; right-wing populist narrative); 1 percent, 35, 61; protection from competition, 56–57; taxes paid by, 10, 57, 68–70, 71. *See also* chief executive officers (CEOs); professional class
emerging markets. *See* narratives, non-Western
emissions, 152, 153*f*, 158, 162; coronavirus and, 254; inequality and, 251; responsibility for, 160, 161, 162*f*, 246–247. *See also* climate change
empathy, 16
empirical claims, 31. *See also* facts
employment: types of, 48–50, 82–83. *See also* adjustment; job loss; manufacturing jobs
enemy, identifying, 175–180
Energy Charter Treaty, 115
England. *See* Brexit; United Kingdom (UK)
environment, 152–163. *See also* climate change
environmental nationalism, 273–276
environmental standards, 99, 100. *See also* corporate power narrative
equality, 208. *See also* distribution; income inequality; inequality
establishment narrative, 29, 81, 131, 147; adjustment in, 44–47, 53, 77, 82; Biden's

trade agenda and, 19; ceding of control and, 95; challenges to, 47, 55–57, 270, 281 (*see also* Brexit; Trump, Donald J.); China and, 47–53, 142; climate change and, 249, 274–278, 297; on connectivity, 145; coronavirus and, 255; criticism of, 35; defense of specialization, 48; described, 6–7, 8; dominance of, 295–296; efficiency in, 212, 263–264; Elephant Graph and, 20–22; on free trade, 36–38, 41, 48, 52, 80; free trade agreements in, 111; on free trade alternatives, 52–53; on "good" jobs, 104; interdependence in, 131; international research/cooperation in, 182–183; lack of diversity and, 289; left-wing populist narrative compared to, 208; losers in, 44–45; on lower prices, 73; main features of, 166*t*; on manufacturing job loss, 81–82; market capitalism in, 40–41; NAFTA and, 191–193; in non-Western countries, 221; pain-gain package, 44–45; people as consumers in, 205–206; on poverty, 39–40, 236; on productivity, 49; on productivity-wage gaps, 59; on protecting workers vs. jobs, 53; protectionist narrative compared to, 204; on relocation, 85; renegotiation of NAFTA and, 194*f*, 198*f*, 199*f*, 201*f*; right-wing populist narrative and, 97, 204; risks and rewards in, 215; schematic representation of, 13*f*; security in, 124, 129, 212; Somewheres vs. Anywheres split and, 87–88; on standard of living, 39–40; summary of, 53; tax havens and, 102; trade agreements and, 35, 41–43; two-step approach to integration, 290; US trade policy and, 184–191, 202; values and, 292–293; winners in, 7, 105, 144; wireless networks in, 134; workers in, 263–264, 266. *See also* narratives, globalization

EU (European Union). *See* Brexit; European Union (EU)

euro crisis (2009), 4

Europe: anti-immigration sentiment in, 91; corporate power narrative in, 9; immigration in (*see* immigration); income inequality in, 59*f*; right-wing populist narrative in, 10, 79. *See also* European Union (EU); West; *individual countries*

European Central Bank (ECB), 63, 64

European Commission, 63–64; antitrust regulation, 174–175; on benefits of free trade, 52; New EU-US Agenda for Global Change, 142; relationship with China, 141

European Green Deal, 276–277

European Union (EU): CETA and, 112; China and, 133, 139, 141–142; climate change and, 277; eastern Europe in, 42–43; immigration and, 96 (*see also* Brexit); loss of control to, 95; peace and, 42–43; regulations adopted by, 108–109; supply chains and, 272; US-Chinese relationship and, 140. *See also* Brexit; *individual countries*

executives, 9, 66–68. *See also* elites

Expert Political Judgment (Tetlock), 282

Extinction Rebellion, 156

Facebook, 117, 118–119, 120, 171, 173. *See also* Big Tech

facts, 20–21, 22, 27. *See also* empirical claims

Farage, Nigel, 95, 96

Farrell, Henry, 131

Ferguson, Victor, 190

financial crises, 4; Argentinian debt crisis, 4, 225; global financial crisis (2008), 7, 35, 42, 55, 62–64, 65, 149; Greek crisis, 63–64, 69

financial institutions, 62–64, 65–66, 73, 225. *See also* International Monetary Fund (IMF); World Bank

financialization of economy, 66, 76, 208, 267

5G technology, 133–136, 214, 215. *See also* Huawei

Five Eyes, dependence on China, 129
flu pandemic, 146
Flying Geese paradigm of development, 237
Ford, Christopher Ashley, 135, 137
Ford, Doug, 148, 266
Foroohar, Rana, 65, 100
fossil fuels, 152. *See also* climate change; global threats narratives
fox-like thinking, 280, 281–282. *See also* perspectives, multiple
Frame Analysis (Goffman), 25
framing, 25–26, 27, 169. *See also* levels of analysis; narratives, overlapping; narratives, switching; units of analysis
France: diesel tax in, 251; geographical divides in, 84; National Front, 88; National Rally, 255; right-wing populists in, 94; tax evasion/avoidance in, 69
Frank, Thomas, 30
freedom of movement, 96. *See also* immigration
Freeland, Chrystia, 192
free trade: alternatives to, 52–53; democracy and, 122; disconnect between elite and working class on, 94; economists on benefits of, 37; in establishment narrative, 80, 111; positive view of, 3; social sustainability of, 53. *See also* establishment narrative; liberalization, economic; neoliberalism; trade agreements
free trade agreements. *See* trade agreements
Friedman, Milton, 205
Friedman, Thomas, 43–44, 54
Friel, Sharon, 158
fungibility, 205–207
Future Is Asian, The (Khanna), 220

G20 (Group of 20), 52, 53
gains: distribution of (*see* distribution; income inequality; inequality); in globalization narratives, 166–168*t*; trade-offs between absolute and relative, 211–212, 213*f*
Gardner, Howard, 283
Gates, Bill, 146, 183
GATT (General Agreement on Tariffs and Trade), 41–42, 223
Gauland, Alexander, 93
Gell-Mann, Murray, 283
gender, 89–90, 252, 267
General Agreement on Tariffs and Trade (GATT), 41–42, 223
General Motors, 85–87, 88*f*, 89, 90
geoeconomic narrative: analytical structure of, 168*t*; antitrust regulation and, 173–175; battles for technological supremacy in, 136–138; China's rise and, 124–127; climate change and, 252–253, 278, 297; coronavirus and, 254, 257–258; data in, 136; described, 10–11; on digital authoritarianism, 133; on distributive effects, 291; efficiency vs. security in, 210; EU and, 140–142; 5G technology and, 133–136 (*see also* Huawei); foreign investments and, 138–140; global threats narrative combined with, 182; interdependence in, 129, 148; international research/cooperation in, 182–183; resilience narrative compared to, 148, 271–272, 273; risk in, 215, 216; schematic representation of, 13*f*; security in, 129–131; self-reliance and, 271–273; supply chains and, 273; switching from, 181–182; in US, 124; US-Chinese rivalry and, 122–123; US trade policy and, 185–189, 190–191, 202; "villains" in, 175, 176–178, 179; virtues vs. vices in, 178; weaponized interdependence, 131–133. *See also* narratives, globalization; security
geoeconomics, use of term, 124
Georgia, 43
Germany: Alternative für Deutschland (AfD), 88, 92, 93, 94, 251, 252; clean growth in, 250*f*; coronavirus and, 148; corporate power narrative in, 109; immigration in, 79, 92–94; protests of trade agreements in, 113–114; reunification of,

232; review of foreign acquisitions, 139; Vattenfall dispute, 115, 116; workers in, 266
Gertz, Geoffrey, 191
Ghana, 225–226
Gibson, Rosemary, 257
Gilding, Simeon, 134
Gilpin, Robert, 29
global financial crisis (2008), 7, 35, 42, 55, 62–64, 65, 149. *See also* financial institutions
globalization: centrist consensus on, 5; complexity of, 242; emergence of rival narratives about, 5, 7–8 (*see also* narratives, globalization); positive view of, 6 (*see also* establishment narrative); prevailing view of, 3–4. *See also* development
global threats narratives: analytical structure of, 168*t*; Biden's trade agenda and, 19; concentration vs. diversification in, 149–150; connectivity and contagion in, 146–147; described, 11–12; efficiency vs. redundancy in, 150–151; geoeconomic narrative combined with, 182; interdependence vs. self-reliance in, 147–148; international research/cooperation in, 182–183; left-wing populist narrative's overlap with, 257; losers in, 163; outside West, 221, 259; resilience narratives, 144–151; risk and, 216; schematic representation of, 13*f*; summary of, 163; sustainability narratives, 152–163; switching to, 181–182; values and, 293. *See also* climate change; coronavirus; narratives, globalization; sustainability narrative
global warming. *See* climate change; global threats narratives
Goffman, Erving, 25
Golden Arches Theory of Conflict Prevention, 43–44
Goldin, Ian, 146
Goodhart, David, 87
Google, 117, 118–119, 120, 178. *See also* Big Tech
governments: corporations' right to sue [*see* investor-state dispute settlement (ISDS)]; help for losers, 46–47 (*see also* adjustment)
Grabow, Colin, 50
Great Britain. *See* Brexit; United Kingdom (UK)
Great Recession (2008), 42. *See also* global financial crisis (2008)
Greece, 63–64, 69, 133
Greencon coalition, 278
Greenhouse, Steven, 71
Green New Deal, 273–276, 277, 278
Greider, William, 106
gross domestic product (GDP): of China, 126*f*; emphasis on, 8; happiness/wellbeing and, 158–159; by region, 227*f*
Group of 20 (G20), 52, 53
growth, economic, 162, 206, 208
growth, green, 273–276
Guatemala, 197
Guilluy, Christophe, 84, 91
Guterres, António, 144
Gysi, Gregor, 172

H-1B visa category, 91
Haidt, Jonathan, 16, 294
Hanson, Pauline, 96
happiness, 158–159
Harris, Jennifer, 124
Hayden, Michael, 135
health, right to, 208, 209
healthcare, 55, 73, 75–76
hedgehogs, 280–281, 282
hegemony, 222; narratives against Western hegemony, 18, 230–235, 260–261
Hickel, Jason, 162
Hillbilly Elegy (Vance), 88, 205
Hochschild, Arlie Russell, 295
Höcke, Björn, 92
hockey stick of global carbon emissions, 152, 153*f*
hockey stick of inequality, 61
hockey stick of prosperity, 38–39, 297

home appliances, affordability of, 50–52, 51*f*
homophily, 286
hostility, redirecting, 172. *See also* narratives, switching
housing, 55, 73, 75–76, 287
Huawei, 134, 177, 190, 210, 214, 235
Hull, Cordell, 41
Hulme, Mike, 245
Hungary, 133

ideas, 28
identity, 86
identity formation, othering in, 180. *See also* "villains"
Iglesia, Pablo, 69
IMF (International Monetary Fund). *See* International Monetary Fund (IMF)
immigration: backlash against, 78, 91, 92–94, 96 (*see also* autonomy; right-wing populist narrative); Brexit and, 4, 10, 79, 91; climate change and, 276, 278; competition for public services and, 92; coronavirus and, 256; cultural identity and, 10, 93–95; disconnect between elite and working class on, 94; fear of, 4; in Germany, 79, 92–94; importation of low-wage workers, 91; as threat to security of one's group, 90–93; into welfare state, 91–92. *See also* competition; other; right-wing populist narrative; "villains"
imperialism, economic, 226. *See also* neocolonial narrative
income, 26*f*; changes in, 231*f*, 238*f*, 239 (*see also* Elephant Graph); educational attainment and, 71; gender and, 89–90; growth in, 20–22, 38–39; hockey stick of human prosperity, 38–39, 297. *See also* distribution; wages
income inequality, 57, 59–62; CEOs and billionaires, 66–68; hockey stick of inequality, 61; left-wing populist narrative and, 57–62, 69; in Russia, 230–232; wage stagnation, 57–60, 65
India: awakening-giants narrative, 228; climate change and, 248; on multilateralism, 223; narratives in, 221; share of world economy, 229*f*
industrial breadwinner masculinity, 251–252
industrial communities, 78, 85–87, 89. *See also* job loss; manufacturing jobs; right-wing populist narrative; Trump, Donald J.; working class
Industrial Revolution, 38–39, 246
inequality: climate change and, 246, 249–251; coronavirus and, 256–257; increase in, 9, 35; in Russia, 230–232. *See also* income inequality; left-wing populist narrative
information technology, 134. *See also* 5G technology; Huawei; technology industry
in-group identification, 91
innovation, 83–84, 138. *See also* Big Tech; technology; technology industry
integration, 7; as an analytical step, 16; peace and, 42–43; selectivity in, 56–57; between West and China, 211. *See also* European Union (EU); globalization
integrative approach, 16–17, 283–286
intellectual property, 111–113, 197, 209, 224; concentration and, 117; medicines and, 112, 201; NAFTA and, 193; tax evasion/avoidance and, 102–103
interdependence: coronavirus and, 144, 150, 214, 254, 257, 269, 271; in establishment narrative, 131; peace as precondition for, 129; policymaking and, 270–273; vs. self-reliance, 147–148, 151; vulnerabilities, 131; between West and China, 211. *See also* globalization; integration; self-reliance; supply chains
interdisciplinary approach, 283–286
Intergovernmental Panel on Climate Change, 217, 218
international economic order, defense of, 35. *See also* establishment narrative
International Monetary Fund (IMF), 7, 52, 53, 63–64, 102, 225, 231

internet, China's regulatory approach to, 133
Internet of Things, 136
investment decisions. *See* corporate power narrative
investment protection, international, 224–225
investments, foreign, 138–140
investment treaties, 114
investor-state dispute settlement (ISDS), 113–116, 195, 197–198, 225
Ireland, 103, 278
ISDS (investor-state dispute settlement), 113–116, 195, 197–198, 225
Italy, 63, 84, 96

Japan, 125
job loss: automation and, 48; corporate power narrative and, 103; educational attainment and, 48; effects of, 78; gender and, 89–90, 267; immigration and, 10; industrial breadwinner masculinity and, 251–252; lack of mobility and, 85–86; No Differentiation School, 46; right-wing populist narrative and, 10; Trade Is Special School, 46–47; training replacements and, 87, 91; Trump on, 204; in United States, 10. *See also* adjustment; deindustrialization; manufacturing jobs; offshoring; right-wing populist narrative; workers
jobs: concentration of in cities, 83–85; gains through trade with China, 48–50. *See also* adjustment; job loss; manufacturing jobs
jobs-as-property metaphor, 86–87, 204
Johnson, Boris, 95
Joske, Alex, 182
Juncker, Jean-Claude, 138
justice, distributive, 161–163

kaleidoscopic method, 242, 243, 245; alliances and, 262–279; climate change and, 246–254; coronavirus and, 254–261. *See also* policy/policymaking

Kant, Immanuel, 43
Karaganov, Sergey, 233–234
Kay, John, 14
Kenyatta, Uhuru, 237
Keohane, Robert, 180, 214
Khan, Lina, 100, 174
Khanna, Parag, 220, 228
King, Mervyn, 14
Kiribati, 248
Klein, Matthew, 173
Klein, Naomi, 153, 156, 159–160
knowledge-based economy, 118. *See also* intellectual property; skills; technology industry
Kosovo, 233
Krugman, Paul, 40, 110–111

labor, organized, 70–71, 196, 264. *See also* AFL- CIO
labor standards, 110, 196–197, 201. *See also* safety standards; standards; working conditions
language of globalization narratives, 166–168*t*
Lansley, Stewart, 57
Lauterbach, Karl, 76
leadership, stable, 233
Lee Hsien Loong, 140
left behind narratives, 18, 222, 236–239
left-wing populist narrative, 14; analytical structure of, 166*t*; climate change and, 249–251, 274–278, 297; coronavirus and, 254, 256–257, 266; on cost of middle-class staples, 72–76; described, 8–9; distribution of wealth in, 69, 291; elites in, 9, 60–62, 66–70, 79; establishment narrative and, 55–57, 208; on financial sector, 65–66; global financial crisis and, 62–64; global threats narratives' overlap with, 257; on healthcare, 76; income inequality/wage stagnation and, 57–62, 69; losers in, 60; numbers in, 77; on private equity companies, 65–66; right-wing populist narrative's overlap with, 268; rise of, 36; schematic

left-wing populist narrative (*continued*)
representation of, 13*f*; on specialization, 55; summary of, 77; supply chains and, 273; surveillance capitalism in, 175–176; on taxes paid by elites, 68–70; on unions, 70–71; in US presidential election, 22; values and, 208; "villains" in, 175, 179; virtues vs. vices in, 178; on wages, 57–62, 69, 71–73; winners in, 24*f*, 60 (*see also* elites); workers in, 19; work-related measures and, 270. *See also* narratives, globalization; populism; Sanders, Bernie; Warren, Elizabeth
left-wing populists, switching narratives by, 172–173
legal entitlements, 99, 100, 108–116. *See also* corporate power narrative
Lehman Brothers, 62, 149
Leonard, Mark, 131
Le Pen, Marine, 86, 94
levels of analysis: changing, 169, 171, 173, 179–180 (*see also* narratives, switching); of globalization narratives, 25, 166–168*t*; identifying "villains," 175–180
liberalization, economic, 3, 36, 80–82. *See also* free trade; globalization; neoliberalism; trade agreements
liberal perspective, 29. *See also* establishment narrative
Lighthizer, Robert, 125, 193, 195, 197, 200
Lim, Darren, 190
Limbaugh, Rush, 94
Lind, Michael, 62, 91, 110, 173
living conditions, 107, 220
Lordstown, Ohio, 85–87, 89, 90
losers, 13; changing perception of, 171 (*see also* narratives, switching); compensation of, 290–291; from coronavirus, 258; in corporate power narrative, 100–101, 104; developing countries as, 226; in establishment narrative, 44–45; in global threats narrative, 163; in left-wing populist narrative, 60; in narratives, 166–168*t*; in right-wing populist narrative, 23*f*
Lucas, Robert, 291
Luttwak, Edward, 124

machine learning, 119. *See also* technology
MacLeish, Archibald, 154
Macron, Emmanuel, 148, 251, 269
Mahbubani, Kishore, 220, 228
Mankiw, Gregory, 37
manufacturing jobs, 4; in Africa, 236; anti-union laws/practice and, 70–71; automation and, 48; coronavirus and, 257; decline of, 46, 81–82; as "good" jobs, 103; industrial breadwinner masculinity and, 251–252; multiplier effect of, 82–83; in non-Western perspectives, 222; productivity and, 48, 49; protectionist view of, 82–83; renegotiation of NAFTA and, 193–195; self-reliance and, 269–270, 271–273; Trump on, 90. *See also* competition; deindustrialization; industrial communities; job loss; NAFTA; offshoring; workers; working class
Mariathasan, Mike, 146
market, in establishment narrative, 6
market capitalism, 40–41
market concentration, 116–120, 149–150, 258. *See also* antitrust policy/enforcement; Big Tech
market outcomes, redistribution of. *See* distribution
market power, 99, 100, 116–120. *See also* concentration; corporate power narrative
Markovits, Daniel, 62
Marsh, Rick, 89
Martin, Joseph, 79–80
Martin, Roger, 145, 284
Marx, Karl, 175
Marxist perspective on multinational corporations, 29
Matthew effect, 118
May, Theresa, 86, 87
Mazzucato, Mariana, 65
McDonald's restaurants, 43
McKay, David, 148
McKenna, Catherine, 252

McMichael, Anthony, 157
medical supplies, 147–148, 214, 254, 255, 257, 269
medicines, 112, 193, 197, 201, 211, 254, 257
Mélenchon, Jean-Luc, 69, 76
mercantilist perspective on multinational corporations, 29
mergers, 174. *See also* antitrust policy/enforcement
meritocracy, 62
Merkel, Angela, 93, 142, 148, 269
meta-narratives, potential, 295–297
metaphors, 28, 166–168t
metrics of evaluation, 25–26
metropolitan centers, 83–85, 88
Mexico, 106–108, 136, 191, 196, 201; NAFTA, 99, 104–105, 106, 107, 114–115, 191–202
Meyer, Timothy, 53
Microsoft, 117. *See also* Big Tech
middle class, 9, 20, 55, 72–76. *See also* left-wing populist narrative
Milanovic, Branko, 3, 15, 20
Mills, C. Wright, 57
Milroy, Aurora, 220
Mishra, Pankaj, 221
Mitchell, Edgar, 154
mobility, geographical, 85–86, 87–88, 90
mobility, social, 62, 76–77, 287
mobility, worker. *See* adjustment; skills
models, 28, 217–218
Modi, Narendra, 221, 228
monopolies. *See* antitrust policy/enforcement; Big Tech
monopsony power, 119
Montero, Irene, 69
Montesquieu, 43
moral, of narratives, 27. *See also* policy/policymaking
morals, 69. *See also* values
Moretti, Enrico, 83
Morgan, Gareth, 28
Morrison, Scott, 152
multilateralism, neocolonial critique of, 222–223
multiplier effect, 82–83
Muslim immigration, 4. *See also* immigration

Nader, Ralph, 99–100, 107, 110
NAFTA (North America Free Trade Agreement), 99, 104–105, 106, 107, 114–115, 191–202
Narain, Sunita, 221
narrative economics, 12
narratives: building blocks of, 23–27; importance of, 5, 12, 14, 20; multiple, 27–29 (*see also* perspectives, multiple); single, danger of, 28
narratives, globalization, 3, 8; actors and, 14, 169; analytical structure of, 166–168*t* (*see also* levels of analysis; losers; units of analysis; winners); blind spots/biases of, 222 (*see also* narratives, non-Western); construction of, 14; empirical claims of, 31, 33, 34; illustrative proponents of, 166–168*t*; importance of, 15–16, 20–32; normative commitments of, 33–34; schematic representation of, 13*f*; using to understand complex and contested issues, 243 (*see also* climate change; coronavirus; policy/policymaking); winners in, 166–168*t*. *See also individual narratives*
narratives, non-Western, 18; Asia-rising narratives, 18, 226–230, 260–261; coronavirus and, 260–261; left behind narratives, 18, 222, 236–239; narratives against Western hegemony, 18, 230–235, 260–261; neocolonial narrative, 18, 222–226, 236. *See also* perspectives, non-Western
narratives, overlapping, 18–19, 169–170, 243; coalitions, 187–188; conflict and, 184, 188–189; motivations for, 184; renegotiation of NAFTA and, 191–202; sabotage and, 184, 189–191; Trump's trade policies and, 184–191. *See also* perspectives, multiple
narratives, reconciling, 170. *See also* trade-offs

narratives, switching, 169; antitrust policy and, 173–175; climate change and, 181–182; Facebook's China argument, 171, 173; identifying "villains," 175–180; by left-wing populists, 172–173; redirecting hostility from China, 179–180; virtues vs. vices and, 178
nationalism, 78, 252. *See also* right-wing populist narrative
nationalizations, 224–225
National Security Agency, 135
nativism, 91. *See also* autonomy; immigration; right-wing populist narrative
NATO, 44
natural resources, sovereignty over, 224–225
nature. *See* climate change; environmental standards
Navarro, Peter, 82, 83, 129, 130, 148, 178
negotiations. *See* narratives, overlapping
neocolonial narrative, 18, 222–226, 236
neoliberalism, 70, 71, 225–226
Netflix, 117. *See also* Big Tech
network effects, 117–118
New America/New America Foundation, 62, 144
Newman, Abraham, 131
news, Big Tech and, 120
New York Times, 119
New Zealand, 116, 129, 158–159, 252
99 percent, 60–61
Ninsin, Kwame, 225
Nkrumah, Kwame, 225
No Differentiation School, 46
North American Free Trade Agreement (NAFTA), 99, 104–105, 106, 107, 114–115, 191–202
nuclear power, 115
Nye, Joseph, Jr., 181, 214

Obama, Barack, 29, 30, 125–126
Ocasio-Cortez, Alexandria, 67, 172, 252, 256
Occupy Wall Street, 4, 60–61
O'Connor, Sarah, 265, 266
OECD (Organisation for Economic Co-operation and Development), 52, 120, 146, 276
offhand remarks, 29–30
offshoring, 78, 104–108, 204. *See also* competition; deindustrialization; job loss; jobs-as-property metaphor; manufacturing jobs; North American Free Trade Agreement (NAFTA)
Okonjo-Iweala, Ngozi, 259
Olojede, Dele, 259
1 percent, 35, 61. *See also* elites
O'Neil, Shannon, 151
ontological security (*Weltvertrauen*), 94
Opium Wars, 234
orbit, sustainable, 157–159
Organisation for Economic Co-operation and Development (OECD), 52, 120, 146, 276
other, 79, 180, 252. *See also* immigration; "villains"
out-group hostility, 91. *See also* immigration
outsourcing. *See* job loss; manufacturing jobs; offshoring
overlaps among narratives. *See* narratives, overlapping
Oxfam, 66, 161

Page, Scott, 286
Pakistan, 114
Pampinella, Stephen, 181
pandemics, 129, 146. *See also* coronavirus; security
patriotic capitalism, 178
patriotism, 86
pay. *See* income; wages
peace, 11, 41–43, 124–125, 129. *See also* conflict; security
Pelosi, Nancy, 202
Peña Nieto, Enrique, 198
Pence, Mike, 127, 178
perspective, single, 280–281, 282
perspectives, 17. *See also* narratives
perspectives, multiple, 280–282; consciously adopting, 284; distribution and, 290–292; diverse teams, 286–290;

integrative approach, 283–286; values and, 292–295
perspectives, non-Western, 220–222, 246–248. *See also* narratives, non-Western
Pettis, Michael, 173
Philip Morris, 115–116
Philippon, Thomas, 119, 258
Piketty, Thomas, 262
place, 85–86, 87–88, 256
platform firms, 119
plot, developing, 26–27
polarization, 16, 281
policy/policymaking: adjustment assistance, 7, 46–47, 53; climate change and, 251, 273–278; degrowth, 34, 249, 258, 273–276; disagreement with, 34; distribution and, 290–292; diversification of supply chains, 271–273; diversity and, 245, 286–290; framing and, 27; interdependence and, 270–273; job loss and, 46–47; Made in China 2025, 129, 235; multiple perspectives and, 281–282; overlaps among narratives and, 243; self-reliance and, 269–270; specialization in, 283; by supranational bodies, 95 (*see also* autonomy; European Union (EU); right-wing populist narrative); trade-offs and, 203; union decline and, 71; workers and, 264–270. *See also* narratives, overlapping
political outsiders, 35–36. *See also* Trump, Donald J.
poor, 9, 20–22. *See also* income; income inequality; poverty
populism, 31, 55. *See also* left-wing populist narrative; right-wing populist narrative
poverty: in Africa, 236, 237*f*, 239; climate change and, 251; reduction in, 39–40, 220, 228, 236, 291; in Russia, 230–232. *See also* income; income inequality; poor
poverty jobs, 72–73
Power, Samantha, 183
Power of Resilience, The (Sheffi), 146
precautionary principle, 108–109
privacy, digital, 174
private equity companies, 65–66
probabilities, trade-offs involving, 215–219
problems, reframing. *See* narratives, switching
production, 204–207, 267
production decisions. *See* corporate power narrative
productivity, 48, 49, 55. *See also* automation
productivity-wage gaps, 57, 58*f*, 59, 60
professional class, 9, 62; climate change and, 278; income inequality and, 68; lack of diversity in, 287, 289; moving for work and, 86. *See also* elites
professional jobs, 82–83
property, intangible, 102–103. *See also* intellectual property
prosperity, 206, 267
protectionism, 41–42, 78; agriculture and, 206–207, 223, 224; climate change and, 252; NAFTA and, 192; security and, 130, 188–189, 190; workers and, 266. *See also* right-wing populist narrative; tariffs
protectionist narrative, 80, 187; blame for offshoring in, 105; establishment narrative compared to, 204; renegotiation of NAFTA and, 193–195, 198–200, 201*f*; self-reliance and, 271–273; threats in, 136; US trade policy and, 185–189, 202; view of manufacturing jobs, 82–83; work-related measures and, 270. *See also* right-wing populist narrative
Public Citizen's Global Trade Watch, 110
Putin, Vladimir, 232, 233

Quadri, Lorenzo, 256
quantum computing. *See* technology

"race to the bottom," 99, 100, 101, 102*f*, 107. *See also* corporate power narrative
Rajan, Raghuram, 221
rare earth market, 130, 211
Raworth, Kate, 157, 158
Reagan, Ronald, 70, 71
realist school, 210
Rebel Ideas (Syed), 286
Reciprocal Trade Agreements Act, 79–80

reconciling different narratives, 170. *See also* trade-offs
Redefining Europe's Economic Sovereignty (report), 141
redistribution of market outcomes. *See* distribution; income; income inequality
redundancy, 150–151, 219
Reeves, Richard, 75
reframing. *See* narratives, switching
refugees, 4. *See also* immigration
regulations, 100, 101, 108–109, 116, 160. *See also* autonomy; standards; working conditions
Republican Party, 195. *See also* Trump, Donald J.
research, international, 182–183
resilience narratives: concentration vs. diversification, 149–150; connectivity and contagion, 145–147; efficiency vs. redundancy, 150–151; interdependence in, 147–148; self-reliance and, 147–148, 269–270, 271–273; supply chains and, 219, 273; workers in, 264–266
resources, natural, 236, 238, 251–252
Ricardo, David, 38, 210
rights, individual, 208–209, 233
right-wing populist narrative, 14; adjustment in, 83; analytical structure of, 167*t*; blue-collar workers' move to, 278; causal claims of, 33; climate change and, 251–252, 274–278, 297; control and, 95–96 (*see also* autonomy); coronavirus and, 254, 255–256; described, 9–10; on distribution, 291; on elites, 79; establishment narrative and, 97, 204; in Europe, 10, 79; gender and, 89–90, 252; horizontal threats and, 11; immigration and, 93–95; industrial decline and, 78; jobs-as-property metaphor in, 86–87; left-wing populist narrative's overlap with, 268; losers in, 23*f*; manufacturing jobs in, 82–83, 222; on offshoring, 70; patriotism and, 86; renegotiation of NAFTA and, 200; rise of, 36; schematic representation of, 13*f*; security of one's group and, 90–93; self-reliance in, 269–270; summary of, 97; Trump's trade policies and, 185–189; Trump's use of, 172; in US, 10, 22; values and, 86, 88–90, 293; winners in, 23; workers in, 19, 264–266. *See also* Brexit; immigration; narratives, globalization; nationalism; populism; protectionism; protectionist narrative; Trump, Donald J.
risk, 215, 216
Rodrik, Dani, 14, 31, 106, 109, 111, 209–210
Romney, Mitt, 29, 268
Roos, Jerome, 64
Roosevelt, Franklin D., 79
Ross, Wilbur, 188, 273
Roy, Arundhati, 221
Rubik's cube metaphor, 5, 12, 17, 241, 243
Rubio, Marco, 130, 257, 271
Russia, 44, 221, 230–234

sabotage, overlaps among narratives and, 184, 189–191
Sachs, Jeffrey, 179–180
Saez, Emmanuel, 68–69
safety nets, 53. *See also* adjustment
safety standards, 100. *See also* labor standards; working conditions
Salvini, Matteo, 96
Sandel, Michael, 87, 266, 295
Sanders, Bernie, 257; election narrative, 22, 25, 27; framing by, 208; on income inequality, 68; level of analysis used by, 25; on living wage, 72; on Vattenfall dispute, 116. *See also* left-wing populist narrative
Saran, Shyam, 248
Sassen, Saskia, 68
scene, setting, 24–26. *See also* framing
Schadlow, Nadia, 183
Schmidt, Eric, 258
Schuman, Robert, 42
scientific collaboration, international, 182–183
Section 232 of Trade Expansion Act of 1962, 188–189

Section 301 of Trade Act of 1974, 187–188, 189
security, 10; Biden administration on, 130; China and, 125, 174, 235; economics and, 124, 129–131, 215–216, 217*f*; vs. efficiency, 210–214; Huawei and, 134, 177, 190, 210, 214, 235; pandemics' threat to, 146; protectionism and, 130, 188–189, 190; risk and, 215; Trump on, 130. *See also* geoeconomic narrative; peace
security, global, 144, 248. *See also* global threats narratives
security policy, economization of, 123. *See also* geoeconomic narrative
self-interest, voting and, 30–31, 295
self-reliance, 147–148, 151, 235, 269–270, 271–273. *See also* interdependence
semiconductors, 135
service sector, 72–73, 255, 256–257, 263–264. *See also* coronavirus; left-wing populist narrative; wages; workers
shareholders, 98
Sheffi, Yossi, 146
Shiller, Robert, 12
Shiva, Vandana, 154, 221
Shobert, Benjamin, 180
Shue, Henry, 161
Silicon Valley Consensus, 113
Singapore, 260
Singh, Jagmeet, 76
skills, 59–60, 68. *See also* adjustment
Slaughter, Anne-Marie, 144, 146
slavery, 236
Sleeping Giant (Draut), 268
smile curve, 50, 51*f*
Smoot-Hawley Tariff, 41
Snow, John, 264
Snowden, Edward, 135
social contract, 86–87
social responsibility, tax evasion/avoidance and, 103
solutions. *See* manufacturing jobs; policy/policymaking; tariffs
Sommer, Theo, 129, 133, 141
sourcing decisions. *See* corporate power narrative; supply chains
South, US, 70–71, 94
sovereignty, national, 95–96, 208, 209–210. *See also* Brexit; nativism
Soviet Union, 125, 131, 132*f*, 210, 230, 233
Spain, 63, 64, 69, 95–96, 251, 256
Spalding, Robert, 122
Spanish flu pandemic, 146
specialization, 37, 38, 44, 48, 55, 283
Sperling, Gene, 266, 269
Srinivasan, T. N., 221
standard of living, 39–40. *See also* poverty
standards, 104, 108–110. *See also* environmental standards; regulations; working conditions
stealth war, 122
Stern, Nicholas, 218
stifling strategy, 137, 138
Stiglitz, Joseph, 101, 103, 231
Streinz, Thomas, 113
Suedfeld, Peter, 17
suicide, 232. *See also* deaths of despair
Sullivan, Jake, 127, 182
Summers, Larry, 245
Sunstein, Cass, 184
supply-chain contagion, 149
supply chains, 12, 124–125; coronavirus and, 144, 150, 254, 257, 271; disruptions to, 147–148, 216; diversification of, 271–273; efficiency and resilience in, 219; global crises and, 146; lean, 150; peace and, 43; redundancy in, 219; security and, 129–130. *See also* China; interdependence
surveillance, 177
surveillance capitalism, 175–176
Suslov, Dmitry, 234
sustainability, 12, 156
sustainability narrative, 152–163; climate change and, 246–248, 252–253, 258, 274–278; coronavirus and, 258; sustainable orbit, 157–159; values and, 293
swans, black, 220
Swanson, Ana, 187
Sweden, emissions per capita, 161

Switzerland, 256
Syed, Matthew, 286
Syria, refugees from, 4

Tai, Katherine, 202, 207–208, 285
Taleb, Nassim, 151, 215, 220
Tan Tarn How, 260–261
tariffs, 41–42, 52–53, 79–80, 185, 187–191, 193, 223. *See also* protectionism
taxes, 9, 10, 19, 57, 68–70, 71, 99, 101–103, 277
Tax Justice Network, 103
teams, diverse, 286–290
technology, 11; China and, 138, 211, 212, 235; investment in, 37; rivalry in, 122–123, 136–138 (*see also* geoeconomic narrative); trade-offs and, 212. *See also* automation; competition; Huawei
technology industry, 100, 113, 117–118, 119, 136, 211. *See also* antitrust policy/enforcement; Big Tech
Temin, Peter, 60
Tetlock, Philip, 16–17, 282
textile industry, 46, 90. *See also* manufacturing jobs
Thaler, Richard, 205
Thatcher, Margaret, 70
threat multiplier, climate change as, 253
threats. *See* geoeconomic narrative; global threats narratives; security
Thunberg, Greta, 155, 158, 161, 163, 252
Thwaites, Thomas, 38
Tong, Anote, 248
Toyota, 150
TPP (Trans-Pacific Partnership), 110–113, 126
trade, 38. *See also* integration
trade agreements, 113; CETA, 112, 113–115; concentration and, 117; in corporate power narrative, 111; CPTPP, 113; data flows and, 113, 118; GATT, 41–42, 223; intellectual property rights in, 111–113; ISDS, 113–116, 195, 197–198, 225; labor standards and, 196–197; medicines and, 112; NAFTA, 99, 104–105, 106, 107, 114–115, 191–202; peace and, 41–43; Reciprocal Trade Agreements Act, 79–80; support for, 35; TPP, 126; TRIPS, 112, 209; TTIP, 9, 109, 113–115; USMCA, 191, 201. *See also* free trade; liberalization, economic
Trade Is Special School, 46–47, 53
trade-offs, 170; between absolute and relative gains, 211–212, 213*f*; consumption vs. production, 204–207; coronavirus and, 203; economics vs. environmental risks, 217–219; economics vs. security, 215–216, 217*f*; efficiency vs. equality, rights, and democracy, 208–210; efficiency vs. security, 210–214; involving different probabilities, 215–219; values and, 18, 203, 204–214
Trade-Related Aspects of Intellectual Property Rights (TRIPS) agreement, 112, 209
trade restrictions, 41. *See also* protectionism; tariffs
Trade Wars Are Class Wars (Klein and Pettis), 173
Transatlantic Trade and Investment Partnership (TTIP), 9, 109, 113–115. *See also* trade agreements
Trans-Pacific Partnership (TPP), 110–113, 126
TRIPS (Trade-Related Aspects of Intellectual Property Rights) agreement, 112, 209
troika, 63–64
Trudeau, Justin, 198–200
Trump, Donald J., 4, 78, 198–200; appeal to emotions, 95; appeal to manufacturing communities, 82; on Brexit, 95; campaign of, 171–172; China and, 126–127, 180, 186–188, 190–191, 234, 255; climate change denial and, 251; coronavirus and, 203, 254, 255, 256, 257; defeat of, 19; election of, 47, 281, 289; geoeconomic agenda of, 183; immigration and, 91, 256; inaugural address, 79; on job loss, 204; level of analysis used by, 25; on manufacturing jobs, 90; narratives used by, 22, 25, 27,

79; on security, 130; on self-reliance, 148; support for, 95; tax reform of, 68, 277; trade policies of, 184–191; use of jobs-as-property metaphor, 87. *See also* manufacturing jobs; right-wing populist narrative; United States
Tsipras, Alexis, 64
TTIP (Transatlantic Trade and Investment Partnership), 9, 109, 113–115
Tucker, Jonathan, 212
Twitter, 120. *See also* Big Tech; concentration

UK Independence Party (UKIP), 91, 95
Ukraine, 44
underemployment, 72
unemployment. *See* adjustment; competition; job loss; manufacturing jobs; offshoring
Uninhabitable Earth, The (Wallace-Wells), 156
unions, 70–71, 196, 264. *See also* AFL- CIO
United Kingdom (UK): concerns about control in, 96; coronavirus in, 151; dependence on China, 129; focus on, 17; geographical divides in, 84; hospitals in, 151; housing in, 75–76; income inequality in, 59*f*; narratives in, 9; right-wing populist narrative in, 10 (*see also* Brexit); UKIP, 91, 95; unionized workers in, 70. *See also* Brexit; Europe; West
United Nations, 145, 154, 246
United States, 4; dependence on China, 129; focus on, 17; GDP of, 126*f*; income inequality in, 57, 58*f*, 59–62; interdependence with China, 131, 132*f*; lack of redistribution in, 56; narratives in, 9; perception of China's economic rise and, 127–129; right-wing populist narrative in, 10; rivalry with China, 10–11, 122–123, 136 (*see also* geoeconomic narrative; technology); surveillance by, 177; unions in, 70–71. *See also* Biden, Joe; Trump, Donald J.; West
United States–Mexico–Canada Agreement (USMCA), 191, 201. *See also* North American Free Trade Agreement (NAFTA)
units of analysis, 25, 166–168*t*, 169, 171, 181
universities, 283, 284. *See also* educational attainment
upper middle class, 9, 61. *See also* elites
Uruguay Round, 99, 100, 223–224
USMCA (United States–Mexico–Canada Agreement), 191, 201. *See also* North American Free Trade Agreement (NAFTA); trade agreements

value extraction, 65–66
values: anti-immigrant sentiment and, 93; conflicts among, 204–214; consumption vs. production, 204–207; coronavirus and, 208–209; cosmopolitan, rejection of, 86; differences in, 31; efficiency vs. equality, rights, and democracy, 208–210; efficiency vs. security, 210–214; establishment narrative and, 292–293; geographical divides and, 10; plural approach to, 292–295; right-wing populist narrative and, 88–90, 293; trade-offs and, 18, 203, 204–214; traditional, 88–89; of working class, 78, 85–86. *See also* cultural differences; educational attainment; morals; trade-offs
Vance, J. D., 88, 205, 206, 267, 271
Varoufakis, Yanis, 64
Vestager, Margrethe, 100, 120
"villains," 175–180. *See also* China; immigration
violence, anti-immigrant sentiment and, 92
viruses. *See* coronavirus
Vogt, Jeffrey, 105
von der Leyen, Ursula, 141

wages, 100; anti-union laws/practice and, 70–71; concentration and, 119–120; corporate power narrative and, 100, 103–108; establishment narrative and,

wages (*continued*)
263–264; left-wing populist narrative on, 57–62, 69, 71–73; living wage, 72–73, 263, 264; in Mexico, 108*f*, 196; minimum wage, 70, 72–73, 264, 268; NAFTA and, 196; productivity and, 263; productivity-wage gaps, 57, 58*f*, 59, 60; race to bottom in, 99, 100 (*see also* corporate power narrative)
wage stagnation, 57–60, 65. *See also* income inequality
wage subsidy, 268
Wallace-Wells, David, 153, 156, 245, 251, 296
Wallach, Lori, 110
Wall Street. *See* debt; financial institutions; global financial crisis (2008)
Walt Disney Company, 91
Wang Huiyao, 228
war. *See* conflict; peace
Warren, Elizabeth, 65, 69, 73, 75, 100, 116, 117, 172, 173
wealth, 9, 83–85. *See also* distribution; income; income inequality; wages
Weder di Mauro, Beatrice, 149
welfare state, immigration into, 91–92
Wertheim, Stephen, 181
West: allegations of hypocrisy against, 233–234; arrogance of, 220; China and, 11, 210 (*see also* geoeconomic narrative); consumption patterns in, 153; emissions and, 160; influence of, 221; loss of control to supranational bodies, 95 (*see also* autonomy; right-wing populist narrative); perspectives from outside of, 221 (*see also* narratives, non-Western); tax evasion/avoidance in, 69. *See also* Europe; United Kingdom (UK); United States
Western corporations, 122
Western hegemony, narratives against, 18, 230–235
What's the Matter with Kansas (Frank), 30
Wilkinson, Will, 88
Williams, Joan, 86
winners, 13*f*; Asian countries as, 226; changing perception of, 171 (*see also* narratives, switching); compensation of losers by, 290–291; from coronavirus, 258; in corporate power narrative, 9, 104–106; in establishment narrative, 7, 105, 144; in globalization narratives, 166–168*t*; in left-wing populist narrative, 24*f*, 60 (*see also* elites); in right-wing populist narrative, 23*f*
WIPO (World Intellectual Property Organization), 111–112
wireless networks. *See* 5G technology; Huawei
Wolf, Martin, 40
work, value of, 207–208
worker mobility. *See* adjustment
workers: anti-union laws/practice and, 70–71; in Biden's trade agenda, 19; climate change and, 278; coronavirus and, 264–266; in corporate power narrative, 110; dignity of, 266–269; in establishment narrative, 263–264, 266; impact of corporate power on, 100; indifference to, 264; in left-wing populist narrative, 19; policymaking and, 264–270; protecting, 53 (*see also* adjustment); in right-wing populist narrative, 19. *See also* adjustment; competition; job loss; manufacturing jobs; offshoring; service sector
worker solidarity, 107–108
working class: changes in income, 20, 22; climate change and, 278; competition for public services and, 92; declining opportunities for, 78, 89; demographics of, 72; dignity of, 266–268; distrust of elites, 94; healthcare costs and, 76; in left-wing populist narrative, 9; union decline and, 71; values of, 78, 85–86; wage stagnation, 57–60. *See also* job loss; manufacturing jobs
working conditions, 100, 104, 106–108, 208, 264. *See also* safety standards; standards; wages

World Bank, 7, 52, 53, 225, 276
World Happiness Report, 158
World Health Organization (WHO), 143, 183, 257
World Intellectual Property Organization (WIPO), 111–112
World Trade Organization (WTO), 7; on adjustment, 53; China and, 48, 234; on communication of free trade benefits, 52; coronavirus and, 255; on decline in manufacturing jobs, 48; establishment of, 99, 224; peace and, 42; perspectives on, 221; protests against, 4; regulations and, 109; right to health and, 209; Trump's trade policies and, 186
World War I, 44
Wray, Christopher, 128
Wright, Thomas, 131
WTO (World Trade Organization). *See* World Trade Organization (WTO)
Wu, Tim, 100, 119, 171, 173, 174
Wuhan. *See* coronavirus
Wuttke, Jörg, 150

Xi Jinping, 182, 211, 221, 228, 234, 235

Yeltsin, Boris, 233
Yugoslavia, 44

zeitgeist, changing, 295–297
ZTE, 235
Zuboff, Shoshana, 175–176
Zuckerberg, Mark, 171
Zucman, Gabriel, 68–69, 101, 102